Learn at Home
Grade 2

From the Editors of American Education Publishing

Table of Contents

Learn at Home, Grade 2

Table of Contents

Welcome!

Whatever your reason for educating your child at home, you have an exciting adventure ahead of you. As you look forward to the challenge of learning together, you may be a little nervous. Although the scope of the project may seem intimidating, help is on the way. The *Learn at Home* curriculum will guide you through skills and activities on a day-to-day basis and give you confidence that you are covering the second-grade standard curriculum. Use the curriculum as a guide, but, whenever possible, supplement the curriculum with events and activities that arise out of opportunities and your child's curiosity. Also, read aloud to your child every day, creating a love of books that will inspire life-long learning.

Set up an inviting learning environment. It should be attractive, yet a place where your child knows he/she is expected to "conduct daily business." The environment might include a dry-erase board or chalkboard; one or more bulletin boards; table(s) for various centers, displays and projects; a desk for your child; an easel; special "nook" for curling up to read; chairs; and shelves for books and storage. Hang a calendar and clock in the room.

The Learn at Home Series

The *Learn at Home* curriculum is an easy-to-use resource. It includes an introductory section called **Background Information and Supporting Activities** which contains an overview of the instructional program and skill objectives to be mastered by your child. Following this are the 36 weeks of **Lesson Plans**. The final section contains **Answer Keys** to each of the activity sheets from the **Lesson Plans** section.

The **Lesson Plans** section contains three subsections: 36 weeks of lesson plans, background and supporting activities and activity sheets. The lesson plans include activities for six curricular areas: reading, language skills, spelling, social studies, math and science. The plans are brief, with further explanation referenced in the **Teaching Suggestions and Activities** section. Each lesson could include one or more of the following to guide your planning: an assessment of the child's understanding, a parent-directed lesson and/or an independent activity.

The **Teaching Suggestions and Activities** section follows each lesson plan. This section provides helpful background information on each topic introduced and further directions for specific activities mentioned in the lesson plans. Review the **Background Information and Supporting Activities** at the beginning of each week and prior to the beginning of the school year. The activity sheets follow each week's teaching suggestions and activities.

The final section contains **Answer Keys** to the activity sheets, included for your convenience.

Background Information and Supporting Activities

LANGUAGE SKILLS

▶ BACKGROUND

Language includes reading, spelling and language skills. Language skills should be taught in real context in all subject areas, rather than in isolation. Included in the Language Skills section are the process of writing, parts of speech, vocabulary development, sentence structure, punctuation, capitalization, sequencing, letter-writing skills and handwriting skills.

Keep a folder of your child's writing and provide a spiral notebook that will be a journal in which your child will make daily entries which are usually anecdotal and personal. Devote at least one-half hour per day to writing, creative or curriculum based. Many daily lessons include writing activities.

▶ LANGUAGE SKILLS INSTRUCTION DEFINITIONS

The writing process is ongoing and follows a given set of procedures. These include:

Prewriting	The writer brainstorms ideas, gathers and organizes information.
Drafting	The writer composes or writes a rough draft using prewriting ideas. Your child should not worry about mistakes. The emphasis is on fluency, not accuracy. Date the drafts and keep them in a folder.
Revising	The writer rereads the draft looking for fluency, interest and focus on topic. Then, he/she reads the rough draft to one or more persons who offer feedback about word choice, fluency, clarity and interest. The writer makes changes as needed.
Editing	Together the parent and child proofread the revised piece of writing for spelling, capitalization and grammar.
Publishing	The writer copies the corrected proof and prepares to present it.

▶ TEACHING LANGUAGE SKILLS

You will have plenty of opportunity to help your child learn the language skills he/she needs to develop. In doing so, your child will write daily for a variety of purposes. He/she will learn to write meaningful sentences and paragraphs about a specific topic. Your lessons will focus on helping your child use correct capitalization and punctuation, focusing on periods, question marks, exclamation points, commas and apostrophes. He/she will learn to apply the writing process to written ideas.

As the year progresses, your child will be able to produce a piece of writing that stays on topic, includes supporting ideas and has a beginning, middle and end. Also, he/she will develop a variety of appropriate word choices and clear language. You will begin to see your child improve as he/she orally expresses him/herself more effectively—socially as well as academically. To help your child chart his/her progress, have him/her keep a daily journal and writing folder of all writing activities.

SPELLING

▶ BACKGROUND

Spelling should be integrated across the daily curriculum, as your child encounters new words in all subject areas. Throughout the year, your child will move from "invented spelling" (the result of an attempt to spell a word whose spelling is not already known) to "conventional spelling" (an accepted spelling practice), for example, "luv" meaning "love."

The lessons are designed specifically to help your child make this transition. As your child progresses, he/she will begin to develop an ability to recognize letter and word patterns that will enable her/him to form and spell new words correctly. Along with phonic patterns, he/she will develop the ability to recognize correct and incorrect spelling. He/she will exhibit learning as he/she applies conventional spelling to daily writing in all subject areas.

▶ TEACHING SPELLING SKILLS

All spelling lessons will follow the general weekly plan outlined below. You may wish to write the routine on a poster for reference. Any activity sheets or special instructions will be listed or explained in the lesson plans. Make personalized spelling lists out of words that your child is using in his/her writing. You may also use words included in reading, science and social studies vocabulary.

▶ SPELLING DICTIONARY

Have your child maintain a dictionary of words. The dictionary should contain at least 26 pages, one for each letter of the alphabet. As your child encounters a new word, he/she enters it on the appropriate page. Teach your child to enter a pronunciation and definition for each word.

Your child may refer to the dictionary . . .

1. when he/she wants to look up the spelling for a writing project.

2. when he/she wants to learn the meaning of a word.

3. when he/she is looking for words to add to the current spelling list.

You may set other goals for the dictionary as well. You may stress vocabulary development, parts of speech or pronunciation.

▶ GENERAL WEEKLY PLAN FOR SPELLING LESSONS

Monday

1. Give your child a pretest of the new word list on lined paper.

2. Read each word and spell it aloud as your child corrects his/her own test. Any words your child already knows need not be practiced that week.

3. To make the list complete, add words from science vocabulary, reading, personal writing or previously misspelled words.

4. Go through the list together in the following manner: Read the first word, spell the word and read the word again. Repeat with the entire list. Define any words if necessary.

5. Identify and teach the specific spelling or phonics skill of the lesson.

Learn at Home, Grade 2

6. Have your child make an accurate copy of the spelling list from which he/she will study.

Tuesday

1. Have your child use each spelling word in a meaningful sentence. Your child may dictate the sentences and then copy them or your child may first write the sentences using invented spelling (except the spelling word) and then copy them after you have edited the sentences.

Wednesday

1. Complete the provided activity sheet. Have your child write his/her additional words on back.

2. Practice spelling each word aloud while singing, dancing, marching, clapping or using another physical motion.

Thursday

1. Complete an activity that involves repeatedly writing, forming, tracing or reading the words.

Friday

1. Administer a test of your child's spelling list. Any missed words should be added to the list of the following week.

2. Add a "challenge" to the spelling test by having your child write simple sentences or write words that rhyme with those on his/her list. Remind your child to use correct punctuation and capitalization.

READING

▶ BACKGROUND

Teach reading through books that fit your child's ability and interests. Use a basal reader or a variety of books obtained through a bookstore or a library. A tremendous quantity and variety of books are included in the daily lesson plans. Feel free to substitute other literature as long as it relates to the subject matter.

When introducing a new book, discuss with your child his/her knowledge of the content. Read books aloud to your child that are at a higher level than his/her independent reading level. Read aloud time should also continue after your child is reading independently. Your child will keep a running record of all books read every 9 weeks.

▶ READING INSTRUCTION DEFINITIONS

Language Experience: Stories written in your child's own words and used as a reading text build proficiency with language because they are in his/her own words. Reading his/her own writing also builds confidence in becoming a successful reader.

Building Vocabulary: A student may use three different cues when encountering a new word: *context*. Analyze the *syntax* or the arrangement and relationship of the words. For example, if the word comes after the word "the," it must be a thing or a noun. Sound out the word *phonetically*, using word-pattern rules. Introduce dictionary skills and parts of speech, synonyms, homophones, antonyms and idioms as a part of building vocabulary.

Phonemic and Phonic Awareness: Phonemic awareness is the recognition of sounds that make up spoken words. Phonics is a way of teaching reading and spelling that stresses symbol-sound relationships. Teach the following skills in context: beginning, middle and ending sounds; blends and digraphs; rhyming words; vowel sound families; contractions; compound words; possessives; and common prefixes and word endings.

Listening: Listening is to speaking as reading is to writing. All four are important elements of language. Provide ample opportunities to listen to songs, poetry and stories.

Structural Analysis: The identification of word meaning elements, such as *re* and *read* in the word *reread*. These elements include word endings, contractions, compound words, possessives, prefixes, suffixes and syllabication that help your child to identify word elements.

▶ TEACHING READING SKILLS

Your child will develop reading confidence as he/she learns more reading skills this school year. He/she will progress in reading silently and constructing meaning from the text. He/she will also develop reading orally and fluently with expression, as he/she portrays various characters. The lessons are designed to guide your child to respond to literature through writing and creative activity.

As the year progresses, your child will improve in many other aspects of reading. He/she will be able to recognize the cause and effect relationships of different situations, draw conclusions, as well as to infer information. He/she will be able to read, write and perform a series of events in a sequential order. Your child will distinguish fiction and nonfiction, fact and opinion. As your child progresses, he/she will recognize important elements such as the main idea, supporting details, characters, settings and plots. By the end of the year, your second grader will even be able to compare and contrast various books looking at points of view, information, storyline, themes, etc.

Reading skills help develop better reasoning as well. You will notice that your child will become more realistic when predicting outcomes before completing the book. He/she will start to apply critical thinking skills to reading experiences and better evaluate the information read. Finally, your child will improve at following oral and written directions in all circumstances.

Remember to keep reading fun and interesting. It is also important to model reading in your own life. This will go a long way in helping your child develop a positive attitude toward life-long reading.

Learn at Home, Grade 2

MATH

▶ BACKGROUND

Math is everywhere and surrounds us continuously. During the 36 weeks of math instruction, your child will realize how math affects his/her daily life. The application of math concepts will be learned through different meaningful math experiences, including hands-on and active learning, the use of manipulatives, literature, writing about math, traditional written and oral assessments, and the strategies in solving a problem.

The math concepts are described in the weekly lesson plans and the Teaching Suggestions and Activities section.

The areas of instruction include addition and subtraction facts through 18; missing addends, subtrahend and minuend in equations through 18; the commutative property of addition; patterns, number order and odd and even numbers; place value—ones, tens and hundreds; 2- and 3-digit addition with regrouping and no regrouping; column addition; geometry—shapes, tangrams and symmetry; greater than, less than; fractions; time; graphing; ordinal numbers; checking answers using opposite operations; measurement; estimation; multiplication to 5's; and problem solving using different strategies.

▶ TEACHING MATH SKILLS

Your child will develop many basic math skills and concepts throughout this year. Although your child may appear to understand a concept, based on the fact that he/she can correctly perform the skill, you need to be sure to build conceptualization. To do this, use all the steps including the manipulatives and writing assignments when teaching your child. Proving the relevance of math, many of these math skills will be used—and even taught—in other subject areas.

The year will begin with your child practicing addition and subtraction facts up to 18. Then, he/she will learn how to find missing addends, subtrahends and minuends in equations through 18. Using these skills, your child will begin to learn the concepts of the commutative property of addition, patterns, number order and the greater than/ less than concept. As the year progresses, your child's understanding of place value will as well. Soon, he/she will be able to do 2- and 3-digit addition and subtraction with regrouping and without regrouping. Your child's year will end with him/her learning the concept of multiplication. Practice will involve multiplication up to 5's.

Aside from computation, your child will exhibit mathematical knowledge with other types of skills as well. Much time will be spent on geometry throughout the curriculum including working with shapes, tangrams and symmetry. Other math skills found in many subject areas are graphing, problem solving and linear measurement.

SOCIAL STUDIES

▶ BACKGROUND

Social studies involves people and their relationship to their social and physical environments. The primary purpose of this instruction is to encourage your child to become fully engaged in the activities of society and to discover the interdependence among others in the community and around the world. The variety of ways of living in the United States will help your child become more aware of the nature and accomplishments of our society as he/she plans for the future.

Areas of concentration include the neighborhood; the various kinds of communities; shelters around the world from the past to the present; a 10-week study of the 50 states, including the presidents; global awareness, highlighting people in other societies around the world; immigration; transportation and communication.

Many social studies themes will be integrated with other subject areas through the frequent use of related literature. The awareness and discussion of current local, state, national and international events should be a daily occurrence.

▶ TEACHING SOCIAL STUDIES SKILLS

The second-grade social studies program covers a wide range of topics. Fashion your lesson as your child shows interest in certain areas. Pattern your lessons after the given guidelines, and remember that tangents can be valuable lessons for your child. This year begins with a general community study which broadens in scope. Your child will learn the attributes of different neighborhoods and communities. Then, he/she will become aware of the diversity in lifestyles through shelters of different communities. Through this experience, he/she will also become aware of multi-cultures around the world.

History—both personal and national—will also be studied. You will help your child research his/her family heritage. Your child will begin American history by studying ten past and present presidents of the United States. You will then help your child understand the term immigration and how it has affected our society. By the end of the year, your child will better understand how the development of transportation and communication has affected the lives of everyone throughout the world.

Finally, you will guide your child on a study of geographic features of our Earth. He/she will be able to recognize and compare the seven continents of the world. To develop this, your child will do much with reading and interpreting different kinds of maps and globes. You can also personalize the special unit to help your child become aware of the different features of each of the fifty states. Along with that, your child will review geographical areas in relation to where he/she lives.

Learn at Home, Grade 2

SCIENCE

▶ BACKGROUND

Science is the process of wondering, and a good scientist asks lots of questions. The Scientific Method promotes exploring. Your child will construct his/her own knowledge based upon experience. The more experience you provide, the clearer and more accurate will be his/her understanding. Your child will develop a natural curiosity as he/she explores the environment through scientific activities. The interrelationships among the sciences, society and technology are discovered through the integration of earth, life and physical sciences. Many opportunities to investigate and explore scientific inquiry will encourage life-long learning with the parent as the facilitator.

▶ SCIENCE INSTRUCTION DEFINITIONS

The Scientific Method

1. A science lesson may begin with a question that sparks the curiosity of your child. For example, *I wonder what will happen if I leave this half-eaten apple on the counter?* Encourage your child to state a possible *hypothesis*.

2. Follow the question with an *exploration* involving observation, play, debate, experimentation and other methods of inquiry. Encourage your child to use descriptive language, measure appropriately and keep a journal of observations.

3. The next step involves proposing *explanations* and *solutions* for the initial question. The explanation may prove or disprove the earlier hypothesis. This is a time of writing, talking and evaluating. After this step, your child may need to return to the second step of the cycle, exploring the topic further.

4. *Applying* the knowledge to your child's world makes the event more meaningful. *Where have you seen this happen before? What will you do differently because of the experiment?* This fourth step can also spark a new question that begins the cycle again.

▶ TEACHING SCIENCE SKILLS

After working with the Scientific Method, your child will be able to apply it to any and all science. Having your child keep a Science Log will help him/her methodically work through experiments and other problems.

This year, your child will learn the unusual properties of water. You will start by teaching your child the attributes of solids, liquids and gases. Then, he/she will study the water cycle of evaporation, condensation and precipitation. Along with that, your child will conduct experiments to discover the properties of salt and fresh water.

The science program will also cover biology, chemical/physical science and geology. Your child will learn to observe the physical qualities of a bird and the function of the feathers as well as kinds of birds and their habitats. You will expose your child to geology as he/she collects, observes and classifies rocks. The year will end with a study of electricity including experiments to help your child recognize and even construct a complete circuit.

Language Skills	Spelling	Reading
Monday **Handwriting** Demonstrate how to write correctly. Teach your child to form letters touching the top and bottom lines of the rule. Starting on the top line, form several large *O's* that fill the writing guidelines. *See* Language Skills, Week 1, number 1.	Pretest your child on these spelling words: bad gas mad wag sat rag pat had bat bag Review the consonant-vowel-consonant pattern and short *a* vowels.	**Parts of Speech** Read together *Q Is for Duck; an Animal Guessing Game* by Mary Elting and Michael Folsom. Have your child pick out the nouns and point to them on each page. Teach your child that a noun names a person, place or thing. Have your child write the animal nouns and add some animals of his/her own.
Tuesday Demonstrate how to form tall straight lines. Begin each line at the top and move down to the bottom rule. Have your child try this and repeat. Remind him/her to practice forming straight lines that fit the rule.	Have your child write the spelling words in sentences.	With your child, create names for each animal from yesterday's list. Have your child write the names (proper nouns). Make sure each proper noun begins with a capital letter. Have your child complete **Common Nouns** (p. 17) and **Proper Nouns** (p. 18).
Wednesday Teach your child to form letters between the dotted line and the bottom line of the writing guidelines. Have him/her practice forming small *o's* and straight lines. *See* Language Skills, Week 1, number 2.	With your child, spell each word aloud while clapping the consonants and tapping the vowels. Have your child complete **Catch an Act!** (p. 16).	Have your child change each singular animal noun in *Q Is for Duck* into a plural noun. Have your child write the singular and plural nouns. Have your child complete **Singular Nouns** (p. 19) and **Plural Nouns** (p. 20).
Thursday Each day, until the whole alphabet is learned, teach your child to form one to three letters correctly. Follow the guidelines in Language Skills, Week 1. Teach lower-case letters first, and give your child plenty of guided practice. *See* Language Skills, Week 1, number 3.	Together, brainstorm a list of other words ending in *ad, ag, as* and *at*. Write rhymes using these words. Keep the spelling lists and rhymes in a folder for further reference.	Teach your child about verbs. (A verb is an action word.) Have your child pick out the verbs in *Q Is for Duck* and write them in ABC order.
Friday Have your child begin a journal. The first writing assignment topic: *Write about something that makes you feel happy.* *See* Language Skills, Week 1, number 4.	Give your child the final spelling test.	Have your child write an original noun/verb book using the proper nouns from Tuesday.

Learn at Home, Grade 2

Math	Science	Social Studies
Assessment and Review Have your child count large numbers of objects, such as shells, etc. Ask your child to count objects several more times, grouping and counting by twos, fives and tens. Have your child write numbers on lined paper, counting by ones, twos, fives and tens.	**Water** Show your child how to make an entry in his/her Science Log with today's exploration: What is a drop of water like? *See* Science, Week 1, number 1. Have your child observe a drop of water on wax paper.	**Neighborhood** With your child, brainstorm attributes of a neighbor. Copy the **Topic Web** (p. 23) for helping your child organize his/her thoughts as you both brainstorm.
From the collections counted yesterday, count out two sets with a total of ten for your child to add together. Then, create a subtraction fact using the same two sets. *See* Math, Week 1, number 1. Have your child complete **Addition Facts to 10** (p. 21).	Put drops of water and other liquids (i.e., syrup and juice) on wax paper. Have your child observe and compare. Bump the wax paper lightly so each liquid moves slightly. Have your child draw and label each drop in his/her Science Log and write any other observations.	Brainstorm the attributes of your neighborhood. Use another **Topic Web** (p. 23) to help your child organize his/her thoughts as you brainstorm with your child.
Use addition flash cards to 10 to assess which facts your child needs to practice. *See* Math, Week 1, numbers 2 and 3.	Add food coloring to water. Put a drop on the wax paper with a drop of oil nearby. Ask what will happen when the oil and water mix. Have your child write his/her hypothesis in the Science Log. Then, move the paper so the drops come together. Have your child draw and label what happened in his/her Science Log.	**Art:** Have your child paint, color or draw a picture of him/herself in the neighborhood, working or playing with a neighbor (or neighbors).
Read *Domino Addition* by Lynette Long with your child. Then, with real dominoes, create addition and subtraction facts for the number of pips (dots) on each domino. Have your child complete **Subtraction Facts to 10** (p. 22).	**Art:** Use red, yellow and blue tempera paints and a straw to make a blow painting. *See* Science, Week 1, number 3.	Help your child compose an acrostic poem about a special person in your neighborhood. Write NEIGHBOR or the person's name vertically in capital letters. Think of descriptive words or phrases that tell about that person for each letter of his/her name. *See* Social Studies, Week 1, number 1.
Continue using flash cards to assess which facts your child needs to practice. Then, have your child match the addition and subtraction flash cards to form fact families.	With your child, explore the property of cohesion. (Your child does not need to know this word.) The question for today may be *How does water act when you try to pull it apart?* Have your child complete his/her Science Log entry for today.	Propose some common neighborhood problems. Discuss ways to solve them. Emphasize the importance of cooperation and compromise. *See* Social Studies, Week 1, number 2.

Learn at Home, Grade 2

TEACHING SUGGESTIONS AND ACTIVITIES

LANGUAGE SKILLS (Handwriting)

There are different methods of teaching handwriting. You will need to explore and choose the appropriate method for your child. The teaching suggestions given below are appropriate for any method.

▶ 1. Have your child hold the pencil correctly and practice writing in the proper form. Make sure the desk and chair are comfortable. Have your child write on ruled paper with a middle dotted line. Instruct your child to stay within the lines.

▶ 2. In manuscript, review writing all lower- and upper-case letters. Practice writing the featured nouns and verbs in *Q Is for Duck* by Mary Elting and Michael Folsom.

▶ 3. Your child can create and write original ABC riddles.

▶ 4. Start a journal with your child. With your child, brainstorm some strategies for coming up with writing topics. The easiest story to write is one that tells about something your child knows about or has done. Respond to your child's writing with specific positive comments.
Example: "When you used the word _____, I could really see what you were talking about."

READING (Parts of Speech)

As your child is exposed to print in stories, poems, books or on the computer, he/she gains a sense of syntax, the way words make up a sentence. Use the vocabulary of parts of speech: nouns, verbs, adjectives and adverbs in context as you read with your child.

▶ 1. Center: Make a four-column chart on the inside of a folder. At the top of the columns write the headings: NOUN, VERB and ADJECTIVE. Write nouns, verbs and adjectives on small cards. Have your child place the cards in the correct columns.

▶ 2. Choose tongue twisters to read from *Six Sick Sheep: 101 Tongue Twisters* by Joanna Cole and Stephanie Calmenson. Have your child chart the nouns, verbs and adjectives on the chart used for the center in number 1.

▶ 3. Cut pictures of singular and plural nouns from newspapers, magazines, catalogs, etc.
Example: Cat-cats, girl-girls, boy-boys, car-cars, etc. Glue all singular-noun pictures, labeled, on one set of cards and plural-noun pictures, labeled, on the other set of cards. Have your child play a game matching the cards.

MATH (Assessment and Review)

BACKGROUND
Assessment is an ongoing process that provides you with valuable information about your child. Assessments take many forms—from observing your child working to a formal test. When you assess your child, look for accuracy not only in response but also his/her thought processes and strategies and how your child meets and deals with obstacles. You can learn about how he/she learns through assessment. You also gain perspective on which concepts come easily and which need more practice. Assess your child regularly throughout the year and adjust your teaching to match the needs of your child.

You, as parent, should incorporate each of the following activities on a daily, or at least weekly, basis:

▶ 1. Practice counting orally by twos, fives and tens to memorize the sequences. While you and your child recite each number, make a physical motion such as marching while counting by twos.

Learn at Home, Grade 2

Common Nouns

A **common noun** names a person, place or thing.

Example: The **boy** had several **chores** to do.

Fill in the circle below each common noun.

1. First, the boy had to feed his puppy.
   ○   ○   ○   ○

2. He got fresh water for his pet.
   ○   ○   ○ ○

3. Next, the boy poured some dry food into a bowl.
   ○   ○   ○   ○

4. He set the dish on the floor in the kitchen.
   ○   ○   ○   ○

5. Then, he called his dog to come to dinner.
   ○   ○   ○

6. The boy and his dad worked in the garden.
   ○   ○   ○   ○

7. The father turned the dirt with a shovel.
   ○   ○   ○   ○

8. The boy carefully dropped seeds into little holes.
   ○   ○   ○   ○

9. Soon, tiny plants would sprout from the soil.
   ○   ○   ○   ○

10. Sunshine and showers would help the radishes grow.
    ○   ○   ○ ○

Proper Nouns

A **proper noun** names a specific or certain person, place or thing. A proper noun always begins with a capital letter.

Example: Becky flew to **St. Louis** in a **Boeing 747**.

Put a ✔ in front of each proper noun.

_____ 1. uncle

_____ 2. Aunt Retta

_____ 3. Forest Park

_____ 4. Gateway Arch

_____ 5. Missouri

_____ 6. school

_____ 7. Miss Hunter

_____ 8. Northwest Plaza

_____ 9. New York Science Center

_____ 10. Ms. Small

_____ 11. Doctor Chang

_____ 12. Union Station

_____ 13. Henry Shaw

_____ 14. museum

_____ 15. librarian

_____ 16. shopping mall

Underline the proper nouns.

1. Becky went to visit Uncle Harry.

2. He took her to see the Cardinals play baseball.

3. The game was at Busch Stadium.

4. The St. Louis Cardinals played the Chicago Cubs.

5. Mark McGwire hit a home run.

18

Learn at Home, Grade 2

Singular Nouns

A **singular noun** names one person, place or thing.

Example: My **mother** unlocked the old **trunk** in the **attic**.

If the noun is singular, **draw** a line from it to the trunk. If the noun is not singular, **draw** an **X** on the word.

teddy bear	hammer	picture	sweater
bonnet	letters	seashells	fiddle
kite	ring	feather	books
postcard	crayon	doll	dishes
blocks	hats	bicycle	blanket

19

Plural Nouns

A **plural noun** names more than one person, place or thing.

Example: Some **dinosaurs** ate **plants** in **swamps**.

Underline each plural noun.

1. Large animals lived millions of years ago.

2. Dinosaurs roamed many parts of the Earth.

3. Scientists look for fossils.

4. The bones can tell a scientist many things.

5. These bones help tell what the creatures were like.

6. Some had curved claws and whip-like tails.

7. Others had beaks and plates of armor.

8. Some dinosaurs lived on the plains, and others lived in forests.

9. You can see the skeletons of dinosaurs at some museums.

10. We often read about these animals in books.

Learn at Home, Grade 2

Topic Web

Write the topic of the web in the center oval. **Write** four subheadings in the small ovals. **Write** details of each subheading on the spokes.

	Language Skills	Spelling	Reading
Monday	Continue to observe and correct, when necessary, your child's handwriting skills throughout all written activities this week. (The Social Studies activity involves a written project all week.)	Pretest your child on these spelling words: wet tell fell pen best men rest well met set Review the short *e* vowel sound. Notice that each word contains only one vowel and one syllable.	With your child, read *Tacky the Penguin* by Helen Lester. Teach your child about verbs. Ask him/her to find and name some of Tacky's actions. Have your child write five sentences that tell what Tacky and the other penguins do. Have your child complete **Action Verbs** (p. 29).
Tuesday	If there are particular numbers or letters your child needs to practice more, give him/her ruled paper to use for extra practice.	Have your child write the spelling words in sentences.	Discuss the present- and past-tense of verbs. Reread the story and have your child decide when the actions happen. Teach your child to change past-tense sentences to present tense. *See* Reading, Week 2, numbers 1–3.
Wednesday	Have your child continue to practice writing skills.	Have your child spell each word aloud while tapping his/her foot. Have your child complete **Nestlings** (p. 28).	With your child, brainstorm a list of regular present-tense verbs to change to past tense by adding *ed*. Then, make another written list of irregular verbs. *See* Reading, Week 2, numbers 4 and 5. Have your child complete **Irregular Verbs** (p. 30).
Thursday	Have your child continue to practice writing skills.	With your child, brainstorm a list of other words ending in *et, en, ell* and *est*. Have your child write rhymes using these words.	Tell your child that every sentence must contain a verb. Notice with your child that not all sentences contain action. Introduce linking verbs. Find examples in *Tacky the Penguin*. Have your child complete **Linking Verbs** (p. 31).
Friday	Have your child continue to practice writing skills.	Give your child the final spelling test.	Find verbs that end in *ing*. Ask your child to identify the root word. The *ing* ending often is preceded by a linking verb. Help your child make finger puppets to act out the story. Have your child complete **Playing in the Summer Sun** (p. 32).

24

Learn at Home, Grade 2

Math	Science	Social Studies
Addition and Subtraction Use flash cards from Week 1 to assess your child's accuracy and speed with addition and subtraction facts through ten. Help your child with unknown facts. Have your child complete **Addition and Subtraction Facts to 10** (p. 33).	**Surface Tension** With your child, explore the property of surface tension. (Your child does not need to know this word.) Lead your child to discover that water has a tough surface. *See* Science, Week 2, number 1. The question for today may be *How does water act when you try to pull it apart?* Have your child complete the Science Log entries for today.	Have your child create and discuss a book about your neighborhood. It can include drawings, photos and written descriptions. Brainstorm its contents and list ideas. Take pictures of your neighborhood for the book and have them developed as soon as you can.
Have your child use manipulatives to create addition and subtraction facts up to 10. Show how addition and subtraction facts are related in fact families. **Example:** $6 + 4 = 10$ $4 + 6 = 10$ $10 - 4 = 6$ $10 - 6 = 4$	*See* Science, Week 2, number 2. Have your child complete the Science Log entry for today's lesson.	**Writing:** Have your child interview and write a story about a neighbor who has lived in your neighborhood for awhile. *See* Social Studies, Week 2, numbers 1 and 2. Have your child use **Getting To Know You** (p. 35) for interview question ideas.
Have your child repeat Tuesday's lesson by using manipulatives to form fact families. Play dominoes and apply addition and subtraction facts as each domino is played.	*See* Science, Week 2, number 3. Have your child complete the Science Log entry for today's lesson.	Have your child work on the neighborhood book. Have your child write descriptions for the photos from Monday on lined paper.
Look for objects that your child can add, especially ones that come in parts and make up a whole, such as the holes in an outlet. The vocabulary, "parts and whole," shows the relationship of addition and subtraction. *See* Math, Week 2, number 1.	*See* Science, Week 2, number 4. Have your child experiment with bubbles and examine how soap acts in water.	Have your child continue working on the neighborhood book. Have him/her write a description on lined paper and draw pictures of different highlights of your neighborhood on plain paper.
Help your child memorize the facts that he/she had trouble with on the flash cards. Have your child complete **Addition and Subtraction Facts to 10** (p. 34). Compare results to Monday's assessments.	Have your child create his/her own surface tension experiment today. Have your child complete the Science Log entry for today's lesson.	Have your child publish an original neighborhood book by organizing the pages designed this week into a book. Have your child share the book with family and friends.

25

TEACHING SUGGESTIONS AND ACTIVITIES

READING (Parts of Speech)

BACKGROUND

A verb is the action word in a sentence. To form the past tense of a regular verb, add *ed*. **Example:** talk–talked. The past tense of irregular verbs is spelled differently. **Example:** draw– drew. Linking verbs show no action but link the subject with a description. They are always in some form of the verb **to be**. **Example:** The dog **is** funny.

▶ 1. Copy or make up ten sentences that include either a past- or present-tense verb. It may help to include clue words, such as *currently, yesterday* and *now*. Have your child underline the verb and tell whether it is past- or present-tense. You may also have your child write the past and present verbs in categories to find patterns, such as *ed* endings.

▶ 2. Write a present- or past-tense verb on each of twelve cards. Have your child sort the cards into two groups: past and present tense. Have your child use each verb in a sentence or combine two verbs (from the same tense), in one sentence.

▶ 3. Create an activity sheet of sentences with the verb missing. Provide a present- and past-tense verb choice for your child to fill in the blank.
Examples:
Let's wait while the boys _____ their shoes.
tie   tied
After school yesterday, Suzie _____ on her homework.
works worked

▶ 4. Write *come, make, take* and *ride* on the chalkboard. Have your child dictate a sentence using each present-tense verb. Ask your child to dictate a second sentence for each verb, converting each to the past tense. Ask if there is a pattern among the past-tense verbs. (Irregular verbs do not take the *ed* ending in the past tense.)

▶ 5. Keep a chart in the classroom of irregular verbs your child comes across in his/her reading. Have your child write the present- and past-tense form of each verb.

MATH (Addition and Subtraction)

▶ 1. Have your child trace his/her hand ten times on drawing paper. Write a number from 1 through 10 on the palm of each hand. Have your child write addition and subtraction equations in each finger whose sums and differences equal the number written on the palm. **Example:** A hand with 4 on the palm could have 1 + 3, 2 + 2, 9 – 5, 8 – 4 and 5 – 1 on the fingers.

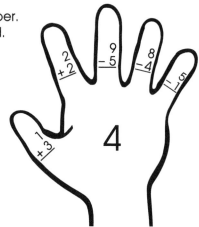

Learn at Home, Grade 2

SCIENCE (Surface Tension)

Through various experiments, your child will learn that water has a tough surface.

▶ 1. On a sturdy surface, place a penny on a paper towel or tissue. Spark your child's curiosity by having him/her predict how many drops of water will fit on the penny. Using an eyedropper, your child will add and count drops of water until the water spills onto the paper towel. Allow your child to repeat the experiment many times, each time recording the results (dry the penny between tries). Your child may propose variations such as turning the penny over or using a nickel. Ask your child to observe the water on the penny and propose why he/she thinks the water acted as it did.

▶ 2. Fill a glass to the brim with water and place it on a sturdy table. (Place a paper towel under the glass on the table first.) Ask your child to predict how many small paper clips he/she will be able to place in the glass before the water overflows. During and after the exploration, have your child propose explanations. Vary this experiment by dropping pennies into the glass of water. Try the experiment using a different liquid. Have your child record observations in his/her Science Log. **Extension:** A paper clip normally sinks in water. However, your child may be able to make a small paper clip rest on the surface of the water. Ask your child to propose an explanation. (It is not floating: the strong surface tension is supporting the very light paper clip.)

▶ 3. Fill a shallow dish with more than 1" of water. Ask your child to predict what will happen when you sprinkle some cinnamon or talcum power over the surface. Ask your child to observe what happened to the powder. Dip a toothpick in some detergent. Dip its soapy tip into the center of the dish. Ask your child to describe what happened and propose an explanation. **Extension:** try the penny exploration (number 1, above) with soapy water.

▶ 4. Mix a $\frac{1}{2}$ cup of dishwashing detergent and 1 quart of water in a dishpan. Allow your child to explore and have fun playing with the bubbles.

SOCIAL STUDIES (Neighborhood)

Your child should become familiar with his/her own neighborhood and interview a neighbor.

▶ 1. Coach your child before you have him/her make an appointment to interview a neighbor. Discuss interview etiquette. Your child should be polite. He/she should introduce him/herself clearly and explain the purpose of the interview. Use **Getting To Know You** (p. 35) as an interview guide or design your own interview questions. You may wish to tape record the interview so you do not have to write while you listen (ask permission before taping). If you are comfortable with this neighbor, allow your child to go alone. Remind your child to thank the neighbor for his/her time and send a follow-up thank you note.

▶ 2. **Writing:** Based on the information from the interview, have your child write a story about the neighbor. Edit the story first for fluency and then for accuracy in grammar, spelling and punctuation. Have your child make a "neat sheet" of the story. Share the published story with the neighbor.

Nestlings

wet   fell   tell

men   rest   well   set

met   best   pen

Write the spelling words that rhyme with the pictures.

 _____

_____

_____

 _____

_____

 _____

 _____

_____

Complete the puzzle.

Across

3. Please ____ the vase on the table.
5. Mom won a prize for baking the ____ pie.
6. Ted has a bad cold and does not feel ____ .
7. We ____ Grandmother downtown.
8. Betsy wrote the letter with a ____ .

Down

1. You should ____ if you are sick.
2. He tripped on a rock and ____ down.
4. Please ____ them we will be late.
6. The puppy ran through the sprinkler and got all ____ .
7. Five ____ help coach the baseball team.

28

Learn at Home, Grade 2

Action Verbs

A **verb** is a word that can show action.

Example: I **jump**.   He **kicks**.   He **walked**.

Underline the verb in each sentence. **Write** it on the line.

1. Our school plays games on Field Day.   _____

2. Juan runs 50 yards.   _____

3. Carmen hops in a sack race.   _____

4. Paula tosses a ball through a hoop.   _____

5. One girl carries a jellybean on a spoon.   _____

6. Lola bounces the ball.   _____

7. Some boys chase after balloons.   _____

8. Mark chooses me for his team.   _____

9. The children cheer for the winners.   _____

10. Everyone enjoys Field Day.   _____

Irregular Verbs

Verbs that do not add **ed** to show what happened in the past are called **irregular verbs**.

Example: Present   Past
        run, runs   ran
        fall, falls   fell

Jim **ran** past our house yesterday.
He **fell** over a wagon on the sidewalk.

Fill in the verbs that tell what happened in the past in the chart. The first one is done for you.

Present	Past
hear, hears	heard
draw, draws	
do, does	
give, gives	
sell, sells	
come, comes	
fly, flies	
build, builds	
know, knows	
bring, brings	

Learn at Home, Grade 2

Name: _____ **Date:** _____

Address: _____

Why did you choose to live in this neighborhood?

_____

_____

Who else lives with you here?

_____

_____

Describe your work.

_____

_____

Tell about your interests and hobbies.

_____

_____

Describe any changes you have seen in the neighborhood.

_____

_____

What do you think would make this neighborhood a better place to live?

_____

_____

Language Skills	Spelling	Reading

Monday

Language Skills

Adjectives
Cut out four pictures of cars (or people, flowers or houses) from a magazine or draw. Each car (object) should be different from the others. Ask your child to identify a car by its attributes. **Example:** *Find the red car. Find the car with four doors. Find the small car.* Teach your child that the words that add information about the car are adjectives.

Spelling

Pretest your child on these spelling words:

fix	still	sit
win	tin	fit
hit	will	hill
	bill	

Review the phonics skill of short *i* vowels.

Reading

Pick objects and describe them using adjectives. Teach your child that these descriptive words are called adjectives. They can tell about size, texture, number, appearance and kind. Have your child write descriptions about the objects.

Tuesday

Language Skills

Describe a simple picture for your child to draw. *See* Language Skills, Week 3, number 1. Have your child write a description of a simple picture using many adjectives.

Spelling

Have your child write the spelling words in sentences.

Reading

Go for a walk in your yard or around the neighborhood. Talk about what you see, encouraging your child to describe things using adjectives. **Examples:** I see *two brown* squirrels. I see a *gold* car. The road is *rocky*. The sky is *blue*. Have your child draw a picture of some of the things you saw on your walk. Label the picture with adjectives and nouns.

Wednesday

Language Skills

Choose several objects around the home to describe. Then, have your child write sentences describing the objects. *See* Language Skills, Week 3, number 2.

Spelling

Have your child complete **It's a Dilly!** (p. 40).

Reading

Read with your child, various tongue twisters using adjectives in *Six Sick Sheep: 101 Tongue Twisters* by Joanna Cole and Stephanie Calmenson. Discuss the adjectives. Have your child write tongue twisters using adjectives. **Example:** *Sally saw seven silly slippery silver seals swimming.*

Thursday

Language Skills

Adjectives make writing more interesting. They help you "show" rather than "tell" about your topic. Adjectives can describe color, size, shape, number, personality and texture. Brainstorm with your child adjectives that fit in each category. Then, have your child write a description of an animal using adjectives that describe size, personality, color, size, shape and texture.

Spelling

Have your child brainstorm and list other words ending with *in, it* and *ill*. Then, have him/her write rhymes using these words.

Reading

Have your child describe his/her toys using adjectives. *See* Reading, Week 3, number 1.
Have your child complete **Adjectives** (p. 41).

Friday

Language Skills

With your child, make a reference book of adjectives to use in writing. Brainstorm with your child several adjectives and discuss how they can be categorized for easy reference. They could be organized as in Thursday's lesson or alphabetized, for example. Have your child copy the adjectives and make a book. Have him/her leave spaces on each list for adding more adjectives.

Spelling

Give your child the final spelling test.

Reading

Play a game with your child in which you try to guess the object he/she is describing with an adjective. *See* Reading, Week 3, number 2.
Write a description of each item, using the adjectives from the game.
Have your child complete **Add the Adjectives** (p. 42).

Learn at Home, Grade 2

Math	**Science**	**Social Studies**
Missing Addends Teach your child to identify the numbers of an equation and place them in a part-part-whole frame. *See* Math, Week 3, number 1. Place the following math sentences in part-part-whole frames: $4+5=9$ $3+4=7$ $2+7=9$ $6+2=8$ $6+3=9$ $5+2=7$ $3+3=6$ $4+4=8$ $3+2=5$ $3+5=8$ $4+2=6$ $1+5=6$	**Sink or Float** Gather many common objects for this exploration. Provide a dishpan with water. Your child will test the objects for buoyancy. He/she should sort the objects into two piles: things that might float and things that might sink. Have him/her try each object one-by-one and draw the object in the correct box. Have your child complete **Buoyancy** (p. 44).	Read with your child, *This Is the Way We Go to School: A Book About Children Around the World* by Edith Baer. Compare and discuss the different neighborhoods: city, urban, rural, downtown, suburb, village and town.
Using the part-part-whole frames that your child created yesterday, hide one part and ask your child to figure out what number is missing. Ask your child to explain how he/she figured it out. Write the equation as a missing addend. *See* Math, Week 3, number 2. **Example:** $6 + \_\_\_ = 8$	Tightly crumple up a 5" x 5" sheet of foil and drop it in the water. Then, place a flat sheet of foil on the surface of the water. Ask your child to tell why he/she thinks this happened. Have him/her find out at what point the foil sinks. Fold the foil once and check whether it floats, fold twice and check, and so on. Each time, have your child record the results in his/her Science Log.	With your child, read the fable *The Town Mouse and the Country Mouse*. Have your child imagine and describe how the mice would fare in your neighborhood.
Teach how to "count on" to find the missing addend. **Example:** In $5 + \_\_\_ = 7$, your child says 5, then counts on his/her fingers to 7. The number of fingers is the missing addend.	Look at pictures of boats. Discuss of what they are made and why they float. Today's exploration: *What shape boat will hold the greatest number of pennies without sinking?* Allow your child time to explore with foil. One sheet of foil may be reshaped many times before it tears. Explore the question and have your child complete the day's log entry.	Take your child to visit your local government offices. Look at a large map of the area and identify your neighborhood. Arrange to have a tour and talk to someone about community projects, problem solving and area growth. Have your child write a personal thank you note to anyone who took time to talk to you on your field trip.
Teach your child to look for familiar skip-counting in missing addends. **Examples:** $5 + \_\_\_ = 10$ (counting by fives) $6 + \_\_\_ = 8$ (counting by twos) $40 + \_\_\_ = 50$ (counting by tens)	*See* Science, Week 3, number 1. Have your child complete the log entry for today's exploration.	Read the community newspaper with your child and talk about local issues. Cut out interesting articles and maintain a "Community News" bulletin board, folder or scrapbook. Have your child complete **City Streets** (p. 45).
Teach your child how to subtract to find the missing addend. **Example:** $4 + \_\_\_ = 9$. The answer can be found by $9 - 4 = \_\_\_$. Have your child check the answer by placing it in the original problem. Have your child complete **Something's Missing** (p. 43).	Using scraps of wood, plastic, foam, cloth, etc. build with your child a vessel to float in water. In his/her log, have your child write how you built the vessel and its movement in water.	Visit the reference department of a local library and view the different phone books available from urban and rural areas. Compare and contrast the yellow and white pages information.

Learn at Home, Grade 2

TEACHING SUGGESTIONS AND ACTIVITIES

LANGUAGE SKILLS (Adjectives)

▶ 1. While you look at a simple picture that your child cannot see, describe what you see to your child without naming the objects. Describe it again while your child attempts to draw a picture of what you are describing. Use many adjectives to help your child "see" the picture as you do. Use adjectives that describe the size, color, texture and number of objects in the picture. Then, switch roles, with your child describing a picture while you draw.

▶ 2. Your child may describe a familiar tree, as in the following sentences: The tree is as tall as our house and has many long branches. *The leaves are large and green all summer long. Sometimes I scrape my bare knees on the rough bark.*

READING (Parts of Speech)

▶ 1. Gather several toys, such as stuffed animals, blocks, a ball and a game. Ask your child to identify toys by their attributes. For example, ask your child which is the soft blue toy. After a few examples, ask your child to describe each toy using several adjectives. Repeat this activity with other groups of objects, such as foods, nature pictures, clothes and books.

▶ 2. Help your child gather a wide variety of objects. Play a game in which your child identifies each object with a noun. Write it on a card and place the card next to the object. Then, have your child say an adjective that describes one object. Write the adjective on a card and place the card by the object you think it describes. If the adjective describes more than one object, write that adjective on more cards and place the cards by all the appropriate objects. Ask your child to use another adjective that clearly identifies one object. Have your child continue providing adjectives until you have placed cards by all the objects. Some objects may have several adjectives. Then, have your child write a description of each object, using the accumulated adjectives.

MATH (Missing Addends)

Teaching the skill of finding missing addends reinforces your child's understanding of the relationship between addition and subtraction. Teach your child to think of the sum as a whole and the addends as the parts. Teach more than one strategy for finding the missing addend. Your child should adopt the strategy that makes the most sense to him/her.

▶ 1. Write an addition sentence on the board. Draw dots in a horizontal row to illustrate the sum of the problem. Draw dots representing one addend directly below the original row, aligning the dots carefully. Draw a vertical line and continue drawing the dots representing the second addend. Note that the two rows of dots are the same except for the vertical line which divides the bottom row into two parts. Have your child identify which number in the equation each set of dots represents. Draw a frame around the dots. This frame is called a part-part-whole frame. Write other addition sentences and have your child fill in a part-part-whole frame to illustrate the problem.

Learn at Home, Grade 2

Adjectives

An **adjective** is a word that describes a noun. It tells **how many**, **what kind** or **which one**.

Example: Yolanda has a **tasty** lunch.

Color each space that has an adjective. **Do not color** the other spaces.

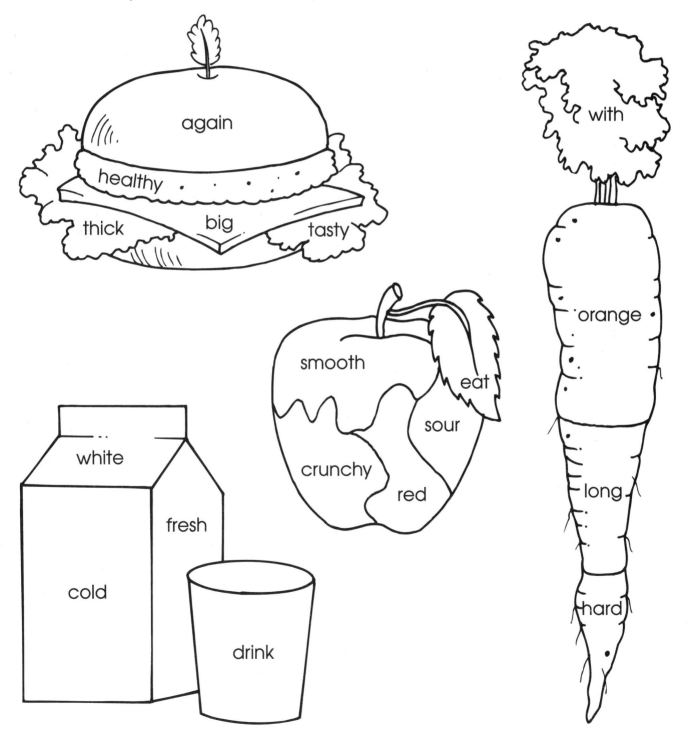

41

Add the Adjectives

Write a describing word on each line. **Draw** a picture to match each sentence.

high mountain

The _____ flag waved over the _____ building.

A _____ lion searched for food in the _____ jungle.

We saw _____ fish in the _____ aquarium.

Her _____ car was parked by the _____ van.

The _____ dog barked and chased the _____ truck.

The _____ building was filled with _____ packages.

42

Learn at Home, Grade 2

Something's Missing

In the forest, 10 animals have a picnic. Skunk brings 8 sandwiches. How many sandwiches should Raccoon bring so that each animal can have one?

$$8 + \text{?} = 10$$

What number added to 8 equals 10?
To find the missing addend, find the difference of 10 and 8.
That is, subtract the given addend (8) from the sum (10).

$$10 - 8 = 2$$

Since $10 - 8 = 2$, then $8 + 2 = 10$.
Raccoon should bring 2 sandwiches.

Find the missing addends.

$\underline{3} + 6 = 9$ $\underline{2} + 7 = 9$

$9 + \underline{1} = 10$ $5 + \underline{5} = 10$

$\underline{3} + 5 = 8$ $3 + \underline{7} = 10$

Things I think will sink:
(Place them here.)

Things I think will float:
(Place them here.)

Things I know sink:
(Draw a picture of each here.)

Things I know float:
(Draw a picture of each here.)

Learn at Home, Grade 2

Every town has some interesting street names. Streets can get their names in many different ways. They are often named after presidents, states, trees and flowers. What are some of the interesting street names in your town?

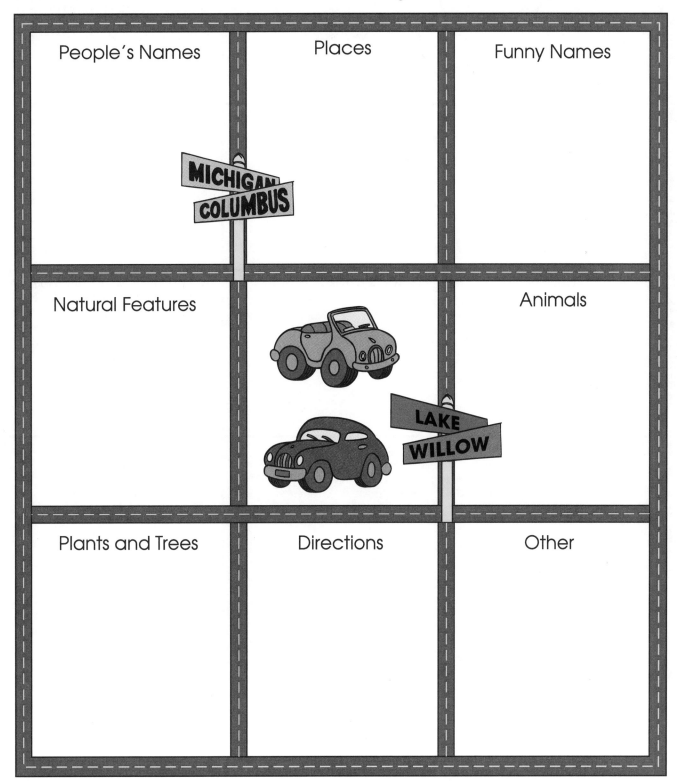

People's Names

Places

Funny Names

Natural Features

Animals

Plants and Trees

Directions

Other

	Language Skills	Spelling	Reading
Monday	**Nouns and Subjects** Take sentences from your child's writing. Have your child underline all the nouns (persons, places and things). Have your child try to write a sentence that does not contain a noun. (It can be done as a command because the noun is implied, not always stated.)	Pretest your child on these spelling words: job pop box rock got sock cob lot fox hop Review the phonics skills of short *o* vowels, the *ck* sound and the letter *x*.	**Vowels** Review the short vowel sounds and rules. *See* Reading, Week 4, number 1. With your child, read "Spring" in *Frog and Toad Are Friends* by Arnold Lobel. Have your child look for words that fit the rules. Have your child write a list using these words.
Tuesday	Teach your child to identify the subject of a sentence. Write several sentences on the chalkboard and guide your child as he/she underlines each subject. Have your child complete **Subjects of Sentences** (p. 50).	Have your child write the spelling words in sentences.	With your child, read "The Story" in *Frog and Toad Are Friends*. Have your child look for words that use the long vowel sounds and rules. Have your child write a list using these words.
Wednesday	Write ten individual sentences on sentence strips. Have your child determine each sentence's subject. Cut the subject of each sentence away from the rest of the sentence strip. Have your child mix and match the strips. They will probably form silly sounding sentences. Save these sentence strips for next week.	Have your child complete **Rocketing Off!** (p. 51).	With your child, read "The Lost Button" from *Frog and Toad Are Friends*. Review the long vowel sounds and rules. *See* Reading, Week 4, numbers 2–6. Write a list using these words. Have your child complete **Short and Long** (p. 52).
Thursday	Teach your child dictionary skills. Teach him/her what kind of information is available in a dictionary and how to look up words. He/she can look up unfamiliar words from the book read in Social Studies today. *See* Language Skills, Week 4, numbers 1.	With your child, brainstorm a list of words ending in *ob, ock, op, ot* and *ox*. Help your child write rhymes using these words.	With your child, read "A Swim" from *Frog and Toad Are Friends*. Have your child look for words that fit the short and long vowel rules. Have your child add to his/her lists using these words.
Friday	*See* Language Skills, numbers 2 and 3. Have your child brainstorm many possible topics for writing and keep a topic list for a time when he/she needs a topic. **Ideas:** Help your child think of favorite things he/she could write about, such as a toy, game, book or stuffed animal. Help him/her think of special people to write about? Encourage him/her to tell about a place to visit.	Give your child the final spelling test.	With your child, read "The Letter" from *Frog and Toad Are Friends*. Have your child write a letter to a friend. He/she can use a copy of the activity sheet (p. 232) for the correct form if needed.

     Learn at Home, Grade 2

Math	Science	Social Studies
Missing Subtrahends and Minuends Have your child identify numerals in a subtraction problem and place them in a part-part-whole frame. **Example:** 9−4=5 (9 is the whole and 4 and 5 are parts.) *See* Math, Week 4, numbers 1 and 2. Place the following subtraction sentences in part-part-whole frames: 9−5=4 7−5=2 8−4=4 6−2=4 9−6=3 6−3=3 5−1=4 8−5=3 6−1=5 7−3=4 9−4=5 4−2=2	**Observing Solids, Liquids and Gasses** Gather a variety of solid objects for your child to test following the questions in Science, Week 4, numbers 1 and 2. Have your child prepare a chart in his/her log with each question written along the left side of a grid. Have him/her write the name of each object along the top. Have your child make his/her observations.	**Cities** On a map of your state, point out the cities. Refer to the map legend to determine the relative size of the cities. Select a city near you to study for the week.
Using the part-part-whole frames that your child created yesterday, hide one of the parts or the whole and ask your child to figure out what number is missing. Ask your child to explain how he/she figured it out. Write the subtraction equation as a missing subtrahend or minuend. **Examples:** $7 - \underline{} = 2$ $\underline{} - 4 = 5$	Gather a variety of safe liquids for your child to test following the questions in Science, Week 4, number 1. Have your child prepare another chart in his/her log with each question written along the left side of a grid. Have him/her write the name of each liquid along the top and make his/her observations.	At the library, teach your child how to find information and maps for the chosen city. Have your child complete **City Research** (p. 55).
Write subtraction problems with the minuend (the top number) missing. Discuss ways your child could solve the problem. Have your child chose a strategy and find the answer. Repeat with other problems. **Example:** $\underline{} - 9 = 0$ $\begin{array}{r} \underline{} \\ -\,4 \\ \hline 5 \end{array}$ Have your child complete **Missing Subtrahends and Minuends** (p. 53).	Capture a gas (*see* Science, Week 4, number 2) for your child to test following the questions in Science, Week 4, number 1. Have him/her continue the chart in his/her log with each question written along the left side of a grid and the name of each gas along the top. Have your child make his/her observations.	If possible, visit a city. Visit the library, museum, downtown and other points of interest. Have your child write about his/her impressions of the city including a description using all the senses.
Game: Practice subtraction facts with missing subtrahends and minuends using concrete models. *See* Math, Week 4, number 3. Have your child complete **Food Fun** (p. 54).	Demonstrate that air (a gas) takes up space. *See* Science, Week 4, number 3. Have your child complete today's entry in his/her log.	With your child, read *City Seen From A to Z* by Rachel Isadora.
Review all processes learned this week involving missing subtrahends and minuends. Write word problems with these missing numbers. **Example:** I had ___ books. I had 10 grapes. I read 4 books. I ate ___ grapes. I had 2 left to read. I had 7 left. What is the missing What is the missing minuend? subtrahend?	Have your child review the three charts produced this week to determine the attributes common to all. Ask your child: *What are the attributes common to all solids? What are the attributes common to all liquids? What are the attributes common to all gases?* Have your child record his/her observations in his/her log.	With your child, read *The Adventures of Taxi Dog* by Debra and Sal Barracca. Discuss how Maxi's life in the city is similar to and different from yours.

47

TEACHING SUGGESTIONS AND ACTIVITIES

LANGUAGE SKILLS (Nouns and Subjects)

The subject tells who or what does something. It always contains a noun.

▶ 1. Buy or borrow a children's dictionary. Teach your child how to "look up" words by using the first letter of each word.

▶ 2. Start a writing folder with two pockets for your child. Your child should keep all his/her writing in the folder. Keep the topic list in the front of the pocket or in the three-hole binder for quick reference. Your child may also want to keep blank paper and a pencil in the folder so everything needed for writing is readily available.

▶ 3. Using the sentence strips from Wednesday, have your child choose his/her favorite silly combination sentence formed to illustrate.

READING (Vowels)

There are some predictable patterns with long and short vowels. There are also many "exceptions to the rule." At this point, it is best to teach the words that fit the long and short vowel patterns. Teach the words that do not fit as they come up. In context, your child will probably be able to read the word even if the vowel sound is different than the rule he/she learned.

▶ 1. Teach the following clue words to help your child remember the short vowel sounds: *a*–apple, *e*–egg, *i*–inch, *o*–octopus and *u*–umbrella. The long vowel sounds are the same as the letter names.
   Vowel rules:
   a. In a single-syllable word, if a single vowel is followed by one or two consonants, the vowel is short. **Examples:** *cat, fun, tent, rot* and *lint*
   b. In a single-syllable word with two vowels, the first vowel is long and the second vowel is silent. This is found when the two vowels are next to each other, as in *sweet, coat, train* and *read*. This is also true when the second vowel is an *e* at the end of the word, as in *tile, fame, poke* and *cube*.
   c. Finally, if a word has only one vowel, but the vowel is not followed by a consonant, the vowel is long, as in *so, we, hi* and *me*.

▶ 2. Ask your child what sound the letter *a* makes in *apple*. Have your child name some other words in which he/she hears a short *a*. Write the words on the chalkboard. Underline the *a* in each word. Repeat with the other short vowel sounds.

▶ 3. **Art:** Have your child paint a 6" *a* in the middle of a 18" x 24" piece of sheet and decorate it. While it is drying, have your child go through old magazines looking for pictures of objects that include a short *a* sound. Repeat with other short vowels.

▶ 4. Make ten vowel cards. Write the short vowels on five cards and the long vowels on each of the other cards. Give the cards to your child. When you say or write a word, have your child hold up the matching vowel sound card.

▶ 5. Use the spelling lists of rhyming words created during Weeks 1–4 and Week 5's short *u* spelling list, to read short vowel words. Then, add another vowel to the words, so they now have a long vowel sound. **Example:** *men-mean, hop-hope, cut-cute.*

▶ 6. **Poetry:** Reread the spelling rhymes that your child wrote during Weeks 1–4. Then, have him/her write rhymes using the long vowel words from activity 5.

Learn at Home, Grade 2

MATH (Missing Subtrahends and Minuends)

▶ 1. Write a subtraction problem on the board. Ask your child to identify each numeral of the equation as either a part or a whole. Have your child illustrate the number sentence by drawing dots in a part-part-whole frame.

▶ 2. Draw a part-part-whole frame with dots representing parts and the whole. Have your child write one or two subtraction sentences using the given parts and whole.

▶ 3. **Game:** Place five pebbles in a row on the table and have your child count them. Use your hand to cover some of the pebbles. Have your child identify the number of hidden pebbles by count-ing the number of pebbles that are still visible. Repeat with other numbers.

SCIENCE (Observing Solids, Liquids and Gases)

BACKGROUND
Attributes are the observable physical characteristics that are a part of an object or person. Your attributes include your size; your hair, eye and skin color; the way you smell; the texture of your skin; and the sound of your voice. The goal of this week's lessons is to have your child observe the attributes of solids, liquids and gases. In the following weeks, your child will observe water in each form.

▶ 1. For each object your child observes, he/she should answer the following questions in his/her log about its attributes. From the similarities, your child will be able to select the attributes that describe any solid, liquid or gas.
   • Is it a solid, liquid or gas?
   • What does it look like?
   • How does it act?
   • Does it keep its shape when it's put in a plastic bag?
   • Does it tip the balance scale?
   • Does it take up space?
   • Does it fill the balloon?
   To test the last question, put the solid, liquid or gas in an uninflated balloon. If the balloon inflates, you can answer yes. Gases will fill up any available space. This is one attribute that makes gas unique from liquid.)

▶ 2. Carbon dioxide is produced by exhaling. Capture your breath in a balloon or plastic bag. Carbon dioxide gas is also produced when vinegar and baking soda are mixed. Your child can capture the gas in a balloon. Put vinegar in a soda bottle. Put 1 tablespoon of baking soda in a balloon. Secure the opening of the balloon around the mouth of the soda bottle and empty the baking soda into the vinegar. Capture the gas in the balloon.

▶ 3. Put water in a large glass bowl or aquarium. Stuff one paper towel in the bottom of a glass. Ask your child to predict what will happen to the paper towel when you put the glass in the water. Turn the glass upside down. (The paper towel should not fall out.) Bring the glass straight down into the water without tipping. The towel does not get wet. Lead your child to propose that there is air in the glass. The air takes up the space and the water cannot fill the same space.

Subjects of Sentences

The **subject** of a sentence tells **who** or **what** does something.

Example: Some people eat foods that may seem strange to you.

Underline the subject of each sentence.

1. Some people like crocodile steak.

2. The meat tastes like fish.

3. Australians eat kangaroo meat.

4. Kangaroo meat tastes like beef.

5. People in the Southwest eat rattlesnake meat.

6. Snails make a delicious treat for some people.

7. Some Africans think roasted termites are tasty.

8. Bird's-nest soup is a famous Chinese dish.

9. People in Florida serve alligator meat.

10. Almost everyone treats themselves with ice cream.

Learn at Home, Grade 2

City Research

City's Name _____

Population _____

Area _____

Region in the U.S. _____

State _____

Founded _____

Other _____

_____

Main Industries/Businesses _____

_____

Types of Transportation Available _____

_____

Museums/Special Points of Interest _____

_____

Physical Description _____

_____

Learn at Home, Grade 2

	Language Skills	Spelling	Reading
Monday	**Verbs and Predicates** Take sentences from your child's writing. Have your child underline all verbs. Ask your child if he/she can write a sentence that does not contain a verb.	Pretest your child on these spelling words: sub but sun run bus fun nut cut tub cup Review the phonics skill of short *u* vowels.	Before reading, ask your child to think of different types of weather in your area. With your child, read *Cloudy With a Chance of Meatballs* by Judi Barrett. Have your child draw a picture of his/her favorite food raining down on the house and write a descriptive sentence of the picture using weather report vocabulary.
Tuesday	Teach your child to identify the predicate of a sentence. The predicate tells what the subject is or does. Write several sentences on the chalkboard and guide your child as he/she underlines each subject and circles each predicate. The predicate of the sentence contains the verb. *See* Language Skills, Week 5, number 1.	Have your child write the spelling words in sentences.	Discuss other weird weather events that could have occurred in the story. Have your child create his/her own town with an unusual weather storyboard. *See* Reading, Week 5, number 1.
Wednesday	Using the sentence strips from last week, have your child identify the subject and predicate of each sentence. Have your child complete **Predicates of Sentences** (p. 60).	Have your child spell each word aloud in a singing voice. Have your child complete **Submerging Subs** (p. 62).	Discuss Grandpa's character. Review long vowel sounds. *See* Reading, Week 5, numbers 2 and 3. Have your child write a description of Grandpa. He/she could also underline any words with long vowels sounds in them.
Thursday	Have your child build sentences using the subject and predicate wheel from **Wheelies** (p. 61).	With your child, brainstorm words ending in *ub, un, up, us* and *ut*. Then, have him/her write rhymes using these words.	Discuss nutrition and a balanced diet. Refer to the food pyramid. Analyze with your child whether the people of Chewandswallow were eating a healthy diet before the change in weather. Have your child plan and report a weather forecast for the people of Chewandswallow that contains appropriate foods for a nutritious and balanced day of eating.
Friday	Have your child write about something he/she has done with family or friends using many action words to describe the event.	Give your child the final spelling test.	Write each vowel rule at the top of a column on lined paper. Have your child look in the book for words that apply to each rule. Have your child write the words in the appropriate columns. *See* Reading, Week 5, number 4.

56

Learn at Home, Grade 2

Math	Science	Social Studies
Addition and Subtraction Facts to 18 Have your child group flash cards in meaningful categories. **Examples:** facts with same addends (6 + 6), facts with one-different addends (6 + 7), facts with even sums or facts with an even and an odd addend. *See* Math, Week 5, numbers 1 and 2. Have your child complete **Ride the Rapids** (p. 63).	**Water as a Gas** Ask your child to predict what will happen when heat is applied to a pan of water. Put a pan of water on the stove and heat until your child observes a change. Discuss the change. Ask your child to propose an explanation for where water goes when it leaves the pan. *See* Science, Week 5, number 1. Have your child complete today's log entry.	**Shelters** Discuss the meaning of the word *shelter*. Then, have your child look it up in the dictionary. Have your child look through old magazines to find examples of different kinds of shelters (from mansions to grass huts). Have him/her cut out, glue and label the pictures on construction paper.
Go through the flash cards one by one with your child. Set aside the facts that need more practice. Teach your child a strategy for each fact that needed more practice.	This experiment will take several days. Put three jars of water in the room. Have your child make a hypothesis and observe the changes to the water. *See* Science, Week 5, number 2. Measure and mark the water level in each jar every day. Have your child record his/her observations in his/her log.	With your child, read *Where Indians Live: American Indian Houses* by Nashone. Study and compare the different kinds of homes with your child.
Game: Using two blank dice or wooden or plastic cube blocks, write 1, 2, 3, 4, 7 and 9 on the faces of one die or block and 2, 4, 5, 6, 8 and 9 on the other. To play, your child rolls two dice or cubes and adds the numbers. To make your own dice for this game, use **Multipurpose Cube** (p. 65). Your child then writes the addends and sums on **The Numbers Game** (p. 64).	Have your child continue the observations from this week.	Have your child construct a model tepee. *See* Social Studies, Week 5, number 1. Your child can use **The Plains Tepee Pattern** (p. 67).
Play "The Numbers Game" again. Then, have your child complete **Addition Facts to 18** (p. 66).	Follow the directions in Science, Week 5, number 3. Discuss where the water goes when it evaporates. *Why is the plastic bag still full of water?* Have your child complete the log entry.	Have your child read different stories and legends about Native Americans to learn more about their lifestyle.
Using manipulatives or collections of objects, have your child "build" equations with sums between 10 and 18. Have him/her write the equations he/she built. Then, have your child write the equations in groups with the same sum.	Have your child continue the observations from this week.	Have your child write or diagram, in sequence, how he/she constructed the tepee home.

TEACHING SUGGESTIONS AND ACTIVITIES

LANGUAGE SKILLS (Verbs and Predicates)

▶ 1. Write the following sentences on the chalkboard:
The two little puppies rolled over each other.
The two little puppies were ten weeks old.
Ask your child to identify and underline the subject in both sentences. Have your child circle the rest of the sentence (or the predicate). Discuss what a predicate tells.

READING (Vowels)

▶ 1. Have your child create his/her own storyboard for **Cloudy With a Chance of _____**.
Fold a 12" x 18" sheet of construction paper into fourths.
In box 1, write "Cloudy With a Chance of _____" by _____.
In box 2, write "In the town of _____ it _____ _____ every morning."
In box 3, write "In the afternoon it _____ ."
In box 4, write "In the evening it _____."
Then, have your child draw pictures to describe each statement.

▶ 2. Write a list of one-syllable words that contain two vowels next to each other. **Examples:** *tail, boat, eat, eel, rain, meat, tied, seem, jail, feel, road, team, oat* and *pie*. Have your child read the list and tell how many vowel sounds can be heard in each word. Have your child identify the vowel sound and ask what letter does not make a sound. Have your child draw a line under the vowel he/she hears and an X on the silent vowel. Ask your child to use his/her own words to state a rule for these words.

▶ 3. Write a list of one-syllable words that have a vowel-consonant-vowel pattern. **Examples:** *make, time, woke, mule, came, mice, like, hope* and *pole*. Have your child read the list and tell how many vowel sounds can be heard in each word. Have your child identify the vowel sound and which
letter does not make a sound. Have your child draw a line under the vowel he/she hears and draw an X on the silent vowel. Ask your child to use his/her own words to state a rule for these words.

▶ 4. Discuss the following with your child: *Suppose the town's weather brought money rather than food. How would the story change? Write your own story about the town.* Ask what else the weather might bring.

MATH (Addition and Subtraction to 18)

Learning the addition and subtraction facts to 18 can be accomplished using some of the same activities that were suggested in the first 4 weeks, including missing addends, subtrahends and minuends.

▶ 1. Create flash cards for addition facts with sums to 18. Write equations vertically and horizontally so your child gains familiarity with working problems both ways. Write the answers on the back for self-checking.

▶ 2. Have your child group flash cards into categories that you propose, such as facts that add up to 13 or even sums and odd sums.

Learn at Home, Grade 2

SCIENCE (Water as a Gas)

BACKGROUND
Your child is already very familiar with water in its liquid form. Now he/she will study water in its gaseous form. Evaporation is the process that changes water from a liquid to a gas. Evaporation requires some source of heat. As water is heated, the liquid molecules move more rapidly until they are moving so rapidly that they move into the air, taking up the available space there. Steam is the first stage of liquid water turning into gas. At that point, the water is not always visible, but it is still present.

▶ 1. Put cold water in a saucepan and put it on the stove. Ask your child to draw a picture of the pan on the stove and describe what will happen when the water is heated. Observe the water and have your child describe what is happening as it heats. After the water has boiled for 10 minutes, ask your child to draw a second picture of the pan and label the changes. Ask your child to write an explanation for where the water is now.

▶ 2. Gather three wide-mouth jars for this experiment. Put 1 cup of water in each jar. Place one jar by a sunny window. Place another jar near a heat source. Place the third jar in a dark, cool location. Have your child draw each jar and describe its location. Your child may find it easier to observe change if he/she measures the height of the water in each jar with a centimeter ruler. Place the ruler along the side of the jar and note the water level in centimeters up from the table top. Use dry-erase markers to mark the level on the jar. Have him/her observe and measure the water level for several days.

▶ 3. Pour a half-cup of water on a plate and set it in a sunny window. Pour a half-cup of water in a plastic bag, seal it and set it in a sunny window. After 3 or 4 days, have your child pour the water from the plate into the half-cup measure and observe the water level. Then, have him/her pour the water from the plastic bag in the half-cup measure and observe. Ask your child to draw a conclusion.

1	3
2	4

SOCIAL STUDIES (Shelters)

BACKGROUND
Shelter is one of life's three necessities. Shelters are found in every neighborhood in the world. What form a shelter takes depends on the availability of materials, the climate and the needs (or desires) of the residents. For the next four weeks, you and your child will explore the variety of shelters in history and throughout the world. Learning about shelter broadens your child knowledge of cultures and diversity. If you have experience with other communities and their shelters, teach about that rather than those provided. Respond to your child's interest and enthusiasm. The point is to learn about diversity in lifestyle through the shelters of different communities.

▶ 1. Each book in the new series, *A New True Book*, published by Children's Press of Chicago, focuses on a different Native American group. The text and photos are an excellent resource.

▶ 2. Have your child read different stories and legends about Native Americans to learn more about their lifestyle.

Learn at Home, Grade 2

Predicates of Sentences

The **predicate** of a sentence tells what the subject is or does. It is the verb part of the sentence.

Examples: Sally Ride **flew in a space shuttle**.

She **was an astronaut**.

Underline the predicate in each sentence.

1. She was the first American woman astronaut in space.

2. Sally worked hard for many years to become an astronaut.

3. She studied math and science in college.

4. Ms. Ride passed many tests.

5. She learned things quickly.

6. Sally trained to become a jet pilot.

7. This astronaut practiced using a robot arm.

8. Ms. Ride used the robot arm on two space missions.

9. She conducted experiments with it.

10. The robot arm is called a remote manipulator.

Learn at Home, Grade 2

The Plains Tepee Pattern

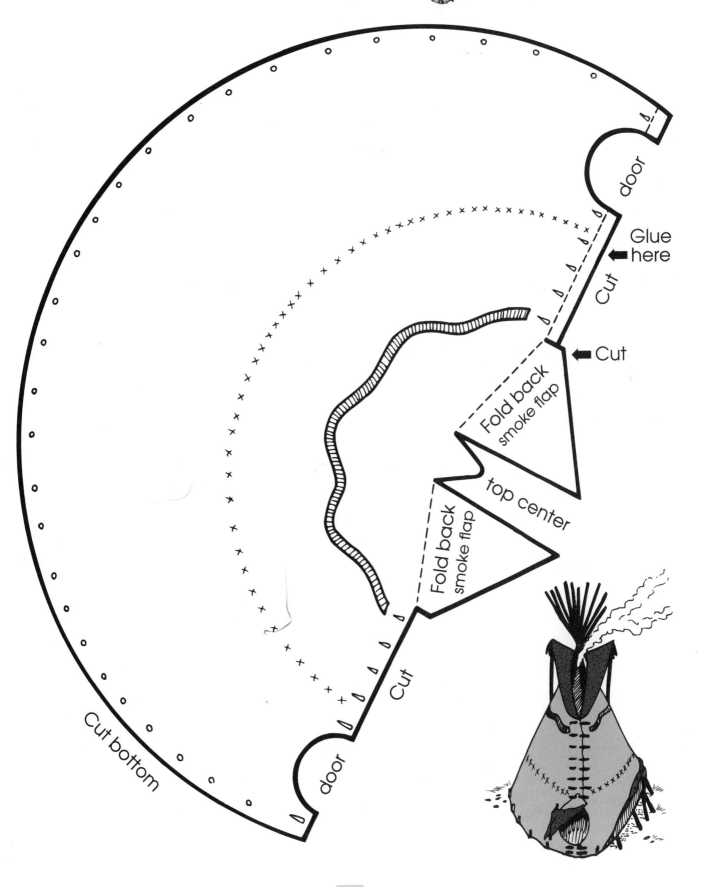

door

Glue here

Cut

Cut

Fold back smoke flap

top center

Fold back smoke flap

Cut

door

Cut bottom

	Language Skills	Spelling	Reading
Monday	A sentence is a group of words that tells a complete idea. It contains a subject and a predicate. Write some complete and incomplete sentences on the chalkboard. Have your child read each and identify the complete sentences. Have your child complete **Complete Sentences** (p. 72).	Pretest your child on these spelling words: way pain rain wait say lay pay sail day nail Review the phonics skill of long *a* vowels.	**Double Consonants/Adding Endings** Write the following words with double consonants: *buzz, toss, puff, sell, pass, call* and *drill*. Teach your child to recognize the double consonant in short vowel words. With your child, read a Nate the Great book by Marjorie Sharmat this week. *See* Reading, Week 6, numbers 1 and 2.
Tuesday	Write five incomplete sentences on the chalkboard. A sentence fragment may be missing a predicate or a subject. Have your child copy each incomplete sentence from the chalkboard, adding the words necessary to make them complete sentences.	Have your child write spelling words in sentences.	Write the list of short vowel words whose final consonant must be doubled before adding an ending. *See* Reading, Week 6, number 3. Teach your child that the final consonant must be doubled so the vowel remains short. Have your child look for words that follow this rule in the Nate the Great book and write them in a list. Have him/her circle the added endings and underline the root words.
Wednesday	Teach your child to identify a run-on sentence. Have your child write a brief story about a recent experience. Then, have her/him read the story to you without stopping, unless there is a period. Then, reread it with your child, and place periods where needed.	Have your child complete **Sail Away** (p. 73).	Teach your child that the root word does not change when there are already two consonants or the ending does not begin with a vowel. Discuss applying this concept while reading. *See* Reading, Week 6, numbers 4–6. Have your child look for words that follow this concept in the Nate the Great book read on Mon. and add them to Tues.'s list. Have your child complete **Double or Nothing** (p. 74).
Thursday	With your child, cut ten pictures from an old magazine. Have your child write a sentence about each picture and underline the subject and circle the predicate.	With your child, brainstorm and list other words ending in *ay, ait, ail* and *ain*. Then, have him/her write rhymes using these words.	Review the rules learned in the lists from Tuesday and Wednesday. Have your child use some of the words from each list to write sentences. *See* Reading, Week 6, number 7.
Friday	Have your child choose one of the pictures from yesterday's lesson and write a complete story about it.	Give your child the final spelling test.	Teach your child that, on long vowel words, you do not double the ending consonant. When a word ends with a silent *e*, drop the *e* before adding an ending, such as *ed* or *ing*. **Examples:** hope + *ed* = hoped hope + *ing* = hoping Have your child state the rules for these short/long vowel words when adding an ending. Have your child add endings to this week's spelling words.

68

Learn at Home, Grade 2

Math	Science	Social Studies
Have your child group flash cards in meaningful categories. **Examples:** facts with the same subtrahend and difference ($12 - 6 = 6$), facts with one-different "parts" ($13 - 6 = 7$), facts with even "parts" or facts with an odd minuend. *See* Math, Week 6, number 1. Have your child complete **Connect the Facts** (p. 75).	**Water As a Solid** Ask your child if he/she has ever seen water in its solid form. Have him/her propose how to change liquid water into a solid. Follow his/her plan. Check the process periodically and observe the changes as the water becomes ice. Have your child record his/her observations and draw pictures in his/her log.	Have your child construct a Native American community using last week's tepee model. Use a large box to display the project.
Go through the flash cards one by one with your child. Set aside the facts that need more time. Teach your child a strategy for each fact that needed more practice. Have your child complete the first twenty problems of **Subtraction Facts to 18** (p. 76).	Copy **Water Wizard Gameboard** (pgs. 78, 79) and prepare the game. *See* Science, Week 6. The object of the game is to reinforce the three states of water. Play the game with your child.	Have your child add any details that make a realistic scene for the model from yesterday.
Review the flash cards from yesterday that were not memorized. Use manipulatives to reinforce these facts. Finish the remaining twenty problems of **Subtraction Facts to 18** (p. 76).	Play the "Water Wizard Game" together.	Compare, contrast and di ss the differences between you ild's community and the Native Ameri ommunity studied yesterday. Ask: *Ho e they different? Which one would rather live in? Why?*
Have your child create "Fact Family" cards for all facts 11–18. **Example:** $4 + 7 = 11$ $11 - 7 = 4$ $7 + 4 = 11$ $11 - 4 = 7$ *See* "Fact Family" Game, Math, Week 6, number 2.	Brainstorm careers that have a connection with water. Ideas include a sailor, river boat or barge captain, oceanographer, swimming instructor, diver, lifeguard and scuba diver. Discuss each briefly. Have your child select one of the careers and research it.	Di s the homes built by the early icans and settlers in the West. Ask: at type of homes did they build and why? ave your child build a log cabin using toy logs, if available. Brainstorm how doors and windows were made. Ask your child how the settlers would have kept warm with the cracks between the logs allowing cold air to come in. *See* Social Studies, Week 6.
Play the "Fact Family" game from yesterday. Then, pick different facts and write word problems for your child to illustrate.	Have your child use the c earch from yesterday to write He/she may give the r lly or write it on **Ocean J /**).	Have your child propose the kinds of tools the settlers may have brought with them. Also, ask why there were not many doors or windows.

TEACHING SUGGESTIONS AND ACTIVITIES

READING (Double Consonants/Adding Endings)

BACKGROUND
A root word is the smallest form of a word without changing its meaning. It is the word before any suffixes or prefixes are added. For example, the root word of *rereading* is *read*. When adding an ending, such as *ing* or *ed*, your child may need to change the root word slightly so as not to change the vowel sound.

▶ 1. Add endings such as *ed* or *ing* to root words. Then, ask your child if the vowel sound has changed. Have your child underline the root word (review with him/her if necessary) and circle the endings.

▶ 2. While reading the Nate the Great book by Marjorie Sharmat, challenge your child to anticipate Nate's next question and solve the case along with him.

▶ 3. On the chalkboard, write these short vowel words whose final consonant must be doubled before adding an ending: *pat, wag, stop, hop, sit, run, get, win, bus, sun, sag, cut* and *step.* Have your child read the list of words on the board. Ask your child to identify the vowel sound in each word. (They are all short.) Add *ed* to *pat* without doubling the consonant. Change *wag* to *wagged.* Ask your child to read each word. Hopefully, *pated* will look odd to your child. Explain that the final consonant needs to be doubled to keep the vowel short. Without the double consonant, *pated* looks like the vowel-consonant-vowel rule (silent *e* rule). Have your child draw a line under the root word *pat* and circle the *ed* ending. Repeat this with the remaining words: *wagging, stopping, hopped, sitting, running, getting, winning, bussing, sunning, sagged, cutting, stepped.*

▶ 4. Show your child that when *s* is added to a short vowel word, the root word does not change. **Examples:** *caps, mitts* and *tens.* Have your child circle the ending and underline the root word.

▶ 5. Show that when there are two consonants at the end of a word, the root does not change. Write some of the following words to demonstrate this: *ending, rested, pushed, backing, kicked, sending* and *thinking.* Have your child circle the ending and underline the root word.

▶ 6. Write words your child may not be familiar with, such as *drugged, cramming, huffed, massed, humming, jammed* and *pulled.* Have your child circle the endings of all the words. Then, have your child read the word. Ask if the final consonant was doubled before the ending was added. While reading, if your child comes upon a word that he/she does not recognize, instruct him/her to cover the ending and see if he/she recognizes the root word.

▶ 7. Write a sentence, leaving out the verb. Draw a line to show where the word is missing. Write the root word of the missing word under the sentence. Have your child write the word in the blank, adding the appropriate ending and doubling the final consonant if necessary.
Example: The baseball player _____ the ball.
bat

Learn at Home, Grade 2

MATH (Addition and Subtraction to 18)

▶ 1. Create flash cards for subtraction facts with minuends through 18. Write equations vertically and horizontally so your child becomes familiar with solving problems both ways. Write the answers on the back for self-checking.

▶ 2. **Fact Families:** Create "Fact Family" flash cards with the addition facts on one side and the subtraction facts on the other. Write them vertically and horizontally.

Example:

$$
\begin{array}{cc}
4 \\
+7 \\
\hline
11
\end{array}
\qquad
\begin{array}{cc}
7 \\
+4 \\
\hline
11
\end{array}
\qquad\qquad
\begin{array}{cc}
11 \\
-7 \\
\hline
4
\end{array}
\qquad
\begin{array}{cc}
11 \\
-4 \\
\hline
7
\end{array}
\qquad\qquad
\begin{array}{l}
8 + 5 = 13 \\
5 + 8 = 13
\end{array}
\qquad
\begin{array}{l}
13 - 5 = 8 \\
13 - 8 = 5
\end{array}
$$

Hold up one card at a time and have your child tell you the related facts.

SCIENCE (Water as a Solid)

▶ 1. On the outside of a manila folder, write "Water Wizard Game."
Have your child color the copies of the two gameboard
pages and glue them inside the folder.
Duplicate the spinner base and tokens below on heavy paper.
Have your child color each token a different color. Your child
should cut out the tokens and spinner base. Glue the spinner
base to a plastic lid. Put a brad through a large safety pin
(the spinner) and the center of the lid.

  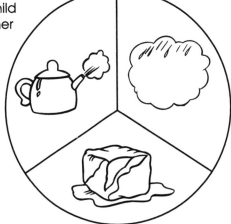

Directions for Two Players:
Each player chooses a token and places it on START. Player One spins the spinner and moves to the first space that matches the picture (form of water) on the spinner. He/she does what is indicated in the space. Players take turns spinning. The first player to reach FINISH is the Water Wizard.

SOCIAL STUDIES (Shelters)

▶ 1. When the early Americans sailed from Europe, they could bring very little with them. Discuss why and what they most likely brought. Ask your child to imagine moving to a new land. What would he/she take in one suitcase? Show on a map where the first settlers landed. Discuss what materials they might have used to build their first shelters. Discuss how the early Americans had to work together to get this accomplished. Settlers who moved west in the U.S. had similar needs. They could only carry what fit in a covered wagon or on a horse's back.

Complete Sentences

A **sentence** is a group of words that tells a whole idea. It has a subject and a predicate.

Examples: Some animals have stripes.
(sentence)
Help to protect.
(not a sentence)

Write S in front of each sentence. **Write No** if it is **not** a sentence.

_____ 1. There are different kinds of chipmunks.

_____ 2. They all have.

_____ 3. They all have stripes to help protect them.

_____ 4. The stripes make them hard to see in the forest.

_____ 5. Zebras have stripes, too.

_____ 6. Some caterpillars also.

_____ 7. Other animals have spots.

_____ 8. Some dogs have spots.

_____ 9. Beautiful, little fawns.

_____ 10. Their spots help to hide them in the woods.

Learn at Home, Grade 2

Sail Away

way   pain   rain

wait   pay   say   lay

sail   day   nail

Write the **ai** words that make the **long a** sound.

_____   _____   _____

_____   _____

Write the **ay** words that make the **long a** sound.

_____   _____   _____

_____   _____

Write the missing spelling word in the boxes.

1. It is a good _____ to fly a kite.

2. Did Mom _____ we may go to the show?

3. Please _____ here for the bus.

4. Sam does not know which _____ to go now.

5. Ray and Mable will _____ for the tickets.

6. Be careful when you hammer the _____ in the wall.

7. The _____ splashed in the puddles.

8. You may _____ your toy boat in the pond.

9. She felt _____ when the bee stung her.

10. Please _____ the blankets on the bed.

73

Double or Nothing

Circle the endings in the words below. **Draw** a line under each root word.

tripped	helped	classes	jetting	planned	drummed
matted	dressed	bagging	flagged	jammed	guesses
cuffs	pinned	cutting	zipped	tugging	tells
popped	sitting	plugged	hunted	tanned	starting

Write each word in the correct column.

Only ending added to the root word	Final consonant doubled before adding ending

Learn at Home, Grade 2

Ocean Jobs

Water Wizard Gameboard

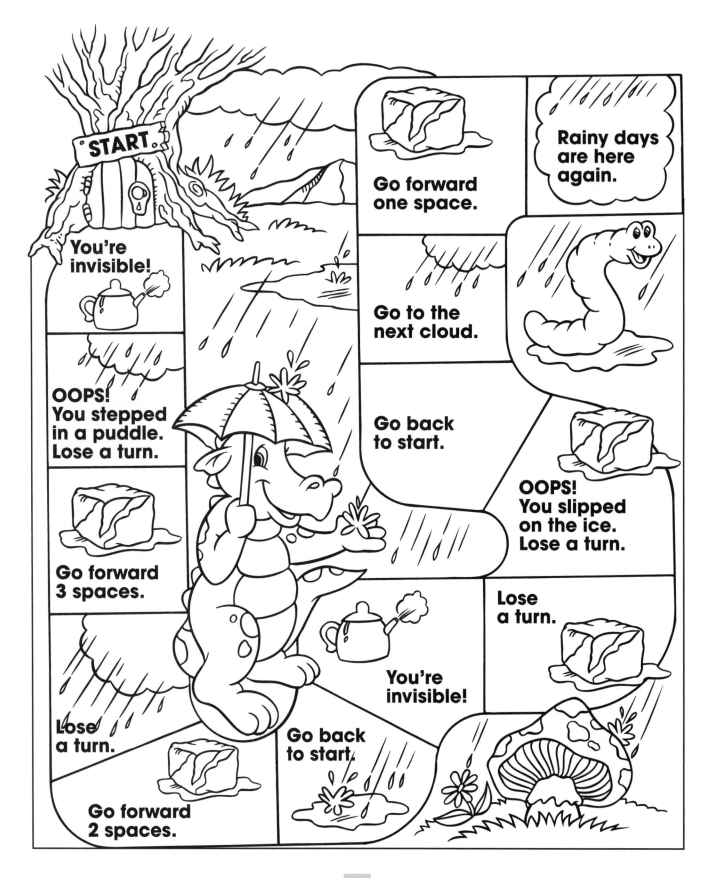

START

You're invisible!

OOPS! You stepped in a puddle. Lose a turn.

Go forward 3 spaces.

Lose a turn.

Go forward 2 spaces.

Go forward one space.

Go to the next cloud.

Go back to start.

Rainy days are here again.

OOPS! You slipped on the ice. Lose a turn.

Lose a turn.

You're invisible!

Go back to start.

78

Learn at Home, Grade 2

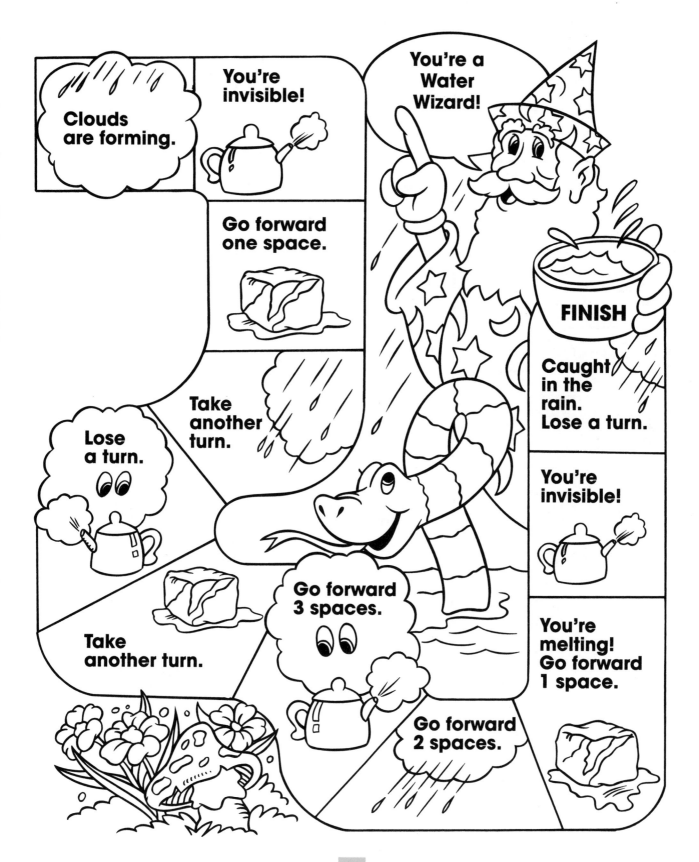

	Language Skills	**Spelling**	**Reading**
Monday	**Compound Subjects and Predicates** A compound subject has two or more subjects joined by the word *and.* Write several sentences on the chalkboard. Include some with compound subjects. Have your child circle the compound subjects. Have your child complete **Compound Subjects** (p. 84).	Pretest your child on these spelling words: eat　　mean　　sea team　　neat　　seat meat　　read　　beam 　　　　lean Review the phonics skill of long *e* vowels followed by a silent vowel.	**Y as a Vowel** Review the sound of *y* as consonant. *Y* makes its consonant sound at the beginning of a word or syllable. *See* Reading, Week 7, number 1. With your child, read *Lyle, Lyle, Crocodile* by Bernard Waber. Have your child identify the characters, setting, problem, events and solution in the story.
Tuesday	The following two sentences have the same predicate: *The boys went to the park. The girls went to the park.* They could be combined to form one sentence with a compound subject. *The boys and girls went to the park.* Write several pairs of sentences that have the same predicate. Have your child write each pair of sentences as one sentence with a compound subject.	Have your child write the spelling words in sentences.	Teach the long *i* sound of *y*. *See* Reading, Week 7, number 2. Find examples in the book where Lyle demonstrates that he is not to be feared. Have your child write a letter to Mr. Grumps explaining why he should give Lyle a chance.
Wednesday	A compound predicate has two or more predicates joined by the word *and.* Write several sentences on the chalkboard. Include some with compound predicates. Have your child circle the compound predicates. Have your child complete **Compound Predicates** (p. 85).	Have your child write each word in large letters, then outline the vowels with a crayon and trace over the letters with his/her finger several times. Have your child complete **Seeing the Sea Life** (p. 86).	Teach the long *e* sound of *y*. *See* Reading, Week 7, numbers 3 and 4. Have your child complete **A Fork in the Road** (p. 87).
Thursday	Look through familiar books for sentences with compound subjects and predicates. Have your child create and write sentences using compound subjects and predicates.	With your child, brainstorm a list of words ending in *eat, ean, ead, ea* and *eam.* Write rhymes using these words.	As you look through the book with your child, find words containing the letter *y*. Use the words to make a word search for your child.
Friday	When planning "Lyle" story for Reading, your child should include compound subjects and predicates in his/her writing.	Give your child the final spelling test.	Review the story elements described on Monday. Help your child plan an original story by changing some of the story elements from *Lyle, Lyle, Crocodile*. For example, your child may plan a story that takes place in Lyle's neighborhood but with a different animal. The problem may be the same or the animal may not be as friendly as Lyle. Help your child write the story he/she planned.

Learn at Home, Grade 2

Math	**Science**	**Social Studies**
Missing Addends, Subtrahends and Minuends: *See* Math, Weeks 3 and 4 for activities. Extend the activities to include equations whose sums (or minuends) are between 11 and 18. Play the "Numbers" game again with your 1–9 dice (from Math, Week 5, Wednesday).	**Water Cycle** With your child, read aloud poems and books about water. For some suggested titles, see Science, Week 7, number 1.	Inspect your house with your child to determine building materials and tools used. *See* Social Studies, Week 7, number 1. Have your child complete **My Special Home** (p. 89).
Create triangular flash cards for practicing fact families 11–18. List and write the different facts in each family. A fact family consists of the facts that come from one set of numbers. *See* Math Week 7, number 1. Use flash cards to have your child practice addition and subtraction facts 11–18.	Brainstorm the uses of water. Some ideas are listed below to get you started. drinking cleaning Have your child record the list in his/her log. Have your child draw a picture of him/herself using water.	In the book, *Homemade Houses, Traditional Homes From Many Lands* by John Nicholson, read chapter 2 "Houses of Reed, Grass and Bamboo." On a world map locate where these houses are located.
Use triangular flash cards to assess your child's speed and accuracy with addition and subtraction facts 11–18. Have your child complete the first two sections of **Missing Numbers** (p. 88).	With your child, read *The Magic School Bus at the Waterworks* by Joanna Cole. Review with your child, the ten water facts explored in this book.	Look at pictures of homes made of grass or leaves. Have your child draw a picture of one, including its surroundings. With your child, speculate on the home's stability and cost of replacement. Find out why some grass houses are on stilts.
Orally present problems that have a missing subtrahend. Use manipulatives (bottle caps, markers, pebbles, etc.) so your child can see what is happening. **Example:** Put 12 pebbles in a line and say, "Andy found twelve pebbles on his hike, but when he got home, he only had 7 left in his pocket." Line up 7 pebbles below the 12. "How many pebbles did he lose?"	**Water Cycle:** Review evaporation. Explore the evidence of condensation. *See* Science, Week 7, number 2. Have your child think of other times he/she has seen water drops form on a cold surface. Have your child write about it in his/her log.	Have your child make a paper house. Materials he/she may use include construction paper, blocks, tinker toys, a deck of cards or wooden logs.
Practice any facts from Wednesday's assessment for which your child needs more time. Have your child complete the third section of **Missing Numbers** (p. 88).	Demonstrate the formation of clouds. *See* Science, Week 7, number 3. Have your child draw a picture of the experiment and describe his/her observations.	**Field Trip:** Visit a building materials store, an architect's office and/or a building site. Discuss how homes are built. Look at the exterior materials (wood, brick or stucco), (presence or absence of) basements, number of levels and heating or cooling needs. Have your child write a thank you letter to the people he/she visited today.

TEACHING SUGGESTIONS AND ACTIVITIES

READING (Y as a Vowel)

BACKGROUND

Y takes on different jobs when it is found in the beginning, middle or end of a word. When y acts as a vowel, it usually makes the sound of a long e or a long i.

▶   1.   Write *yard, year, yak, yell, yarn, yum* and *you* on the chalkboard. Have your child read each word and single out the sound of y. Explain that this is the sound y makes as a consonant at the beginning of words.

▶   2.   Explain that y may make the same sound as the long i. It makes the long i sound in two cases: 1) If y is found at the end and it is the only vowel in the word, as in *by, fry, cry* and *my*. 2) If y is in the middle of the word and the only other vowel is *a* silent e, as in *byte* and *Lyle*.

▶   3.   Teach your child that y makes the long e sound at the end of two-syllable words, such as *jolly, sandy* and *friendly*.

▶   4.   Write *make, gate* and *hive* on the chalkboard. Have your child read the words and identify the vowel sound as long or short (vowel-consonant-vowel pattern). Write *pony, lazy* and *baby* on the chalkboard. Tell your child that the vowel-consonant-vowel pattern exists here too, but when y is at the end of a word, it is not silent.

MATH (Missing Addends, Subtrahends and Minuends)

▶   1.   To make triangle flash cards, cut out 20 construction paper (equilateral) triangles with 3–4 inch sides. For each equation, write the addends and sum on the three corners of a triangle. Write the addends in one color and the sum in a different color. Repeat for each of the facts up to 18. To practice, hide one corner of the triangle. Your child must name the hidden number. **Hint:** If the two numbers your child can see are the same color, he/she adds them. If the numbers are different colors, subtract.

9

15   6

Learn at Home, Grade 2

SCIENCE (Water Cycle)

BACKGROUND
The water of Earth goes through a continuous cycle. It moves from the land to the sky and back again by means of evaporation, condensation and precipitation.

▶ 1. A sampling of books about water are listed below.
Ardley, N., *The Science Book of Water*. Orlando, FL: Harcourt Brace Jovanovich, 1991.
Branley, F., *Floating and Sinking*. New York: Thomas Y. Crowell, 1967.
Evans, D. and C. Williams, *Water and Floating*. New York: Dorling Kindersley, Inc., 1993.
Peters, L., *Water's Way*. Boston, MA: Little, Brown and Company, 1991.
Reidel, M., *From Ice to Rain*. Minneapolis, MN: Carolrhoda Books, Inc., 1981.
Seixas, Judith S., *Water, What It Is, What It Does*. New York: Greenwillow Books, 1987.
Wheeler, Jill., *The Water We Drink*. Edina, MN: Abdo and Daughters, 1990.
Wyler, R., *Raindrops and Rainbows*. Morristown, NJ: Julian Messner, 1990.

▶ 2. Put ice water in a jar. Add food coloring and put the cover on. Ask your child to observe the jar for changes. Your child should observe that water drops form on the outside of the jar. Ask your child to propose from where the water drops came. They must have come from the air. Remind your child that heat made liquid turn to gas. The water as gas was still present in the air. The cold water cooled the water in the air and made it condense into its liquid form.

▶ 3. Fill a wide-mouth jar halfway with boiling water. Tell your child to quickly put the lid upside-down on top of the jar and place a bag of ice cubes on top of the lid. Clouds should soon be visible. Ask your child to recall what happened to the water as it was heated. How are the ice cubes affecting the water in its gaseous form? Have your child connect this to the formation of real clouds. If the clouds are not visible, sprinkle some fine particles of chalk dust in the jar and quickly put the lid back in place. Turn the lights off and shine a flashlight in the jar. The droplets of water will "stick" to the dust particles and be easier to see.

SOCIAL STUDIES

▶ 1. Have your child write a paragraph about his/her home using one of the topic sentences or sentence starters below.

My home is special for several reasons.
I like my home for two reasons.
If I could change one thing about my house, . . .
Living in my house is. . . .

83

Compound Subjects

A **compound subject** has two or more subjects joined by the word **and**.

Example: Owls are predators. **Wolves** are predators.
Owls and wolves are predators. (compound subject)

If the sentence has a compound subject,
write CS. If it **does not**, write **No**.

_____ 1. A predator is an animal that eats other animals.

_____ 2. Prey is eaten by predators.

_____ 3. Robins and bluejays are predators.

_____ 4. Some predators eat only meat.

_____ 5. Crocodiles and hawks eat meat only.

_____ 6. Raccoons and foxes eat both meat and plants.

Combine the subjects of the two sentences to make a compound subject.
Write the new sentence on the line.

1. Snakes are predators. Spiders are predators.

_____

2. Frogs prey on insects. Chameleons prey on insects.

_____

84

　　　　　　　　　　　　　Learn at Home, Grade 2

Compound Predicates

A **compound predicate** has two or more predicates joined by the word **and**.

Example: Abe Lincoln was born in Kentucky. Abe Lincoln lived in a log cabin there.
Abe Lincoln **was born in Kentucky and lived in a log cabin there.**

Kentucky

If the sentence has a compound predicate, **write CP**. If it **does not, write No**.

_____ 1. Abe Lincoln cut trees and chopped wood.

_____ 2. Abe and his sister walked to a spring for water.

_____ 3. Abe's family packed up and left Kentucky.

_____ 4. They crossed the Ohio River to Indiana.

_____ 5. Abe's father built a new home.

_____ 6. Abe's mother became sick and died.

_____ 7. Mr. Lincoln married again.

_____ 8. Abe's new mother loved Abe and his sister and cared for them.

Seeing the Sea Life

> neat   read   eat
>
> sea   mean   seat   beam
>
> team   meat   lean

Write the two letters that make the **long e** sound. _____

Write the spelling words that rhyme with each word below. **Circle** the letters in each word that make the same sound.

1. wheat _____

_____

_____

_____

2. tea _____

3. seam _____

_____

4. bead _____

5. bean _____

Write the correct spelling word from the word box.

1. Another word for ocean _____

2. Opposite of messy _____

3. Flashlights throw a _____ of light. _____

4. You sit on this. _____

5. You use books to do this. _____

6. Something you can eat _____

7. You use your mouth to do this. _____

8. A group of players _____

9. Opposite of kind _____

10. Ladders do this against the side of a house. _____

Learn at Home, Grade 2

A Fork in the Road

Write the words below on the correct "road."

sky   jelly   try   kitty   fly   my

fry   cry   funny   dry   penny

candy   by   sleepy   happy   lazy   baby

sly   fuzzy   shy   many   why

_____   _____

_____   _____

_____   _____

_____   _____

_____   _____

_____   _____

_____   _____

_____   _____

_____   _____

_____   _____

Y sounds like **long e**.   **Y** sounds like **long i**.

Learn at Home, Grade 2

Missing Numbers

Fill in the missing addend.

$9 + \bigcirc = 17$ $\bigcirc + 5 = 12$ $8 + \bigcirc = 14$ $5 + \bigcirc = 11$

$7 + \bigcirc = 13$ $8 + \bigcirc = 16$ $\bigcirc + 6 = 12$ $\bigcirc + 9 = 18$

Fill in the missing subtrahends.

$12 - \underline{} = 3$ $\qquad\qquad$ $11 - \underline{} = 4$

$14 - \underline{} = 6$ $\qquad\qquad$ $17 - \underline{} = 5$

$17 - \underline{} = 8$ $\qquad\qquad$ $15 - \underline{} = 10$

$16 - \underline{} = 9$ $\qquad\qquad$ $15 - \underline{} = 6$

$18 - \underline{} = 9$ $\qquad\qquad$ $15 - \underline{} = 9$

Fill in the missing subtrahends and minuends.

15	18	12	13	15
− 6	− 9	− 6	− 7	− 8
9	9	6	6	3

13	15	10	13	25
− 8	− 7	− 4	− 9	− 9
5	8	6	4	6

Learn at Home, Grade 2

My Special Home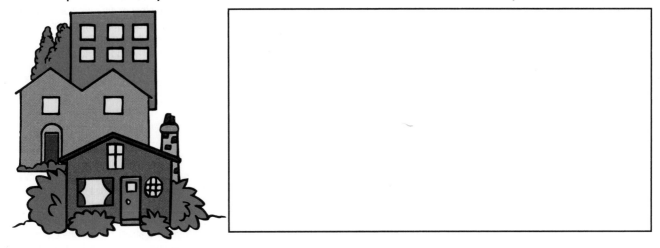

Draw a picture of your home in the box. Then, **answer** the questions.

1. How old is your home? _____

2. What building materials were used for your home?

_____

_____

3. Does your home have special features to make it attractive?
   (Examples: paint trim, walkway, decorated door.) List them.

_____

_____

_____

4. What do you like best about your home?

_____

_____

5. Do you think there are homes similar to yours in other parts of the country?
   Why or why not?

_____

_____

	Language Skills	**Spelling**	**Reading**
Monday	**Compound Sentences** Introduce compound sentences. To make writing more interesting, sometimes you use compound sentences and sometimes simple sentences. *See* Language Skills, Week 8, number 1. Have your child write the compound sentences he/she formed last week.	Pretest your child on these spelling words: thirteen fourteen forty fifteen sixteen sixty seventeen seventy twenty eighteen eighty thirty nineteen ninety fifty Review number words one to twelve. *See* Spelling, Week 8.	**R-Controlled Vowels** Tell the story of the rude *r* and provide examples of words that contain *r*-controlled vowels. *See* Reading, Week 8, number 1 and Background. With your child, read *Gregory, the Terrible Eater* by Mitchell Sharmat.
Tuesday	Have your child look in books for compound sentences that contain the word *and*.	Have your child write the spelling words in sentences.	Find examples of words that contain *r*-controlled vowels in the book. Have your child make a list of words, sorted by sound. With your child, read *Gregory, the Terrible Eater* again. Have your child think of a time when he/she did not want to eat what you prepared. Ask: *How did the cook react? How did you react?* Discuss this and make a plan for next time this comes up.
Wednesday	Teach your child to use the connecting word *but* to form compound sentences. **Example:** *All the girls were given a flower to hold while they danced. Mary dropped hers.* *All the girls were given a flower to hold while they danced, but Mary dropped hers.* See Language Skills, Week 8, number 2.	Have your child complete a copy of **Numbers and Number Words** (p. 94).	Refer to the book *The Scholastic Rhyming Dictionary: Over 15,000 Words* by Sue Young. Make a list of rhyming words with *a, e, i, o* and *u* followed by *r*. **Examples:** far, jar, car, germ, perm, term, girl, twirl, squirrel, bore, roar, soar fur, blur, purr
Thursday	Have your child look in reading books for compound sentences that contain the connecting word *but*.	Have your child write three addition word problems and three subtraction word problems using words from the spelling list. Have him/her also make an answer key for his/her story problems and/or illustrate the word problems to show the solutions.	With your child, read *A Day at Damp Camp* by George Ella Ryon. Look for words with the *r*-controlled vowels. Then, have your child use Wednesday's list to form sets of two rhyming words to illustrate. **Example:** far car, germ perm, twirl girl, bore roar, fur purr
Friday	Write the first part of several compound sentences on the chalkboard. Have your child finish each sentence. **Examples:** *I gave Tim a new book,* **but** _____ . *We sat down by the river,* **and** _____ . *Susie was coming to my house,* **but** _____ .	Give your child the final spelling test.	Have your child draw a picture of the contents of Gregory's refrigerator after he started eating a balance of what he likes and what his parents like.

Learn at Home, Grade 2

Math	Science	Social Studies
Commutative Property Place five objects in one pile and eight objects in another. Ask your child to count the total. Physically switch the piles. Ask your child to add them again. Ask why it was the same sum. Repeat with other numbers. Assess your child's understanding by observing whether your child adds the numbers each time they are switched. If your child does recount, continue teaching. *See* Math, Week 8.	**The Water Cycle** Demonstrate precipitation. *See* Science, Week 8, number 1. Discuss the different types of precipitation. Have your child record his/her observations in his/her log.	For thousands of years, Eskimos have lived in harmony in a harsh, snowy climate for 9 months of the year. Locate Alaska on the map. Discuss climate in relation to its location and read with your child "Inuit Igloo" in the book, *Homemade Houses: Traditional Homes from Many Lands* by John Nicholson. Have your child construct an igloo with play dough, clay, etc.
Use "Fact Family" flash cards from Math, Week 6, number 2. Hold up one side of the card and have your child tell you the other related facts. Have your child complete **Training With Facts** (p. 95).	Discuss the formation of clouds. *See* Science, Week 8, number 2. Go outside and observe the clouds together. Have your child write adjectives to describe them in his/her log.	With your child, read *Eskimo Boy: Life in an Inupiaq Eskimo Village* by Russ Kendall. Have your child compare and contrast Norman's life to his/hers. **Example:** parents' occupations, school, transportation, recreation, food, etc.
Fact Families With your child, read and discuss *12 Ways to Get to 11* by Eve Merriam. Then, choose other numbers from 12 to 18 and write lists of equations that equal these numbers.	With your child, read *The Cloud Book* by Tomie dePaola. Review the cloud descriptions in the book. Then, go outside and observe the different kinds of clouds. Have your child draw pictures of them in his/her log.	Review the Inupiaq Eskimo words in the glossary. Have your child choose five to write and illustrate.
Have your child create his/her own *12 Ways to Get to 11* book. Have him/her choose one of the lists from yesterday and change the title to "____ Ways to Get to ____." Have your child design and illustrate a page describing each equation. The book can be centered on a theme such as animals, holidays, games, sports, etc.	Have your child draw a picture of the water cycle. *See* Science, Week 8, numbers 3 and 4.	Have your child think over all the types of shelters he/she has studied. Ask what type of shelter he/she would like to live in for 1 year. Have him write about and explain his/her choice.
Have your child complete the math book from yesterday.	**Art:** On blue construction paper, glue cotton balls to resemble one type of cloud. The cotton balls can be pulled apart to form wispy clouds. Using crayons, have your child draw a picture below the clouds. The people in the picture should be dressed for the type of weather the clouds signify.	With your child, read *A House Is a House for Me* by Mary Ann Hoberman. Have your child design an appropriate house for a living being or non-living thing. Then, have your child write a paragraph explaining how the home fits its needs.

TEACHING SUGGESTIONS AND ACTIVITIES

LANGUAGE SKILLS (Compound Sentences)

▶ 1. Write two related sentences such as the following:
Bob saw flames shooting out of the windows of his neighbor's house.
He called the fire department.
Have your child read the sentences. Show your child how to replace the first period with a comma, add the connecting word *and* and change the *H* to a lower-case *h*. Write the sentences as one: *Bob saw flames shooting out of the windows of his neighbor's house, and he called the fire department.*
Have your child read it and decide if the meaning has stayed the same. Repeat this activity with other pairs of sentences. Guide your child through combining the two sentences into one compound sentence.

▶ 2. Write the words *and* and *but* on the chalkboard. Write the following two sentences:
Father fixed the roof.   The roof leaked last night during the rainstorm.
Ask your child which connecting word *and* or *but* would make more sense in this example. Have your child rewrite the sentences as one sentence, using *but* as a connecting word. Discuss when each connecting word would be more appropriate. Provide other sentences for your child to combine.

SPELLING

▶ 1. Write the number words *one* through *twelve* on the chalkboard in a column. Write the number words *thirteen* through *nineteen* in a column adjacent to *three* through *nine* so you can discuss the similarities and differences in spelling. Write the number words *twenty* through *ninety* in a third column. Discuss the root words and suffixes.

one		
two		twenty
three	thirteen	thirty
four	fourteen	forty
five	fifteen	fifty
six	sixteen	sixty
seven	seventeen	seventy
eight	eighteen	eighty
nine	nineteen	ninety
ten		
eleven		
twelve		

READING (R-Controlled Vowels)

BACKGROUND
There are many exceptions to the vowel rules learned in previous lessons. The first exception is when any vowel is followed by the letter *r*. The following story may help your child remember the *r*-controlled vowel sounds: The letter *r* is very rude. Whenever it is present after a vowel, it interrupts the vowel and forces it to make a different sound. It is most rude with the letter *a*. As you can hear in the word *far*, the *a* has lost its identity completely. The *r* seems to be saying its own name in that word. The *r* is impressed with the roundness of the letter *o* and lets it keep much of its identity. When the *r* follows the letter *o*, the sound is like the word *or*, as in *for* and *pork*. The rude *r* seems to show no favoritism with the letters *e*, *i* and *u*. When *r* interrupts these letters, all they can say is "er," as in *mother, bird* and *further.*

Learn at Home, Grade 2

Training With Facts

Use the numbers on each train to **write** the fact families.

___ + ___ = ___

___ + ___ = ___

___ − ___ = ___

___ − ___ = ___

___ + ___ = ___

___ + ___ = ___

___ − ___ = ___

___ − ___ = ___

___ + ___ = ___

___ + ___ = ___

___ − ___ = ___

___ − ___ = ___

___ + ___ = ___

___ + ___ = ___

___ − ___ = ___

___ − ___ = ___

95

	Language Skills	**Spelling**	**Reading**
Monday	**Review Week** Review the parts of speech: nouns, verbs and adjectives. Have your child write five sentences using a noun, verb and adjective in each.	**Review Week** Review vowel sounds. Dictate spelling words from Weeks 1–8. Have your child spell the words orally and identify the vowel sound.	**Review Week** Review the parts of speech. With your child, brainstorm a list of nouns, a list of verbs and a list of adjectives. Write the words on index cards and have your child form sentences using words from each part of speech. *See* Reading, Week 9, number 1. Have your child complete **Down to Basics** (p. 101).
Tuesday	Review subjects and predicates. Have your child complete **Predicates of Sentences** (p. 100).	**Game:** Play vowel bingo. *See* Spelling, Week 9, number 1.	Help your child write a tongue twister in the past tense. Have your child circle the nouns, draw an **X** over each verb and draw two lines under all adjectives.
Wednesday	Review complete sentences. **Center:** Write *Complete* at the top of one side of a manila folder and *Incomplete* at the top of the other side. On twenty index cards, write original complete and incomplete sentences or cut phrases from magazine and newspaper ads. Have your child sort the cards and place them on the correct side of the manila folder. Check your child's work.	Have your child choose two or three words from each weekly spelling list Weeks 1–8, and write seven sentences using these words.	Review vowel rules. Dictate to your child ten one-syllable words. Some words may have long vowels, sounds and some may have short vowel sounds. After you say each word, have your child identify the vowel sound verbally. *See* Reading, Week 9, numbers 2 and 3.
Thursday	Have your child write a list of five compound subjects. You write a list of five compound predicates. Then, together match the subjects with the predicates.	With your child, review and read the rhymes written from Weeks 1–8.	Review the jobs of *y* as a vowel and *r*-controlled vowels. *See* Reading, Week 9, numbers 4 and 5. Have your child complete **Y as a Vowel** (p. 102).
Friday	Review compound sentences. With your child, read *Just for You* by Mercer Mayer. Have your child write some original sentences following the pattern in the book.	Have your child choose three rhymes to illustrate. On paper, have him/her type the rhyme at the top and illustrate it.	Have your child list all the books he/she has read in the past 8 weeks. Cut 12" x 18" construction paper in half lengthwise (each piece will produce two 18" x 6" strips). Help your child accordion-pleat each strip into 6" squares. Glue the strips together to create as many squares as books read, plus one more square. For further instructions, *see* Reading, Week 9, number 6.

96

Math	**Science**	**Social Studies**
Review Week Use **Gameboard** (p. 104) to review addition and subtraction. *See* Math, Week 9, number 1 for game directions. Have your child complete **A Hidden Message** (p. 103).	**Review Week** Review the properties of water. Repeat some of the experiments from the first few weeks. Your child will enjoy them and may come away with a new perspective.	**Review Week** Review community vocabulary. Create a list of these words from the lessons of the past 8 weeks. Have your child define each word.
Test your child's speed and accuracy with **Addition Facts to 18** (p. 105). When finished, use **Gameboard** (p. 104). *See* Math, Week 9, 1a, 1b and 1c.	Continue with yesterday's lesson.	Discuss the importance of shelter. With your child, read *Fly Away Home* by Eve Bunting and *Uncle Willie and the Soup Kitchen* by DyAnne DiSalvo Ryan. Compare and contrast the main idea in both books.
Test your child's speed and accuracy with **Subtraction Facts to 18** (p. 106). When finished, use **Gameboard** (p. 104), Math, Week 9, 1d, 1e and 1f.	**Art:** Allow your child to experiment with watercolors. Show him/her how to make a color wash with a lot of water. Let the wash dry before adding paint applied with less water.	Choose a local park, street or other public area. Have your child ask a friend to help you both pick up all the litter. *See* Social Studies, Week 9.
Test your child's speed and accuracy with missing addends, minuends and subtrahends. Review the commutative property of addition. *See* Math, Week 9, numbers 2 and 3.	Look at a world map with your child. Have your child name large bodies of water. Look for large lakes and long rivers around the world.	With your child, read poems aloud from *Neighborhood Odes* by Gary Soto. Discuss the poems and have your child practice reading them with expression.
Using a part-part-whole frame, have your child write four facts (two addition and two subtraction). Have your child complete **All Aboard** (p. 107).	**Creative Writing:** Have your child write a story about the journey of a raindrop or snowflake as it moves through the water cycle. It may have interesting excursions in different countries, such as landing on interesting plants or being drunk by an unusual animal.	Have your child choose his/her favorite poem from *Neighborhood Odes*. Have him/her copy the poem neatly and draw a picture of it.

TEACHING SUGGESTIONS AND ACTIVITIES

SPELLING

▶ 1. **Game:** To prepare for vowel bingo, draw a five-by-five grid on drawing paper. Have your child write words from spelling weeks 1–7 randomly in the boxes. On ten index cards, write the five short vowels and five long vowels. To play the game: Choose a vowel card and state the sound, such as "short a." Have your child find one word on the game card that contains that vowel and place a bingo chip on it. Choose another vowel card and continue play until your child has covered five boxes in a row, column or diagonal.

READING

▶ 1. For this activity you will need four colors of index cards. Write one word on each card. Write all the nouns on blue cards. Write all the verbs on pink cards. Write all the adjectives on yellow cards. You may mix up the cards and have your child randomly pick one of each color and make a sentence using the three words. Or, your child may carefully choose three cards at a time to make a sentence.

▶ 2. Write twelve one-syllable words on the chalkboard. Divide a sheet of lined paper into four columns. Have your child copy the words from the chalkboard, grouping them on the paper by vowel sound and pattern. Have your child label each category appropriately. **Sample word list:** *goat, chat, go, rip, sent, brave, pod, plead, hut, be, yet* and *hunt.*

▶ 3. Write some regular and irregular verbs in present tense on the chalkboard. Use each word in a sentence. Ask your child to use the past tense of the same word in a similar sentence. Have your child write the past tense of each verb beside the original on the chalkboard. Discuss the changes made to the verbs. Look for patterns.

▶ 4. Write a list of one- and two-syllable words ending in *y*. Divide a sheet of lined paper into two columns. Have your child sort and write each word according to the sound that *y* makes.

▶ 5. Provide a list of words containing *r*-controlled vowels. Have your child read each word.
   Sample word list:

person	cursor	ward	form	gargle	warp
turnip	worsen	herd	sharp	worship	forest

▶ 6. This accordion-pleated banner will grow throughout the year as your child continues to read. Seeing the growing number of books he/she has read can be exciting and motivating to your child. Come up with a catchy title and illustration with your child. On the first square, write the title and have your child decorate appropriately. Below are suggestions for titles with ideas for illustrations in parentheses.

   Reading Passport (map)
   I ♥ Reading (books)
   Dino-mite Reading! (dinosaur)

   Rock and Roll with Reading (musical instruments)
   Reading Is Out of This World (solar system)
   Exercising My Mind (sports-related pictures)

   To complete the banner, have your child complete one square for each book read. On the square, your child should write the title of the book, one sentence about the book and a drawing that illustrates the main idea or a favorite scene from the book.

Learn at Home, Grade 2

MATH

▶ 1. **Game/Center:** Reinforce the following addition and subtraction skills using **Gameboard** (p. 104). Store each gameboard and the cards in a large envelope.

   a. **Addition:** Write numerals between 1 and 9 randomly in the spaces on the gameboard. On eight to ten index cards, write instructions such as "___ + 5," "+ 4," or "double the number." Provide a regular die and a game piece. Put the cards facedown on the designated place on the gameboard.
   Directions for your child: *Roll the die and move the marker the number of spaces indicated. Look at the number landed on. Pick the top card and add the number on the card to the number on the gameboard. Write the problem and its answer on a separate sheet of paper. When you have reached "finish," have me check your paper.*

   b. **Subtraction:** Use the gameboard from the addition game above. On nine index cards, write
   "15 – ___," "12 – ___," "18 – ___," and other sentences using numbers 10–18 as minuends. The number on the gameboard is subtracted from the number on the card. Have your child write the equation and answer on a separate sheet of paper. Use the same materials as above.

   c. **Addition and Subtraction:** Cards from the above games can be combined so your child can practice both operations at the same time.

   d. **Missing Addends:** On nine index cards, write the following equations: ___ + ___ = 10, ___ + ___ = 11, ___ + ___ = 12, ___ + ___ = 13, and so on through 18. Have your child roll the die, move to the designated space and read the number there. He/she should also choose a card from the pile, fill in the number from the gameboard as one of the addends, then solve the equation for the missing addend. Have your child write the equations on lined paper throughout the game.

   e. **Missing Minuend:** Use the same gameboard, game parts and directions as above. The nine cards should read as follows: ___ – 9 = ___, ___ – 8 = ___, ___ – 7 = ___, ___ – 6 = ___, and so on to – 1. Your child should fill in the number from the gameboard as the final difference and solve for the missing minuend.

   f. **Missing Subtrahend:** Use the same gameboard, game parts and directions as above. The nine cards should read as follows: 18 – ___ = ___, 17 – ___ = ___, 16 – ___ = ___, and so on. Your child should fill in the number from the gameboard as the final difference and solve for the missing subtrahend.

▶ 2. Hold up addition flash cards without answers one at a time (sums through 18). Have your child respond each time with the related addition problem and the answer (commutative property).

▶ 3. Write three numbers (fact family) on the chalkboard, such as 5, 12 and 7. Ask your child to identify which numbers are the addends and which is the sum. Have your child write an addition problem on board using these numbers.

SOCIAL STUDIES

▶ 1. Have your child wear gloves while handling trash. While he/she is working, have him/her notice what type of litter is found. Have your child make a poster asking the neighbors not to litter. Include pictures on the poster of the type of litter found. Laminate the poster and hang it up at a nearby store.

Predicates of Sentences

The **predicate** of a sentence tells what the subject is or does.

Example: Cars **pollute the air**.
Cars **are helpful machines**.

Color each piece **red** that holds a predicate. **Color** the other pieces **blue**.

our next car

a steering wheel

the engine

four new tires

electric cars

air pollution

some vans

a battery

uses gasoline

adds to smog

is used everyday

carries people

burns fossil fuels

looks neat

goes fast

costs a lot of money

makes pollution

100

Learn at Home, Grade 2

Down to Basics

In each sentence, **circle** the nouns, **draw** an **X** above the verbs and **draw two lines** under all adjectives.

1. The children saw a black cloud in the sky.

2. Rain fell from the enormous black cloud.

3. Lightning flashed and thunder crashed.

4. The rain made puddles on the ground.

5. Moving cars splashed water.

6. The children raced into the house.

7. Ten boys and six girls belong to the Wildcat team.

8. The Wildcats played the Greyhounds from Central City.

9. The Wildcats won the big game.

10. The coach said, "The Wildcats made two more goals than our team."

11. The circus came to town on Thursday.

12. On Friday, the circus had a parade.

13. The silly monkeys rode in a cage and did tricks.

14. The huge elephants pulled heavy wagons.

15. People laughed at the funny clowns.

Y as a Vowel

Y as the long sound of **e**.
Y as the long sound of **i**.

Color the spaces:
purple – **y** sounds like **i**.
yellow – **y** sounds like **e**.

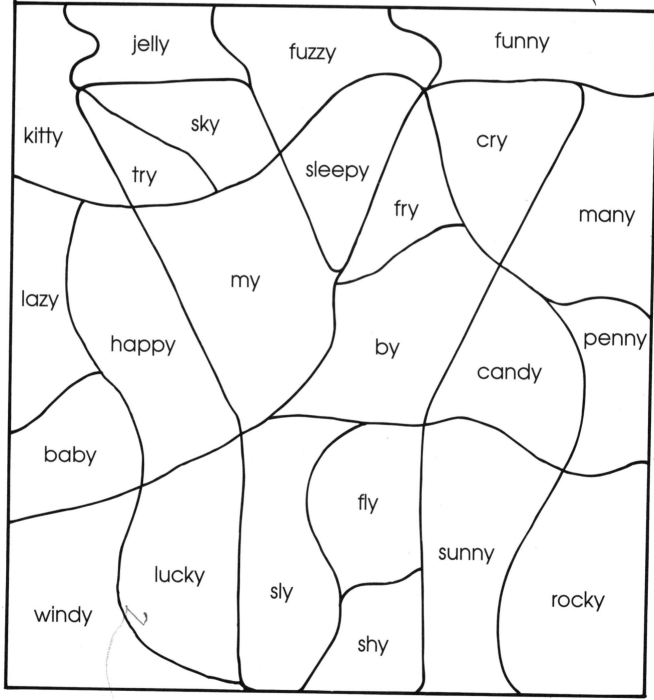

jelly

fuzzy

funny

kitty

sky

cry

try

sleepy

fry

many

my

lazy

happy

by

penny

candy

baby

fly

sunny

lucky

sly

rocky

windy

shy

102

Learn at Home, Grade 2

Addition
Facts to 18

3	7	9	5	7
+3	+4	+6	+6	+4

9	4	4	5	2
+3	+6	+8	+5	+4

5	1	9	6	8	5	3	8	4	6
+8	+7	+3	+8	+9	+6	+8	+7	+3	+7

5	7	9	3	2	7	4	3	9	3
+9	+3	+4	+6	+8	+6	+5	+9	+7	+4

8	3	5	9	8	8	6	9	7	8
+6	+5	+7	+9	+6	+5	+7	+8	+9	+4

Learn at Home, Grade 2

Subtraction
Facts to 18

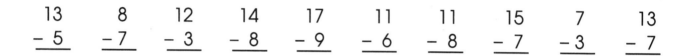

6 − 3	11 − 4	15 − 6	11 − 6	11 − 4

12 − 3	10 − 6	12 − 4	10 − 5	6 − 4

13 − 5	8 − 7	12 − 3	14 − 8	17 − 9	11 − 6	11 − 8	15 − 7	7 − 3	13 − 7

14 − 9	10 − 3	13 − 4	9 − 6	10 − 8	13 − 6	9 − 6	12 − 9	16 − 7	7 − 4

14 − 6	8 − 5	12 − 7	18 − 9	14 − 6	13 − 8	13 − 6	17 − 8	16 − 9	12 − 4

Learn at Home, Grade 2

Add or subtract. Match the related facts.

5 + 9 = __14__ •   • 6 + 9 = _____

8 + 7 = _____ •   • 14 – 9 = __5__

15 – 9 = _____ •   • 15 – 7 = _____

17 – 8 = _____ •   • 14 – 7 = _____

7 + 7 = _____ •   • 9 + 8 = _____

Add or subtract. **Color** spaces brown with answers greater than 12.
Color the rest green.

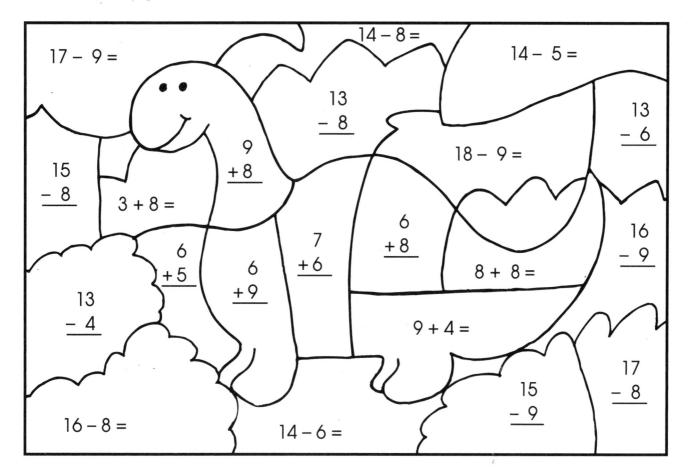

	Language Skills	**Spelling**	**Reading**
Monday	**Writing Sentences** Teach your child that a statement tells. Provide examples. Point out the capital letter at the beginning and the period at the end of each statement. Have your child complete **Summer Camp** (p. 112).	Pretest your child on these spelling words: kind mile side wind mind line bike fine find time Review the silent *e* rule. The other words in this list also contain the long *i* sound, but they do not follow a phonics rule.	**Blends** Write each of the following blends on half of an index card: *sc, st, sw, sl, sp, sn, sk, sm, br, fr, tr, pr, gr, cr, dr, pl, bl, fl, cl* and *gl*. Read through the cards with your child. Teach him/her to say each blend. Give examples of words containing each blend. Save the cards for Week 18. *See* Reading, Week 10, numbers 1 and 2.
Tuesday	Show your child a photograph. Have him/her tell something about the picture in one sentence and write the sentence on lined paper. Provide up to ten pictures for your child to write about.	Have your child write the spelling words in sentences.	Write each of the following word parts on half of an index card: *at, ame, eed, an, ate, ew, op, ide, ied, eep, y, oke, ay, ip* and others you think of. Have your child match blends and word chunks to make and read words. With your child, read *Frederick* by Leo Lionni. Have your child look for words in *Frederick* that begin with blends learned on Monday.
Wednesday	Choose two photos from yesterday. Then, write five statements about each photo including *Who* (is in the picture), *What* (is happening), *Why* (is it happening), and *When* (is it happening). Remind your child to begin each sentence with a capital and end each with a period.	Have your child spell each word aloud as he/she finger spells the word on a rough surface. Have your child complete **Wind It Up!** (p. 113).	Sometimes the *s* blends combine with another consonant and form a three-letter blend. Write the following: *spring, splash, scream, stripe, streak, scram, sprout, split*. Read the words with your child and isolate the blend sound. Have your child make a list of three-letter blends. He/she may find more three-letter blends in the reading. *See* Reading, Week 10, numbers 3 and 4.
Thursday	With your child, read yesterday's sentences and have him/her underline the subject and circle the predicate in each sentence. Have your child list words that begin with blends.	Have your child look for his/her spelling words in the newspaper and circle them.	With your child, read and choose three tongue twisters from *Six Sick Sheep: 101 Tongue Twisters* that use blends. Have your child write the tongue twisters and then illustrate them.
Friday	Sometimes while reading, you come across a sentence that does not make sense. When you reread it, you realize you read it wrong originally and now it makes sense. Teach your child to read for understanding. If a sentence does not make sense, he/she should stop and reread it before going on. When writing, reread what was written to make sure it says what was intended. *See* Language Skills, Week 10, numbers 1 and 2.	Give your child the final spelling test.	With your child, read *Frederick* again. Discuss the value of Frederick's contribution. Discuss the importance of people having a variety of talents. Discuss the importance of accepting others and valuing their uniqueness. Have your child create his/her own poem about his/her favorite season.

Learn at Home, Grade 2

Math	Science	Social Studies
Patterns and Number Order Have your child look around your home, inside and outside, for simple patterns. **Example:** wallpaper, floor tile, furniture, dishes, plants, carpet, etc. Discuss what constitutes patterns. Then, have your child create patterns using manipulatives. *See* Math, Week 10, number 1.	**Oceans** Study the oceans on a world map or globe. *See* Science, Week 10, number 1.	**Geography** Study the continents. Observe a globe with your child. Talk about what it represents. *See* Social Studies, Week 10, numbers 1 and 2.
Continue with Monday's patterning activities. When your child is comfortable making and identifying patterns, go on to number patterns. *See* Math, Week 10, number 2.	With your child, read or watch *The Magic School Bus On the Ocean Floor* by Joanna Cole. Have your child draw a chart of the ocean floor. *See* Science, Week 10, numbers 2 and 3.	Compare the globe to a map of the world. Have your child read each continent name and trace the outline of the continent with his/her finger. Have your child complete **Count the Continents** (p. 115).
With your child, read *Even Steven and Odd Todd* by Kathryn Cristaldi. Discuss concept of odd and even numbers. Have your child choose and complete follow-up activities from the end of the book.	Why is the ocean salty? Conduct a salt water experiment. *See* Science, Week 10, number 4.	Have your child create his/her own "Continent Collage" on a 12" x 18" sheet of blue construction paper. Help him/her tear and glue shapes of each continent, each in a different color, in their proper location.
Start with a chart numbered up to 100. Put it in front of your child and eventually remove it. Ask your child questions such as, *What number comes after 45? What number comes between 76 and 78?* If your child answers this type of question with confidence, add questions such as *What number comes two after 63?* Have your child complete a copy of **Unpack the Teddy Bears** (p. 114).	Conduct another salt water experiment. *See* Science, Week 10, number 5. Have your child record his/her observations in the Science Log.	With your child, read and discuss *Maps and Globes* by Harriett Barton. Help your child recognize physical features on a world map and learn to read the map key.
Play a number riddle game. Give clues to your child so he/she can guess your number. Repeat several times. Then, let your child make up the riddles. **Example:** *I'm thinking of an odd number that is between 50 and 64. You can count by fives to get to this number.* (55)	Have your child observe Wednesday's salt water experiment and record observations in his/her log. Then, have him/her locate and name the four oceans: Pacific, Atlantic, Indian and Arctic. Have him/her write their names on the "Continent Collage" map. *See* Social Studies, Week 10, Wednesday.	With your child, look again at a world map in an atlas or use **Count the Continents** (*see* Tuesday).

Learn at Home, Grade 2

TEACHING SUGGESTIONS AND ACTIVITIES

LANGUAGE SKILLS (Writing Sentences)

A *statement* is a telling sentence.

▶ 1. Changing the word order of a sentence can make it either unclear or easier to understand. Write the following sentence on the chalkboard: Very slowly the man old walked. Have your child rearrange the words so the sentence is clearer. Write other sentences out of order. Have your child write the sentences on paper in the correct order.

▶ 2. A sentence should make sense. Write a paragraph for your child to read. Include a sentence that does not make sense and have your child identify it. Then, ask him/her to rewrite it so that it makes sense. **Example:** My family took a trip to Yellowstone. We rode in the car for a week to get there. We were very cramped in the car, and sometimes we argued. When we finally got to the campground, I like animals that cuddle on my lap. The next day, we drove to Old Faithful and the other geysers. We liked the bubbling mud pots best of all.

READING (Blends)

A blend may be made up of two or three consonants that are read as a unit while each letter retains its sound. The letters of a blend are never divided by syllables.

▶ 1. Give your child only the blend cards that begin with *s*. Prepare a list of words that contains *s* blends. Read one word at a time from the list and have him/her listen for the blend. He/she then holds up the appropriate blend card. If he/she shows you the wrong blend, write the word on the chalkboard and underline the blend. Repeat this activity with the remaining blend cards.

▶ 2. Write some unfamiliar words that begin with blends. Have your child read the words in isolation. If this is too difficult for your child, put each word in a sentence where context will also help him/her figure out the word.

▶ 3. Write some unfamiliar words that begin with three-letter blends. Have your child read them aloud. Put them in sentences if necessary.

▶ 4. Combine the three-letter blends with the word chunks from Tuesday's lesson to form new words.

MATH (Patterns and Number Order)

BACKGROUND
Patterns form the basis of mathematics. Finding those patterns increases your child's comprehension of math and math reasoning. Patterning involves some kind of repetition or predictability. The ability to recognize patterns in numbers requires experience first with simple patterns and concrete materials. Increase the complexity of the patterns with concrete materials and provide opportunities for your child to discover the many patterns in numbers as well. Numbers written in the base-ten system have repetition from 0–9 in the tens and ones places. Seeing this pattern will give your child confidence with numbers and number order from 1 to 100.

▶ 1. Choose from the following activities to provide concrete experience with patterns before working with number patterns.

Learn at Home, Grade 2

a. Your child can copy, repeat or design patterns using manipulatives, such as blocks, keys, macaroni shapes and buttons. Ask him/her to copy a pattern using a different manipulative. Patterns can be simple or complex and involve colors, positions or shapes. Your child will enjoy extending a pattern across the floor, repeating the basic pattern several times.

b. Have your child recreate a pattern using words or noises in place of concrete materials. **Example:** Do the actions *clap, snap, stomp, clap, snap, stomp.*

▶ 2. Provide a hundred chart (matrix) and a simple number pattern. Ask your child to continue the pattern. Here are some number patterns to get you started:

2, 4, 6, 8, 10, . . .   5, 10, 15, 20, 25, . . .   4, 14, 24, 34, 44, . . .

SCIENCE (Oceans)

The four oceans are interesting to study for their enormous size, salty water and fascinating animal and plant life. Each ocean has its own particular characteristics that you can read about in books and the encyclopedia.

▶ 1. Look at a world map or a globe together. Notice that the four oceans are connected, although the continents break them up into distinct bodies. Have your child identify the largest ocean. Each ocean also includes smaller bodies of water formed where the land creates seas, gulfs or bays. Help your child copy names of oceans and seas in his/her Science Log.

▶ 2. Ask your child to imagine what the ocean floor might look like. Your child may be surprised to find that the ocean floor is not flat. In fact, the longest mountain range in the world lies at the bottom of the Atlantic Ocean. Most of the mountains in the ocean are not visible but some rise above the water and form islands. Scientists have mapped and named the mountains and valleys on the ocean floor.

▶ 3. Ocean water contains many minerals, including salt. The salt comes from rocks. The rocks on land contain salt and other minerals. As the water washes over the rocks, it wears away the surface and the minerals dissolve in the oceans. The water may be saltier in some areas of the oceans. Near the equator, the water is very salty because the hot Sun evaporates away the fresh water.

▶ 4. Dissolve as much salt as you can in a half-cup of water. Pour the salt water in a plate and put it in a sunny window. Predict what will happen. Check the salt water in a few days and record what has happened to the water and the salt. Have your child make a connection to what happens to ocean water when it is exposed to the Sun.

▶ 5. Dissolve 1 teaspoon of salt in 1 cup of water. Prepare a second cup with the same amount of fresh water. Drop a very light object in both cups. A small piece of carrot works. If you can cut the carrot piece to just the right size, it will float in the salt water and sink in the fresh water. If you have ever been swimming in the ocean, you know that it is easier to float in salt water than fresh water because salt water is more dense.

SOCIAL STUDIES (Geography)

Geography is the study of locations, people and how people relate to their environment.

▶ 1. Show your child a globe. Teach him/her to recognize the features of land and water. Ask your child to guess whether there is more land or water on Earth.

▶ 2. Teach your child to recognize the large land masses as continents. Name each of the continents. Have your child repeat the names after you.

Summer Camp

A **statement** is a telling sentence. It begins with a capital letter and ends with a period. **Write** each statement correctly on the lines.

1. everyone goes to breakfast at 6:30 each morning

_____

2. only three people can ride in one canoe

_____

3. each person must help clean the cabins

_____

4. older campers should help younger campers

_____

5. all lights are out by 9:00 each night

_____

6. everyone should write home at least once a week

_____

Learn at Home, Grade 2

Wind It Up!

Write the missing spelling word in the boxes.

side   wind   mind

mile   line   kind   bike

fine   find   time

1. The ball bounced on the other _____ of the fence.

2. It is almost _____ to go to school.

3. We have to walk one _____ to the swimming pool.

4. The men painted a _____ down the middle of the road.

5. Do you ride your _____ to school?

6. Always _____ your parents.

7. Bill can't _____ his other sneaker.

8. It is a _____ day for a picnic in the park.

9. Mike's toy car races along the floor if you _____ it up.

10. Everyone should be _____ to his/her pet.

Unpack the Teddy Bears

Cut out the bears at the bottom of the page. **Glue** them where they belong in number order.

Learn at Home, Grade 2

Count the Continents

Color:

Europe – green
Asia – purple
Australia – red
Africa – yellow

North America – orange
South America – brown
Antarctica – blue

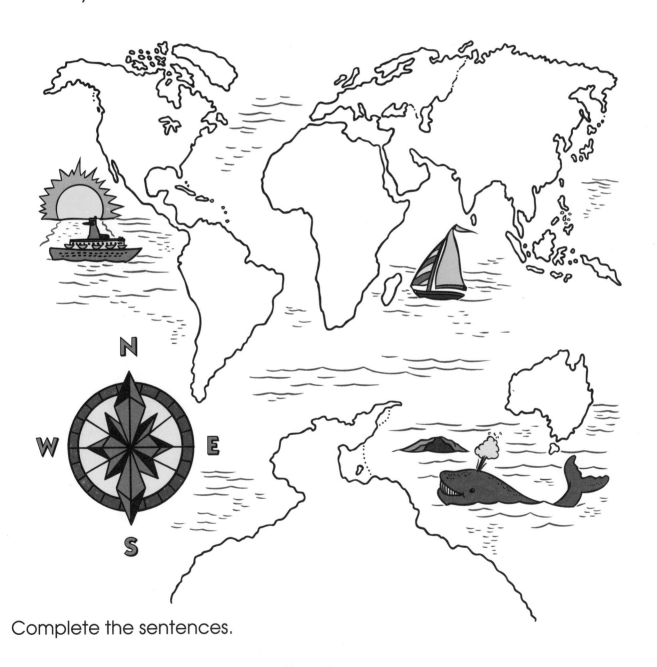

Complete the sentences.

1. There are _____ continents.

2. We live on the continent of _____ .

	Language Skills	**Spelling**	**Reading**
Monday	**Questions** A *question* is a sentence that asks. Write examples of questions on the chalkboard. Point out the capital letter at the beginning of the sentence and the question mark at the end. You may need to teach your child how to form the question mark. Have your child complete **Questions** (p. 120).	Pretest your child on these spelling words: sky might dry by night sight cry light right fly Have your child write the two new ways of spelling the long *i* sound (*y* at the end of a one-syllable word and *igh*).	**Digraphs** Teach your child the sounds of the following digraphs: *ch, th, sh* and *wh*. Give examples of words that contain these digraphs. With your child, read *The Day Jimmy's Boa Ate the Wash* by Trinka Hakes Noble.
Tuesday	A riddle can be a question that gives clues to one answer. With your child, read a riddle book or *Pets in Trumpets and Other Word Play Riddles* by Bernard Most. Look for words that begin riddles. Have your child write his/her own riddles with answers.	Have your child write the spelling words in sentences.	Teach your child the sounds of the following "sleepy" digraphs: *gn, wr, kn* and *ck*. In each of these digraphs, one letter is sleepy (silent), while the other makes its typical consonant sound. Provide examples of words that contain these digraphs. Reread *The Day Jimmy's Boa Ate the Wash* and write the events of the field trip in order.
Wednesday	With your child, brainstorm words that can begin a question. Include *who, what, where, why, how* and *when. See* Language Skills, Week 11, number 1. Have your child complete **More Questions** (p. 121).	Have your child spell each word aloud and write in the air. Have him/her use his/her index finger like a pencil and write using large arm movements. Have your child complete **Lighting the Sky** (p. 124).	Write a list of words that contain digraphs. Have your child read the list and underline each digraph. With your child, read *The Day Jimmy's Boa Ate the Wash* and study the pictures. Have your child write a description of the character telling the story, including her name.
Thursday	Teach your child that a question can be formed simply by changing the word order of a statement. *See* Language Skills, Week 11, number 2. Have your child complete **Word Order in Statements and Questions** (p. 122).	Have your child create five questions using this week's spelling words. Have him/her write each spelling word in two colors, choosing one color for consonants and another color for vowels.	Sometimes a digraph and consonant are read as a unit, such as *shr* and *thr*. Write a list of words containing these combinations for your child to read independently. *See* Reading, Week 11, numbers 1–3.
Friday	In your child's Language Skills story, have him/her include two people having a conversation. Have him/her use several questions in the story. Have your child complete **Completing Sentences** (p. 123).	Give your child the final spelling test.	Call attention to the structure of *The Day Jimmy's Boa Ate the Wash*. Note that the whole story is told in a conversation between two people. Discuss ideas for a story your child can tell in the same manner. Have him/her write an adventure story from the point of view of one character. Have him/her write it so that character tells the story to someone who was not there and has many questions.

Learn at Home, Grade 2

Math	**Science**	**Social Studies**
Place Value Use small manipulatives, dried beans, raisins, macaroni, etc. to group into sets of ten. Put each group of ten in small nut cups. Then, move the groups around to show 10, 20, 30, 40, 50, 60, 70, 80, 90 and 100. Add single pieces to display numbers with 1–9 in the tens place and 1–9 in the ones place. **Examples:** 75, 62, 37, 88 and 50.	If the oceans pick up debris from the shore, what types of materials might be in the ocean and found on the ocean floor? In a jar, mix water, salt, sand, small rocks and pieces of shell. Put the lid on and shake the jar. Have your child draw a picture of the jar after it was shaken, then after it settled. Have him/her compare this activity to what happens on the ocean floor.	With your child, read *This Is Our Earth* by Laura Lee Benson. Discuss and list Earth's physical features described in this book.
Write a list of any ten numbers from 10 to 99. Have your child display these numbers using the manipulatives from Monday. Prepare and explain the place-value board to your child. *See* Math, Week 11, numbers 1 and 2. Have your child pick different numbers from 10–99, then use a copy of the **Place-Value Parts** (p. 125) to display these numbers on the place-value board.	With your child, discuss the types of things people leave at the shore that may get into the ocean. Ask: *How might these things cause a problem?* Put some scraps of paper, plastic and soap or oil in the jar from yesterday. Have your child shake the jar and watch how the pollution acts.	Learn the "This Our Earth" song at the end of the book, *This Is Our Earth*.
Create "place-value art." *See* Math, Week 11, number 3. Write a word problem describing the picture. **Example:** I had 4 tens and 7 ones in the picture of a friend. What was the number? (47)	Discuss ways in which the ocean can be polluted and the danger of pollution in water. Make sure your child realizes that pollution occurs on land as well as in the water. Have your child write a definition of pollution in his/her log. Discuss ways pollution can occur in the ocean and how people can prevent it from happening.	Study geographic features over the next 2 weeks. Each day you will read several of the 63 physical features described in the book, *Geography From A to Z, a Picture Glossary* by Jack Knowlton. With your child, locate the features on a terrain map. Today's words: atoll badland bay beach butte
Look in newspapers, magazines, catalogs; on bottles, boxes, license plates, etc. for numbers from 10 to 99. Make a list of these numbers and tell how many tens and ones are in each number.	With your child, read *Oil Spill* by Melvin Berger. After reading, list the ways oil spills can be prevented.	Play the "Grand Canyon Suite" by Ferde Grofé as music while reading *Grand Canyon: A Trail Through Time* by Linda Vierira. Discuss how the music makes the story come alive. Today's words: canyon cape cave cliff continent continental divide continental shelf
Create a "place-value art" picture using hundreds, tens and ones. *See* Math, Week 11, Number 3. Write a word problem describing the picture. **Example:** I had 1 hundred, 2 tens and 6 ones in my house picture. What is the number? Then, have him/her create a title for the picture.	Have your child draw a beach scene in which people are not polluting.	Today's words: crevasse delta desert dune fjord ford forest geyser glacier

```
╭─────────────────────────────────────────────╮
    TEACHING SUGGESTIONS AND ACTIVITIES
╰─────────────────────────────────────────────╯
```

LANGUAGE SKILLS (Questions)

▶ 1. Write the five *w words* (*who, what, why, where* and *when*) on a chart with five columns. Discuss the type of answer expected from each question word (person, thing, time, place and reason). Brainstorm with your child possible answers for each word. **Example:** In the *who* column, answers may include a girl or basketball player.

▶ 2. Write a statement such as *Some monkeys are trained to do tricks.* Have your child read it. Show your child how you can switch the subject and helping verb to form a question. *Are some monkeys trained to do tricks?* Write other statements and questions on the chalkboard. Have your child change the word order to create the opposite kind of sentence.

READING (Digraphs)

A consonant digraph is a pair of consonants read as a unit. A digraph differs from a blend. In a blend, both consonants retain their sounds. In a digraph, the two letters form a new sound. Sometimes the two consonants of the digraph make the sound of only one of the letters.

▶ 1. Tell your child to listen carefully as you say the following words. Have your child tell you what three letters make up the first sound in each word. Have him/her identify the digraph.

   shrimp   shrill   shrink   three   through   threat

▶ 2. Write the following words on the chalkboard. Have your child read each word and underline the digraph and consonant combination.

   shred   shrine   shrug
   thrill   thread   throat

▶ 3. Sometimes a consonant precedes a digraph at the end of a word. This does not create a blend, but it is helpful for your child to become familiar with these words. Write the following words on the chalkboard for your child to read. Have him/her underline only the digraph. Look for *r*-controlled vowels in this group of words.

   harsh   marsh   munch
   church   birth   porch
   earth   crunch

MATH (Place Value)

Although your child may count easily to 100 and beyond and recognize that 47 represents forty-seven things, he/she may not understand that 47 is made up of groups of numbers such as 4 tens and 7 ones. As adults, we see things in sets and groups more readily than children. Provide experiences that help your child see numbers as sets of ten as well as groups of tens called one hundred, one thousand and so on. After counting 4 tens and 7 ones, it is important to count the objects as 47 single objects, as well as write the numeral so your child makes the connection between the different ways to say the same number.

▶ 1. Make a place-value board by taping together two sheets of 9" x 12" paper along the 12" edge. To distinguish the tens and ones places, use a blue or other colored paper for the tens place (left) and a white paper for the ones place.

Learn at Home, Grade 2

▶ 2. Place-Value Parts: Refer to patterns on page 125. On three different colors of paper, make multiple copies of Place-Value Parts.
Example: yellow—hundreds, blue—tens, green—ones
Cut out the hundred; cut the other hundred into strips of tens and cut the ten strip into ones.
Example:

Hundreds: Tens: Ones:

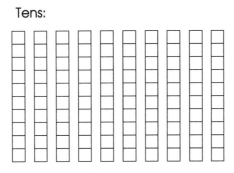

▶ 3. **Place-Value Art:** Using strips of ten and single ones squares, create a picture by gluing the parts onto construction paper. Then, design a picture. Below the picture, write the number it portrays.

▶ 4. Make a drawing of tens and ones on the chalkboard: ᴑᴑᴑᴑᴑᴑᴑᴑᴑᴑ   ᴑᴑᴑᴑᴑᴑᴑᴑᴑᴑ   ᴑ ᴑ ᴑ
Ask your child to count how many designs there are. If your child counts by ones, put another sample up until he/she discovers that there are ten in a bundle. If your child continues to count by ones, put a large amount up so it would be tedious to count by ones. Ask him/her if there might be a quicker way to count these.

Social Studies (Geography)

If you cannot get a copy of *Geography From A to Z*, by Jack Knowlton, look up, with your child, the geographical definitions for each word listed that day.

Learn at Home, Grade 2

Questions

A **question** is an asking sentence. It begins with a **capital letter** and ends with a **question mark**.

Write each question correctly on the line.

1. is our class going to the science museum

_____

2. will we get to spend the whole day there

_____

3. will a guide take us through the museum

_____

4. do you think we will see dinosaur bones

_____

5. is it true that the museum has a mummy

_____

6. can we take lots of pictures at the museum

_____

7. will you spend the whole day at the museum

_____

Learn at Home, Grade 2

Write five questions about the picture.

_____

_____

_____

_____

_____

Word Order

in Statements and Questions

When the order of the words
in a sentence changes,
the meaning of the sentence
often changes.

Example: Many earthquakes do happen each year. (statement)
Do many earthquakes happen each year? (question)

Change the word order to make each statement into a question and each
question into a statement. **Write** the new sentence on the line.

1. Scientists do study earthquakes.

_____

2. Can earthquakes be dangerous?

_____

3. Earthquakes can happen in many places.

_____

4. Do some schools have earthquake drills?

_____

5. Will we practice getting under our desks?

_____

6. Children do practice what to do.

_____

Learn at Home, Grade 2

Completing Sentences

Read each sentence. **Write** a word or words to tell **who** or **when** on each line.

1. Mary's little _____ is starting her first

   day at school _____ .

2. Aunt _____ is moving to Florida _____ .

3. It was almost _____ when _____

   arrived at the party.

4. Mr. _____ wants to meet with the

   soccer team next _____ .

5. We have an appointment at _____ to have

   our teeth checked by Dr. _____ .

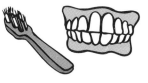

6. _____ and _____ are going

   to the movies _____ instead of _____ .

Learn at Home, Grade 2

Lighting the Sky

| sky | might | dry | by | night |
| sight | cry | light | right | fly |

Write the **igh** words that make the **long i** sound.

_____   _____

_____   _____   _____

Write the spelling words ending in **y** that make the **long i** sound.

_____   _____

_____   _____   _____

Circle the misspelled word in each sentence. Then, **write** the word correctly on the line.

1. We will liht the campfire when it gets dark.   _____

2. Hang the wet towel on the rack so it will dri.   _____

3. Diane likes to walk bi the candy store.   _____

4. The Moon and stars can be seen on a clear nite.   _____

5. Bright flashes of lightning lit up the dark sci.   _____

6. A baby will kri when it is frightened.   _____

7. You can see a deer behind the tree on the rite.   _____

8. Wild geese fli to the river every morning.   _____

9. Mike mite catch the bus if he runs.   _____

10. Quickly, the groundhog jumped into the hole and was out of syte.   _____

Learn at Home, Grade 2

hundreds

ones

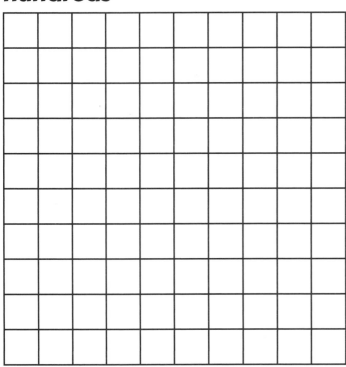

tens

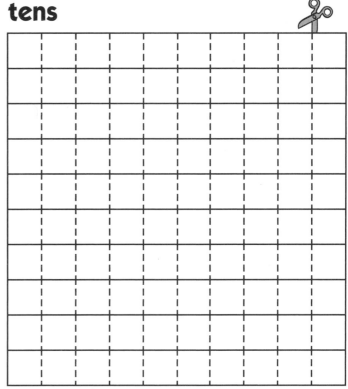

Learn at Home, Grade 2

	Language Skills	Spelling	Reading
Monday	**Commands and Exclamations** A *command* tells someone to do something. Often the subject in a command is missing, but it is understood to be *you*. **Examples:** *Wash your hands. Come home. Read ten pages before dinner.* Have your child find examples of commands in the book he/she is currently reading.	Pretest your child on these spelling words: own hope know sow show woke hole grow joke pole Review the silent *e* rule and teach that the letters *ow* sometimes make the long *o* sound.	**Hard and Soft Sounds** Teach the hard *c* sound. Provide examples of when to use *c* rather than *k*. *See* Reading, Week 12, number 1. Several times this week, read *Alexander and the Terrible, Horrible, No Good, Very Bad Day* by Judith Viorst. With your child, list some things that have happened on a bad day.
Tuesday	Write a list of instructions in command form. Read the instructions over with your child and discuss what makes these sentences commands rather than statements. Have your child write a list of instructions in command form. The instructions can be for cleaning a room, playing a game, following a recipe or another procedure.	Write the spelling words in command and exclamatory sentences.	Teach the soft *c* sound. Provide examples of when to use *c* rather than *s*. *See* Reading, Week 12, number 2. With your child, write a story, modeled after Alexander's story, that tells about a wonderful, terrific, all good, excellent day.
Wednesday	An *exclamation* shows surprise or strong feeling. See if you can find examples in the book you are currently reading. *See* Language Skills, Week 12, number 1. Look at pictures in a magazine. Imagine what people in the pictures are thinking or feeling. Cut out and glue pictures on drawing paper. Have your child write what each person might be saying under the pictures.	Have your child spell each word aloud while acting out the meaning of the word. Have your child complete **Sow and Grow** (p. 130).	Finish the story started yesterday. Edit your child's story. Talk about the parts that made you laugh. Point out words that show what the character is feeling/thinking/doing. Take out sentences that don't seem to fit. Find one area that needs reworking. Encourage your child to listen to your suggestions and make the story better.
Thursday	Learn a story well enough to tell it from memory. After telling it, ask your child to recall some of the events from the story. Write the events in sentence form. Have your child read each sentence and fill in details (orally) about the story. This is the first step in storytelling.	Help your child plant herb seeds in a pot. Have your child keep a log of the seedlings' growth. *See* Spelling, Week 12.	Teach the hard and soft sounds of *g*. *See* Reading, Week 12, number 3. Have your child check his/her story carefully for spelling and punctuation errors. Then, you check his/her work too. Have him/her make a neat copy of the story and create a cover, remembering details to make it look like a professionally published book.
Friday	Have your child practice some storytelling techniques. Have him/her fill in the outline with exclamations, questions and statements to make the telling interesting. *See* Language Skills, Week 12, number 2.	Give your child the final spelling test.	Have your child complete **Hard and Soft c and g** (p. 131).

Learn at Home, Grade 2

Math	Science	Social Studies
Using the place-value board and **Place-Value Parts** from Week 11. Have your child count by twos up to 50. When reading from the place-value board, the number 32 is read *3 tens 2 ones*. Have your child record each number as he/she builds it.	**Sea Animals** Help your child get started with the **Ocean Animal Research Project** (*see* Science, Week 12). Find the books, make a plan and provide the appropriate paper for the final product. This project will continue over several weeks.	Continue reading six to ten physical features from *From A to Z: A Picture Glossary* by Jack Knowlton Then, *see* Social Studies, Week 12 for activities. Today's words: grassland gulch gulf headwater or source highland hill iceberg island
Say a number between 10 and 99 and ask your child to model it on the place-value board. Vary the the way you request it: sometimes saying *twenty-seven* and sometimes saying *2 tens 7 ones* or *two groups of tens and 7 groups of ones*.	Demonstrate that salt water physically supports large fish and mammals better than fresh water. *See* Science, Week 12, number 1. Have him/her record the experiment in his/her log.	Today's words: isthmus jungle key lake marsh meander mountain mountain pass mountain range
Using the place-value board and manipulatives, have your child count backward from 50. When your child removes one object, he/she should read what is on the place-value board and record it on a copy of **Numbers Small and Large** (p. 132).	With your child, read *The Ocean Alphabet Book* and *The Underwater Alphabet Book* by Jerry Pallotta. Have your child pick four favorite creatures from the books and write three or four facts about each. Then, he/she should create an ocean picture which includes all four creatures.	Today's words: mouth ocean ocean ridge palisade peninsula plain plateau promontory or headland
Teach your child to tally in tens and ones by counting pennies; first grouping them into fives and then combining groups of five into a group of tens. Then, say the numbers. Have your child complete **Tens and Ones** (p. 133).	Have your child complete **A Fish Story** (p. 135).	Today's words: rapids reef river sandbank or sandbar sea sea cave seamount sound strait
Have your child roll three dice and arrange them to form the smallest possible number and then arrange them to form largest possible number. Have your child use a copy of **Numbers Small and Large** (p. 134).	Have your child label the basic parts of a fish. *See* Science, Week 12, number 2.	Today's words: stream swamp tundra valley volcano waterfall zone

127

TEACHING SUGGESTIONS AND ACTIVITIES

LANGUAGE SKILLS (Commands and Exclamations)

▶ 1. Examples of exclamations include "That is wonderful!" "Way to go!" "Fantastic!" and "What a book!"

▶ 2. A storyteller remembers the main ideas of a story in order and enhances the story with statements, questions and exclamations. Let your child select a favorite story. Read it several times with him/her. Ask your child to recall the main ideas in order. Have your child copy the main ideas on paper, leaving space between each one to fill in details. Then, have your child write a sentence after each main idea that provides more details. Your child may refer to this written outline when telling the story. The telling should be filled with expression and varied sentence forms.

SPELLING

▶ 1. After following directions on the seed packet, your child can make predictions about germination and speed of growth. Your child should keep a log of predictions and observations as the plants grow. Teach your child to write the date before each entry in the log. Your child may also include a description of any care, such as watering, moving the plant or adding fertilizer. Have your child make an additional list of gardening words such as *seeds, plant, hoe* and *weed*.

READING (Hard and Soft Sounds)

Your child will be introduced to the idea that some consonants make more than one sound. (We have already discussed that vowels make more than one sound.)

▶ 1. Have your child read the following list of words that begin with *c:*
      call, cart, clown, come, crane, coat and *cutting*
   Ask your child what sound the *c* makes.
   Have your child read the following list of words that begin with *k:*
      keep, kite, kettle, kin, key and *kiss*
   Ask your child what sound the *k* makes.
   Discuss why the words are spelled with different letters if they make the same sound. Lead your child to discover that the letter *c* precedes the vowels *a, o* and *u* and is used in blends. The letter *k* precedes the vowels *i* and *e.*

▶ 2. Have your child read the following list of words that begin with *c:*
      cent, circle, certain, circus, center and *city*
   Ask your child what sound the *c* makes.
   Have your child read the following list of words that begin with *s:*
      sat, supper, spot, sore, sneaky and *smile*
   Ask your child what sound the *s* makes.
   Discuss why the words are spelled with different letters if they make the same sound. Lead your child to discover that the letter following *c* is either an *i* or an *e.* (When *c* is followed by *i* or *e,* it makes the *s* sound.) The letter *s* is combined with other letters to form blends and precedes the vowels *a, o* and *u.*

Learn at Home, Grade 2

▶ 3. Have your child read the following list of words that begin with *g*:

giant, grow, gentle, gave, got, gusty, gem, gal, gum, go and gin

Ask your child what sound the *g* makes in each word.

Lead your child to discover that when the letter following *g* is either an *i* or an *e*, the *g* is soft (makes the sound of the letter *j*).

SCIENCE (Sea Animals)

BACKGROUND

The oceans and seas are home to many forms of animal life. Your child may not realize that not only fish but mammals, reptiles, mollusks, crustaceans and other unique marine animals also live in the sea. There are also many aquatic birds that depend on the sea for survival.

Ocean Animal Research Project: Over the next five weeks, give your child the responsibility of writing and illustrating a book about ocean animals. The book will be divided into chapters. Each chapter will feature a different group of ocean animals: mammals, fish, reptiles, crustaceans, mollusks and benthos (bottom dwellers). Provide library books about sea animals for your child to use. Each chapter should include several examples of animals (picture and sentence) from the group. Also, write about the group in general. At the end of the 5 weeks, bring the chapters together; create a cover, title page, table of contents; and number the pages.

▶ 1. Pour 1 cup of distilled water into a glass bowl. Gently lower a "fish" (a fresh egg) into the water. Have your child describe and draw his/her observations. Next, pour a cup of water into a glass bowl and stir in 2 tablespoons of salt until dissolved. Ask your child to make a hypothesis for what will happen when a fresh egg is lowered into the salt water. Gently lower the "fish" into the salt water and have your child describe and draw his/her observations. Ask your child to predict what will happen if another tablespoon of salt is added. Have your child remove the egg, add the salt and stir until dissolved and put the egg back into the salt water. Discuss what happened. Have your child write about the connection to a large fish or mammal swimming in salt water compared to fresh water.

▶ 2. Draw a large model of a fish on chart paper. Ask your child to help you label the following parts of the fish: gills, mouth, eye, nostril, fins and backbone. Have your child feel his/her own backbone. Talk about how fish breathe through their gills while we breathe with our lungs.

SOCIAL STUDIES (Geography)

▶ 1. Make an alphabet book of geographic features. First, staple a book together and label 26 pages with the letters of the alphabet. Challenge your child to think of one geographic feature (general or specific) for each letter. Your child should draw a picture of the feature and write its name on the correct page.

▶ 2. Have your child write riddles about geographic features. The riddles are in the form of three clues that lead to a feature. Your child should write the most general clue first and the most specific one last. Have him/her read the clues to you to guess.

▶ 3. Talk about selected geographic features and what kind of wildlife and animal life live in or near each one and why.

Sow and Grow

sow	own	hope	know	show
woke	hole	grow	joke	pole

Write the spelling words ending with **e** that make the **long o** sound.

_____   _____   _____

_____   _____

Write the **ow** words that make the **long o** sound.

_____   _____   _____

_____   _____

Read each sentence. **Write** the missing spelling word on the line.

1. We all laughed at the funny _____ .

2. Did you _____ your mother your pictures?

3. The loud siren _____ up the baby.

4. He wants to use his _____ bike for the race tomorrow.

5. Water and sunshine will make the plants _____ .

6. A tiny gray mouse ran into the _____ in the ground.

7. They will _____ the corn seeds in the spring.

8. Grace helped raise the flag to the top of the _____ .

9. Does she _____ that her report is due today?

10. Cole and Roberta _____ that they did well on the test.

Learn at Home, Grade 2

Circle as many words in each word search as you can find. List them in the correct column. Hint: the words going up and down have the hard sound, and the words going across and backwards are soft.

g

Hard ⬇

t	s	g	e	m	n	r
e	l	t	n	e	g	p
g	n	s	g	e	r	m
i	t	o	a	h	o	f
r	i	h	p	r	a	o
l	e	g	i	a	n	t

Soft ➡

_____

_____

_____

_____

_____

Two words in the **c** word find go diagonally. They have both a hard and a soft **c** sound.

c

Hard ⬇

c	e	n	t	e	r	c
a	i	c	r	a	i	a
s	x	r	a	r	g	r
t	n	e	c	l	f	p
p	y	u	a	l	n	e
a	s	r	n	s	e	t
c	i	t	y	o	m	u

Soft ➡

_____

_____

_____

Both Hard and Soft

_____   _____

Numbers
Small and Large

Smallest **Number**

Largest **Number**

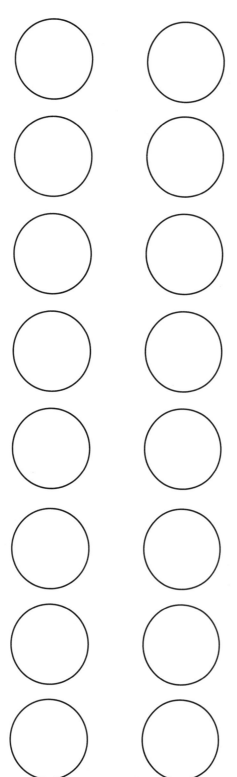

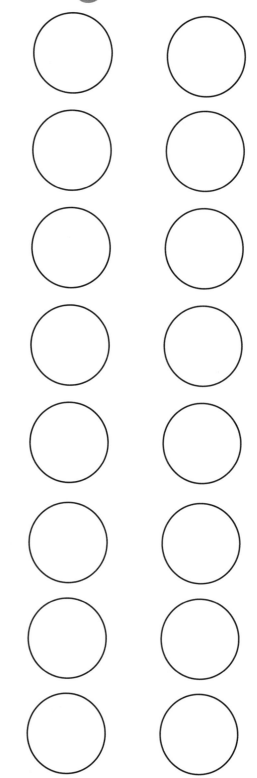

132

Learn at Home, Grade 2

Tens and Ones

Write the number indicated by tally marks.

 _____    _____

 _____    _____

 _____    _____

Using tally marks, **draw** the numbers named.

35	**41**
15	**22**
45	**7**
11	**29**
30	**26**
18	**10**

Smallest **Number**   ## **Largest** Number

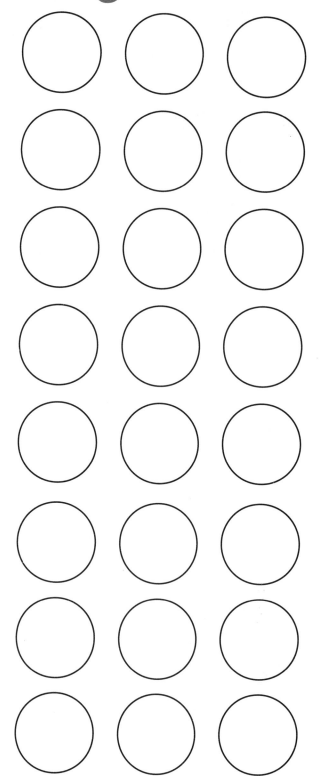

134

A Fish Story

Fish live almost anywhere there is water. Although fish come in many different shapes, colors and sizes, they are alike in many ways.

 All fish have backbones.

 Fish breathe with gills.

 Most fish are cold-blooded.

 Most fish have fins.

 Many fish have scales and fairly tough skin.

Use the clues to unscramble the fish names. **Write** each name correctly at the top of the bubble. Then, use your imagination to draw each fish.

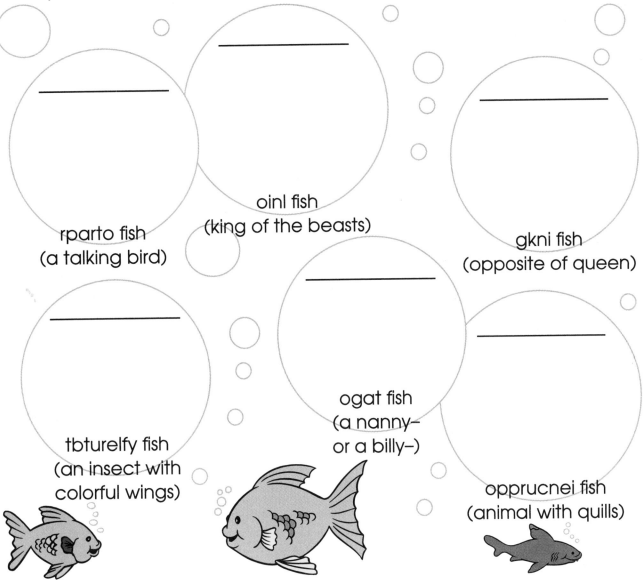

rparto fish
(a talking bird)

oinl fish
(king of the beasts)

gkni fish
(opposite of queen)

tbturelfy fish
(an insect with colorful wings)

ogat fish
(a nanny–
or a billy–)

opprucnei fish
(animal with quills)

135

	Language Skills	**Spelling**	**Reading**
Monday	Have your child identify questions and statements read aloud. On one index card, draw a large question mark. On another, draw a large period. Read statements and questions aloud and have your child hold up the appropriate end punctuation with each sentence. Have your child complete **Kinds of Sentences** (p. 140).	Pretest your child on these spelling words: coat boat cold road load fold hold gold told goat Review the long *o* sound (followed by a silent vowel). Also teach your child that the long *o* sound is heard in the word chunk *old*.	**Compound Words and Contractions** Teach how to form compound words. With your child, read *The Mysterious Tadpole* by Steven Kellogg. Have your child find and list the compound words in the book. Have your child complete **Book Evaluation** (p. 144).
Tuesday	**Center:** To prepare the game, write questions on twelve index cards. Write the answers on twelve other index cards. Mix up the cards. **Directions:** Sort the cards into statements and questions. Match each question to the appropriate answer. Have your child complete **Writing Sentences** (p. 141).	Have your child write the spelling words in sentences.	Have your child form compound words from clues. *See* Reading, Week 13, number 1. Have your child complete **Compound Your Effort** (p. 145).
Wednesday	Review four kinds of sentences: *statement, question, command* and *exclamation.* Your child gives examples of each. Have your child complete **Four Kinds of Sentences** (p. 142).	Have your child spell each word aloud and jump on two feet while saying the consonants and jump on one foot while saying the vowels. Have your child complete **Loading Cargo** (p. 143).	Have your child write the story elements for *The Mysterious Tadpole.* Discuss story elements (plot, setting, characters, etc.).
Thursday	Reread *The Case of the Missing Birthday Party* from Monday's Math. As the book is read, indicate the four kinds of sentences and how they are used in the story.	Sometimes a word's shape helps your child remember word order. Make letter boxes that show the shape of each spelling word. Have your child fill in the word that fits each shape. *See* Spelling, Week 13.	Introduce contractions. Contractions are a shortened form of two words. If your child has trouble identifying the original two words, explain that an apostrophe shows where at least one letter has been left out. Often the missing letter(s) come from the second word. *See* Reading, Week 13, numbers 2 and 3. Have your child complete **Contractions** (p. 146).
Friday	Role play a phone conversation in which you ask and answer questions. Tell your child that he/she must respond and ask questions in complete sentences.	Give your child the final spelling test.	Have your child complete **Alphonse's First Year** (p. 147).

Learn at Home, Grade 2

Math	Science	Social Studies
Review place value. With your child, read The *Case of the Missing Birthday Party* by Joanne Rocklin. Discuss and have your child complete one of the activities at the end of the book.	You may call the National Wildlife Federation to obtain information about protecting whales. Call 1-800-822-9919 for a brochure on "Save the Whales." Help your child make a poster promoting awareness of the needs of whales. Also, have your child continue the Sea Animal Book.	**Music/Art:** Sing American folk songs, such as *She'll Be Comin' 'Round the Mountain, Sourwood Mountain,* and *Down in the Valley* with your child. Have your child visualize the picture each song "paints." Have your child paint a picture of the image each song brings up.
2-Digit Addition, No Regrouping: Teach your child to add 2-digit numbers using two place-value boards and manipulatives. *See* Math, Week 13, number 1. Then, dictate some 2-digit problems that require no regrouping. Have your child complete problems on a copy of **Recording Sheet** (p. 149).	With your child, read and discuss *Humphrey The Lost Whale: A True Story* by Wendy Tokuda and Richard Hall. On a map, have your child locate the setting and terrain as pictured on the end covers.	With your child, write an original verse for one of the songs above.
Provide a copy of **Circus Fun** (p. 148). Have your child add the 2-digit addition problems (no regrouping) without manipulatives. Allow him/her to use manipulatives if needed. Have your child check his/her own answers by building each problem on the place-value board.	Use resource materials to find names and lengths of whales. In his/her log, have your child list them from the shortest to the longest.	**Writing:** Talk about life in a cave or forest. Discuss how it would look, feel and sound. Have your child write a cave or forest adventure story.
Teach your child to solve 2-digit addition problems (no regrouping) using mental math. *See* Math, Week 13, numbers 2 and 3.	Make a graph comparing lengths of whales. Give your child a sheet of $\frac{1}{2}$" graph paper. Have your child number from 0–100 counting by fives and write the names of the whales alphabetically along the bottom. He/she should color in boxes above each whale's name to show how long each one is.	Help your child make a relief map. Reproduce an outline of the United States. Make mountains and trees that project out from the flat map. *See* Social Studies, Week 13.
Dictate some addition problems that require no regrouping. Have your child write them on a copy of the **Recording Sheet** (p. 149).	Have your child estimate how much longer the blue whale is than him/her. *See* Science, Week 13, number 1.	Continue yesterday's work.

TEACHING SUGGESTIONS AND ACTIVITIES

SPELLING

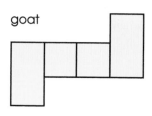

goat

▶ 1. To make word shapes, make a box for each letter. The box is the shape of the letter. Letters such as *h, b, l* and *t* are tall letters and make tall boxes. Letters such as *a, r, n* and *o* are short letters and make short boxes. Letters such as *j, g* and *y* are low letters. The low boxes start at the height of the short boxes and extend below the line. See the example to the right for the word *goat*. Also, see examples of word shapes on pages 16, 40, 73.

READING (Compound Words and Contractions)

BACKGROUND

Compound words and contractions are alike in that they are made up of two words. However, when the two words of a compound word are joined, no change takes place to either word. When two words are put together in a contraction, letters are removed and an apostrophe is substituted.

▶ 1. With your child, read each sentence below. Have your child fill in the blank with a compound word. The words that make up the compound word can be found within the sentence.
   • The time to go to bed is called _____.
   • You run to the base after you hit the ball when you play _____.
   • A pole for raising the flag is called a _____.
   • A coat worn to keep off the rain is called a _____.
   • A storm that produced snow is called a _____.
   • A shelf for books is called a _____.
   • The room where your class meets is called a _____.
   • If you walk up the stairs, you go _____ .
   • A box to hold sand is called a _____.
   • A tie worn around your neck is called a _____.
   • The light from the sun is called _____.

▶ 2. Write these words on the chalkboard.

I'm	he's	can't	isn't
I'll	he'll	didn't	doesn't
I've	she's	don't	shouldn't

Have your child tell what two words make up each contraction. Write the two words next to each contraction. Have your child compare the words and tell in what way the words changed when they formed a contraction.

▶ 3. Write one contraction on each of fifteen index cards. Write the two words that make up the contractions on separate index cards. Mix up the cards and place them facedown in an array. Play a game of "Memory" where you take turns turning over two cards, attempting to match the contraction and its components.

Learn at Home, Grade 2

MATH (2-Digit Addition, No Regrouping)

With a sound understanding of place value, learning to add without regrouping is very easy. If it is not easy, your child probably needs more time building and naming 2-digit numbers. Teach your child to see an equation such as 24 + 35 as 2 tens 4 ones plus 3 tens 5 ones.

▶ 1. Make a second place-value board using two sheets of 9" x 12" construction paper in blue and white. Place both place-value boards on the table, one above the other. Model the number 24 on the first board and 32 on the second board using tens and ones. Tell your child that to add these numbers you bring the ones together and the tens together on one place-value board. Ask your child to name the resulting number. Write the equation vertically on the chalkboard, lining up the tens and ones. Go over the process step by step with your child: *First, you add 4 ones and 2 ones and write 6 ones below the line. Then, you add 2 tens and 3 tens and write 5 tens below the line. The sum is 56.*

▶ 2. Say a number to your child between 10 and 50. Ask your child to visualize the number in tens and ones. Have him/her describe what he/she pictures. Repeat several times to help your child learn the skill of visualizing.

▶ 3. Ask your child to add two 2-digit numbers together mentally. He/she should visualize both numbers as tens and ones, then add the ones and add the tens together. Do this several times. Do not include problems that involve regrouping for this mental math activity.

SCIENCE (Sea Animals)

▶ 1. On the sidewalk, measure the length of the blue whale and make a chalk line to mark it. Have your child lie down with feet touching one end of the line. Mark the top of his/her head on the sidewalk. Have your child get up and put his/her feet where his/her head was and lie down again. Mark the top of his/her head on the sidewalk. Continue counting until you reach the other end of the whale length. Have your child record the number in his/her log. Discuss how close your child's guess was.

SOCIAL STUDIES (Geography)

▶ 1. Your child should refer to a terrain map for accurate placement of features. Have your child complete the directions below. Label the features with your child as he/she works.
With a blue crayon or marker, have your child draw in major rivers such as the Mississippi, Rio Grande, Colorado, Missouri and Ohio. With a brown crayon, color the Mojave and Painted Deserts. With a green crayon, color the Great Plains. Color the major lakes blue, including the Great Salt Lake and the five Great Lakes.
Cut out 3-D mountains and help your child glue them in the appropriate spots to show the Appalachian Mountains, the Rocky Mountains and the Cascade Range.

139

Kinds of Sentences

A **statement** ends with a period. ▪ A **question** ends with a question mark. **?**
Write the correct mark in each box.

1. Would you like to help me make an aquarium ☐

2. We can use my brother's big fish tank ☐

3. Will you put this colored sand in the bottom ☐

4. I have three shells to put on the sand ☐

5. Can we use your little toy boat, too ☐

6. Let's go buy some fish for our aquarium ☐

7. Will twelve fish be enough ☐

8. Look, they seem to like their new home ☐

9. How often do we give them fish food ☐

10. Let's tell our friends about our new aquarium ☐

Learn at Home, Grade 2

Every sentence begins with a capital letter.

Come to the Fourth of July Picnic.
Town Park—All Day

Write three statements about the picture.

_____

_____

_____

Write three questions about the picture.

_____

_____

_____

Learn at Home, Grade 2

A **statement** tells something. A **question** asks something. An **exclamation** shows surprise or strong feeling. A **command** tells someone to do something.

Example: The shuttle is ready for takeoff. (statement)
Are all systems go? (question)
What a sight! (exclamation)
Take a picture of this. (command)

Use the code to color the spaces.

Code
statement—**yellow**
question—**red**
exclamation—**blue**
command—**gray**

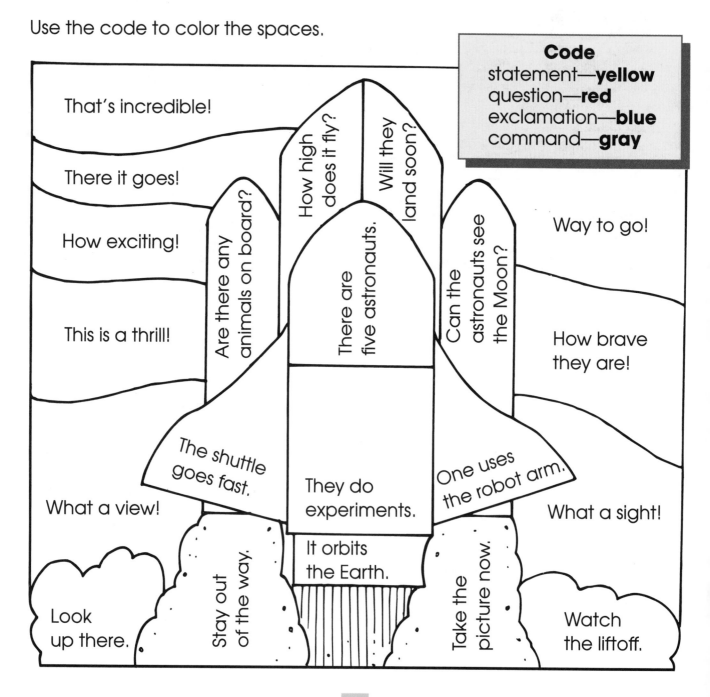

That's incredible!

There it goes!

How exciting!

This is a thrill!

How high does it fly?

Will they land soon?

Are there any animals on board?

There are five astronauts.

Can the astronauts see the Moon?

Way to go!

How brave they are!

The shuttle goes fast.

They do experiments.

One uses the robot arm.

What a sight!

What a view!

Stay out of the way.

It orbits the Earth.

Take the picture now.

Look up there.

Watch the liftoff.

Learn at Home, Grade 2

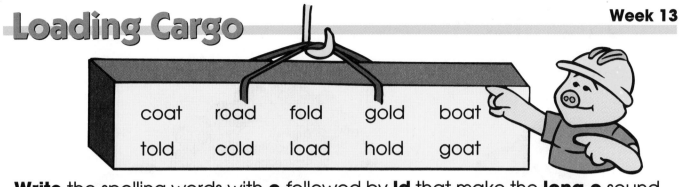

coat	road	fold	gold	boat
told	cold	load	hold	goat

Write the spelling words with **o** followed by **ld** that make the **long o** sound.

_____ _____ _____

_____ _____

Write the **oa** words that make the **long o** sound.

_____ _____ _____

_____ _____

Complete the puzzle.

Across

1. An animal
3. Opposite of hot
6. A ship
7. To fill
8. A street

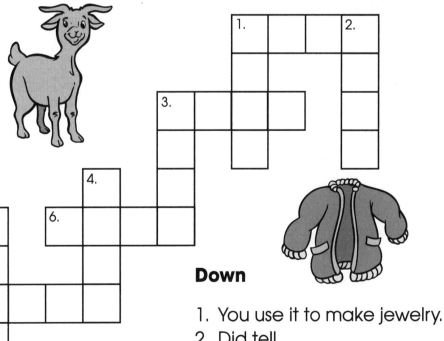

Down

1. You use it to make jewelry.
2. Did tell
3. Something to wear
4. You use your hands to do this.
5. To bend something over

Book Evaluation

Write an evaluation of the book.

The Mysterious Tadpole is a good title for this book because _____

_____

_____

_____

Another good title might be _____

Write three things you would teach Alphonse if he were your pet.

1. _____

2. _____

3. _____

Why would you teach Alphonse to do these tricks?

_____

_____

Draw a tadpole around the word that tells how you feel about this book.

boring   okay   good   excellent

Compound Your Effort

Find the word in the word box that goes with the words numbered below to make a compound word. Cross it out. Then, **write** the compound word on the line.

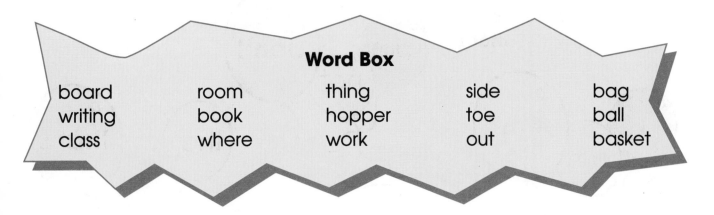

Word Box

board	room	thing	side	bag
writing	book	hopper	toe	ball
class	where	work	out	basket

1. coat _____

2. snow _____

3. home _____

4. waste _____

5. tip _____

6. chalk _____

7. note _____

8. grass _____

9. school _____

10. with _____

Look at the words in the word box that you did not use. Use those words to make your own compound words.

1. _____

2. _____

3. _____

4. _____

5. _____

Learn at Home, Grade 2

Contractions

A **contraction** is a word made up of two words joined together with one or more letters left out. An **apostrophe** is used in place of the missing letters.

Examples: I am—**I'm**
do not—**don't**
that is—**that's**

Draw a line to **match** each contraction to the words from which it was made. The first one is done for you.

1. he's	we are	6. they'll	are not
2. we're	cannot	7. aren't	they will
3. can't	he is	8. I've	you have
4. I'll	she is	9. you've	will not
5. she's	I will	10. won't	I have

Write the contraction for each pair of words.

1. you are _____

2. does not _____

3. do not _____

4. would not _____

5. she is _____

6. we have _____

7. has not _____

8. did not _____

Learn at Home, Grade 2

Alphonse's First Year

Number the sentences in the correct order. Then, **draw** a picture to go with each set.

_____ There was a tadpole in the jar.

_____ Louis opened the door.

_____ There was a knock at the door.

_____ The postman handed Louis a jar.

_____ Alphonse grew and had to be moved to the sink.

_____ Louis named his pet Alphonse.

_____ Alphonse kept growing and had to be moved to the bathtub.

_____ Eventually, he was even too big for the bathtub.

_____ They used the money to build a swimming pool for Alphonse.

_____ Miss Seevers, the librarian, had an idea to help Louis and Alphonse.

_____ She located information about a sunken treasure.

_____ Alphonse brought up the treasure.

Circus Fun

Add. Remember to add the ones first.

tens	ones
2	5
+ 1	4

tens	ones
5	3
+ 3	2

tens	ones
7	1
+ 2	8

tens	ones
4	4
+ 3	2

tens	ones
5	1
+ 3	7

tens	ones
2	6
+ 5	2

tens	ones
2	6
+ 4	2

tens	ones
3	7
+ 5	1

tens	ones
1	9
+ 3	0

Learn at Home, Grade 2

tens	ones

tens	ones

tens	ones

tens	ones

tens	ones

tens	ones

tens	ones

tens	ones

tens	ones

tens	ones

tens	ones

tens	ones

Learn at Home, Grade 2

	Language Skills	**Spelling**	**Reading**
Monday	**Capitalization and Punctuation** Brainstorm with your child categories of words that are capitalized regularly. Include the first word in a sentence, proper nouns, titles, holidays, days of the week, months and streets. Under each heading established above, write several specific examples of capitalized words.	Pretest your child on these spelling words: story park corn part north horse far farm hard start Teach your child to recognize the *ar* and *or* sounds.	**Pronouns and Proper Nouns** Teach your child to identify and capitalize proper nouns. *See* Reading, Week 14, number 1. With your child, read *Night Tree* by Eve Bunting. Have him/her look for proper nouns in the book. Compile ten copies of **Christmas Around the World** (p. 157) into a booklet. Each day read and discuss a different holiday book, and have your child complete a page in the booklet.
Tuesday	Write a sentence on the chalkboard that is not capitalized properly. Have your child erase the lower-case letters and write in the appropriate capital letters. Have your child complete **A Sensational Scent** (p. 154).	Have your child write the spelling words in sentences.	With your child, read and discuss *My First Kwanzaa Book* by Deborah M. Newton Chocolate. Review the seven principles of Kwanzaa. With your child, list the proper nouns in the book. Remember to have your child complete **Christmas Around the World** for this story.
Wednesday	Review end punctuation with your child. Have your child complete **Punctuation Magic** (p. 155).	Have your child spell each word aloud while walking in a circle. Step once for each letter. Have your child complete **Horsing Around** (p. 156).	Teach that pronouns replace nouns without changing meaning. Write a sample sentence with a noun repeated two or three times. Show your child how to substitute a pronoun. With your child, read, discuss and complete the activity sheet for *Nine Days to Christmas: A Story of Mexico* by Marie Hall Ets. Look for different pronouns in the book. Have your child complete **Picking Pronouns** (p. 158).
Thursday	Write the following run-on sentence. *The cat ran through the yard and the birds flew away to save their lives.* Read it to your child without taking a breath until you reach the period. Discuss the subject of the sentence. Lead your child to discover that this should be two sentences since *birds* is a new subject. Teach your child how to convert the sentence to two sentences. Repeat with other run-on sentences.	Write a spelling word on an index card with a black marker. Have your child use a different color crayon or marker to write the word again, shadowing the first spelling. Use a third color and trace the word again. Repeat several times, creating a rainbow word. Repeat with all the spelling words.	Teach your child to use the apostrophe to show ownership. *See* Reading, Week 14, number 3. With your child, read discuss and complete the activity sheet for *Too Many Tamales* by Gary Soto (Mexico). Look for possessives in the story. Have your child complete **Add an Apostrophe** (p. 159).
Friday	Teach your child how to proofread his/her own writing. Have your child read aloud one of his/her own writing pieces, looking for run-on or incomplete sentences. Have him/her circle the end punctuation that needs to be changed and underline the letters that need to be capitalized. Put a strike through a capital letter that should be lower-case.	Give your child the final spelling test.	Teach the possessive pronouns. Write *The branch belongs to the tree.* Ask your child to write a shorter version of this phrase using a possessive word. After he/she has written the word, have him/her use it in a sentence. With your child, read, discuss and complete an activity sheet for *An Amish Christmas* by Richard Ammon. Look for proper nouns, possessives and possessive pronouns.

Learn at Home, Grade 2

Math	**Science**	**Social Studies**

2-Digit Addition With and Without Regrouping
Through the use of manipulatives and two place-value boards, teach your child how to add with regrouping. *See* Math, Week 14, number 1.
	Art: Have your child paint an undersea picture. Allow your child to cut out pictures of sea creatures from old issues of *National Geographic* and glue them on the background.	**United States**
		In the next ten weeks, study the US states. *See* Social Studies, Week 14.
		Washington **WA**
		          named after George Washington
		          nicknamed The Evergreen State
		capital city - Olympia
		landmarks - Mt. St. Helens (erupted in 1980)
		                    Grand Coulee Dam
		                    Seattle
		biggest apple producer

Repeat yesterday's lesson using different manipulatives. While your child works on the place-value board, demonstrate how to solve the problem on paper. Talk about what you are doing while you work.	**Music:** Play the song "Baby Beluga" by Raffi. Teach your child the words and sing along together. Have your child continue to work on the Ocean Animal Research Project.	*Oregon* **OR**
		          French name meaning *hurricane*
		          nicknamed The Beaver State
		capital city - Salem
		landmarks - Crater Lake
		                    Sea Lion Caves
		                    Portland

Have your child add 2-digit numbers using nuts and cups for manipulatives. First, use manipulatives to work the problems. Then, solve the problem on paper.
Have your child pretend the nuts are acorns as he/she completes **Nutty Addition** (p. 160).
	With your child, read Sim *Chung and the River Dragon: A Folktale from Korea* by Ellen Schecter. Discuss how this "sea monster" helped Sim Chung to fulfill her wish.	*Idaho* **ID**
		          named from Indian word for *daybreak*
		          nicknamed The Gem State
		capital city - Boise
		landmarks - Craters of the Moon National
		                    Monument
		                    Hell's Canyon
		largest potato producer

Use a die to determine the number of manipulatives to add to a 2-digit number.
Have your child record the equations and answers on a copy of the **Recording Sheet** (p. 149). *See* Math, Week 13, number 2.
Have your child use the place-value boards to solve the first seven problems on **Just Like Magic** (p. 161).
	Creative Writing: Long ago, people believed there were sea monsters that performed terrifying acts such as swallowing entire ships or causing violent waves that overturned ships. Have your child write a story about a sea creature who helps a child to fulfill a dream. Include all the story elements: setting, characters, problem, events and a solution.	*California* **CA**
		          named after a fictional treasure island
		          nicknamed The Golden State
		capital city - Sacramento
		landmarks - Hollywood
		                    Los Angeles
		                    San Francisco
		                    Redwood National Park
		                    Joshua Tree National Monument
		                    Golden Gate Bridge

Have your child solve the last seven problems on paper when completing **Just Like Magic** (p. 161).	Have your child finish writing the sea creature story begun yesterday.	*Nevada* **NV**
		          named *snow-covered* in Spanish
		          nicknamed The Silver State
		capital city - Carson City
		landmarks - Las Vegas
		                    Hoover Dam
		                    Lake Tahoe
		                    Sierra Nevada Mountains

TEACHING SUGGESTIONS AND ACTIVITIES

READING (Pronouns and Proper Nouns)

BACKGROUND
A pronoun may replace a noun and keep the same meaning. A pronoun can refer to persons or things previously mentioned or understood from the context. Using too many pronouns can make the meaning of a sentence unclear.

Special names for people, places and things are proper nouns. Proper nouns are always capitalized.

▶ 1. Have your child write his/her full name and address, capitalizing the first letter of each proper noun. The words are capitalized because they name a special person, place or thing.

▶ 2. Write a list of pronouns:

I	we	me	us
you	you	you	you
he, she, it	they	him, her, it	them

Teach your child to recite sentences using the different pronouns. (**Examples:** I am going to a party. You are going to a party. He is going to a party. We are going to a party.)

▶ 3. Have your child write two sentences about a friend. In the second sentence, use a pronoun in place of the friend's name. Teach your child that the pronoun refers to the friend's name.

He   She   It   They

Possessives: A possessive is a word that tells who or what owns something and is usually formed by adding 's. **Example:** Tail of a cat—cat's tail.
Possessive pronouns do not need the apostrophe. They are *mine, its, his, hers, ours, yours* and *theirs*.

▶ 4. Write: *the branch belongs to the tree.* Ask your child to write a shorter version of this using a possessive (the tree's branch). Repeat with other phrases that show ownership. For example, *the tail of the kite and the stars of the flag.* When your child has written the possessives, have him/her use each in a sentence.

▶ 5. Write ten pairs of sentences such as the example below. Write a list of possessive pronouns on the chalkboard. Have your child read a pair of sentences and select a possessive pronoun to write in the blank.
The dog's paw was hurt.
_____ paw had to be bandaged. (His)

Learn at Home, Grade 2

MATH (2-Digit Addition With and Without Regrouping)

Use manipulatives throughout this lesson. This is the time for your child to fully understand the concept of trading tens for ones. Early use of manipulatives gives your child a solid foundation for future work. Your children can visualize the early experiences for later concepts. It is very important that you mix problems that need regrouping with problems that do not require regrouping. This requires your child to think about why he/she is regrouping, rather than placing the number 1 over the tens place automatically.

▶ 1. Use the two place-value boards as in last week's lesson. Write the equation 26 + 37 vertically on a sheet of paper. Have your child build the number 26 on the first board and the number 37 on the second board. Tell your child to move and combine all the ones on one place-value board. Your child will see that there are more that ten manipulatives on the ones side.
Have your child count and bundle up 10 of the sticks and move the 10 to the top of the tens place temporarily. Temporarily place a 1 on your written equation in the same place that your child placed the 10 on the place-value board. Write the 3 below the line to match the 3 in your child's ones place. Now have your child combine the tens, including the 1 ten placed at the top. Write 6 below the line in the tens place on your written equation. Have your child read how many tens and ones are on the place-value board. Go over how the sum was found on the written equation. Do several more examples in this manner. Be sure to include some problems that do not require regrouping.

SOCIAL STUDIES Weeks 14–23 (United States)

You may add to these lessons to fit your experiences and your child's interest. Over the next 10 weeks, create an awareness of the 50 states. Refer to a variety of maps and help your child become familiar with places and their major attractions. Choose from the activities below for each state. Present one state per day. General information is provided for each state.

▶ 1. Provide your child with a folder for collecting and organizing state information. Reproduce **Map of the United States** (in separate pages throughout these weeks) and glue it to the cover of the folder. Your child may color each state as he/she learns about it. The blanks by each capital city are to number them according to the key.

▶ 2. Look at the compass rose on **Map of the United States** (when completed from various pages). Teach your child to use the direction words (North, South, East and West). In what part of the United States is the state found (North, South, East or West)?

▶ 3. Use the information provided as you wish. Have your child research for the information itself. Your child may want to add the landmarks onto the maps provided. You do not have to use all the information provided.

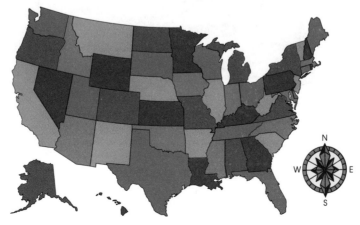

A Sensational Scent

Week 14

Circle the letters that should be capital letters. Then, **write** them in the matching numbered blanks below to answer the question.

1. eddie, Homer's friend, lives on elm Street.

2. Homer's aunt lives in kansas City, kansas.

3. are you sure Aunt aggie is coming?

4. old Rip Van Winkle came to town.

5. The doughnuts were made by homer Price.

6. Miss terwillinger and Uncle telly saved yarn.

7. *Homer Price* was written by robert McCloskey.

8. Uncle ulysses owned a lunch room.

9. The super-Duper was a comic book hero.

10. Doc pelly lived in Homer's town.

11. money was stolen by the robbers.

12. now you have the answer to the question.

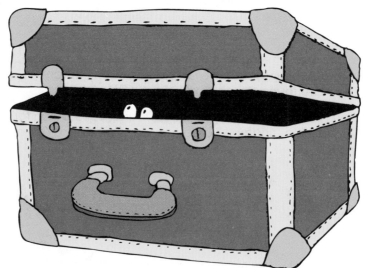

Who is hiding in the suitcase?

__ __ __ __ __   __ __ __   __ __ __   __ __ __ __ __
3 7 4 11 3   6 5 1   10 1 6   9 2 8 12 2

154

Learn at Home, Grade 2

Punctuation Magic

Write the sentences correctly. Be sure to use capital letters, periods and question marks.

1. mrs paris talked to richard, alex, matthew and emily about the trip to the museum

_____

_____

2. the children read a story about a king who was greedy

_____

_____

3. everyone but richard drew a picture about the story

_____

_____

4. why was drake sick

_____

5. mrs gates asked matthew to take homework to drake

_____

_____

6. did richard's wish make drake sick

_____

Horsing Around

story	park	corn	part	north
horse	far	farm	hard	start

Write the spelling words with the same vowel sound as in **horn**. Then, **circle** the letters that make that sound.

_____ _____ _____ _____

Write the spelling words with the same vowel sound as in **jar**. Then, **circle** the letters that make that sound.

_____ _____ _____

_____ _____ _____

Complete the puzzle.

Across

1. Opposite of near
2. A place to play
3. Opposite of stop
4. A yellow vegetable
7. An animal you can ride

Down

1. A place to raise animals and crops
2. A piece of something
3. Something you can read or write
5. Opposite of south
6. Opposite of soft

Learn at Home, Grade 2

1. Title _____

2. Author _____

3. Illustrator _____

4. Country _____

5. Continent _____

6. New words I learned _____

_____

_____

_____

7. I learned that _____

_____

_____

_____

 _____

Learn at Home, Grade 2

Picking Pronouns

The words **he**, **she**, **it** and **they** can be used in place of a noun.

Write the correct pronoun in each blank.

He   She   It   They

1. John won first place.

   _____ got a blue ribbon.

2. Janet and Gail rode on a bus.

   _____ went to visit their grandmother.

3. Sarah had a birthday party.

   _____ invited six friends to the party.

4. The kitten likes to play.

   _____ likes to tug on shoelaces.

5. Ed is seven years old.

   _____ is in the second grade.

Learn at Home, Grade 2

Add an Apostrophe

Add **'s** to a noun to show who or what **owns** something.

Circle the correct word under each picture.

The _____ nose is big.

clown   clowns   clown's

This is _____ coat.

Bettys   Betty's   Betty

I know _____ brother.

Burt's   Burt   Burts

The _____ hat is pretty.

girl   girl   girl's

That is the _____ ball.

kitten's   kitten   kittens

My _____ shoe is missing.

sisters   sister   sister's

The _____ coach is Mr. Hall.

team   team's   team

The _____ cover is torn.

book's   books   book

Sam Squirrel and his friend Wendy were gathering acorns. When they gather 10 acorns, they put them in a bucket. The picture shows how many acorns Sam and Wendy each gathered. **Write** the number that tells how many.

tens	ones

_____

tens	ones

_____

How many acorns did Sam and Wendy gather in all?

1. Put numbers on ten's and one's table.

tens	ones
3	6
+ 2	7

2. Add ones first.

tens	ones
1	
3	6
+ 2	7
	3

3. Add tens.

tens	ones
1	
3	6
+ 2	7
6	3

Sam and Wendy gathered _63_ in all.
Add and regroup as needed.

tens	ones
3	8
+ 4	6

tens	ones
5	4
+ 2	7

tens	ones
4	9
+ 1	3

tens	ones
2	6
+ 1	7

Just Like Magic

Add.

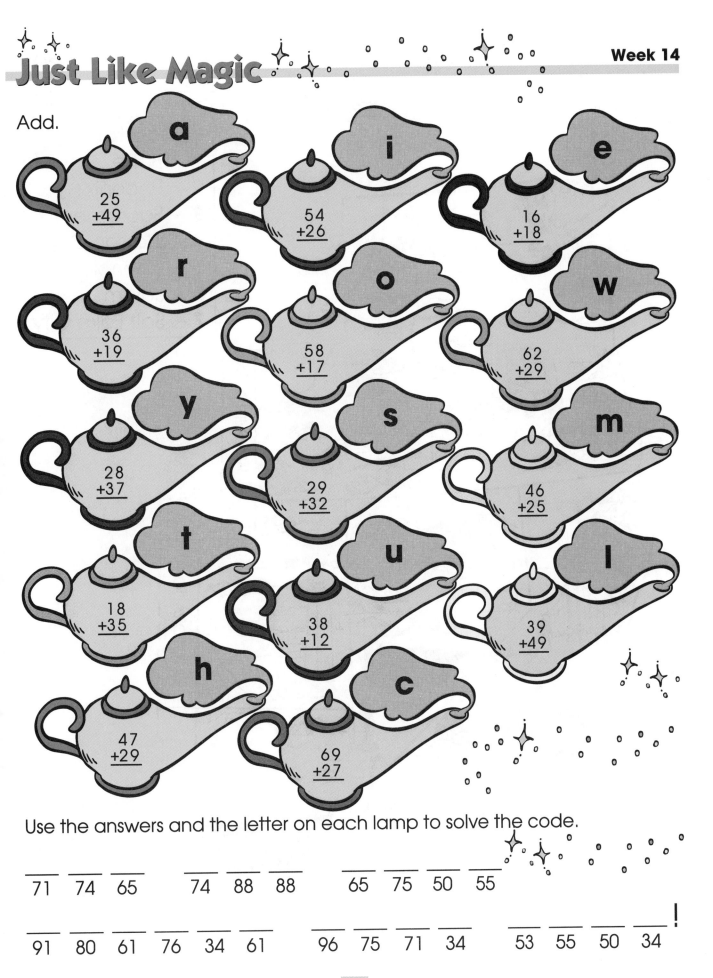

a 25 +49

i 54 +26

e 16 +18

r 36 +19

o 58 +17

w 62 +29

y 28 +37

s 29 +32

m 46 +25

t 18 +35

u 38 +12

l 39 +49

h 47 +29

c 69 +27

Use the answers and the letter on each lamp to solve the code.

____ ____ ____   ____ ____ ____   ____ ____ ____ ____
71   74   65   74   88   88   65   75   50   55

____ ____ ____ ____ ____ ____   ____ ____ ____ ____   ____ ____ ____ ____!
91   80   61   76   34   61   96   75   71   34   53   55   50   34

161

U.S. Map Puzzle
SECTION 1

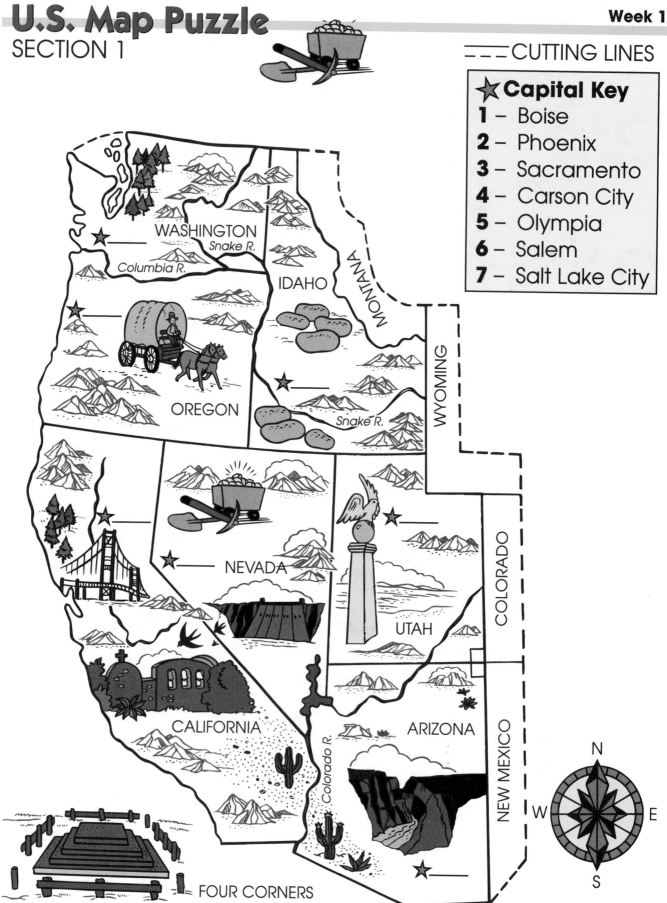

---- CUTTING LINES

⭐ **Capital Key**
1 – Boise
2 – Phoenix
3 – Sacramento
4 – Carson City
5 – Olympia
6 – Salem
7 – Salt Lake City

WASHINGTON
Snake R.
Columbia R.
IDAHO
MONTANA
OREGON
Snake R.
WYOMING
NEVADA
COLORADO
UTAH
CALIFORNIA
Colorado R.
ARIZONA
NEW MEXICO
FOUR CORNERS

N
W E
S

162

Learn at Home, Grade 2

U.S. Map Puzzle
SECTION 2

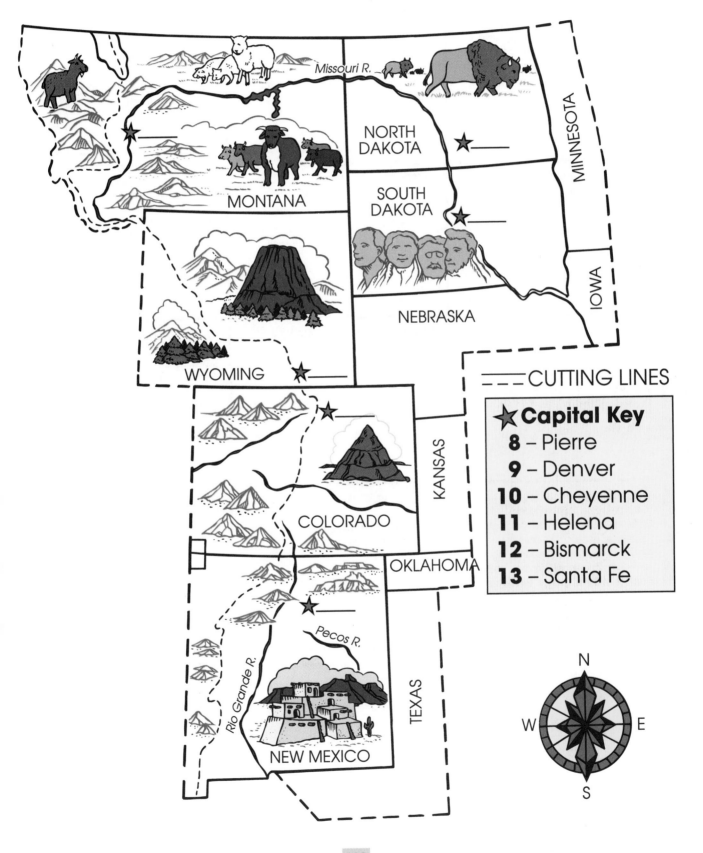

Missouri R.

NORTH DAKOTA

MINNESOTA

MONTANA

SOUTH DAKOTA

IOWA

NEBRASKA

WYOMING

KANSAS

COLORADO

OKLAHOMA

Pecos R.

Rio Grande R.

TEXAS

NEW MEXICO

— — — CUTTING LINES

⭐**Capital Key**
8 – Pierre
9 – Denver
10 – Cheyenne
11 – Helena
12 – Bismarck
13 – Santa Fe

N
W   E
S

Learn at Home, Grade 2

	Language Skills	Spelling	Reading
Monday	**Review pronouns** Teach your child that certain pronouns make more sense at the beginning of a sentence. *See* Language Skills, Week 15, number 1. Have your child write examples of sentences that begin with the following pronouns: *I, you, he, she, it, we* and *they.* Have your child underline the pronoun in each written sentence.	Pretest your child on these spelling words: stir, girl, verb, skirt, herd, her, clerk, first, bird, jerk. Teach your child to recognize the sound made by *ur, ir* and *er.*	**Syllabication** Clap the number of syllables in the names of family members and friends. Model a couple first. Say some familiar words to your child and have him/her clap the number of syllables in each word. *See* Reading, Week 15, numbers 1 and 2. With your child, read, discuss and complete the activity sheet (p. 157) for *A Baker's Dozen: A St. Nicholas Tale* by Aaron Shepard (Dutch).
Tuesday	Write 10 statements with specific subjects (not pronouns). Underline the subject in each sentence. **Examples:** Rebecca ate three hot dogs at the picnic. My dog chased the neighbor away from our fence. Grandma and Grandpa will come over for Thanksgiving. Have your child replace each underlined subject with a subject pronoun. Have your child complete **Subject Pronouns** (p. 168).	Have your child write the spelling words in sentences.	Have your child read familiar words to you and identify the number of syllables in each word. *See* Reading, Week 15, number 3. With your child, read, discuss and complete **Christmas Around the World** (p. 157) for *The Trees of the Dancing Goats* by Patricia Polacco (Hanukkah).
Wednesday	Write examples of sentences that contain the following pronouns in the predicates: *me, you, him, her, it, us* and *them. See* Language Skills, Week 15, number 2 for examples. Have your child underline the pronoun in each written sentence.	Have your child complete **Stir Up a Dessert** (p. 170).	With your child, read, spell and identify two-syllable words. Look for patterns where syllables are separated. *See* Reading, Week 15, numbers 4 and 5. With your child, read, discuss and complete the activity sheet for *O Christmas Tree* by Vashanti Rahaman (West Indies).
Thursday	Write ten statements with specific nouns in the predicate (not pronouns). Underline the noun in each predicate. **Examples:** Rebecca ate three hot dogs at the picnic. My dog chased the neighbor away from our fence. Grandma and Grandpa will visit Shelby. Have your child replace each underlined noun with an object pronoun. Have your child complete **Object Pronouns** (p. 169).	Have your child spell words using individual letters cut from old magazines, newspapers and workbooks. Your child can glue the words on paper.	With your child, read, discuss and complete the activity sheet for *Tree of Cranes* by Allen Say (Japan).
Friday	Have your child proofread the Christmas story he/she wrote in Reading and share it with someone.	Give your child the final spelling test.	With your child, read, discuss and complete the activity sheet for *Silver Packages: An Appalachian Christmas Story* by Cynthia Rylant. Have your child write a Christmas story.

Learn at Home—Grade 2

Math	Science	Social Studies
Review 2-digit addition with and without regrouping. List five to ten problems using both methods for your child to complete. **2-Digit Subtraction Without Regrouping:** With the use of manipulatives and two place-value boards, teach your child how to count backward to subtract without regrouping. **Example:** $26 - 10 = 16$ $\begin{array}{r}78\\-\,13\\\hline 65\end{array}$	Allow your child sufficient time to work on the Ocean Animal Research Project. (*See* Science, Week 12.)	Continue to study the 50 states. *See* Social Studies, Week 14. **Utah** **UT** named for the Ute Indians nicknamed The Beehive State capital city - Salt Lake City landmarks - Promontory hosted completion of the first trans-continental railroad Arches National Park Great Salt Lake
Repeat Monday's lesson (starting at different numbers) until your child is confidently counting backward and recording the numbers on his/her own. *See* Math, Week 15, number 1.	**Art:** Help your child carve a small sea animal using a bar of soap and a variety of non-sharp kitchen utensils.	**Arizona** **AZ** name means *small spring* nicknamed The Grand Canyon State capital city - Phoenix landmarks - The Grand Canyon Flagstaff Painted Desert Tucson Colorado River
Have your child subtract 2-digit numbers with and without regrouping, using nuts and cups for manipulatives. Write the problems on a copy of the **Recording Sheet** (p. 149). Then, have your child use the nuts and cups to solve the problems. $\begin{array}{r}37\\-\,5\\\hline 32\end{array}$	Provide a poinsettia plant. Discuss its characteristics. Then, read *The Legend of the Poinsettia* by Tomie dePaola. Create a tissue paper collage of a poinsettia.	**Montana** **MT** named *mountainous* in Spanish nicknamed The Treasure State capital city - Helena landmarks - Rocky Mountains Missouri River Little Bighorn National Monument Grasshopper Glacier National Bison Range
Have your child use the place-value boards and manipulatives to solve the first seven problems in **Just Like Magic . . . Again** (p. 171).	Have your child make the cover for his/her ocean animal book. *See* Science, Week 12. Decorate it with animals researched and write a title followed by your child's name as author. Have the book ready to read and share on Monday, Week 16.	**Wyoming** **WY** named *upon the great plain* in Indian nicknamed The Equality State capital city - Cheyenne landmarks - Rocky Mountains Old Faithful Geyser Independence Rock Devil's Tower Fort Laramie Buffalo Bill Historical Center
Have your child try to solve the last six problems on paper only when completing **Just Like Magic . . . Again** (p. 171).	Have your child create an ocean aquarium with two of the ocean animals he/she researched or have him/her make stick puppets of two of the animals. *See* Science, Week 15, number 1.	**North Dakota** **ND** named *allies* in Sioux (Dakota) Indian nicknamed The Flickertail State capital city - Bismarck landmarks - Fort Abercrombie Rugby, the geographic center of North America International Peace Garden United Tribes Powwow

165

TEACHING SUGGESTIONS AND ACTIVITIES

LANGUAGE SKILLS (Pronouns)

▶ 1. Pronouns may take the place of nouns. They are often used so that a noun is not overused. This makes the writing more varied. Certain pronouns make more sense replacing the subject of a sentence. Other pronouns make more sense in the predicate part of the sentence, replacing the object. Experience and good modeling will teach your child when each type of pronoun is to be used. Provide lots of examples of subject and object pronouns in context.

▶ 2. Have your child underline the pronoun in the predicate of each sentence.
   My brother eats them every day.
   Ruth carried it to school.
   Karen rode with her all the way to Grandma's house.
   Yeta told us about the trip yesterday.

READING (Syllabication)

BACKGROUND

Each syllable has only one "working" vowel. (A silent vowel is not a working vowel.) Review the long and short vowel rules. Teach your child to recognize that longer words can be made of chunks called syllables. Practice clapping syllables of familiar words. Knowing the skill of syllabication is helpful when attacking new words of more than one syllable.

▶ 1. Write the numbers 1, 2, 3 and 4 on four cards to be used as category headings. Write one-, two-, three-, and four-syllable words on other cards. Read each word to your child. He/she should clap and count the syllables he/she hears and put the word card under the correct number card. If your child misplaces a word, say it again slowly and have your child clap and count again.

▶ 2. Prepare cards as in number 1. Use different words. Instead of reading words to your child, let your child read words independently and listen for syllables. Then, have your child sort word cards by the number of syllables in the word.

▶ 3. Provide an auditory experience when identifying syllables. Instruct your child to fold a 9" x 12" sheet of paper to make six boxes. Have your child number the boxes 1–6. Read one of the six sentences below. Tell your child to listen for a word with three syllables and draw it in the first box. Repeat with the other five sentences, drawing one picture in each box.

   • Sammy the Seal and Ellie the Elephant went for a walk after the zoo closed for the night.
   • They saw their friend, the chimpanzee.
   • The chimp was in a tree eating a banana.
   • He joined Sammy and Ellie and off they all went to find the kangaroo.
   • Kelly Roo was away paying a call on Artie Anteater, so they went to Artie's.
   • Sammy, Ellie, the chimp, Kelly Roo and Artie all went to visit Annie the Antelope.

▶ 4. Write ten familiar two-syllable words, each on an index card. Cut each card into two pieces, separating the syllables. Mix up cards. Have your child put two syllables together to make a word. Have your child read and write each word.

▶ 5. Make a list of two-syllable words on the chalkboard. At this time, use only easily divided words such as those with two consonants in the middle and compound words. Have your child draw a line between the two syllables. **Examples:** cat|tle, tooth|paste and mem|ber

166

6. **Poetry:** Have your child pick a subject for a poem, such as a pet, a feeling or a food. Have your child write a one-syllable word about the subject on the first line, a two-syllable word about the subject on the second line, a three-syllable word about the subject on the third line and a four-syllable word (or phrase) on the fourth line. Your child may continue, if possible. Have your child draw a picture about the subject and rewrite the poem neatly on the picture.

MATH (2-Digit Subtraction Without Regrouping)

Use manipulatives to teach this concept even if your child is able to subtract the ones place and the tens place on paper accurately. This will make the transition to regrouping much easier.

1. Ask your child to visualize and solve subtraction problems without paper or manipulatives. Avoid problems involving regrouping.

SCIENCE (Sea Animals)

1. On tagboard or poster board, have your child draw and paint or color ocean animal puppets. Cut them out and staple or tape each to a dowel, stick, paint stirrer or other prop. Hold the puppet sticks and do your puppet presentation.

   Give your child an old gray sock. Show your child how to hold it to make a puppet. Create a mouth with your thumb and fingers inside the sock. Have your child make eyes and other features from felt.

167

Subject Pronouns

I, **you**, **he**, **she**, **it**, **we** and **they** are **subject pronouns**. They take the place of nouns or noun phrases in the subject part of the sentence.

Example: Cinderella is my favorite fairy tale character.
She is my favorite fairy tale character.

Write the pronoun that takes the place of the underlined words.

1. <u>A prince</u> was looking for a wife.

   _____ was looking for a wife.

2. <u>A big ball</u> was held at the palace.

   _____ was held at the palace.

3. <u>Cinderella's stepmother</u> wouldn't let her go.

   _____ wouldn't let her go.

4. <u>Cinderella</u> was left at home to work.

   _____ was left at home to work.

5. <u>A fairy godmother</u> came to help her go to the ball.

   _____ came to help her go to the ball.

6. <u>The prince</u> fell in love with Cinderella.

   _____ fell in love with Cinderella.

7. <u>The prince and Cinderella</u> were married.

   _____ were married.

Object Pronouns

An **object pronoun** replaces a noun or noun phrase in the predicate part of a sentence. **Me**, **you**, **him**, **her**, **it**, **us** and **them** are object pronouns.

Example: Tommy packed **his backpack**.
Tommy packed **it**.

Rewrite each sentence. Replace the underlined words with the correct object pronoun.

1. Tommy packed <u>sandwiches and apples</u>.

_____

2. He saw <u>the trail</u>.

_____

3. Tommy heard <u>the birds</u>.

_____

4. Tommy called <u>Ed and Larry</u>.

_____

5. Rita met <u>Tommy</u> at the trail's end.

_____

6. Tommy gave <u>Rita</u> one of his sandwiches.

_____

7. They ate <u>their lunches</u> under a tree.

_____

169

Stir Up a Dessert

stir   girl   verb

skirt   herd   her   clerk

first   bird   jerk

Write the spelling words with **er** that make the sound you hear in the middle of **fern**.

_____   _____   _____

_____   _____

Write the spelling words with **ir** that make the sound you hear in the middle of **shirt**.

_____   _____   _____

_____   _____

Write the missing spelling word in the boxes.

1. Our class will sing the _____ song in the program.

2. The cowboys will drive the cattle _____ to the range.

3. Sara wore her new _____ to the party.

4. A tiny _____ chirped when it hatched from its egg.

5. A part of speech that describes an action is called a _____ .

6. Trudy met _____ grandmother at the train station.

7. You must _____ the cake batter before you put it in the pan.

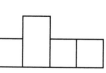

8. The car started to _____ as it ran out of gas.

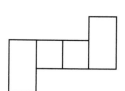

9. Mother paid the _____ for my new shirt.

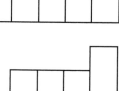

10. That _____ lives next door to me.

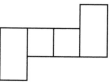

Learn at Home, Grade 2

Just Like Magic . . . Again

Subtract.

i
90
−24

a
52
−15

r
52
−19

o
98
−59

w
43
−29

y
95
−37

s
80
− 8

m
73
−26

n
82
−28

u
93
−48

d
52
−26

h
57
−29

c
81
−38

Use the answers and the letter on each lamp to solve the code.

___ ___ ___ ___   ___ ___ ___ ___
58 39 45 33   14 66 72 28

___ ___   ___ ___   ___ ___ ___ ___ ___ ___ ___ !
66 72   47 58   43 39 47 47 37 54 26

	Language Skills	**Spelling**	**Reading**
Monday	**Articles** Write the following two sentences. *Sally ate a pear. Mark ate an apple.* Have your child underline the article in each one and discuss when to use each article. Have your child fill in the appropriate article before each of the following nouns and use each in a sentence. ___ ant ___ balloon ___ cat ___ egg ___ fire ___ gate ___ house ___ inch ___ jar ___ kite ___ light	Pretest your child on these spelling words: girlfriend baseball everybody maybe today myself sometimes outside lunchbox downtown Discuss the formation of compound words.	Teach your child to split words into syllables. To determine the number of syllables, count the number of vowels that make a sound. Make a syllable split between each working vowel. If there are two consonants, split between them. If there is one consonant, split before the consonant. Never break up blends, digraphs or *r*-controlled vowels. *See* Reading, Week 16, numbers 1–3. **Examples:** po-ta-to, yel-low, steam-er
Tuesday	Explain that *the* is also an article. *The* is more specific than *a* or *an*. *The* can also be used before singular or plural nouns. Have your child think about the difference in meaning between the following two sentences: *I chased after a cat. I chased after the cat. The* tells more specifically which one. *See* Language Skills, Week 16, number 1.	Have your child write the spelling words in sentences.	Continue yesterday's lesson. Provide lots of examples. With your child, read *Arthur's Nose* (The first Arthur book-1976) by Marc Brown, and then read a recent Arthur book, *Arthur's TV Trouble* (1995). Review the story elements for each book. Also discuss how Arthur's looks have changed over 19 years.
Wednesday	Discuss when to use *a, an* and *the*.	Have your child spell each word aloud while you clap each letter. Have your child complete **Mixing a Compound** (p. 177).	Teach your child to separate unfamiliar words into syllables to decode. Each syllable of a word can be read like a one-syllable word. Review vowel rules. With your child, read and discuss *Arthur's Eyes* by Marc Brown. Review the story elements in the book. Then, have your child write a story about a problem he/she had and how it was solved.
Thursday	Have your child complete **Articles** (p. 176).	Write two or three sentences using all the spelling words. Have your child paint a picture of each sentence and glue the sentences to the appropriate paintings.	With your child, read and discuss *Arthur Babysits* by Marc Brown. Review the story elements in the book.
Friday	Have your child share his/her Christmas story with family, friends, relatives, etc. Have him/her get their ideas and then rewrite the story including some of these new ideas. Remind him/her to include a beginning, middle, end and use details. *See* Reading, Wednesday.	Give your child the final spelling test.	With your child, read and discuss *Arthur Writes a Story* by Marc Brown. Your child then shares her/his story from Wednesday with family friends, etc. *See* Language Skills, Friday.

Learn at Home, Grade 2

Math	**Science**	**Social Studies**

2-Digit Subtraction With Regrouping
Review counting backward and ask your child to explain how he/she moves the manipulatives from 30 to 29. Consolidate the process into a few words such as *move a ten to the ones place, dump it out, count the total.* Teach regrouping using place-value materials and a die. *See* Math, Week 16, numbers 1–3.
	Have your child read, present and share his/her Ocean Animal Research Project to a small audience.	Continue to study the 50 states. *See* Social Studies, Week 14.
		South Dakota **SD**
		     named *allies* in Sioux (Dakota) Indian
		     nicknamed The Sunshine State
		capital city - Pierre
		landmarks - Badlands National Park
		         Corn Palace
		         Castle Rock,
		            geographic center of USA

Have your child play the dice game from yesterday. Start at a different number and continue subtracting until he/she reaches zero. Use different manipulatives. You can record the problems while your child uses manipulatives.	Compare sea and land turtles. With your child, read *Sea Turtles* by Caroline Arnold and *Box Turtle at Long Pond* by William T. George.
	Have your child use **Turtle Venn Diagram** (p. 179) to chart the similarities and differences.
		Colorado **CO**
		     named *colored red* in Spanish
		     nicknamed The Centennial State
		capital city - Denver
		landmarks - Rocky Mountains
		         Colorado River
		         Aspen
		         Garden of the Gods
		         US Mint
		         Mesa Verde National Park

As your child moves the tens cup and dumps it into the ones, show him/her how to represent that on paper. Cross out the tens and write how many there are now above. Cross out the ones, count the total and record how many there are now. Have your child complete the page. Give your child assistance as needed. Use **Subtraction With Regrouping** (p. 178) to teach your child how to regroup.	Some sea animals can also live on land. When not swimming, they must walk. With your child, read *Cimru the Seal* by Theresa Radcliffe. Discuss how Cimru and her pup were able to survive living in both areas. *See* Science, Week 16, number 1.	***New Mexico*** **NM**
		     named after Mexico
		     nicknamed Land of Enchantment
		capital city - Santa Fe
		landmarks - Carlsbad Caverns
		         Albuquerque
		         Smokey Bear National Park
		         Four Corners
		         Inscription Rock National Monument
		         Gila Cliff Dwellings National
		            Monument

Create story problems that involve subtraction. Have your child use manipulatives to solve.	Play "water and sea" music and have your child move like different ocean animals. *See* Science, Week 16, number 2.	***Nebraska*** **NE**
		     named *flat water* in Oto Indian
		     nicknamed The Cornhusker's State
		capital city - Lincoln
		landmarks - Omaha
		         Chimney Rock
		         Carhenge
		         Platte River

Subtraction is not just taking away; it can involve comparison of two quantities. Snap together several long trains of Unifix cubes. Choose two trains and ask your child to find out how much longer one train is than the other. Have your child write a subtraction sentence to express the comparison. **Hint:** The trains will be easier to count if ten cubes in a row are the same color.	With your child, read *Out of the Ocean* by Debra Frasier. Choose five or six beach discoveries from the book and read more about them in "An Ocean Journal" at the end of the book.	***Kansas*** **KS**
		     named for Kansa Indians meaning *people of the south wind*
		     nicknamed The Sunflower State
		capital city - Topeka
		landmarks - Kansas City
		         Wichita
		         Dodge City
		         Chisholm Trail
		         Cowboy Capital of the World

Learn at Home, Grade 2

TEACHING SUGGESTIONS AND ACTIVITIES

LANGUAGE SKILLS (Articles)

▶ 1. Write example sentences using *a, an* and *the*. Ask which article precedes plural nouns.

Sally ate a yellow pear.   The boy played a pinball game.
Sally ate the yellow pears.   The boys played the pinball game.
Sally ate an orange.   Sally ate the orange.

READING (Syllabication)

▶ 1. Write the following compound words on the chalkboard.

raincoat   doghouse   football   inside

Have your child read each word and draw a line between the two words that make up each compound word. Have your child say the compound word and tell the number of syllables. Ask what kind of letters the line is drawn between (two consonants). Tell your child when there are two consonants in the middle of a two-syllable word, the syllables are divided between the two consonants.

▶ 2. Write the following two-syllable words on the chalkboard.

little   import   happen   suggest   sentence   merry

Have your child read each word aloud and tell how many syllables he/she hears. Have your child draw a line between the two syllables. Ask what kind of letters the line is drawn between (consonants). Tell your child when there are two consonants in the middle of a two-syllable word, the syllables are divided between the two consonants.

▶ 3. Write the following two-syllable words with only one consonant in the middle.

report   peacock   baker   recent   music   wiper

Have your child read each word aloud and tell how many syllables he/she hears. Have your child draw a line at the end of the first syllable to separate it from the second syllable. Ask, what kind of letter the line was drawn between in each word (after the vowel/before the consonant). Ask your child what kind of a vowel sound he/she hears in the first syllable (long). Tell your child that usually when there is only one consonant between the vowels in a two-syllable word, the first syllable ends with a vowel.

Learn at Home, Grade 2

MATH (2-Digit Subtraction With Regrouping)

BACKGROUND
Provide a variety of experiences with manipulatives to teach regrouping (borrowing). Use different manipulatives and play games involving subtraction. It is very important to mix problems with and without regrouping so your child thinks the process through each time. In real life, problems are mixed, so it's important that your child learns to decide whether this is a time for regrouping or not. If your child really understands the process with manipulatives, he/she will automatically use the correct process when solving the problem on paper.

▶ 1. Have your child "build" 52 with the place-value materials. Roll the die. Help your child think through how to take that number away. **Example:** (52 – 5) *Child:* "We need to take 5 ones away, but there are only 2 ones here." *Parent:* "Where can we get more ones?" *Child:* "From the tens." *Parent and child together:* "Move a ten to the ones place, dump it out, count the total." *Child:* "Now there are 12 ones and I can take 5 away. That leaves 4 tens 7 ones." Roll the die again and repeat. (Your child will not need to "borrow" with each roll.)

▶ 2. Write 32 on the chalkboard to start this activity. Have your child build it. Write –19 under it. Ask your child how many ones are supposed to be taken away. Have your child look at the 32 he/she built and suggest how it can be done. Let your child come up with a solution if he/she can. If not, talk your child through the process. Tell your child that he/she could take a ten from the tens side, exchange it for ten ones and put them on the ones side. Have your child do that and then tell how many ones there are. Ask how many tens now remain. Cross out the 3 on the board and change it to a 2. Ask if your child can now take 9 ones away. Have him/her do it. Ask how many are left. Write 3 under the line in the ones column. Ask how many tens need to be taken away. Have your child remove a ten and ask how many are left. Write 1 under the line in the tens column. Repeat this procedure several times with several problems.

▶ 3. Write subtraction problems on the chalkboard, one at a time. Have your child look at the ones column and decide if regrouping is necessary.

SCIENCE (Sea Animals)

▶ 1. Pour 3 or 4 gallons of water in an empty aquarium. Have your child put one hand in the water with fingers apart and pull his/her hand through the water. Then, have your child try again, forming a cup with his/her fingers. Ask which way would be better for swimming. Relate this to a sea turtle's feet.

▶ 2. Play some "music of the sea." Give your child directions to move like different animals of the ocean.

Swim like a fish.   Creep like a snail.
Paddle like a sea turtle.   Dig like a crab.
Walk like a lobster.   Jet like an octopus.
Dive like a seal.   Leap like a dolphin.

Articles

A, **an** and **the** are special adjectives called **articles**. Use **a** before singular nouns that start with a consonant sound. Use **an** before singular nouns that begin with a vowel sound or a silent **h**. Use **the** before singular or plural nouns.

Examples: a city, **an** apartment, **an** hour, **the** cab, **the** building

Write a or **an** in the blank.

1. My apartment is in _____ skyscraper.

2. I ride _____ elevator to the fifty-seventh floor.

3. I don't have _____ yard to play in, so I go to the park.

4. We played there for _____ hour.

5. The park has a big lake and _____ zoo.

6. I can see _____ elephant everyday if I want.

7. The zoo also has _____ ostrich.

8. There is _____ aquarium at the park, too.

Underline the articles in the sentences.

9. The monkey chattered at the crowd.

10. The little boy waved to the monkey.

Learn at Home, Grade 2

Mixing a Compound

sometimes   downtown   girlfriend

everybody   maybe   myself   lunchbox

baseball   outside   today

Write the correct compound word on the line. Then, use the numbered letters to solve the code.

1. Opposite of inside   — — — — — — —
            1

2. Another word for me   — — — — — —
           2   3

3. A girl who is a friend   — — — — — — — — — —
    4   5

4. Not yesterday or tomorrow, but . . .   — — — — —
           6

5. All of the people   — — — — — — — — —
      7   8

6. A sport   — — — — — — — —
          9

7. The main part of a town   — — — — — — — —
    10   11

8. Not always, just . . .   — — — — — — — — —
  12   13

9. A box for carrying your lunch   — — — — — — — —
          14

10. Perhaps or might   — — — — —
          15

— — — — — — — — — ! — — —
10   8   11   6   15   7   3   1   9   2   8   1

— — — — —   — — —
3   8   1   11   6   13   14   15

— — — — —   — — — — — — — — !
7   5   4   14   13   12   8   9   1   13   5   8   11

Subtraction
With Regrouping

Use manipulatives to find the difference.

1.

Tens	Ones
4	14
5	4
− 1	7
3	7

2.

Tens	Ones
3	3
− 1	5

3.

Tens	Ones
6	1
− 3	3

4.

Tens	Ones
2	7
− 1	6

5.

Tens	Ones
4	2
− 2	4

6.

Tens	Ones
5	2
− 2	6

7.

Tens	Ones
9	4
− 4	8

8.

Tens	Ones
7	7
− 3	4

9.

Tens	Ones
6	5
− 2	6

Learn at Home, Grade 2

Turtle Venn Diagram

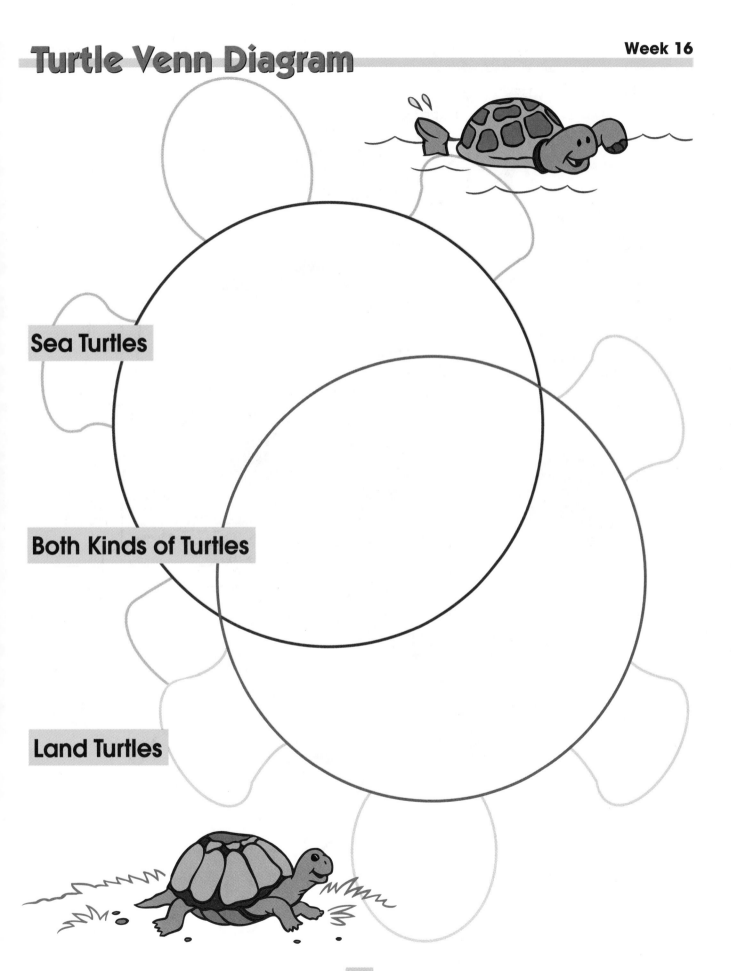

Sea Turtles

Both Kinds of Turtles

Land Turtles

179

SECTION 3

NEBRASKA

Platte R.

IOWA

MISSOURI

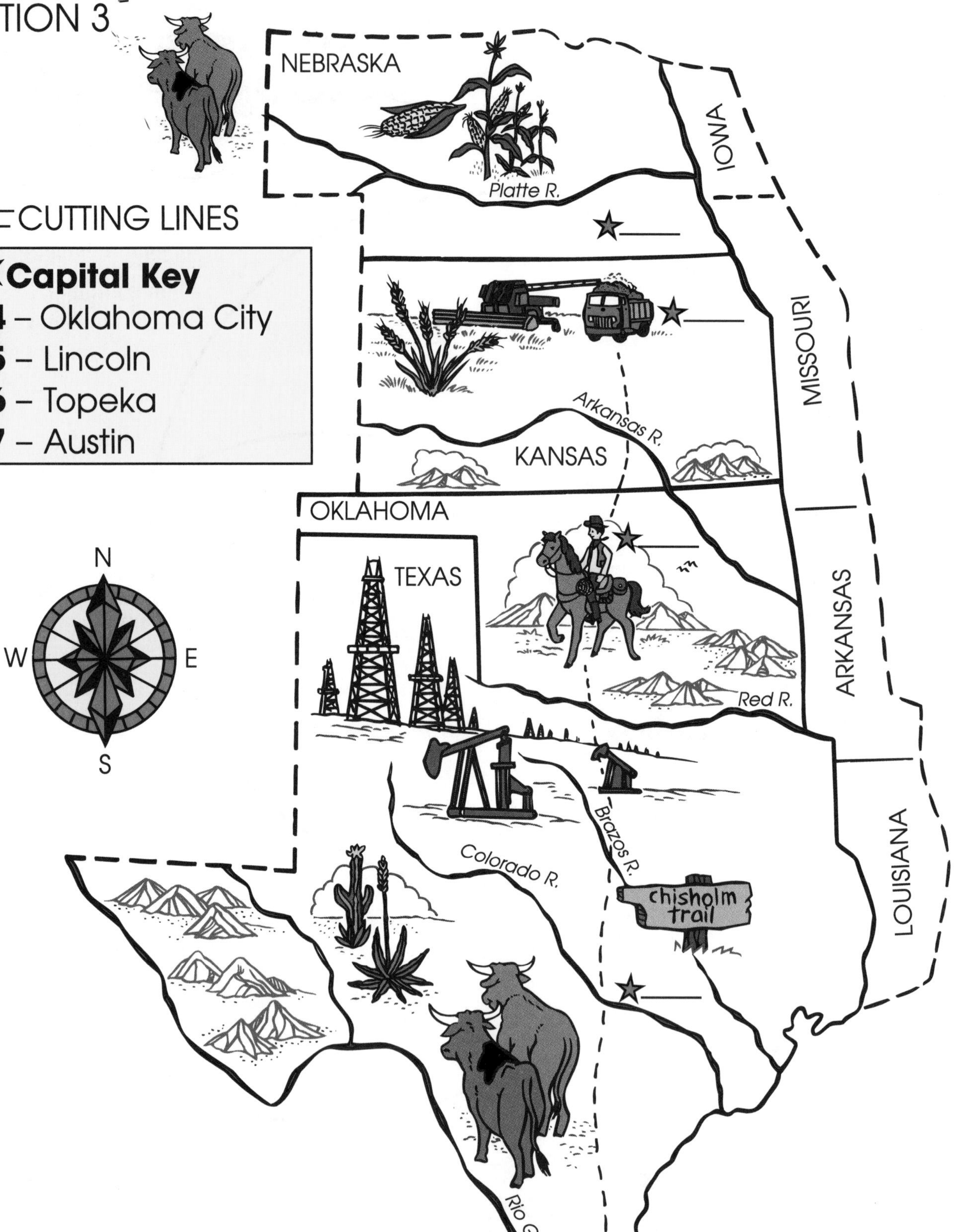

═══ CUTTING LINES

☆ **Capital Key**
14 – Oklahoma City
15 – Lincoln
16 – Topeka
17 – Austin

Arkansas R.

KANSAS

OKLAHOMA

TEXAS

ARKANSAS

N
W E
S

Red R.

Brazos R.

Colorado R.

chisholm trail

LOUISIANA

Rio Grande R.

Learn at Home, Grade 2

U.S. Map Puzzle
SECTION 4

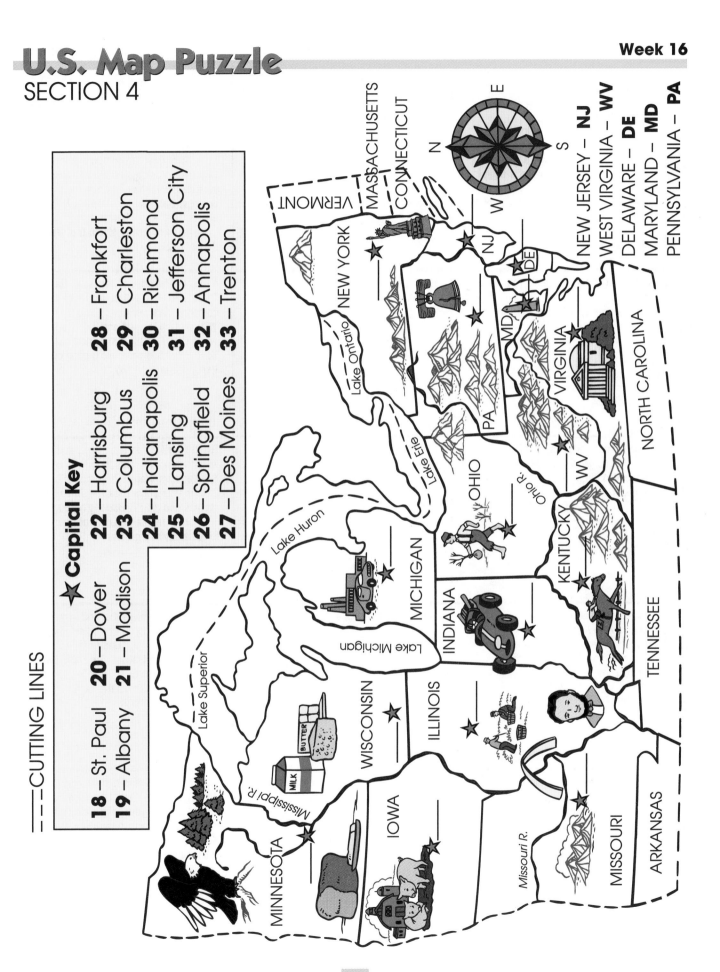

—CUTTING LINES

★ Capital Key

18 – St. Paul   20 – Dover   22 – Harrisburg   28 – Frankfort
19 – Albany   21 – Madison   23 – Columbus   29 – Charleston
24 – Indianapolis   30 – Richmond
25 – Lansing   31 – Jefferson City
26 – Springfield   32 – Annapolis
27 – Des Moines   33 – Trenton

NEW JERSEY – **NJ**
WEST VIRGINIA – **WV**
DELAWARE – **DE**
MARYLAND – **MD**
PENNSYLVANIA – **PA**

VERMONT
MASSACHUSETTS
CONNECTICUT
NEW YORK
NJ
DE
MD
PA
VIRGINIA
NORTH CAROLINA
OHIO
WV
KENTUCKY
Ohio R.
MICHIGAN
INDIANA
TENNESSEE
Lake Ontario
Lake Erie
Lake Huron
Lake Michigan
Lake Superior
WISCONSIN
ILLINOIS
IOWA
MINNESOTA
Mississippi R.
Missouri R.
MISSOURI
ARKANSAS

BUTTER
MILK

Language Skills	Spelling	Reading
Monday **Contractions** Discuss the use of contractions. A contraction is a word made up of two words joined together with one or more letters left out. An apostrophe is used in place of the missing letters. Write several sentences containing contractions for your child to read. Confirm that your child recognizes contractions and their meaning.	Pretest your child on these spelling words: didn't it's who's don't isn't that's she's aren't doesn't he's Discuss how contractions are formed. *See* Spelling, Week 17, number 1.	**Comparative Endings** Place two similar objects in front of your child. The objects should be different sizes so he/she can compare them using words such as big and bigger. Write your child's words and underline the endings. *See* Reading, Week 17, number 1. Have your child complete **Is It a World Record?** (p. 187).
Tuesday Dictate several sentences to your child containing contractions. With your child, read over the written sentences and reteach any contraction spellings necessary.	Have your child write the spelling words in sentences.	A study of assorted versions of "The Three Little Pigs" will be read and compared this week. With your child, read and discuss *The Three Little Pigs* by James Marshall. Have your child complete a copy of **Book Report Form** (p. 188).
Wednesday Write ten sentences containing contractions. Write above each contraction the original two words that formed it.	Have your child spell each word aloud. Have your child complete **Something is Missing!** (p. 186).	Teach your child to use the *est* ending when comparing more than two objects. *See* Reading, Week 17, numbers 2 and 3. With your child, read *The Three Little Wolves and the Big Bad Pig* by Eugene Trivizas. Compare and contrast this story to yesterday's "pigs" book.
Thursday List the contractions in *The Three Little Pigs and the Fox* from Reading, Tuesday. Then, have your child write the original two words that form these contractions.	*See* today's Language Skills lesson.	Show how adjectives that end in *y* change when you add *ed* or *est*. *See* Reading, Week 17, number 4. With your child, read and discuss *The Three Little Pigs and the Fox* by William Hooks. Compare and contrast this book to the first two "pigs" books.
Friday Have your child write a story about his/her "Tangram Collage" from Math, Thursday. Remind your child to have a beginning, middle, end and details. Have him/her share and discuss the story with someone.	Give your child the final spelling test.	With your child, read and discuss *The True Story of the Three Little Pigs* by Jon Scieszka. Have your child pick his/her favorite "pigs" book to read this week. Have your child write a commercial telling why everyone should read this book.

Learn at Home, Grade 2

Math	Science	Social Studies

Geometry
Provide shapes for your child to explore and sort. Ask your child to explain how he/she sorted the shapes. *See* Math, Week 17, number 1. Provide pattern blocks or pattern block stickers. Tell your child to create a repeating design or picture with the shapes. On 1 inch graph paper, help your child graph how many of each shape used in the picture.
	Discuss fishing. Why do people fish? Look at pictures of industrial fishing boats. Find out what happens to the fish. Some fish may be processed into fish oil or meal that is used in pet and farm animal food.	Continue to study the 50 states. *See* Social Studies, Week 14.
		Oklahoma **OK**
		          named after the Chocotaw Indians
		          meaning *red people*
		          nicknamed The Sooner State
		capital city - Oklahoma City
		landmarks - Tulsa
		          Chisholm Trail
		          Rush Springs

With your child, read *The Silly Story of Goldie Locks and the Three Squares* by Grace Maccarone. Choose different activities at the end of the book to complete.	**Field Trip:** Visit a fish market and a livestock/pet supply store. *See* Science, Week 17, numbers 1 and 2.	*Texas* **TX**
		          named *allies* or *friends*
		          nicknamed The Lone Star State
		capital city - Austin
		landmarks - Rio Grande River
		          Houston
		          Dallas
		          The Alamo, San Antonio
		          San Jacinto Monument

Go on a shape search. Look for geometric shapes within pictures, in man-made objects and in nature. *See* Math, Week 17, number 2. Have your child draw a picture of something from your shape search and color the shapes in the picture.	Create and help your child prepare a meal with a "fish dish" (entree).	*Minnesota* **MN**
		          named *sky-tinted water* in Sioux
		          Indian
		          nicknamed The Gopher State
		capital city - St. Paul
		landmarks - Minneapolis
		          Mayo Clinic
		          Duluth
		          Mall of America
		          Lake Itasca

With your child, read and discuss *Grandfather Tang's Story* by Ann Tompert. As you read, observe the tangram animals. When finished, use a set of paper tangrams to form some of the animals in the book. *See* **Tangram** (p. 189).	With your child, read and discuss *The Freshwater Alphabet Book* by Jerry Pallotta. Have your child choose four or five favorite freshwater fish and write two facts about each on a 3" x 5" card.	*Iowa* **IA**
		          named *beautiful land* or *sleepy ones*
		          after the Ayuhwa Indians
		          nicknamed The Hawkeye State
		capital city - Des Moines
		landmarks - Cedar Rapids
		          Effigy Mounds
		          Sioux City

Have your child design an original tangram collage using characters from yesterday or create his/her own. *See* Math, Week 17, number 3.	Have your child complete Thursday's project and illustrate the fish on the other side of each card. Have him/her share the cards.	*Missouri* **MO**
		          named *town of the long canoes* in
		          Indian
		          nicknamed The Show Me State
		capital city - Jefferson City
		landmarks - Gateway Arch
		          Kansas City
		          Hannibal, Mark Twain's home

TEACHING SUGGESTIONS AND ACTIVITIES

SPELLING

▶ 1. Make sure your child can identify the two words that make up each contraction and what letter is missing in each one. Have your child identify the second word of each contraction. It is usually in the second word of a contraction that a letter is omitted.

READING (Comparative Endings)

BACKGROUND

Words that compare persons, places and things are called comparative adjectives. Comparative adjectives may describe color, texture, size, shape or other attributes. Usually the comparative ending *er* is added to an adjective when two nouns are compared and *est* is added when more than two nouns are compared. Some comparative adjectives are irregular.

▶ 1. Place two potatoes on the table. Ask your child how they are alike. Then, ask how they are different (size, shape or color). Encourage your child to describe each potato using words such as *brown, browner, round, rounder, small, smaller, large, larger* and other appropriate adjectives. Explain that when the attributes of two objects are compared, *er*, rather than *est*, is added to the adjective. Repeat this exercise with other objects.

▶ 2. Place three balls on the floor. Ask your child to describe the balls. Then, roll a ball and say, "This ball rolls fast." Write *fast* on the chalkboard. Roll the second ball a little faster and have your child describe how it moves compared to the first ball. ("This ball rolls faster.") Write *faster* on the chalkboard. Roll the last ball faster than the second ball, say "This ball rolls fastest," and write *fastest* on the chalkboard. Underline the endings. The ending *est* is added to an adjective when more than two nouns are compared. Repeat this activity with three different objects.

▶ 3. Explain there are some adjectives that do not follow the pattern, such as *good, better, best; many, more, most;* and *little, littler, less* or *least.* Also, words with more than two syllables use these words rather than having a suffix added.

Model how to use these words in sentences. **Examples:** "The white cake is good. The yellow cake is better. The chocolate cake is best." Have your child use the other irregular adjectives in original sentences.

Change y to i Before Adding Ending:
Since the comparative endings begin with a vowel, this is a good time to introduce the "*y* changes to *i*" rule. This rule will come up again. When a word ends in *y*, you must drop the *y* before adding an ending that begins with a vowel.

▶ 4. Write the following adjectives on the chalkboard. Ask your child to use each one in a sentence. Then, use each adjective in a comparative example, such as "My brother is happier than he was yesterday." Write the word happier next to happy and compare the spellings.

    happy   crazy   pretty   fancy

Learn at Home, Grade 2

MATH (Geometry)

BACKGROUND

At the elementary level, geometry involves sorting, exploring and describing of physical models. It is important that early experiences include several examples of each shape so your child is aware, for example, that a triangle may be long and skinny, wide, have a very short side, be tiny or large, and so on. The important attributes are 3 corners and 3 sides. With more experience, your child can start describing a shape's properties such as curved, parallel, right angles and symmetrical. Until that point, accept descriptions such as lines going in the same direction, corner like a square and same if you fold it over. Also provide opportunities for your child to put together shapes and create designs.

▶ 1. From heavy paper or cardboard, cut out a large variety of shapes. Ask your child to sort the shapes into groups that are alike. Have your child describe each group. Mix up the shapes and ask your child to group them in different ways. Your child may create groupings such as shapes with corners, shapes with equal sides, shapes with one square corner and shapes with three sides.

▶ 2. Take your child on a walk through your neighborhood looking for familiar shapes. Many shapes can be found on houses and in landscaping. Help your child identify shapes by name. Look for triangles, squares, rectangles, circles, diamonds and trapezoids, as well as cones, cylinders, pyramids, rectangular prisms and spheres.

▶ 3. **Tangram Collage:** *See* **Tangram** (p. 189). Copy the tangram pattern on different colored or patterned 8 1/2" x 11" paper. Cut out the seven parts and arrange them to form a character or characters for a collage, sides or points to be touching, but not overlapping. Create the whole scene on a larger sheet of paper and use torn colored paper to complete the background.

SCIENCE (Sea Animals)

▶ 1. Visit the fish market yourself in advance of taking your child so you know what fish is available. Take along resource books with pictures of the various kinds of fish. Have your child look at the different kinds of fish for sale. Find the pictures of the fish in the books. The person who works at the market may be able to tell your child interesting facts about some of the fish.

▶ 2. At a pet or livestock supply store, have your child look at the labels on the dog and cattle food. With your child, read the labels to see if there are any fish products in the ingredients.

185

Something Is Missing!

doesn't	it's	she's
don't	aren't	who's	he's
didn't	that's	isn't

Write the correct contraction for each set of words. Then, **circle** the letter that was left out when the contraction was made.

1. he is _____

2. are not _____

3. do not _____

4. who is _____

5. is not _____

6. did not _____

7. it is _____

8. she is _____

9. does not _____

10. that is _____

Write the missing spelling word on the line.

1. _____ on her way to school.

2. There_____ enough time to finish the story.

3. Do you think _____ too long?

4. We _____ going to the party.

5. Donna _____ like the movie.

6. _____ going to try for a part in the play?

7. Bob said_____ going to run in the big race.

8. They_____ know how to bake a cake.

9. Tom _____want to go skating on Saturday.

10. Look, _____ where they found the lost watch.

Learn at Home, Grade 2

Is It a World Record?

Write the correct word on the line.

big

bigger

biggest

1. Emmett made a _____ snowball.

2. Sara helped him make it even _____ .

3. The town made the _____ snowball on record.

fast

faster

fastest

1. The snowball started to roll very _____ .

2. It was the _____ rolling snowball anyone had ever seen.

3. It rolled _____ than they could run.

white

whiter

whitest

1. After it snowed all night, the town was the _____ it had ever been.

2. Mr. Wetzel's face turned _____ when he saw the snowball rolling toward his candy store.

3. As the snowball rolled closer, Mr. Wetzel's face became

even _____ .

Book Report Form

Title _____

Illustrator _____

Setting _____

Main Characters _____

_____

Problem _____

Solution _____

Ending _____

Some new words from the book:

1. _____ 4. _____

2. _____ 5. _____

3. _____ 6. _____

I liked the book. (Color one worm.)

Illustrate your favorite part of the book on another sheet of paper.

188

Learn at Home, Grade 2

Tangram

Cut out the tangram below. Use the shapes to make a cat, a chicken, a boat and a large triangle.

	Language Skills	**Spelling**	**Reading**
Monday	**Review Week** Review statements.	**Review Week** Review spelling words learned in the past 8 weeks. Have your child make a tape using the harder words. Have him/her read a word, count silently to ten, spell the word slowly, then repeat the word. Repeat with each word. Play the tape back. Have your child spell the word aloud in the 10-second pause. Have your child use the tape for review throughout the week.	**Review Week** Review blends and digraphs. Use the words from Weeks 10 and 11. Have your child compile a list of words that contain each digraph and blend. Your child may look in books and the dictionary for ideas.
Tuesday	Review questions. Find five interesting pictures from calendars, magazines, newspapers, etc. Have your child write one question and statement about each picture.	Separate the compound words learned in Week 16 into the two words from which they were comprised. Write the words randomly on paper. Using ten colored pencils, have your child circle the two parts of each word the same color. Then, have your child rewrite each compound word with the colored pencils.	Review the sounds *c* makes. *See* Reading, Week 18, numbers 1 and 2. Choose one activity to give your child practice reading words with the hard and soft *c* sounds.
Wednesday	Review pronouns. Look through some of the books read recently and point out pronouns, telling if they are subject or object pronouns. Have your child complete **Pronouns** (p. 194).	Review contractions. Have your child make contractions from two words.	Review compound words. *See* Reading, Week 18, number 3 for game instructions. Have your child complete **Word Magic** (p. 195).
Thursday	Write a paragraph with run-on sentences and containing punctuation and capitalization errors. Have your child proofread and rewrite paragraph correctly.	Review long and short vowels. Have your child write words that rhyme with spelling words from the past 8 weeks. Your child should choose different sets of rhyming words and write rhymes using these sets.	Review common and proper nouns. Have your child look through magazines, books, etc. for proper nouns and write them in a list. Then, help him/her create a common noun that refers to each proper noun. **Examples:** New York - state China - country
Friday	Have your child write directions explaining how to make something. **Example:** How to Make a Banana Split	Review *r*-controlled vowels (*ar, ur, or, ir* and *er*). Have your child sort the spelling words from Weeks 14 and 15 into the different vowel sounds and add other words to each list.	Have your child pick a favorite fiction book read the past 9 weeks and write a book report. Have your child complete another copy of **Book Report Form** (p. 188).

Learn at Home, Grade 2

Math	Science	Social Studies

Review Week
Review patterns. Add the number from one column and one row. Write the sum in the empty box where the row and column meet. Have your child look for patterns in the chart. *See* Math, Week 18, numbers 1 and 2.
Teach your child how to complete the **Addition Chart** (p. 196).
	Review Week
	Observe the difference between fresh water and salt water and what happens to each when they evaporate and freeze. *See* Science, Week 18, number 1.
	Have your child complete **Anti-Freeze** (p. 199).
		Continue to study the 50 states. *See* Social Studies, Week 14.
		Wisconsin **WI**
		    named *gathering of waters* in
		        Chippewa Indian
		    nicknamed The Badger State
		capital city - Madison
		landmarks - Milwaukee
		        Circus World Museum

Use a pair of dice to form small and large numbers using tens and ones. Refer to Math, Week 12.
Have your child complete a copy of **Numbers Small and Large** (p. 134).
	Field Trip: Visit an aquarium, zoo, coastal area or pet store to let your child observe sea animals.	***Illinois*** **IL**
		    named *superior men* in Illini Indian
		    nicknamed The Land of Lincoln
		capital city - Springfield
		landmarks - Lincoln's home
		        Chicago
		        Cahokia Mounds

Review 2-digit addition with and without regrouping. *See* Math, Week 18, number 4.
Have your child complete **Keep on Truckin'** (p. 197).
	Discuss yesterday's field trip.	***Michigan*** **MI**
		    named *great lake* in Indian
		    nicknamed The Wolverine State
		capital city - Lansing
		landmarks - Detroit (Motor City)
		        Four Great Lakes
		        Holland & Windmill Island
		        Sleeping Bear Sand Dunes
		        Upper & Lower Peninsulas
		        Mackinac Island

Review 2-digit subtraction without and with regrouping. *See* Math, Week 18, number 4.
Have your child complete **Subtraction on the Beach** (p. 198).
	Game/Center: Write question and answer cards for each sea animal researched. *See* Science, Week 18, number 2.	***Indiana*** **IN**
		    named after Indians living there
		    nicknamed The Hoosier State
		capital city - Indianapolis
		landmarks - Indianapolis 500 Race
		        Historic Fort Wayne
		        Gary
		        Wyandotte Cave

Review geometry. With your child, read the book *Circles, Triangles and Squares* by Tana Hoban. Cut basic shapes from construction paper and have your child glue the shapes on white paper in a design, pattern or picture.	Finish the experiment from Monday.	***Kentucky*** **KY**
		    named *pasture* in Cherokee Indian
		    nicknamed The Bluegrass State
		capital city - Frankfort
		landmarks - Kentucky Derby
		        Fort Knox Gold Vault
		        Mammoth Cave National Park

TEACHING SUGGESTIONS AND ACTIVITIES

READING

▶ 1. Fold a sheet of lined paper in half lengthwise. Open up the paper and write the following headings at the top of each column: "*c* sounds like *s*" and "*c* sounds like *k*." Have your child look through old magazines and newspapers for words that contain the letter *c*. Have your child cut them out, sort them by sound and glue them in the correct column.

▶ 2. Provide your child with a list of words beginning with *c*: some with the hard sound, some with the soft sound. Have your child fold a sheet of writing paper in half and write "Hard *k*" at the top of one side and "Soft *s*" at the top of the other. Have your child copy the list of words in the correct columns. Have your child explain why *c* makes the sound it does in each column.

▶ 3. **Game: Popcorn Bingo** While the popcorn is popping, have your child fold a sheet of paper in thirds in both directions, forming nine boxes. Write *popcorn* in the center space. Then, have your child write eight of the compound words from the list below in the remaining boxes.

bedtime	raincoat	classroom	sandbox	baseball	flagpole
snowstorm	toothbrush	necktie	bookshelf	upstairs	sunlight

Have your child put a piece of popcorn on the word *popcorn* to mark a free space. Prepare a sentence for each compound word. Read one at a time aloud, omitting the compound word. If your child has a compound word on his/her board that would make sense in the sentence, your child may place a piece of popcorn on the space. When your child has a row of three in any direction, that "game" is over.

MATH

▶ 1. Discuss finished **Addition Chart**. Let your child discover and tell you about patterns that he/she sees. Ask some of the following questions to assist your child's thinking:

   • What do you notice about the first line across and the first column down?
   • What do you notice about the second line across and the second column down?
   • Put your finger on the sum of 0 + 0. Move your finger horizontally to the right. What do you notice about the numbers?
   • Put your finger on the sum of 1 + 1. Move your finger diagonally to the bottom right corner. What do you notice about the number pattern?
   • Put your finger on the sum of 9 + 1 in the top right corner. Move your finger diagonally to the bottom left corner. What do you notice about the numbers?
   • With your child, brainstorm why there is only one zero and one eighteen in the chart.

▶ 2. **Listening:** Say a string of numbers with a pattern. Have your child join in when he/she knows the pattern. **Example:** 2, 4, 6, 8, 10, . . .

▶ 3. Gather several dimes and pennies for this addition practice. Find foods and other objects around the house on which you can realistically put a price tag below 50¢. Have your child choose one object and show its price with dimes and pennies. Have your child select a second object and show its price with dimes and pennies. Your child can then add the pennies and dimes to find the combined cost. Help your child trade pennies for a dime when necessary.

▶ 4. **Subtraction practice:** From a box of craft sticks, have your child grab a handful of sticks and count them by ones. Have your child record the number on lined paper. Then, have your child count the same handful of sticks using the place-value board. When the tens and ones are set up, your child should roll one die to determine how many sticks to take away. Have your child record that number on the lined paper with a minus sign. Your child may or may not have to "borrow" when subtracting the number rolled.

Learn at Home, Grade 2

SCIENCE

▶ 1. Have your child pour 1 cup of distilled water into a glass pie pan and label it "fresh water." Also have your child mix 1 cup of distilled water with 2 tablespoons of salt and dissolve. Then, tell your child to pour it into a second pie pan and label it "salt water." Put both pans near a sunny window. Have your child write a hypothesis about what will happen to both dishes. Have your child observe and draw changes over the next few days.

▶ 2. **Game/Center:** Write a question on an index card such as "What is a Weddell seal?" On a separate card, write three sentences about that animal.
   Examples:
   • It has shiny brown eyes.
   • It lives in Antarctica.
   • It can dive deep and stay underwater as long as 43 minutes.
   Make at least ten sets of cards. Mix them up and store in a labeled envelope. To play, your child matches the question cards with the answer cards.

193

Rewrite each sentence. Replace the underlined words with the correct pronoun.

<u>Tommy</u> packed sandwiches and apples.

_____

Tommy hiked along <u>the trail</u>.

_____

<u>Ed and Larry</u> caught up with Tommy.

_____

<u>Rita</u> met the boys at the trail's end.

_____

Tommy sent <u>Bill</u> one of his photos later.

_____

<u>The boys</u> ate their lunches under a tree.

_____

After lunch, <u>Rita</u> gave the boys a cookie.

_____

Learn at Home, Grade 2

Word Magic

Week 18

Maggie Magician announced, "One plus one equals one!" The audience giggled. So Maggie put two words into a hat and waved her magic wand. When she reached into the hat, Maggie pulled out one word and a picture. "See," said Maggie, "I was right!"

Use the box to help **write** a compound word for each picture below.

ball	door	rain	star	shirt	bell	fish	shoe	book	foot	basket
bow	lace	box	stool	light	sun	cup	mail	tail	cake	worm

_____

_____

_____

_____

_____

_____

_____

_____

_____

_____

_____

195

+	0	1	2	3	4	5	6	7	8	9
0										
1										
2										
3										
4										
5										
6										
7										
8										
9										

Keep On Truckin'

Write each sum. Connect the sums of 83 to make a road for the truck.

$$\begin{array}{r} 17 \\ +66 \\ \hline \end{array} \qquad \begin{array}{r} 48 \\ +26 \\ \hline \end{array} \qquad \begin{array}{r} 42 \\ +19 \\ \hline \end{array}$$

$$\begin{array}{r} 28 \\ +38 \\ \hline \end{array} \quad \begin{array}{r} 64 \\ +19 \\ \hline \end{array} \quad \begin{array}{r} 26 \\ +57 \\ \hline \end{array} \quad \begin{array}{r} 58 \\ +25 \\ \hline \end{array} \quad \begin{array}{r} 17 \\ +75 \\ \hline \end{array} \quad \begin{array}{r} 65 \\ +29 \\ \hline \end{array}$$

$$\begin{array}{r} 37 \\ +39 \\ \hline \end{array} \quad \begin{array}{r} 48 \\ +35 \\ \hline \end{array} \quad \begin{array}{r} 58 \\ +37 \\ \hline \end{array} \quad \begin{array}{r} 65 \\ +16 \\ \hline \end{array} \quad \begin{array}{r} 38 \\ +25 \\ \hline \end{array} \quad \begin{array}{r} 39 \\ +59 \\ \hline \end{array}$$

$$\begin{array}{r} 59 \\ +27 \\ \hline \end{array} \quad \begin{array}{r} 55 \\ +28 \\ \hline \end{array} \quad \begin{array}{r} 39 \\ +44 \\ \hline \end{array}$$

197

Subtraction on the Beach

Subtract. Regroup as needed. **Color** the spaces with differences of:

10–19 **red**   20–29 **blue**   30–39 **green**

40–49 **yellow**   50–59 **brown**   60–69 **orange**

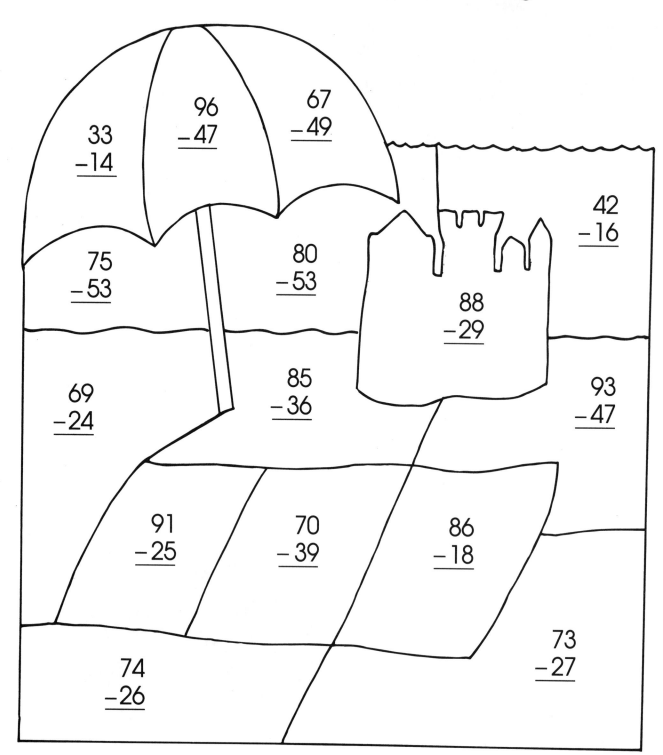

33
−14

96
−47

67
−49

75
−53

80
−53

42
−16

88
−29

69
−24

85
−36

93
−47

91
−25

70
−39

86
−18

74
−26

73
−27

198

Learn at Home, Grade 2

Anti-Freeze

Water turns into a solid at a temperature of 32°F. This is called the freezing point. Does all water freeze at 32°F?

You will need:
2 small paper cups
4 teaspoons of salt
water
marking pen
freezer

1. Fill both cups with water.

2. Mix 4 teaspoons of salt in one of the cups. Write "salt" on that cup.

3. Put both cups in the freezer. Check on them every hour for four hours.

I found out . . .

the cup of plain water _____

_____

the cup of salt water _____

_____

	Language Skills	**Spelling**	**Reading**
Monday	**Writing Sentences** Reteach any skill with which your child had difficulty. Have your child complete **Review of Sentences** (p. 204).	**Homophones** Pretest your child on these spelling words: our too their there by two to here buy near hour Have your child match up the homophone pairs and discuss. *See* Spelling, Week 19.	**Vowel Combinations** Continue the Fairy Tale study. Read with your child Cinderella books this week. *See* Reading, Week 19, number 1. With your child, read and discuss *Cinderella* retold by Barbara Karlin. Teach the sounds of the *oo* combinations. *See* Reading, Week 19, number 2. Have your child complete a copy of **Fairy Tale Trivia** (p. 208).
Tuesday	Write ten sentences, leaving a word or two out of each sentence. **Examples:** Harry was the ___ of the ___ race. He ___ a blue __. Have your child fill in the blanks with words that make sense. Ask your child to identify the parts of speech of the new words (noun, verb or adjective). Discuss with your child the clues that told him/her what kind of word to place in the blank.	Have your child combine each set of homophones into one sentence.	With your child, read and discuss *Cinder-Elly* by Frances Minters. Reread and emphasize the rhyming words. Have your child complete a copy of **Fairy Tale Trivia** (p. 208).
Wednesday	Provide your child with practice combining sentences. *See* Language Skills, Week 19, number 1. Encourage your child to try combining some sentences at the revision stage in his/her own writing. Have your child complete **Sentence Combining** (p. 205).	Have your child spell each word aloud while clapping a rhythm. Have your child complete **Hear It Here!** (p. 207).	With your child, read and discuss *Mufaro's Beautiful Daughters: An African Fairy Tale* by John Steptoe. Have your child complete a copy of **Fairy Tale Trivia** (p. 208).
Thursday	Teach your child to add meaningful details to sentences to make them more interesting. *See* Language Skills, Week 19, number 2. Have your child complete **Better Sentences** (p. 206).	Have your child illustrate each homophone sentence from Tuesday.	Practice the *oo* vowel sounds. *See* Reading, Week 19, numbers 2 and 3 for activity ideas. With your child, read and discuss *Prince Cinders* by Babette Cole. Have your child complete a copy of **Fairy Tale Trivia** (p. 208).
Friday	Have your child write a descriptive paragraph about one of his/her favorite Cinderella characters from the books read this week. Have him/her include details that tell how the character looked and felt.	Give your child the final spelling test.	With your child, read and discuss *The Rough-Face Girl* by Rafe Martin. Have your child complete a copy of **Fairy Tale Trivia** (p. 208). Help your child compare all tales read this week and analyze how they are similar and different.

Learn at Home, Grade 2

Math	Science	Social Studies
Place Value to Hundreds Using **Place-Value Parts** (p. 125) form different 3-place numbers using the ones, tens and hundreds.	**Birds** Ask your child to write in his/her log the names of all the birds he/she can. Go for a walk outside or sit near a bird feeder. Watch for birds. Discuss the features that are common to all birds. What are some features that distinguish different birds? Have your child begin **My Bird List** (p. 210).	Continue to study the 50 states. *See* Social Studies, Week 14. *Ohio* **OH** named *something great* in Iroquois Indian nicknamed The Buckeye State capital city - Columbus landmarks - Cleveland Great Serpent Mound Football Hall of Fame
Teach your child to make hundreds, tens and ones manipulatives. *See* Math, Week 19, number 2. Place value parts (p. 125), base-ten blocks or Unifix cubes can also be used for this week's activities.	Teach your child the different habitats of North American birds. *See* Science, Week 19, numbers 1 and 2.	*Pennsylvania* **PA** named Penn's Woods nicknamed The Keystone State capital city - Harrisburg landmarks - Independence Hall Hershey Chocolate Factory Pittsburgh Gettysburg Flagship Niagara Ground Hog Day Festival
Finish making bean sticks and rafts.	Introduce the bird habitat research project. Start with the urban habitat. Show your child how to use the reference books. *See* Science, Week 19, number 3.	*West Virginia* **WV** named separately after siding with the North in the Civil War nicknamed The Mountain State capital city - Charleston landmarks - Appalachian Mountains Parkersburg Grave Creek Mounds Huntington Potomac River
On index cards, write random numbers between 100 and 999. Have your child pick a card and build the number using the homemade manipulatives. After your child builds the number, have him/her count each (by ones) to confirm. (This is an important connecting step.) Continue having your child build and read 3-digit numbers.	Refer to an encyclopedia and bird guide to compare the features of different birds. Have your child draw and write in his/her log a description of the different bills (beaks) of birds. Explain the special uses of different bills. Have your child complete **The Early Bird Gets the Worm!** (p. 211).	*Virginia* **VA** named for England's Queen Elizabeth I, the Virgin nicknamed Old Dominion capital city - Richmond landmarks - The Appalachian Mountains Arlington National Cemetery Cumberland Gap Chesapeake Bay Monticello, Jefferson's home
Choose an index card from yesterday's lesson. Ask your child to identify which number is in the hundreds place, tens place and ones place. Teach your child the symbols for the hundreds, tens and ones manipulatives and have him/her draw large numbers symbolically. *See* Math, Week 19, number 3. Have your child complete **What Big Numbers!** (p. 209).	Have your child draw and write in his/her log a description of the different feet and legs of birds. Explain the special uses of different feet and legs.	*Maryland* **MD** named for English Queen Maria nicknamed The Old Line State capital city - Annapolis landmarks - Fort McHenry Baltimore US Naval Academy Potomac River Chesapeake Bay

TEACHING SUGGESTIONS AND ACTIVITIES

LANGUAGE SKILLS (Writing Sentences)

▶ 1. Write *It snowed all day yesterday. It snowed all day today.* Ask your child to underline the phrase that is common in both sentences. Discuss with your child ways to make one sentence from the two without changing the meaning. *It snowed all day yesterday and today.* Model and provide examples for other sentence combining. Some sentences are provided below.

Mary's puppy is a poodle.   *Mary's puppy is black.*
Jim lives in the red house.   *Jim lives on Main Street.*
Chicago is in Illinois.   *Chicago is a windy city.*

▶ 2. Write a simple sentence on the chalkboard such as *Lynn went to the store.* Then, write the same sentence below the first but add a detail. *Lynn went to the store yesterday.* Discuss how the word *yesterday* was more specific and made the sentence more interesting. Write the sentence a third time, leaving a blank before *store.* Have your child fill in a descriptive word. Rewrite the sentence as many times as possible to continue adding meaningful details.

Lynn went to the store.
Lynn went to the store yesterday.
Lynn went to the _____ store yesterday.
Lynn went to the ___ store yesterday to buy a jar of ____.
Lynn and ____ went to the ___ store yesterday to buy a ____ jar of ____ .
Lynn and ____ went to the ___ store yesterday to buy a jar of ____ for ____.

SPELLING (Homophones)

BACKGROUND
Homophones are words that sound the same but are spelled differently and have different meanings. All spelling words this week are homophones.

READING (Vowel Combinations)

BACKGROUND
Earlier your child learned the long vowel rule that the first vowel is long and the second is silent (as in *beat, hair* and *pie*). In the next 3 weeks you will teach some exceptions that your child will need to recognize and memorize. The following common vowel combinations do not make the long sound: *oo, ou, ow, au, aw, oi* and *oy.* Provide many examples of words containing these vowel combinations so that your child will become familiar with these spellings and their accompanying sounds.

▶ 1. **Fairy Tale Trivia:** Make enough double sided copies of the activity sheet, page 208, to form a booklet, so each fairy tale book has 2 pages of identical information. After a tale is read, have your child complete the information. In many fairy tales, things happen in number patterns, such as in threes. Next to "Special Number" write events, characters, etc. that appear in number patterns.

▶ 2. Write *look, book, hook* and *shook* on the chalkboard. Have your child read each word and tell what sound *oo* makes. Repeat with *food, moo, tool, boot* and *zoo.* Teach your child that the *oo* spelling can be pronounced both ways. If your child isn't sure which way to pronounce a word while reading, the other words in the sentence will help. He/she can try pronouncing the word with both sounds and see which one makes sense.

▶ 3. Write a list of words that contain *oo.* Have your child read each word. If he/she has trouble reading a word, write a sentence containing that word. Using the word in context should help.

Learn at Home, Grade 2

MATH (Place Value to Hundreds)

Have your child build the manipulatives to be used for this concept. If you build them, your child will not comprehend as fully. After your child makes and uses the ones, tens and hundreds, teach the symbols that can be drawn on paper for a less cumbersome and more readily available "manipulative." Provide concrete experiences now to make the future work with addition and subtraction easier.

▶ 1. Use **Place-Value Parts** *see* Week 11, pages 119 and 125. Use the tens and one ones to show different numbers from 1–99. After 99, add 1 more to get 100. A new unit is formed, a hundred. With the manipulatives, form different 3-digit numbers. **Example:** 234 = 2 hundreds, 3 tens and 4 ones.

▶ 2. To make hundreds, tens and ones manipulatives, you will need a bag of dried beans, wood glue and about 130 craft sticks. Your child should glue exactly 10 beans to approximately 110 craft sticks. These bean sticks are called tens. Your child should keep 18 tens and make the rest of the tens into hundreds. To make hundreds, have your child make rafts holding 100 beans (10 tens). Your child should place 10 bean sticks side by side, beans side down. Then, your child should glue 2 craft sticks (without beans) crosswise on the back of the bean sticks. The 2 craft sticks will hold the 10 bean sticks together. Let the glue dry before handling.

▶ 3. The written symbol for hundreds is a square (raft). The symbol for tens is a line (stick). The symbol for ones is a dot (bean).

SCIENCE (Birds)

BACKGROUND
The bird is an amazing animal. There are about 9,700 kinds of birds. They live in all parts of the world. All birds have feathers and wings but not all can fly. They all hatch from eggs. Birds have two forelimbs (wings) and two hindlimbs (legs). Birds have no teeth but do have beaks for eating and protecting themselves. Most birds cannot make long ocean flights, so the birds of North America are different from the birds seen on other continents. This unit will focus on birds seen in North America. Where a bird lives is determined by its needs for survival: climate, available food and nesting areas. Birds in North America live in seven kinds of habitats: urban, forest, woodland, grassland, brush, desert, inland waters, marshes and seacoasts.

Bird Habitat Research: Over the next 9 weeks, give your child the responsibility of writing and illustrating a book about birds. The book will be divided into the seven habitats of North American birds: urban, forest and woodland, grassland, brush, desert, inland waters, marshes and seacoasts. Provide library books about birds for your child to use. Your child should draw (on construction paper) several birds from each habitat and prepare a written paragraph about the birds and the habitat in general. In the last 2 weeks, your child will paint scenes depicting each of the seven habitats. Then, he/she will attach the appropriate birds to the habitats. The seven pages will be compiled and made into a book with a cover and title page.

▶ 1. Ask your child to explain why he/she did not see all the birds on his/her Science Log list when he/she watched for birds yesterday. Introduce the word "habitat." Look at pictures of birds in their natural habitats.

▶ 2. Some birds migrate. Discuss the reason that some birds move away seasonally and some remain all year.

▶ 3. Encourage your child to look at birds scientifically. Have your child make notes about the bird's habits. Record where the bird was seen (on the ground, on a window ledge, in a tree). Note how each bird moves on the ground and in the air. Have your child draw a close-up of the bird's beak and feet.

Review of Sentences

Underline the sentence that is written correctly in each group.

1. Do Penguins live in antarctica?

   do penguins live in Antartica.

   Do penguins live in Antarctica?

2. penguins cannot fly?

   Penguins cannot fly.

   penguins cannot fly.

Write S for **statement, Q** for **question, E** for **exclamation** or **C** for **command** on the line.

_____ 1. Two different kinds of penguins live in Antarctica.

_____ 2. Do emperor penguins have black and white bodies?

_____ 3. Look at their webbed feet.

_____ 4. They're amazing!

Underline the **subject** of the sentence with one line. **Underline** the **predicate** with two lines.

1. Penguins eat fish, squid and shrimp.

2. Leopard seals and killer whales hunt penguins.

3. A female penguin lays one egg.

Learn at Home, Grade 2

Sentence Combining

Two sentences can become one sentence. **Write** two sentences as one sentence.

The bird lives in a nest.

The bird lives in the tree.

_____

The music teacher is wearing a blue dress.

The music teacher is wearing white pearls.

_____

I will meet you at the park.

I will meet you by the balloon stand.

_____

My name is . . .

My first name is Brian.

My last name is Williams.

_____

Better Sentences

Describing words like adjectives can make a better sentence. **Write** a word on each line to make the sentences more interesting. **Draw** a picture of your sentence.

1. The skater won a medal.

   The _____ skater won a _____ medal.

2. The jewels were in the safe.

   The _____ jewels were in the _____ safe.

3. The airplane flew through the storm.

   The _____ airplane flew through the _____ storm.

4. A fireman rushed into the house.

   A _____ fireman rushed into the _____ house.

5. The detective hid behind the tree.

   The _____ detective hid behind the _____ tree.

1.	2.

3.	4.	5.

Learn at Home, Grade 2

our   too   their   there

by   two   to

here   buy   near   hour

Write the spelling words that rhyme.

1. blue _____ _____ _____

2. care _____ _____

3. deer _____ _____

4. sour _____ _____

5. fly _____ _____

Write the missing spelling word in the boxes.

1. They went to the store to _____ ice cream.

2. The box is _____ small to hold all the toys.

3. Come and see _____ new television set.

4. Speak louder, so everyone can _____ you.

5. Please bring the book _____ .

6. We will go _____ the library today.

7. I think the desk would fit better over _____ .

8. The train blew its whistle as it passed _____ the town.

9. There are _____ eggs in the nest.

10. Sue's plane will take off in one _____ .

11. _____ grandfather and grandmother are coming to visit them.

Fairy Tale Trivia

Title _____

_____

_____

_____

Author_____

Illustrator _____

Setting _____

Beginning Words _____

Royal Characters _____

_____

Evil Characters _____

_____

Special Number _____

Magic_____

_____

Learn at Home, Grade 2

What Big Numbers!

Write each number. The first one has been done for you.

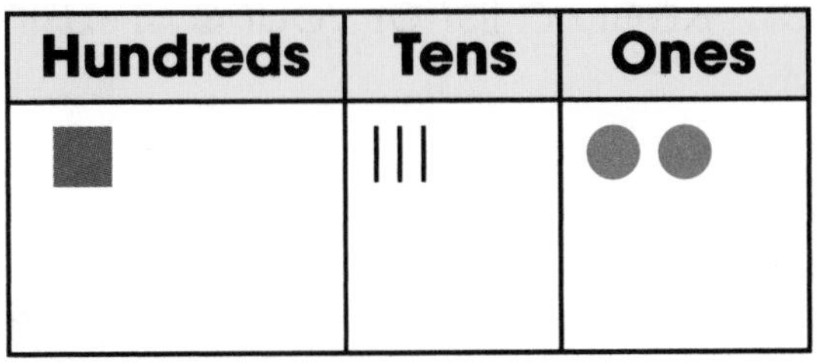

Hundreds	Tens	Ones
■	|||	● ●

__1__ hundreds
__3__ tens
__2__ ones = __132__

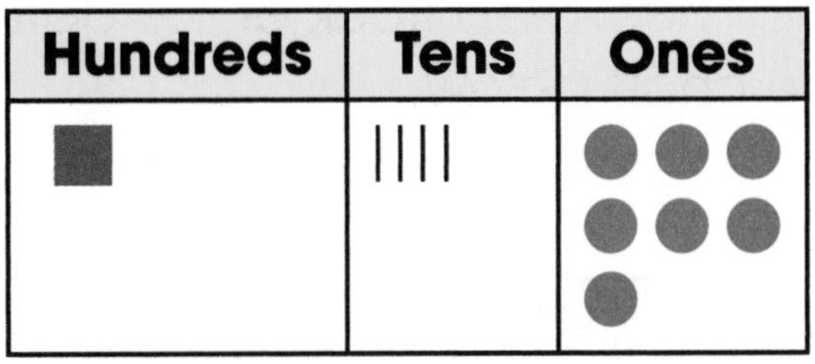

Hundreds	Tens	Ones
■	||||	● ● ● ● ● ● ●

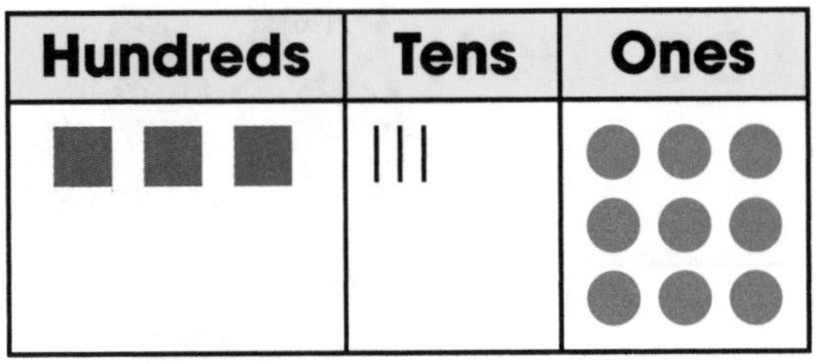

___ hundreds
___ tens
___ ones = _____

Hundreds	Tens	Ones
■ ■ ■	|||	● ● ● ● ● ● ● ● ●

___ hundreds
___ tens
___ ones = _____

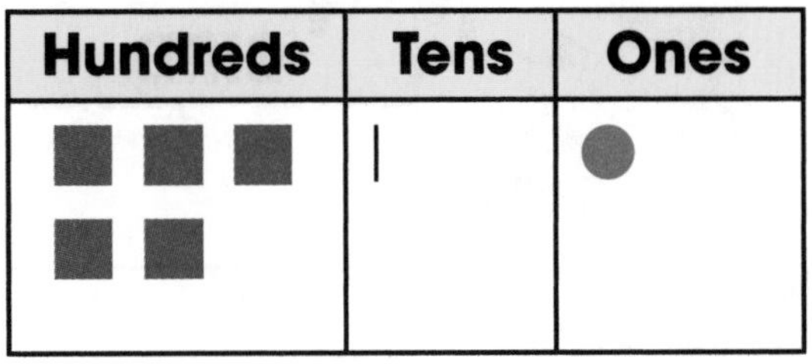 Hundreds	Tens	Ones
■ ■ ■ ■ ■	|	●

___ hundreds
___ tens
___ ones = _____

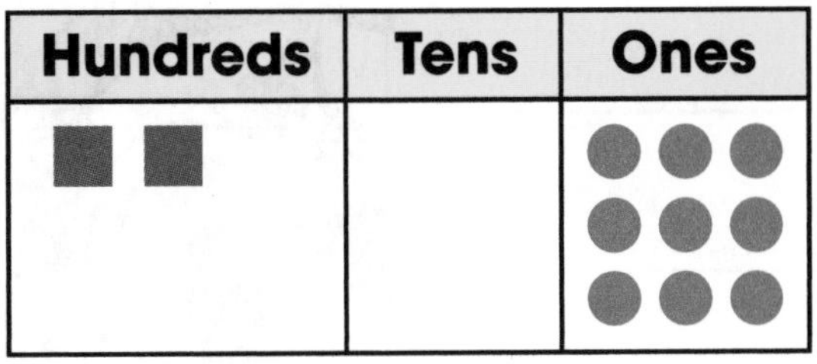 Hundreds	Tens	Ones
■ ■		● ● ● ● ● ● ● ● ●

___ hundreds
___ tens
___ ones = _____

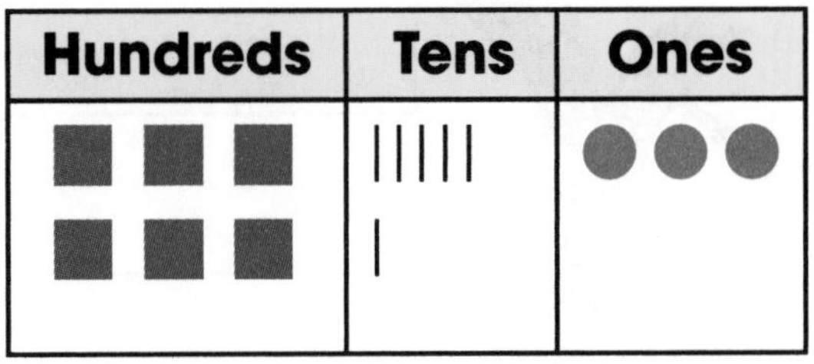 Hundreds	Tens	Ones
■ ■ ■ ■ ■ ■	||||| |	● ● ●

___ hundreds
___ tens
___ ones = _____

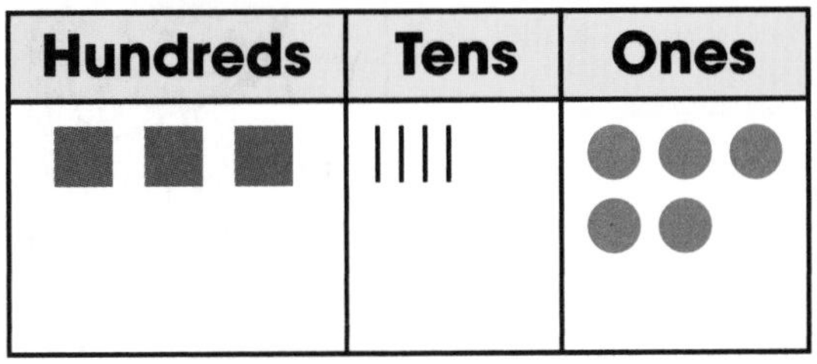 Hundreds	Tens	Ones
■ ■ ■	||||	● ● ● ● ●

___ hundreds
___ tens
___ ones = _____

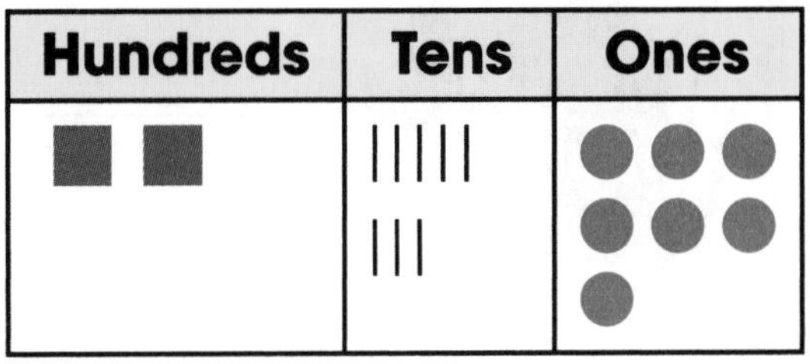 Hundreds	Tens	Ones
■ ■	||||| |||	● ● ● ● ● ● ●

___ hundreds
___ tens
___ ones = _____

My Bird List

Bird watchers keep a list of all the different kinds of birds they have seen. They also keep track of the date and location. Keep a list of your own using the chart below.

BIRD	DATE	LOCATION

Learn at Home, Grade 2

The Early Bird Gets the Worm!

1. Discuss the three types of bird beaks. Each type has functions similar to the tool listed. With an adult, experiment with the tools.

SHAPE			
FOOD	small animals (meat)	flower nectar	seeds, worms
TOOL	pincers (grasp and tear)	straw (sucking action)	pliers (pick and pull)

2. Draw a large beak in the top left portion of a sheet of paper. Use informational books to determine which types of birds have the kind of beak on the paper. Then, draw the rest of the bird's body. Do the same for all three beak types shown above.

	Language Skills	**Spelling**	**Reading**

Monday	**Creative Writing**
	Write sentence starters for your child to complete. A sentence starter can spark an idea for a writing project.
	I thought about _____.
	I was excited when _____.
	When I was two years old, _____.
	A starter may spark more than one idea. You may also use these for journal ideas.
		Pretest your child on these spelling words:
		
		   kite sick key
		   back call cake
		   duck pick king
		           candy
		Discuss the letters that make the *k* sound.
			Introduce the vowel sounds *ow* and *ou*. *See* Reading, Week 20, numbers 1 and 2. With your child, read and discuss a different Amelia Bedelia book (by Peggy Parish) each day this week. Review homophones, idioms and word play, as the books are read. *See* Reading, Week 20, number 3. With your child, read and discuss *Amelia Bedelia*.

Tuesday	Teach your child about paragraphs. *See* Language Skills, Week 20, number 1. Have your child write a paragraph about something he/she knows a lot about. Or he/she may use a sentence starter from yesterday.	Have your child write the spelling words in sentences.	Teach your child that *ow* sometimes makes the long *o* sound. Provide the following examples for your child to read: *show, tow, know, grow, low, bow* (can be read with either sound) and *mow*. If your child attempts to say the ouch sound, the word will not make sense. With your child, read and discuss *Amelia Bedelia and the Baby* by Peggy Parish.
Wednesday	Edit and proofread your child's paragraph together.	Have your child spell each word aloud while jumping rope. Have your child complete **Backpacking** (p. 216).	With your child, read and discuss *Teach Us, Amelia Bedelia*. Have your child compare how Amelia taught and how he/she is taught.
Thursday	Teach your child about alliteration. Let him/her write alliterative sentences, such as *Randy's robots race rodents around the room*. Have him/her save the sentences in his/her writing folder. One of the silly creations may be a spark for a story. *See* Language Skills, Week 20, number 2.	Have your child write tongue twisters using three of the words beginning with *c* or *k*.	Introduce the vowel sounds *au* and *aw*. Both spellings make the sound heard in *launch*. *See* Reading, Week 20, number 4. With your child, read and discuss *Good Driving, Amelia Bedelia* by Herman Parish. Point out the use of homophones in the book.
Friday	Help your child write descriptive sentences telling how he/she prepared the recipe. *See* Reading, Week 20, number 3. **Example:** Next, I quickly mixed the grainy, brown sugar with the soft, creamy butter.	Give your child the final spelling test.	With your child, read and discuss *Bravo, Amelia Bedelia* by Herman Parish. Amelia likes to cook. Help your child find a recipe he/she thinks Mr. and Mrs. Rogers would like. Help your child follow directions and prepare the recipe.

Learn at Home, Grade 2

Math	**Science**	**Social Studies**

Play a riddle game to start the lesson (*see* Math, Week 20, number 1). Each day read, discuss and solve two pages from *Math Curse* by Jon Scieszka and Lane Smith. Have your child solve the problems each day. Today, read, discuss and solve the first four pages with your child.	With your child, observe a bird's feather. Point out the interlocking strands and how the feather can be smoothed in only one direction. Have your child drop water on the feather, then ask how the water reacts. Have your child draw a detailed picture of a single feather.	Continue to study the 50 states. *See* Social Studies, Week 14. ***Delaware*** **DE**
		named for its governor, Lord DeLa Warr
		nicknamed The First State
		capital city - Dover
		landmarks - Delaware Bay
		   Great Cypress Swamp
		   The Octagonal School

Have your child choose an index card from last Thursday's lesson (numbered between 100 and 999) and write the number that comes before it, the number, then write the number that follows it. Repeat with several cards. He/she can use the bean sticks and rafts as necessary. With your child, read, discuss and solve pages 5 and 6 of *Math Curse*.	With your child, discuss the functions of feathers. Feathers help birds fly and regulate body temperature. The coloring of feathers helps a bird hide from its enemies or attract a mate. With your child, read and discuss *Feathers for Lunch* by Lois Ehlert. Have your child draw a colorful bird.	***New Jersey*** **NJ**
		named after the Isle of Jersey in England
		nicknamed The Garden State
		capital city - Trenton
		landmarks - Atlantic City
		   George Washington Bridge
		   Old Barracks

Play a game with place-value manipulatives that teaches your child to think about forming the smallest possible number given 3-digits. *See* Math, Week 20, number 2. Your child may want to use a copy of **Numbers Small and Large** (p. 134 from Week 12). With your child, read and discuss pages 7 and 8 in *Math Curse* and solve addition and birthday graph problems.	With your child, read and discuss *Counting Is for the Birds* by Frank Mazzola, Jr. to learn what birds eat. Have your child list some foods in his/her log. Ask: *Are there foods that are not available to birds in cold weather? See* Science, Week 20.	***New York*** **NY**
		named to honor the Duke of York
		nicknamed The Empire State
		capital city - Albany
		landmarks - Statue of Liberty
		   Wall Street
		   Niagara Falls
		   Lake Placid
		   West Point Military Academy
		   Baseball Hall of Fame

Game: Play the number line game. This teaches sequence and order of large numbers. *See* Math, Week 20, numbers 2–4. Read with your child and discuss pages 9 and 10 in *Math Curse* and solve the counting problems.	Make a bird feeder with your child. *See* Science, Week 20, number 1.	***Arkansas*** **AK**
		named *downstream people* in Sioux Indian
		nicknamed The Land of Opportunity
		capital city - Little Rock
		landmarks - Hot Springs National Park
		   Texarkana
		   MacArthur Park
		   Crater of Diamonds State Park

With your child, read and discuss pages 11 and 12 in *Math Curse* and solve the fraction and measurement problems. Explore the concept of large numbers in our everyday lives. Calculators may be used when counting and adding large numbers. Search the home, inside or out and find things with large numbers. **Example:** Wallpaper patterns, popcorn kernels in a bag, bricks in a house, candies in a bag, etc.	Allow your child sufficient time to work on the bird habitat research project— forest and woodland—from Week 19.	***Louisiana*** **LA**
		named after the French King Louis XIV
		nicknamed The Pelican State
		   also nicknamed The Heart of Dixie
		capital city - Baton Rouge
		landmarks - New Orleans
		   Mississippi Delta
		   Jean Lafitte National Historical Park & Preserve

TEACHING SUGGESTIONS AND ACTIVITIES

LANGUAGE SKILLS (Creative Writing)

A paragraph is an organized group of related sentences. The first sentence often states the subject of the paragraph; it is called a topic sentence. The following sentences support the topic sentence with details and further information.

▶ 1. Following are some starters that will help your child write an organized paragraph:
There are two things I like about summer.
The book I'm reading made me laugh.
My family is special to me for several reasons.
The best pet for me is a dog for three reasons.
The rainforest has three distinct layers of life.

▶ 2. Outline the information your child used in the paragraph from Tuesday. Have him/her rewrite the paragraph with the new structure.

▶ 3. Challenge your child to see how much he/she can expand a sentence by adding descriptive details. Make sure he/she doesn't "run on" too far though!

READING (Vowel Combinations)

The vowel sounds *ow* and *ou* both make the sound heard in *ouch*. When *ow* is found at the end of a word, it may sound like long *o*. Alliteration is the use of same starting sounds. Tongue twisters are a good example of alliterative sentences.

▶ 1. Write words that contain *ow* and *ou* on the chalkboard. Some suggestions include *out, loud, mouse, our, clown, mouth, mouse* and *cow*. Have your child read the words and tell what vowel sound he/she hears in each word. You may wish to call it the "ouch" sound. Have your child identify the letters that make the "ouch" sound in each word.

▶ 2. Tell your child you are going to say some words. Every time he/she hears a word with the "ouch" sound in it, your child is to say "Ouch!" You may say a list of words or speak in sentences. Make sure you include words that contain *ow* or *ou*.

▶ 3. Your children will be introduced to the use of homophones, idioms and word play while reading Amelia Bedelia books. An idiom is an expression having special meaning different than the usual meanings of the words.
Example: "Raining cats and dogs" means raining hard
Homophones were introduced during Week 19 in Spelling. Word play is making use of the various meanings of words in humorous ways. Have your child reillustrate a page from one of the Amelia Bedelia stories.

▶ 4. Repeat activity 1 above using the vowel spellings *au* and *aw*. Some suggestions include *draw, thaw, taught, haul, jaw, saw, paw, Paul, bawl, fault* and *straw*.

MATH (Place Value to Hundreds)

▶ 1. Present riddles for your child to solve using the manipulatives. The riddles should teach the concept that 12 tens is equivalent to 1 hundred 2 tens. **Example:** I have 4 hundreds, 13 tens and 5 ones. Who am I?

Learn at Home, Grade 2

▶ 2. **Game:** Make number cards for the numerals 0–9. Use the place-value board and the rafts, sticks and beans or other base-ten manipulatives from last week or Week 11. To play, your child chooses three cards and looks at the numbers. The goal is to make the smallest number possible using these three digits. If your child chooses 3, 8 and 1, the smallest possible number is 138. Your child should use the rafts, sticks and beans to model the smallest number, then write the number on lined paper. Your child should return the three cards and chooses three new cards. Play continues several times. Game may be played with your child making the largest possible number.

▶ 3. On the chalkboard, draw a number line and mark the end points. The end points can be 0 and 100, 500 and 600 or any other set of 100. On a sheet of paper, write a secret number and mark where on the number line it would fall. Your child should attempt to guess the secret number. If your child makes an incorrect guess, write that number where it would fall on the number line. Your child continues to guess, each time getting closer until he/she is on the exact number. For an extra challenge, do not reveal your end points to your child. He/she guesses the number through trial and error.

▶ 4. **Game/Center:** On each of ten index cards, write a different 2-digit number. Draw a chart with three columns. For each number card, have your child follow these directions:

　　a. Write the number in the middle column.

　　b. Write the number that is ten less in the first column.

　　c. Write a number that is ten greater in the third column.

SCIENCE (Birds)

Birds will live where there is an adequate food supply. Many birds in cold climates must migrate to a warmer climate to find food. Many people set up bird feeders for birds that stay in the winter. Make it clear to your child that if someone begins to provide food for the birds, he/she should continue all winter because the birds rely on it for most of their food supply.

▶ 1. Use an old plastic detergent or milk bottle to make a bird feeder. Wash it out thoroughly. Cut out a large hole two inches from the bottom. Leave the lid on the bottle. Make two holes below it. Tie string through the holes and fill the feeder with bird food. Hang it on a tree. Watch the feeder and use your list to keep a record of the birds that visit.

Backpacking

kite   sick   key   pick   king

back   call   cake   duck   candy

Write the spelling words beginning with **c** that make the **k** sound.

_____   _____   _____

Write the spelling words beginning with **k** that make the **k** sound.

_____   _____   _____

Write the spelling words ending with **ck** that make the **k** sound.

_____   _____   _____   _____

Write the missing spelling word in the boxes.

1. Which _____ will open the lock?

6. Kate had to stay home because she was _____ .

2. The front and _____ of the folder look the same.

7. The _____ and queen live in a castle.

3. A mother _____ waddled to the pond.

8. Buck gave his mom a box of chocolate _____ .

4. Many people are needed to _____ the ripe apples.

9. Let's _____ our friends and invite them to a party.

5. The wind blew the _____ high into the sky.

10. There are eight candles on her birthday _____ .

216

Learn at Home, Grade 2

SECTION 5

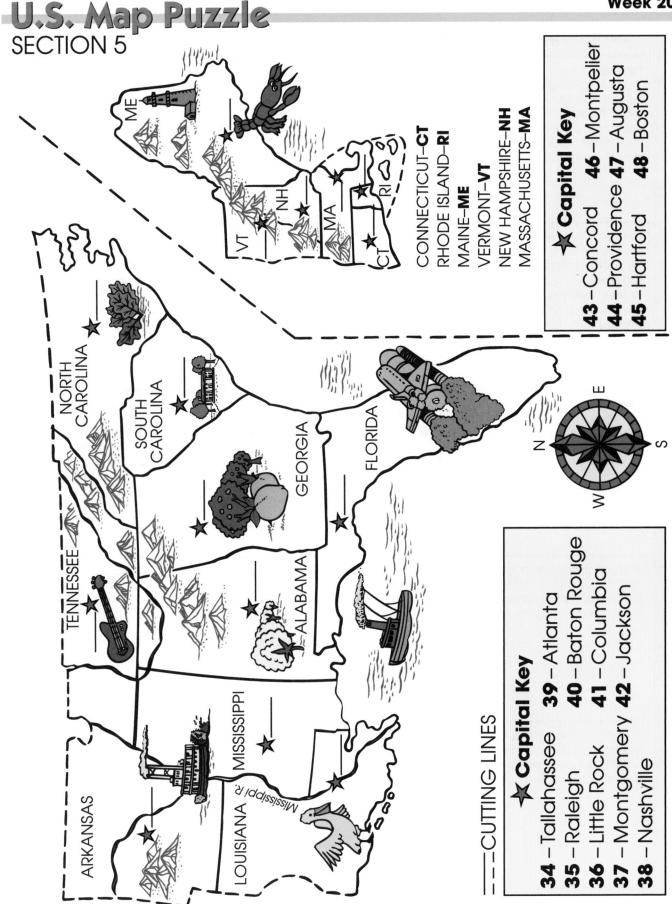

ME

VT
NH
MA
RI
CT

CONNECTICUT–**CT**
RHODE ISLAND–**RI**
MAINE–**ME**
VERMONT–**VT**
NEW HAMPSHIRE–**NH**
MASSACHUSETTS–**MA**

★ **Capital Key**

43 – Concord **46** – Montpelier
44 – Providence **47** – Augusta
45 – Hartford **48** – Boston

NORTH CAROLINA

SOUTH CAROLINA

GEORGIA

FLORIDA

TENNESSEE

ALABAMA

MISSISSIPPI

ARKANSAS

LOUISIANA

Mississippi R.

N E S W

CUTTING LINES

★ **Capital Key**

34 – Tallahassee **39** – Atlanta
35 – Raleigh **40** – Baton Rouge
36 – Little Rock **41** – Columbia
37 – Montgomery **42** – Jackson
38 – Nashville

217

	Language Skills	**Spelling**	**Reading**
Monday	**Paragraphs** Write a paragraph about a familiar topic. Include one sentence that does not belong. Ask your child to read the paragraph and cross out the sentence that does not belong. Write a paragraph about an aunt or other close relative.	Pretest your child on these spelling words: jump pond stamp kind bump hand land send camp ramp Have your child sort the words by their ending sounds.	Introduce the vowel sounds *oi* and *oy*. Both spellings make the sound heard in *oink*. See Reading, Week 21, numbers 1 and 2. Begin reading chapter books this week. With your child, read two chapters a day in *Arthur and the Crunch Cereal Contest* by Marc Brown. Discuss the main idea in each chapter. Today, read with your child chapters 1 and 2. Discuss the main idea.
Tuesday	Find a photo or magazine picture about which you can write a paragraph. Cut the finished paragraph into separate sentences. Give the picture and mixed up sentences to your child. Have him/her organize the sentences in an order that makes sense. *See* Language Skills, Week 21, number 1.	Have your child write the spelling words in sentences.	With your child, read chapters 3 and 4 and discuss how Arthur proceeded to solve his problem of forming the Crunch Bunch band. Talk about how to solve problems. Have your child complete **Forgetful Fred** (p. 224).
Wednesday	Sometimes a paragraph can tell about an event or activity as a sequence. Have your child complete a copy of **Sentence Sequence** (p. 222).	Have your child spell each word aloud while tapping his/her chin. Have your child complete **Bumper Cars** (p. 223).	With your child, read and discuss chapters 5 and 6. In these chapters Arthur was dedicated to writing a jingle. Have your child write a story about how he/she is dedicated to an idea, friend, person, pet, idea, belief, etc.
Thursday	Have your child write a paragraph describing the steps in a familiar activity such as brushing teeth, preparing breakfast or playing a game.	With your child, reread *A Day at Damp Camp* by George Ella Lyon. *See* Reading, Week 8, number 1. Have your child use the spelling word combinations to form two word phrases. **Examples:** camp stamp, jump bump, land hand, camp ramp, etc. Then, have him/her illustrate the phrases.	With your child, read and discuss chapters 7 and 8. Help your child compare the characters in this book. Have your child complete **Our House** (p. 225).
Friday	Have your child write a jingle about a favorite food. Brainstorm rhyming words related to its name. Then, have him/her create a rhyme promoting that food.	Give your child the final spelling test.	With your child, read and discuss chapters 9 and 10. Share ideas and feelings about this book.

Learn at Home, Grade 2

Math	**Science**	**Social Studies**

Greater Than/Less Than
Teach your child the meaning of *greater than* and *less than*. *See* Math, Week 21, numbers 1 and 2. With your child, read and discuss pages 14 and 15 in *Math Curse* and solve the English and Phys. Ed. word problems.
	Have your child think of questions about birds he/she wants answered. Your child should write the questions in his/her Science Log. Provide books that may answer the questions. Work with your child to read and answer the questions this week. *See* Science, Week 21, number 1.	Continue to study the 50 states. *See* Social Studies, Week 14.
		Mississippi **MS**
		    named *big river* in Indian
		    nicknamed The Magnolia State
		capital city - Jackson
		landmarks - Delta Queen
		          Natchez
		          Delta Blues Museum
		          Biloxi

Teach your child to make the greater than and less than symbols. Make < and > cards. Have your child place the correct card between pairs of numbers. *See* Math, Week 21, numbers 3–5. With your child, read and discuss pages 16 and 17 in *Math Curse* and examine the many ways to count.	What are birds of prey and why aren't they coming to the feeder? *See* Science, Week 21, number 2. With your child, read and discuss *Crow and Hawk: A Traditional Pueblo Indian Story* retold by Michael Rosen. Compare fact and fiction. Discuss how the hawk, a bird of prey, reverses her nature and saves the young crows.	***Tennessee*** **TN**
		    named for a Cherokee village
		    nicknamed The Volunteer State
		capital city - Nashville
		landmarks - Grand Ole Opry
		          Graceland
		          Casey Jones Railroad Museum
		          Appalachian Mountains
		          Chattanooga
		          Memphis

Draw a number line on the chalkboard. Circle two numbers on the number line. Have your child write the two numbers on lined paper and draw the correct sign between them. With your child, read and discuss pages 18 and 19 in *Math Curse* and solve the class cupcake problem. Have your child complete **Number Lines** (p. 226).	**Creative Writing:** Compare fact and fiction while reading about the owl, a bird of prey. With your child, read and discuss *Animal Lore and Legend: Owl* retold by Vic Browne. Then, have your child write two facts about the Great Gray Owl, the Great Horned Owl and the Burrowing Owl. *See* Science, Week 21, number 3.	***Alabama*** **AL**
		    named *clearers of the thickets* in
		      Creek Indian
		    nicknamed The Heart of Dixie
		capital city - Montgomery
		landmarks - Mobile
		          Birmingham
		          George Washington Carver
		           Museum

With your child, read and discuss pages 20 and 21 in *Math Curse* and solve the money problems.
Have your child complete **"Mouth" Math** (p. 227).
	Why do birds sing? Sit outside and listen to the variety of calls and songs. With your child, read and discuss *A Nest Full of Eggs* by Priscilla Belz Jenkins. Have your child write ten new facts he/she learned about birds. Allow your child sufficient time to work on the bird habitat research project—grassland—from Week 19.	***North Carolina*** **NC**
		    named for King Charles I
		    nicknamed The Tarheel State
		capital city - Raleigh
		landmarks - Smoky Mountains
		          Cape Hatteras Lighthouse
		          Wright Brothers National
		           Memorial
		          Cherokee Indian Reservation
		          USS North Carolina

With your child, read and discuss pages 22 and 23 in *Math Curse* and solve the end-of-day problems. Then, finish reading the book. Create addition and subtraction facts to 20 using Mayan numerals. *See* Math, Week 21, number 6.	With your child, read and discuss *The Bird Alphabet Book* by Jerry Pallotta. Choose five birds and have him/her describe them in his/her Science Log.	***South Carolina*** **SC**
		    named for King Charles I
		    nicknamed The Palmetto State
		capital city - Columbia
		landmarks - Hilton Head Island
		          Fort Sumter National Monument
		          Southern 500 Race
		          Charleston

TEACHING SUGGESTIONS AND ACTIVITIES

LANGUAGE SKILLS (Paragraphs)

▶ 1. Write a paragraph for each of four pictures. Give your child the pictures, topic sentences and supporting sentences all mixed together. Tell your child to arrange the sentences under the correct pictures and in the correct order.

READING

▶ 1. Write words with the *oi* and *oy* spelling on the chalkboard. Some suggestions include *toy, boy, joy, soil, noise, coin* and *oink*. Have your child read the words and tell what vowel sound he/she hears. You may wish to call this the "oink" sound. Ask what letters make the oink sound in each word.

▶ 2. Tell your child you are going to say some words. Every time a word has the oink sound in it, your child is to say "Oink." Mix the words you say with the *oo, ou* and *au* sounds from the last two week's lessons. Suggestions for *oy* and *oi* words include *Roy, soy, boil, noise, join, point, moist, foil, joint, sirloin* and *coil*.

MATH (Greater Than/Less Than)

BACKGROUND
The *greater than/less than* concept helps your child understand placement of a number within a field of numbers. The symbols greater than (>) and less than (<) can be the most confusing part of this concept. An easy method to help your child remember the greater than/less than concept is that the two symbols look like a greedy alligator opening its mouth. The hungry alligator likes to eat the greatest amount, so its mouth is always open toward the greater number.

▶ 1. Show your child a baseball. Ask your child to describe its size. He/she may do that by comparing it to other objects. Teach your child to use the words *greater* and *less* (in size). Have your child compare a nickel and a dime (by amount and size). Discuss synonyms (larger, bigger, more, over, above and smaller, littler, lower, fewer).

▶ 2. Show two pictures of like objects in differing amounts, such as three cats and six cats or ten squares and twelve squares. Have your child write the number of objects in each picture, compare and tell which number is greater (or less).

▶ 3. Provide manipulatives such as blocks, marbles and pennies. Write number sentences such as 10 > 8. Have your child model the sentence with sets of ten and eight objects and the > card. Teach your child to read the sentence as, "ten is greater than eight."

▶ 4. Provide manipulatives and number sentences such as 8 < 10 for your child to model. Teach your child to read the sentence "eight is less than ten."

▶ 5. Mix the > and < signs. Write a pair of numbers with the symbol missing between. Have your child model the two numbers, compare them and fill in the correct sign. Repeat several times using greater and less than.

▶ 6. **Mayan Numerals:** The Mayan Indians of Central America used number signs. They counted on their fingers and toes; so they used a number system based on twenty. Dots and dashes stood for numbers. Help your child invent his/her own version.

220

SCIENCE (Birds)

▶ 1. Below are some possible questions to get your child thinking:
- What is the smallest bird? the largest bird? the fastest bird?
- How much do birds weigh?
- How do most birds move? What enables them to fly? How fast do birds fly? How far can birds fly?
- What birds do not fly and why? How do they move?
- What do birds eat? Do all birds eat the same thing?
- How do birds protect themselves?
- How do birds communicate?
- Spend the rest of the week answering these and your child's other questions. Some sample lessons are included in the lesson plans.

▶ 2. Show pictures of some birds of prey. Birds of prey include owls, hawks, vultures, eagles, kites and falcons. Discuss how and why their eye placement differs from other birds and reasons for the shape of their beaks and feet. Tell your child birds of prey also rely on hearing to locate prey. Their ears are located on the sides of their heads under their feathers.

▶ 3. **Creative Writing:** Prompt for your child: *Pretend you are a bird of prey scanning the landscape for food. Finally, you see it. Write what you do and what the prey does.*

Sentence Sequence

Sentences can tell a story. **Color, cut out** and **glue** the pictures in order to tell a story. **Write** a sentence on each line that tells what is happening in the pictures.

1	
2	
3	
4	

222

Bumper Cars

jump   pond   kind   hand   land   stamp   bump   send   camp   ramp

Write the spelling words that end with the same consonants as sand.

_____   _____   _____   _____   _____

Write the spelling words that end with the same consonants as stump.

_____   _____   _____   _____   _____

Write the spelling words on the lines. Then, use the numbered letters to solve the code.

1. To run into

    __ __ __ __
       1

2. Not mean

    __ __ __ __
    2 3

3. To live in a tent in the woods

    __ __ __ __
       4

4. A small lake

    __ __ __ __
       5

5. A walkway that slopes

    __ __ __ __
    6

6. To leap

    __ __ __ __
         7

7. The ground

    __ __ __ __
    8

8. A part of your body

    __ __ __ __
    9   10

9. To make or order someone to leave

    __ __ __ __
     11 12

10. You need this to mail a letter

    __ __ __ __ __
    13

Y __ __   __ __ __ __ __ __ __
   5 1   9 4 12 10 8 11 10

__ __   __ __ __ __   __   __ __ __!
3 13   8 3 2 11   4   7 6 5

Forgetful Fred

Each sentence tells about a problem. Think of a way to solve each one. Then, **write** it on the lines.

I was gonna do my homework, but I sorta kind of forgot to remember to do it!

Cathy is always late for school.

_____

_____

Brian forgets his eyeglasses every morning, and his mother has to bring them to school.

_____

_____

Sara can't find her library book when she needs to return it to the school library.

_____

_____

Fred doesn't remember to do his homework.

_____

_____

Our House

Choose two words from the box that describe each character. Then, complete each sentence to tell why you chose those words.

understanding	spoiled	responsible	lazy	helpful	upset	happy
busy	caring	kind	mean	confused	unhappy	patient	nice

The girl is _____ and _____

because she _____

_____

_____

_____

Mother is _____ and _____

because she _____

_____

_____

_____

Father is _____ and _____

because he _____

_____

_____

_____

Number Lines

Write the circled numbers in the correct order on the lines.

A.

_____ > _____

B.

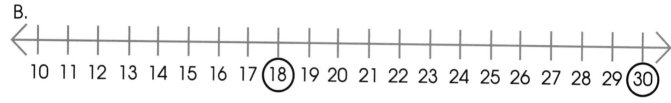

_____ < _____

C.

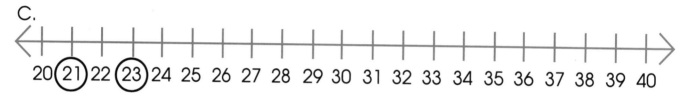

_____ > _____

D.

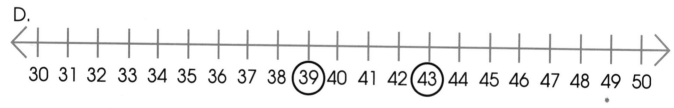

_____ < _____

E.

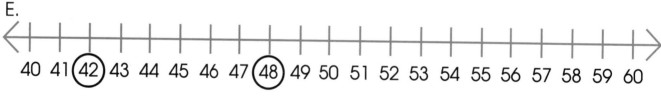

_____ > _____

F.

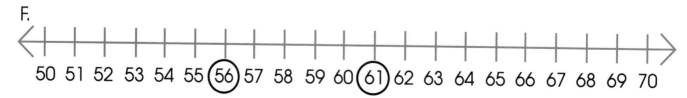

_____ < _____

Learn at Home, Grade 2

"Mouth" Math

Write < or > in each circle. Make sure the "mouth" is open toward the greater number!

36 ◯ 49   35 ◯ 53

20 ◯ 18   74 ◯ 21

53 ◯ 76   68 ◯ 80

29 ◯ 26   45 ◯ 19

90 ◯ 89   70 ◯ 67

227

	Language Skills	**Spelling**	**Reading**
Monday	**Letter Writing** Write a friendly letter to your child in the correct format. Address the envelope correctly and "send" it to your child. Point out the five parts of a friendly letter. *See* Language Skills, Week 22, numbers 1 and 2. Have your child write a letter to someone he/she cares about. Have him/her be sure to include the five parts of the friendly letter.	Pretest your child on these spelling words: free drop truck drive train from grass brag grade bring Teach the *r* blend sounds heard at the beginning of each word.	**Prefixes** Teach your child to recognize prefixes by providing several examples and discussing their meaning. Write *un* words on the chalkboard. Have your child underline the root words. Help your child identify the prefix and its meaning. Read two chapters a day in *Arthur Makes the Team* by Marc Brown. *See* Reading, Week 22, number 1. Have your child use a copy of **Chapter Book Report Form** (p. 234).
Tuesday	**Art:** Have your child design stationery that he/she would like to use. Make copies of the stationery. Allow your child to use or trace over **A Friendly Letter** (p. 232).	Have your child write the spelling words in sentences.	Introduce the prefix *mis*, which, as a prefix, means "wrongly" or "badly." Have your child read *mis* words. If your child does not recognize a word, have him/her cover the prefix and read the root word. *See* Reading, Week 22, number 2. Read chapters 3 and 4 of the Arthur book. Discuss a time you asked for advice or help.
Wednesday	Discuss why people write letters. Allow your child to get the mail each day. Have your child help you sort the mail into categories, such as personal, magazines, advertisements, requests for money and informational.	Have your child form each letter of the spelling words by shaping pipe cleaners. Have your child complete **Right on Track** (p. 233).	With your child, read Chapters 5 and 6 of the Arthur book. Review the word "teamwork" and how the Eagles were working or not working together as a team.
Thursday	Analyze an addressed envelope with your child. Point out the location of the sender's address. Note what words are capitalized. Help your child address the envelope for the letters he/she writes.	Have your child look for *r* blend sounds at the beginning of words in *Arthur Makes the Team*.	With your child, read chapters 7 and 8. Discuss how Arthur and Francine learned to help each other.
Friday	After reading the Arthur book in Reading, have your child pretend that he/she would like to be on the Eagles Team. Have him/her write a letter to Arthur or Francine telling them about him/herself and why he/she would like to be on the team.	Give your child the final spelling test.	With your child, read chapters 9 and 10 of the Arthur book. Review the completed **Chapter Book Report Form**. Then, with your child, make a list of requirements needed for effective teamwork.

Learn at Home, Grade 2

Math	**Science**	**Social Studies**

3-Digit Addition
Review 2-digit addition with and without regrouping. Give your child a problem such as 423 + 246. While he/she solves the problem, have your child talk through the process: "First, I added the ones and got 9, then I added the tens and got 6 and finally I added the hundreds and got 6."
	In his/her Science Log, have your child write a definition of the following words: *migration, ornithologist, habitat* and *bird of prey.*	Continue to study the 50 states. *See* Social Studies, Week 14.
		Georgia GA
		        named for King George II
		        nicknamed The Peach State
		capital city - Atlanta
		landmarks - Martin Luther King's home
		        Savannah
		        Stone Mountain
		        Okefenokee Swamp

Have your child practice adding 3-digit numbers with regrouping. At first, provide problems that only require regrouping in the ones place. Your child should use place-value materials to model each equation. *See* Math, Week 22, number 1.	With your child, read and discuss *Have You Seen Birds?* by Joanne Oppenheim. Then, have your child create his/her own poem about one or more birds and illustrate the poem.	**Florida FL**
		        named *flowery* in Spanish
		        nicknamed The Sunshine State
		capital city - Tallahassee
		landmarks - Key Largo
		        Cape Canaveral
		        Ringling Museum
		        EPCOT Center/Disney World
		        Fort Lauderdale
		        Orlando

Use the symbols learned in Week 19 to model 3-digit addition problems. Prepare several index cards with hundreds, tens and ones symbols (*see* Math, Week 22, number 2). For each problem, have your child choose one of these cards for one addend. For the other addend, have your child choose an index card from the set used in Week 19. Have your child write down and solve the equations created from the above activity.	Have your child write in his/her log the name of each state and its state bird. Ask: *Do the states with the same state bird have similar climates?* Allow your child sufficient time to work on the bird habitat research project—brush—from Week 19.	**Maine ME**
		        name refers to being mainland
		        nicknamed The Pine Tree State
		capital city - Augusta
		landmarks - Portland Head Lighthouse
		        West Quoddy Head Light
		        Mount Katahdin

Copy **Recording Sheet** (p. 235). Have your child use three dice. He/she should roll one at a time to determine how many hundreds, tens and ones. The first roll is hundreds, the second roll, tens and the third roll, ones. Have your child record the numbers as addends in each correct column to form a problem. Then, have your child solve the equations created by this activity.	Discuss birds that are symbols, such as the eagle for strength, the dove for peace and the owl for wisdom. Before tomorrow's field trip, read *Owl Moon* by Jane Yolen. Discuss how the young girl was very quiet while "owling" with her Pa. Have your child select a new bird to be a symbol. Have him/her describe for what it is a symbol and why he/she chose that bird. Have your child draw a picture of the bird.	**New Hampshire NH**
		        named for Hampshire, England
		        nicknamed The Granite State
		capital city - Concord
		landmarks - Mount Washington
		        Old Man of the Mountain
		        Brattle Organ
		        Windsor-Cornish Covered Bridge

Teach your child to recognize a 3-digit number from its number name, standard number and symbolic drawing. On index cards, write one of the three forms of the number. When your child chooses a card, he/she copies the information and adds the other two forms on lined paper.
Example: three hundred
▢▢▢ ‖ ••••••   326   twenty-six
symbolic   standard   number
drawing   number   name
	Field Trip: Go bird watching with your child in a special place. Near a river or swamp may be an excellent location. Tell your child that it is important to be very quiet and still when watching birds. Take binoculars, **My Bird List** (started in Week 19) and a bird field guide. Have your child look for birds and list them using the guide to identify them.	**Vermont VT**
		        named *green mountain* in French
		        nicknamed The Green Mountain State
		capital city - Montpelier
		landmarks - Waitsfield Barn
		        Proctor marble quarries
		        Bennington Battle Monument
		        Concord Academy
		        Windsor-Cornish Covered Bridge

TEACHING SUGGESTIONS AND ACTIVITIES

LANGUAGE SKILLS   (Letter Writing)

▶ 1. On the chalkboard, draw an outline of a letter with boxes representing the five parts of a friendly letter (*see* page 232). Point to each part on your child's letter and label it on the drawing. The five parts are the date, the greeting, the body, the closing and the signature.

▶ 2. Find opportunities for meaningful letter writing.
   - Have your child write a letter to a cousin or friend who lives far away.
   - Have your child write a letter to the Chamber of Commerce in an area he/she would like to visit.
   - Obtain a pen pal from a different state, country or city with whom your child may correspond.
   - Have your child respond promptly to any letters he/she receives.
   - Have your child write a thank you note for any gift he/she receives.
   - Find a resource at the bookstore (or on the Internet) of addresses to which your child may write to obtain free objects.

READING (Prefixes)

BACKGROUND
A prefix is a word element attached to the beginning of a root word.

▶ 1. **Chapter Book Report**

1	4
2	5
3	6

Use a double-sided copy of the **Chapter Book Report Form** (p. 234). Number the front side as shown. Number from 7 to 10 on the back side. Instruct your child to write the title and author. After reading each chapter, write the title and main idea in the matching box. **Example:** Chapter 1 in box 1, etc.

▶ 2. Write *re* on the chalkboard. Explain that when you see the letters *re* at the beginning of a word, they make their own syllable preceding the root word. The prefix *re* changes the meaning of the word. Put several pennies on the table. Have your child count them. Write *count* on the chalkboard. Put a couple more pennies on the table and ask your child to recount the pennies. Write *recount*. The prefix *re* means "again." Have your child underline the root word and circle the prefix. Introduce other words with the *re* prefix. Some suggested words are *rebutton, reread, return, relock* and *refreeze*. Have your child draw a line under each root word, circle the prefix and use each word in a sentence. Discuss the meaning the prefix gives each word.

Learn at Home, Grade 2

MATH (3-Digit Addition)

BACKGROUND
Teach 3-digit addition in the same way as 2-digit addition. Many of the activities suggested in Weeks 13 and 14 may be duplicated during this week's lessons. Don't spend much time on the concept since your child should be able to transfer the process to this level fairly easily. Lead your child to understand that the same process will be used with the thousands place and higher. At first, let your child solve problems with base-ten blocks or other manipulatives.

▶ 1. Write nine 3-digit addition problems on the chalkboard. Some of the problems should require regrouping in the tens place, some in the ones place. Some problems should require no regrouping. Give your child a copy of the **Recording Sheet** (p. 235). Tell your child to copy each problem in the correct columns on the **Recording Sheet**. Discuss how many hundreds, tens and ones are in each addend. Instruct your child to find the sum of each problem using place-value materials. Help your child as needed.

▶ 2. Have your child look at the index card and write the 3-digit number represented by the symbols. **Example:** The drawing to the right represents the number 235.

_____

_____

_____

_____

_____

_____

_____

_____

_____

_____

_____

Learn at Home, Grade 2

Right on Track

free   drop   truck   drive   train

from   grass   brag   grade   bring

Write the spelling words on the lines. Then, use the numbered letters to solve the code.

1. Operate a car

_ _ _ _ _ _
         1

2. Transportation that moves on a track

_ _ _ _ _
2   3

3. To take something to someone

_ _ _ _ _
     4

4. A kind of plant

_ _ _ _ _
   5   6

5. To let fall

_ _ _ _
   7 8

6. At no cost to you

_ _ _ _
   9 10

7. To boast

_ _ _ _
    11

8. Transportation that travels on a road

_ _ _ _ _
   12

9. You are in the second . . .

_ _ _ _ _
    13

10. Opposite of to

_ _ _ _
    14

_ _ _ _ _ !   **Y** _ _   _ _ _
11 9 10 5 2   7 12   5 9 10

_ _ _ _ _ _   _ _   _ _ _   _ _ _ _ _ !
14 7 1 3 4 11   5 2   2 7 8   6 8 10 10 13

233

Chapter Book Report Form

Book Title _____ by _____

Learn at Home, Grade 2

Recording Sheet

Addition of 2-Digit and 3-Digit Numbers

H = hundreds   **T = tens**   **O = ones**

H	T	O

H	T	O

H	T	O

H	T	O

H	T	O

H	T	O

H	T	O

H	T	O

H	T	O

Learn at Home, Grade 2

	Language Skills	**Spelling**	**Reading**
Monday	**Poetry** Expose your child to a wide variety of poetry. Read poetry aloud from different books. Laugh with your child at the playful language available in poetry today. Discuss the meaning of the poems you read. With your child, read a poem and write a list of rhyming words from the poem. *See* Language Skills, Week 23, number 1, for poetry suggestions if you need some.	Pretest your child on these spelling words: sleep small speak snap slow smart spin smile spell snow Teach the *s* blend sounds heard at the beginning of each word.	**Suffixes** Teach your child to recognize suffixes. Provide several examples and discuss their meaning. Introduce the suffix *er*. Write *helper, runner, teacher* and *player* on the chalkboard. Underline the root words. Help your child identify the suffix. Have your child make a list of words that end in *er*. Prompt him/her to think of the jobs and actions of people. **Example:** Someone who paints is a painter.
Tuesday	Brainstorm rhyming words. *See* Language Skills, Week 23, number 2. Copy the lists of rhyming words. Help your child make a book to refer to while writing poetry. A useful resource for rhyming words is the book, *The Scholastic Rhyming Dictionary: Over 15,000 Words* by Sue Young.	Have your child write the spelling words in sentences.	Start reading *Freckle Juice* by Judy Blume. Discussion questions for chapters 1 and 2: *Why did Andrew want freckles? Do you think there is a real freckle juice? Is there anything about yourself you would like to change? In what way did Andrew think the freckle juice would solve all of his problems? How do you think Andrew earned his allowance?*
Wednesday	Help your child write bird riddles that have two-word, rhyming answers. *See* Language Skills, Week 23, number 3. Have your child complete **Loosey Goosey** (p. 240).	Have your child spell each word aloud while thumping the table with his/her knuckle. Have your child complete **Smile, Please!** (p. 241).	Continue reading *Freckle Juice.* Discussion questions for chapter 3: *Would you have waited to read the recipe? Would you have tried it? What changes did Andrew make in the recipe?* Have your child practice reading and identifying suffixes. *See* Reading, Week 23, numbers 1–3 for activity ideas.
Thursday	**Art:** Help your child make a pop-up book. Your child may publish his/her favorite riddle in the pop-up book. *See* Language Skills, Week 23, number 4.	Have your child create two-word rhymes using spelling words. **Example:** snow show, sheep sleep, smart Bart, etc.	Finish reading *Freckle Juice.* Discussion questions for chapters 4 and 5: *Why didn't Andrew want to go to school ever again? Do you think Sharon made Andrew sick on purpose? What do you think Andrew should say to Sharon? What did Miss Kelly do that made Andrew feel better? If you were Andrew, what would you tell Nicky about Sharon's recipes? What do you think Nicky should do about his freckles?*
Friday	Help your child write rhyming couplets. Find examples in poetry books. Point out that each line has the same rhythm and the last word in each line rhymes. *See* Language Skills, Week 23, number 5. Have your child write his/her own couplets.	Give your child the final spelling test.	Have your child invent (and write) a recipe for something he/she would like to change.

Learn at Home, Grade 2

Math	Science	Social Studies
Column Addition Write the following problems: 4 5 2 3 3 5 6 7 +3 +7 +8 +5 Let your child try adding the easy combinations first (doubles and sums of ten), then, in a different order. Let your child discover how much easier it is to add the first way. Have your child complete **Adding Strategies** (p. 242).	Help your child define *threatened, endangered* and *extinct.* Have your child identify birds in each category. *See* Science, Week 23, numbers 1 and 2.	Continue to study the 50 states. *See* Social Studies, Week 14. **Massachusetts MA** named *near the green hill* in Massachusetts Indian nicknamed The Bay State capital city - Boston landmarks - Plymouth Cape Cod Martha's Vineyard & Nantucket
Teach your child to add three 2-digit numbers in a column with and without grouping. Emphasize aligning columns and beginning in the ones column. *See* Math, Week 23, number 1.	With your child, read and discuss *Will We Miss Them: Endangered Species* by Alexandra Wright. Brainstorm solutions for the problem of endangered species of birds.	**Connecticut CT** named *on the long tidal river* in Mohican Indian nicknamed The Constitution State capital city - Hartford landmarks - Gillete Castle Great American Clock & Watch Museum Groton Naval Submarine Base
Teach your child to add 3-digit numbers in a column with and without regrouping. Again emphasize aligning columns and beginning in the ones column, moving onto the tens and then to the hundreds.	Discuss the word extinct. With your child, read and discuss *The Extinct Alphabet Book* by Jerry Pallotta. Have your child research one of the extinct birds in the book. Allow your child sufficient time to work on the bird habitat project—desert—from Week 19.	**Rhode Island RI** named officially Rhode Island & Providence Plantations nicknamed The Ocean State capital city - Providence landmarks - Slater Mill Historic Site Newport The Arcade Southeast Lighthouse
Have your child write and solve his/her own addition problems using 3-digit numbers on a copy of the **Recording Sheet** from Week 22 (p. 235).	Have your child design a poster that raises awareness for one of the threatened or endangered species of birds.	**Alaska AK** named *great land* in Aleutian nicknamed The Last Frontier capital city - Juneau landmarks - Anchorage Point Barrow Mt. McKinley Aleutian Islands Kodiak Yukon River
Review yesterday's assessment on understanding column addition. Then, have your child read and solve the math riddles in *Easy Math Puzzles* by David Adler.	With your child, research ways birds are useful to people (food, insect control, pollination, feathers, etc.). Observe the birds near your home and discuss how they are useful or a problem to you. Have your child write a paragraph about these thoughts.	**Hawaii HI** nicknamed The Aloha State capital city - Honolulu landmarks - Pearl Harbor Mauna Kea Diamond Head Maui Beach Polynesian Cultural Center *See* p. 250.

TEACHING SUGGESTIONS AND ACTIVITIES

LANGUAGE SKILLS (Poetry)

▶ 1. You can easily find many collections of poetry for children in your bookstore or library. Children's poets to look for: Arnold Adoff, Shel Silverstein, Judith Viorst and Jack Prelutsky.

▶ 2. Create lists of word families. Write several familiar words across the top of the chalkboard. Brainstorm with your child words that rhyme with each word. Write the rhyming words in a column below each header word. Read over the completed list with your child. Eliminate lists that do not have many rhymes. Have your child copy the words on separate pages that you compile into a book of lists.

▶ 3. After your child completes **Loosey Goosey** (p. 240), help your child picture the silly birds of the rhymes. With your child, brainstorm some silly riddles that begin "What do you call a bird that . . ."

▶ 4. Give your child these directions for making the pop-up book:
Fold a 9" x 12" sheet of construction paper in half. Make two 1-inch cuts 1 inch apart in the center of the fold. Open the folded paper and push the cut "square" to the inside. This forms the frame on which the pop-up will be glued. Fold a second sheet of 9" x 12" construction paper in half. Glue the first sheet inside the second, keeping the cut pop-up frame free. Write the riddle on the outside paper. Draw a picture of your silly bird on a small sheet of paper and cut it out. Glue the bird on the pop-up frame so it stands up when the paper is opened. Write the answer to the riddle under the pop-up bird.

▶ 5. Write examples of two-line, rhyming couplets. With your child, brainstorm his/her favorite toys, pets, hobbies and clothes. One of these may be the start of a couplet.
Example:
> I like to dig in the sand
> And play the drums in a band.

To model the rhythm and rhyme, write a sample couplet but leave off the final rhyme.
> I can fly a kite
> But not as well at _____.

Allow your child time to play with this format and make up his/her own rhyming couplets.

READING (Suffixes)

BACKGROUND
A suffix is a word part attached to the end of a root word. It can add to or change the meaning of a word.

▶ 1. Write a list of words ending in *er* on the chalkboard. Include words such as *painter, eater, picker, flyer, worker* and *reader*. Have your child read each word and tell you what the words have in common. Explain that *er* is called a suffix. When *er* is added to a word, it may change the root word from an action into the person doing the action. Have your child underline the root word and circle the suffix.

▶ 2. Write *wiper, rider, driver, hiker, writer* and *maker* on the chalkboard. Have your child read each word and identify the root word. Spell the root word above each word as your child says it. Write *er* after the root word. Lead your child to discover that the *e* of the root word was dropped before the suffix was added.

▶ 3. Write *runner, winner, sitter, batter, jogger* and *bidder* on the chalkboard. Have your child read each word and identify the root word. Have your child underline the root word and suffix. Help your child recall the following vowel rule: In order to keep a vowel short in a one-syllable word, the final consonant is doubled before the ending is added.

MATH (Column Addition)

BACKGROUND

Teach your child, when adding numbers in a column, to be thoughtful about which combinations will make the process simpler. Finding two digits that have a sum of 10, for example, makes adding the third addend much easier. Remind your child that the commutative property says that changing the order of addends does not affect the sum.

▶ 1. Write the "doubles" facts on flash cards for your child to practice. The goal is to gain speed and accuracy in recalling the sum of each. The doubles are 1 + 1, 2 + 2, 3 + 3, 4 + 4, 5 + 5, 6 + 6, 7 + 7, 8 + 8, 9 + 9 and 10 + 10.

SCIENCE (Birds)

▶ 1. Discuss what might cause birds to become threatened or endangered. A complete list of endangered birds may be obtained by writing to: Publications Unit, U.S. Fish and Wildlife Service, 113 WEBB, Washington, DC 20240. Endangered birds include the short-tailed albatross, the California condor, the whooping crane, the Hawaiian crow, the paradise parrot and the oriental white stork.

▶ 2. Write to one of the following associations for further information about threatened and endangered birds.
Defenders of Wildlife, 1244 19th Street NW, Washington, D.C. 20036
National Audubon Society, 700 Broadway, New York, NY 10003
National Wildlife Federation, 1400 16th Street NW, Washington, D.C. 20036-2266
Sierra Club, 730 Polk Street, San Francisco, CA 94109

Loosey Goosey

Find the names of the birds at the bottom of the page that will rhyme with the words given.

Example: Loose goose

narrow	_____	bobbin	_____
hairy	_____	dark	_____
men	_____	pinch	_____
pork	_____	muffin	_____
love	_____	beagle	_____
pleasant	_____	frail	_____
perky	_____	hull	_____
soon	_____	lay	_____
luck	_____	howl	_____
darling	_____		

jay   owl
stork   dove
wren   robin
canary

starling
sparrow
pheasant
eagle
turkey

gull
finch
loon
puffin
lark   duck
quail

Learn at Home, Grade 2

sleep small speak snap slow

smart spin smile spell snow

Write the spelling words that begin with the sound you hear at the beginning of the pictures.

_____

_____

_____

_____

_____

_____

_____

_____

Write the missing spelling word on the line.

1. Can you _____ all the words correctly?

2. The clown has a big _____ painted on his face.

3. A baby needs lots of _____ .

4. Steve likes sledding on the fresh white _____ .

5. A _____ white bunny hid behind the bush.

6. Studying and learning will help make you _____ .

7. Bike wheels _____ when you pedal.

8. Do you know how to _____ your fingers?

9. Cars must _____ down near a school.

10. Please _____ louder, so that everyone can hear you.

241

Adding Strategies

When adding three numbers, add two numbers first, then add the third to that sum. To decide which two numbers to add first, try one of these strategies.

Look for doubles.

$$
\begin{array}{r}
8 \\
3 \\
+\ 3 \\
\hline
14
\end{array}
\qquad 6
$$

$$
\begin{array}{r}
4 \\
4 \\
+\ 5 \\
\hline
13
\end{array}
\qquad 8
$$

$$
\begin{array}{r}
2 \\
9 \\
+\ 2 \\
\hline
13
\end{array}
\qquad 4
$$

Look for a ten.

$$
\begin{array}{r}
7 \\
3 \\
+\ 4 \\
\hline
14
\end{array}
\qquad 10
$$

$$
\begin{array}{r}
8 \\
4 \\
+\ 6 \\
\hline
18
\end{array}
\qquad 10
$$

$$
\begin{array}{r}
1 \\
5 \\
+\ 9 \\
\hline
15
\end{array}
\qquad 10
$$

Solve. Look for a 10 or doubles.

5	2	7	3	6
5	6	1	7	2
+ 4	+ 8	+ 7	+ 4	+ 6

7	7	6	5
6	8	7	5
+ 6	+ 3	+ 4	+ 3

Learn at Home, Grade 2

U.S. Map Puzzle
SECTION 8

ALASKA

Haida
plank
house

Peninsula

Kodiak Island

Gulf of Alaska

N
W   E
S

	Language Skills	**Spelling**	**Reading**
Monday	**Poetry** Over the next 2 weeks, read a variety of poetry with your child. Talk about the message of each poem. Talk about the author's choice of words. In a poem, words are chosen very carefully for their meaning and effect. With your child, read poetry just to enjoy it. Find opportunities for your child (and you) to write poetry.	Pretest your child on these spelling words: floor glue blink play glad flag club plant clean blow Teach the *l* blend sound heard at the beginning of each word.	**Biographies/Reading for Details** A biography is a true account of a person's life. When reading, think about the *Who, What, Why, Where* and *When* in the person's life. *See* Reading, Week 24. With your child, read and discuss *Young Christopher Columbus: Discoverer of New Worlds* by Eric Carpenter. Make ten copies and have your child complete **http://WWWWW.biography** on Columbus (p. 249).
Tuesday	Be sure to read poetry with and without rhyme.	Have your child write the spelling words in sentences.	With your child, read and discuss *Young George Washington: America's First President* by Andrew Woods. Have your child complete **http://WWWWW.biography** about Washington (p. 249).
Wednesday	Review alliteration. Alliteration is the repetition of the same sounds, especially at the beginning of words. Have your child practice tongue twisters. Have your child create his/her own tongue twisters.	Have your child spell each word aloud while clapping the consonants and tapping the vowels. Have your child complete **Fluttering Flags** (p. 248).	With your child, read and discuss *Young Rosa Parks: Civil Rights Heroine* by Anne Benjamin. Have your child complete **http://WWWWW.biography** about Parks (p. 249).
Thursday	Some poems have a rhythm or pattern that is easy to mimic. When you find a poem like this, have your child substitute his/her own words into the pattern. If your child is having trouble, try a limerick—it has an easily imitated rhythm.	Have your child design a flag. Then, have him/her write a story about the flag, using as many spelling words as possible.	With your child, read and discuss *Young Martin Luther King Jr. "I Have A Dream"* by Joanne Mattern. Have your child complete **http://WWWWW.biography** about King (p. 249).
Friday	Teach your child to use some of the patterns for writing poetry described in Language Skills, Week 23, numbers 1–5, and Week 25, numbers 1–6.	Give your child the final spelling test.	With your child, read and discuss *Young Abraham Lincoln: Log Cabin President* by Andrew Woods. Have your child complete **http://WWWWW.biography** about Lincoln (p. 249).

Learn at Home, Grade 2

Math	Science	Social Studies
3-Digit Subtraction Have your child to build the number 647 using place-value materials. Give him/her instructions to take away a certain number of tens and ones, such as 2 tens and 5 ones. Ask for the difference. Tell your children to rebuild 647. Then, repeat with different numbers, with no regrouping.	Allow your child sufficient time to work on the bird habitat research project—inland waters—from Week 19. Have your child prepare a paragraph about each habitat and draw birds for each habitat.	**Presidents** Discuss the current president. Ask: *How many presidents served before him? What makes him popular? What is he good at? Who is in his family?* Look for articles and pictures in the newspaper about the president. With your child, read and discuss the articles.
Repeat yesterday's lesson with the original number of 674. Have your child record the four equations with no regrouping on the **Recording Sheet** (p. 235). Then, say "Remove 2 tens and 6 ones" which causes your child to regroup to subtract. Provide your child with remaining subtrahends that generate regrouping. Have your child record five more equations with regrouping on a copy of the **Recording Sheet.**	**Field Trip:** Arrange for a visit to a pet store that specializes in birds. Learn about the various kinds, their origin, care and feeding and special training. Have your child write about the field trip in his/her log.	Learn about the presidents in *Ghosts of the White House* by Cheryl Harness. With your child, read and discuss one president each day. Today, read about George Washington. Have your child complete a copy of **Presidential Facts** (p. 251).
Give your child eight 3-digit subtraction equations to solve including regrouping. Emphasize lining up the numbers in the hundreds, tens and ones columns.	**Writing:** Have your child write a thank you letter to the pet store employee. Your child should include in the letter what he/she learned on the visit. Your child may want to use a copy of page 232.	With your child, read about John Adams. Have your child complete a copy of **Presidential Facts** (p 251).
Create subtraction problems using three dice. *See* Math, Week 24, number 1.	**Art:** Have your child draw pictures of different pet birds using colored pencils.	With your child, read about Thomas Jefferson. Have your child complete a copy of **Presidential Facts** (p. 251).
Write addition and subtraction story problems that involve 3-digit numbers. Have your child solve them on paper and/or with manipulatives.	Have your child make a list of things to do to care for a pet bird. Then, have him/her make list of what must be done to care for a bird that lives in your yard. Have him/her tell which type of bird he/she would rather care for and why.	With your child, read about Abraham Lincoln. Have your child complete a copy of **Presidential Facts** (p. 251).

TEACHING SUGGESTIONS AND ACTIVITIES

LANGUAGE SKILLS (Poetry)

▶ 1. Follow this five-line pattern for writing a sensory poem. See two examples below.

Line 1: Name an emotion or feeling. Finish the line with a color word.	**Example:**	Excitement is bright red. It sounds like the Fourth of July.
Line 2: Tell what it sounds like.		It smells like a firecracker.
Line 3: Tell what it smells like.		It tastes like watermelon.
Line 4: Tell what it tastes like.		Excitement feels like you're
Line 5: Tell what it feels like.		going to EXPLODE!

▶ 2. Follow this pattern for writing an autobiographical poem. See the example below.

Line 1: Your first name	**Example:**	Suzie
Line 2: Three adjectives that describe you		Friendly, kind, smart
Line 3: Your role or relationship		Your child
Line 4: Who loves . . .		Who loves ice cream.
Line 5: Who feels . . .		Who feels happy.
Line 6: Who needs . . .		Who needs hugs.
Line 7: Who fears . . .		Who fears spiders.
Line 8: Who lives in . . .		Who lives in St. Louis.
Line 9: Your last name . . .		Smith

▶ 3. Follow the pattern for an acrostic poem. Notice in the examples the subject of the poem is written vertically. Each line begins with a letter from that word. An acrostic can be made up of single words, small phrases or complete sentences. Help your child select a subject for an original acrostic.

Warm water	**J**ust
Air dry	**A**ctive
Smells clean	**N**eat
Home laundry	**E**xcellent

▶ 4. Copy an example of shape poetry on the chalkboard. Make it more interesting by using colored chalk. Shape poems may or may not rhyme.

▶ 5. See the examples of alphabet poetry below. The words of the poem begin with successive letters of the alphabet. Your child may begin with any letter of the alphabet. The syntax should make sense, although the poem will be silly.

Examples: Able Boys Can Drop Everything For Games.
Even Frogs Grow Hands.

▶ 6. Haiku is Japanese poetry that follows a strict syllabic pattern. The poem is usually about something in nature. In this three-line poem, the first line has five syllables; the second has seven; the third line has five. Study the following example with your child.

The wind does not blow
On this sultry, summer night.
We're too hot to talk.

READING (Biographies/Reading for Details)

BACKGROUND

Reading for details is an important skill, especially when reading nonfiction. Your child should learn to concentrate while reading and recall information when he/she puts the book down. The details are generally written in the text, not implied. Before reading nonfiction, ask your child to think of some questions that might be answered in the text. After reading, you can discuss the answers to those questions.

Learn at Home, Grade 2

Sometimes it helps, before you read a selection, to read over the questions to answer. You may encourage your child to ask his/her own questions before reading. With your child, read the sentences at the bottom of the page first. Then, read the selection. Finally, have your child complete the sentences on the bottom of the page based on the reading. This helps to focus the reader's attention on the first reading.

MATH (3-Digit Subtraction)

BACKGROUND
Teach 3-digit subtraction in the same way as 2-digit subtraction. Many of the activities suggested in Weeks 15 and 16 may be duplicated during this week's lessons.

▶ 1. Instructions for your child: Roll three dice. Arrange the numbers to create the largest possible 3-digit number. Write the number on lined paper and build it with place-value materials. Then, arrange the same numbers to create the smallest possible 3-digit number. Write this number below the first on the lined paper. Subtract this number from the first number and write the difference.

SOCIAL STUDIES (Presidents)

BACKGROUND
Study past presidents to create an awareness of names and interesting facts for which they are most remembered. Included here are facts you or your child may use when learning about each president.

George Washington	1st President served 1789–1797
	born: Feb. 22, 1732 in VA died: Dec. 14, 1799 in VA
Accomplishments:	Held the country together during its early days.
	Proclaimed Thursday, Nov. 26, 1789 as the first national Thanksgiving holiday.
Interesting Facts:	His picture is on the quarter and one-dollar bill.
	His false teeth were made of ivory.

John Adams	2nd President served 1797–1801
	born: Oct. 30, 1735 in MA died: July 4, 1826 in MA
Accomplishments:	Saved the country from an unnecessary war.
	Put the US Navy together.
Interesting Fact:	He was the only president who was the father of another president, John Quincy Adams.

Thomas Jefferson	3rd President served 1801–1809
	born: April 13, 1743 in VA died: July 4, 1826 in VA
Accomplishments:	Bought the Louisiana Territory which doubled the size of the country.
	Invented the American system of money.
Interesting Facts:	He wrote the first draft of the Declaration of Independence.
	He was one of only four presidents to live past 80 years.

Abraham Lincoln	16th President served 1861–1865
	born: Feb. 12, 1809 in KY died: April 15, 1865 in Washington, D.C.
Accomplishments:	Held the nation together during the Civil War.
	Rallied against slavery.
Interesting Facts:	His picture is on the penny and five-dollar bill.
	He was assassinated while seeing a play only days after the Civil War ended.
	He was six foot four inches tall.

Fluttering Flags

floor   glue   blink   play   glad

flag   club   plant   blow   clean

Write the spelling words that begin with the sound you hear at the beginning of the pictures.

_____

_____

_____

_____

_____

_____

_____

_____

_____

Complete the puzzle.

Across

2. Opposite of work
3. To open and close your eyes quickly
4. Part of a room
5. Opposite of dirty
6. Paste

Down

1. Happy
2. To put seeds in the ground
3. The wind can do this
4. A banner
5. A heavy stick

Learn at Home, Grade 2

http://WWWWW.biography

1. **Title** _____

2. **Author** _____

3. **WHO** (is this book about) _____

_____

4. **WHAT** (did he/she do) _____

_____

5. **WHY** (did he/she do this) _____

_____

6. **WHERE** (did he/she achieve fame) _____

_____

7. **WHEN** (did he/she achieve fame) _____

_____

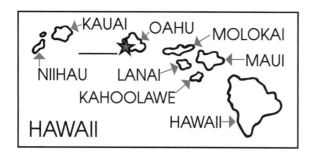

HAWAII

KAUAI · OAHU · MOLOKAI · MAUI · NIIHAU · LANAI · KAHOOLAWE · HAWAII

⭐**Capital Key**
49 - Honolulu

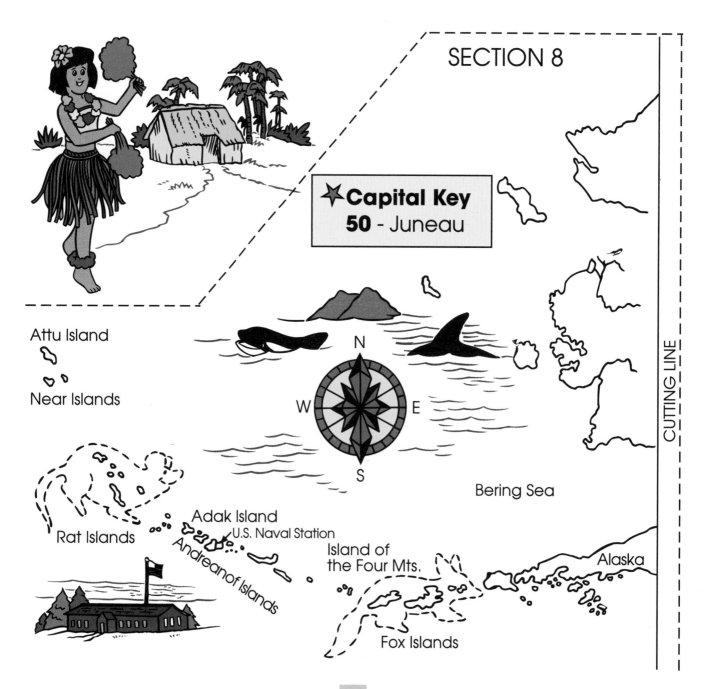

SECTION 8

⭐**Capital Key**
50 - Juneau

Attu Island

Near Islands

N
W   E
S

Bering Sea

Rat Islands

Adak Island
U.S. Naval Station

Andreanof Islands

Island of
the Four Mts.

Alaska

Fox Islands

CUTTING LINE

Learn at Home, Grade 2

Presidential Facts

President _____

From the state of _____

Accomplishment(s) _____

_____

_____

_____

_____

An interesting fact about him is _____

_____

_____

I researched him by using _____

_____

Learn at Home, Grade 2

	Language Skills	**Spelling**	**Reading**
Monday	Help your child memorize his/her favorite poems.	Pretest your child on these spelling words: what　why　rush when　shoe　ship where　cash　sheep 　while Teach the *sh* and *wh* digraphs.	**Dictionary Skills** Hang an alphabet line or cards on the wall for reference. Teach alphabetizing. Pick ten words, beginning with different letters and write them on index cards. Then, have your child arrange them in abc order. With your child, read *Young Jackie Robinson: Baseball Hero* by Edward Farrell. Have your child complete **http:// WWWWW.biography** (p. 249) on Robinson.
Tuesday	Turn a favorite poem (by another author) into an illustrated book. Have your child copy the poem onto several pages, one or two lines per page, and illustrate each page, showing his/her interpretation of the poem. Staple the pages together with a construction paper cover. Have your child write the title of the poem on the cover with the author's name and his/her name as illustrator.	Have your child write the spelling words in sentences.	Teach your child to alphabetize to the second letter. *See* Reading, Week 25, numbers 1 and 2.With your child, read *Young Orville and Wilbur Wright: First to Fly* by Andrew Woods. Have your child complete **http:// WWWWW.biography** (p. 249) on the Wright Brothers.
Wednesday	Have your child keep a folder of his/her original poems. Next week, he/she will put them together in an anthology with illustrations and share the "published" poems with others.	Have your child imagine the floor is very large paper and his/her feet are a pencil. Have him/her walk out the spelling of each spelling word. Have your child complete **Shoe Sale Rush** (p. 256).	Teach your child how to alphabetize when the first two letters are the same. *See* Reading, Week 25, number 3. With your child, read *Young Harriet Tubman: Freedom Fighter* by Anne Benjamin. Have your child complete **http:// WWWWW. biography** (p. 249) on Tubman.
Thursday	Have your child keep pages in his/her poetry folder of words that sound great to him/her. He/she may use this as a reference when writing poetry in the future.	Have your child write poems using all the spelling words.	With your child, read *A Girl Named Helen Keller* by Margo Lundell. With your child, practice "The One-Hand Manual Alphabet" at the end of the book. Find five words in the book to look up in the dictionary. With your child, read each definition and the words defined before and after the word.
Friday	With your child, read and write poetry just for the fun and enjoyment of it. *See* today's Science lesson.	Give your child the final spelling test.	Your child should write an autobiography about his/her own life to the present time. Be sure he/she includes the five "Ws" *who, what, why, where* and *when* in the story.

Learn at Home, Grade 2

Math	**Science**	**Social Studies**
Fractions With your child, read *Eating Fractions* by Bruce McMillan to introduce fractions. Teach your child to identify equal-size parts of a whole (or one). Divide a banana into thirds, an apple into fourths, a cake into halves and so on. Cut something into three uneven parts and discuss why the parts cannot be called thirds. Have your child complete a copy of **Equal and Unequal Parts** (p. 257).	Work with your child to research and construct a birdhouse. *See* Science, Week 25, numbers 1–3.	Ask your child to describe what he/she thinks it might be like to be president. Have your child write a poem about the presidency. *See* Social Studies, Week 25, number 1. Continue reading *Ghosts in the White House* by Cheryl Harness. With your child, read and discuss Theodore Roosevelt. Have your child complete a copy of **Presidential Facts** (p. 251).
Divide objects into fractions, such as halves, thirds, fourths, fifths, sixths, eighths, tenths and twelfths. Count the fractional parts in the following manner: *one-fifth, two-fifths, three-fifths, four-fifths, five-fifths.* If you have two whole objects, such as pizzas, count . . . *five-eighths, six-eighths, seven-eighths, eight-eighths, nine-eighths, ten-eighths.* Your child must be able to see and physically count the fractions.	Continue construction.	With your child, read and discuss Franklin D. Roosevelt. Have your child complete a copy of **Presidential Facts** (p. 251).
Have your child identify given parts of a whole. **Example:** Cut a sandwich into fourths and ask your child to identify one-fourth of the sandwich, two-fourths, three-fourths and four-fourths. Repeat with other objects and fractional parts. Have your child complete **Mean Monster's Diet** (p. 258).	Continue construction. Allow your child sufficient time to work on the bird habitat research project—marshes and sea coasts—from Week 19.	With your child, read and discuss Dwight D. Eisenhower. Have your child complete a copy of **Presidential Facts** (p. 251).
Introduce fractions as parts of a set. A set may be several (same-size) cookies, pencils, manipulatives or pennies. Group the set into fractions. **Example:** twelve cookies can be grouped into fourths (4 groups of 3), sixths, thirds, halves or twelfths. Count the fractions with your child as before (*see* Math, Tuesday). Repeat with several different sets. Have your child complete **Fortunate Fractions** (p. 259).	Have your child put the birdhouse in your yard and record the date. Have your child predict when you will see birds move in. Together keep an account of any bird activity at your birdhouse this season.	In *Ghosts in the White House,* read about the requirements for becoming a president, how he is elected and his duties. With your child, read and discuss John F. Kennedy. Have your child complete a copy of **Presidential Facts** (p. 251).
With your child, read and discuss the use of fractions in *Fraction Action* by Loreen Leedy or *The Doorbell Rang* by Pat Hutchins or *Give Me Half!* by Stuart J. Murphy.	**Poetry:** Have your child write a poem about the bird that will move into the birdhouse.	**Creative Writing:** Have your child write a paragraph beginning with one of these starters: I'm proud to be American because . . . If I were president of the United States, I would . . . Being president must be a hard job because . . .

TEACHING SUGGESTIONS AND ACTIVITIES

READING (Dictionary Skills)

BACKGROUND

The dictionary skills the second grader should master are alphabetical order to the third letter and finding word meanings.

▶ 1. Write two words that begin with the same letter, such as *fire* and *furniture.* Tell your child you want to put the words in alphabetical order, but they both begin with *f.* Ask your child if he/she has any idea how to do it. Guide your child into seeing he/she must look at the second letter in each word in order to put them in alphabetical order. Repeat with other pairs of words.

▶ 2. Write three words, two that begin with the same letter like *truck* and *three* and a third that begins with a different letter such as *neighbors.* Have your child identify the first letter of each word. Ask your child to help you alphabetize the words. If your child does not know where to begin, suggest that you put the words that begin with the same letter together, for now. Place *neighbors* first, then the words that begin with *t.* Then, ask your child if he/she remembers what to do when two words begin with the same letter (above).

▶ 3. Have your child compare two words that begin with the same first two letters. Look at *fun* and *furniture* together. Ask your child how he/she might decide which would come first in the dictionary. Teach your child to look to the first letter that is different when alphabetizing. Look up the words in the dictionary to check.

MATH (Fractions)

BACKGROUND

Expose your child to a variety of representations for fractions. There are three types of models: an area subdivided into smaller parts, a set of objects divided into subsets and lengths divided into parts (lines or physical materials). Use fraction vocabulary, such as *the whole, halves, thirds, fourths, fifths, sixths* and so on. Use these words orally or written out; avoid using symbols or the words one-third or one-eighth at first.

SCIENCE (Birds)

▶ 1. Check out a book from the library about birdhouses. With your child, read to find a bird that will most likely be found in your area. Read about how to construct its birdhouse and where to place the house to attract the birds.

▶ 2. Construct the birdhouse. Each birdhouse has its own special dimensions and characteristics. Follow directions carefully and measure accurately. Always allow only yourself or another adult to handle the cutting tools.

▶ 3. Help your child measure the dimensions of the birdhouse as you work and when it is completed.

Learn at Home, Grade 2

SOCIAL STUDIES (Presidents)

▶ 1. **Poetry:** With your child, read the poem by Arnold Spilka below. Then, write the first and last sentences on chart paper. Have your child fill in three or four sentences that describe what he/she thinks it would be like to be president of the United States.

> I'll tell you what it's like to be president of the United States.
> First, you are inaugurated at an outdoor ceremony
> In January in Washington, D.C.
> You and your family live in the White House,
> Which is very nice and you don't have to cook or clean your room.
> You get to meet famous people, but you have to make a lot of speeches, too.
> You get to ride in helicopters and Air Force One.
> You work with Congress to make laws and you get to sign them.
> You can also veto a law if you don't like it.
> You have to smile even when you don't feel like it.
> That's what it's like to be president of the United States!
>
> *by Arnold Spilka*

Presidential Facts

Theodore Roosevelt 26th President   served 1901–1909
born: Oct. 27, 1858 in NY   died: Jan. 6, 1919 in NY

Accomplishments: Helped keep big businesses from becoming too powerful.
Worked to make the national parks and forests and the Panama Canal.

Interesting Fact: The original Teddy bear was named after him.

Franklin D. Roosevelt 32nd President   served 1933–1945
born: Jan. 30, 1882 in NY   died: April 12, 1945 in GA

Accomplishments: Saw the USA through the Great Depression of the 1930's and World War II.
Brought about great changes despite exhaustion and polio.

Interesting Fact: He was cousin to Teddy Roosevelt and was distantly related to 10 other presidents.

Dwight D. Eisenhower 34th President   served 1953–1961
born: Oct. 14, 1890 in TX   died: Mar. 28, 1969 in Washington, D.C.

Accomplishments: Ended the war in Korea.
Interesting Fact: Was a great military leader as well.

John F. Kennedy 35th President   served 1961–1963
born: May 29, 1917 in MA   died: Nov. 22, 1963 in TX

Accomplishments: Worked for equal rights for all citizens.
Established the Peace Corps.

Interesting Facts: He was the first Catholic president.
He was assassinated in Dallas, TX on his way to make a speech.
He wrote the book *Profiles in Courage* while recovering from a war injury on his back. It won a prize for the best American history book for that year.

Shoe Sale Rush

what why rush when shoe
ship where cash sheep while

Write the spelling words that begin like **shark**.

_____ _____ _____

Write the spelling words that begin like **whistle**.

_____ _____ _____ _____ _____

Write the spelling words that end like **brush**.

_____ _____

Write the correct spelling word on the line.

1. Money _____

2. To hurry _____

3. A word used to tell about two things
   happening at the same time. _____

4. It asks for a reason. _____

5. A large boat _____

6. It asks about a thing. _____

7. It asks about a place. _____

8. A farm animal _____

9. It asks about a time. _____

10. You wear it on your foot. _____

Learn at Home, Grade 2

Cut out each shape below along the solid lines. Then, fold the shape on the dotted lines. Do you have equal or unequal parts? Sort the shapes by equal and unequal parts.

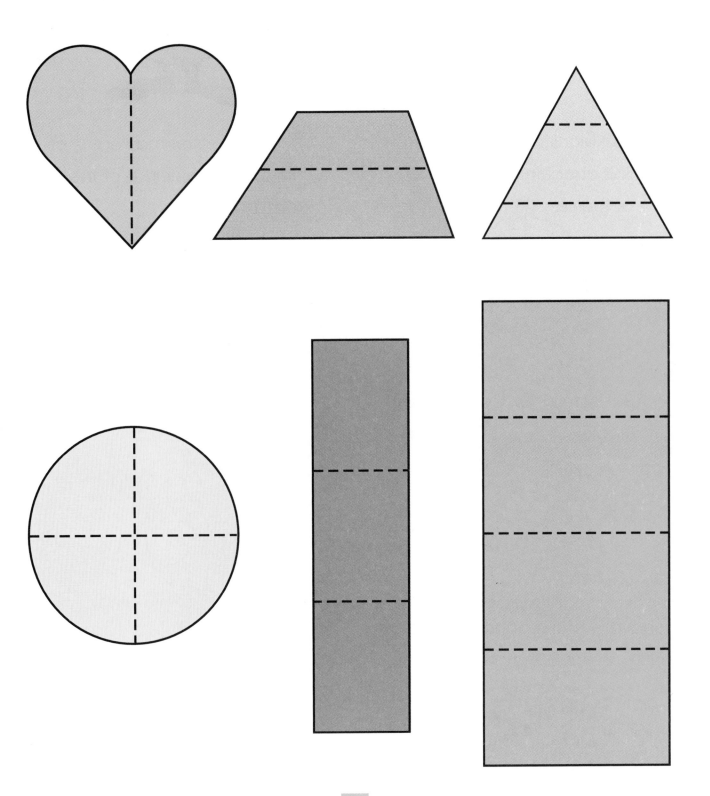

Mean Monster's Diet

Help Mean Monster choose the right piece of food.

1. Mean Monster may have $\frac{1}{4}$ of this chocolate pie. Color in $\frac{1}{4}$ of the pie.

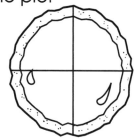

2. For a snack, he wants $\frac{1}{3}$ of this chocolate cake. Color in $\frac{1}{3}$ of the cake.

3. For an evening snack, he can have $\frac{1}{4}$ of the candy bar. Color in $\frac{1}{4}$ of the candy bar.

4. Mean Monster may eat $\frac{1}{3}$ of this pizza. Color in $\frac{1}{3}$ of the pizza.

5. For lunch, Mean Monster gets $\frac{1}{2}$ of the sandwich. Color in $\frac{1}{2}$ of the sandwich.

6. He ate $\frac{1}{2}$ of the apple for lunch. Color in $\frac{1}{2}$ of the apple.

Learn at Home, Grade 2

Fortunate Fractions

Color the correct number of fortune cookies to show each fraction.

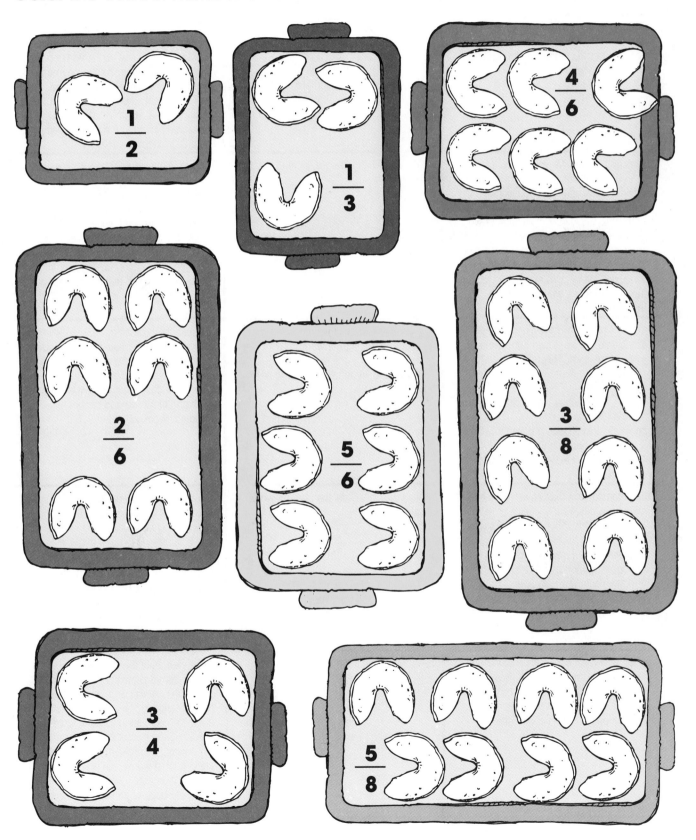

$\frac{1}{2}$

$\frac{1}{3}$

$\frac{4}{6}$

$\frac{2}{6}$

$\frac{5}{6}$

$\frac{3}{8}$

$\frac{3}{4}$

$\frac{5}{8}$

Learn at Home, Grade 2

	Language Skills	**Spelling**	**Reading**
Monday	Find and discuss poems that create an image by comparing two unlike things. The poem "Fog" by Carl Sandburg compares fog to a cat. *See* Language Skills, Week 26, number 1 for the poem.	Pretest your child on these spelling words: think tooth each teach thank child change both inch thing Teach the *ch* and *th* digraphs.	Introduce guide words. Teach your child that guide words help you find the dictionary page you are looking for more quickly. Show your child that the guide words are the same as the first and last words on that page. Turn to any page and have your child read the guide words. Repeat. *See* Reading, Week 26, numbers 1–4. Begin reading *Stringbean's Trip to the Shining Sea* by Vera B. Williams.
Tuesday	*Similies* are easy for your child to learn to write. Similies create clear images for poetry. Teach your child to recognize similies. *See* Language Skills, Week 26, number 2. Have your child think of what he/she wants to describe in the poem. Have him/her think of another thing that shares a characteristic with it. Tell your child that It is okay to exaggerate to help the reader picture what the author intends.	Have your child write the spelling words in sentences.	Choose ten vocabulary words from the first half of *Stringbean's Trip to the Shining Sea* for your child to look up in the dictionary. When your child is looking for the word, encourage him/her to use the guide words as a reference. Have your child write each vocabulary word on lined paper, followed by the guide words found at the top of the page and the page number.

Wednesday	Often in poetry, two things are compared that create a vivid image without the words, *like* or *as*. This is called *metaphor*.
	Read:
	    The dancer was a bird.
	    Alan is a snail.
	    Einstein was a brain.
	    My hands are ice.
	Allow your child to write some poetic comparisons.
		Have your child spell each word in a different voice (high, low, grumpy or excited).
		Have your child complete **Inching Along** (p. 264).
			Discuss the characters in *Stringbean's Trip to the Shining Sea*. Ask: *How do they get along? What can you tell about them from the postcards?*
			Have your child create character webs for both Stringbean and his brother. *See* Reading, Week 26, number 5.

Thursday	*Onomatopoeia* is the use of words that imitate sounds. Pronunciation of words like *buzz, slam, whirr, sizzle, hiss* and *woof* suggests their meaning. Poetry includes such words to create a rhythm or suggest a mood. Look for more onomatopoeic words in poetry. Have your child write a poem that includes onomatopoeia.	Have your child write the spelling words in abc order.	Choose ten vocabulary words from the second half of *Stringbean's Trip to the Shining Sea* for your child to look up in the dictionary. Encourage him/her to use the guide words as a reference. Have him/her write each vocabulary word on lined paper, followed by a brief definition of the word.
Friday	Have your child copy his/her best poems neatly in a homemade book. Have him/her give the anthology a title and share it with others. A neatly published book of poetry makes a nice gift.	Give your child the final spelling test.	Have your child complete a five-line story pyramid describing *Stringbean's Trip to the Shining Sea*. Here's the order for your child to use: a characteristic of the main character using one word, description of the setting of the story in two words, the problem or action of the story in three words, the events in the story in four words, your child's feelings about the book or characters in five words.

Learn at Home, Grade 2

Math	**Science**	**Social Studies**
Time Help your child make a clock face using a large paper plate or pizza wheel. Put the numbers 1–12 around the clock. Then, begin at 12 and put 60 marks around the outside for minutes—every fifth being darker. Make the hands out of colored tagboard and attach with a paper fastener. Number by fives going around the clock. Explain differences between the hour and the minute hands.	Read aloud poems about birds.	With your child, read and discuss *Arthur Meets the President* by Marc Brown. Write an essay about "How I Can Help Make America Great." Write a letter to the president in care of The White House 1600 Pennsylvania Ave. Washington, D.C. 20500.
On the clock, have your child practice showing times on the hour and half hour. Then, show your child how to write the times. **Example:** 3:00 3:30, 10:00 10:30, 7:00 7:30, etc.	Have your child complete the bird habitat research project from Week 19. For the next 2 weeks, paint each habitat and attach the birds that belong in each. Have your child label each habitat in neat letters across the top of the painted page. The size of the paper for the habitats depends on the size and number of birds your child has prepared. A 12" x 18" sheet of construction paper will probably be large enough.	**Music/Physical Activity:** Play patriotic music. Have your child sing and/or march to the music. Include "Hail to the Chief," which is played whenever the president is present at a formal function. Begin reading *The Story of the White House* by Kate Williams.
Review yesterday's lesson. Then, on the clock, give your child practice showing times on the quarter hour. Show your child how to write the times. **Example:** 2:45, 6:15, 11:45, 1:15, etc.	Over the past 7 weeks, your child has been drawing birds for each researched habitat. Now, he/she will prepare the birds to attach them to the painted habitat. For each bird, cut 3" x 1/2" strip of construction paper. Accordion-fold each strip paper. Glue one end of the accordion to the back of the bird. Glue the other end to the back of the habitat. Plan this carefully so the birds are evenly distributed around the habitat.	Finish reading and discussing *The Story of the White House*. Discuss how the White House is different and similar to your house. With your child, read and discuss the "Fun Facts to Know About the Presidents" and "The White House Portraits" at the end of the book.
Review lessons learned in telling time. Then, on the clock, give your child practice showing times involving 5-minute intervals. Show your child how to write the times. **Example:** 2:10, 4:25, 6:40, 10:55, etc. Have your child complete **Turtle Time** (p. 265).	You and your child should continue work on the bird habitats project.	On a map, locate the four state capitals named after presidents (Madison, WI; Jefferson City, MO; Lincoln, NE; and Jackson, MS). Look on your state map. Are there any cities/towns named after presidents? Are there any streets in your city named to honor a president?
Review yesterday's activity and telling time. *See* Math, Week 26, numbers 1–3.	You and your child should continue work on the bird habitat project. Help your child prepare a cover and title page on the same size paper as the habitat. Staple all the pages together along the left side.	Look at coins and dollar bills. Identify the presidents pictured.

LANGUAGE SKILLS (Poetry)

▶ 1. **Fog**
The fog comes
on little cat feet.
It sits looking
over harbor and city
on silent haunches
and then moves on.
by Carl Sandburg

▶ 2. **Center/Game:** In this activity, your child should complete a simile with a word that makes sense. To prepare, write incomplete similes on sentence strips. Write the words to complete the similes on index cards. Have your child match the sentence-strip simile with the word (index card) that completes it.
Similes:

as busy as a . . . (bee)	as straight as an . . . (arrow)	as graceful as a . . . (swan)
as quick as a . . . (wink)	as tough as . . . (nails)	as clumsy as an . . . (ox)
as slow as a . . . (snail)	as soft as a . . . (marshmallow)	as fast as a . . . (jet)
as light as a . . . (feather)	as rough as a . . . (pine cone)	as shiny as a . . . (new penny)
as heavy as a . . . (rock)	as smooth as . . . (silk)	as hungry as a . . . (bear)
as white as a . . . (sheet)	as dark as . . . (midnight)	as dry as a . . . (desert)

▶ 3. Discuss comparisons in the poems your child reads or writes (i.e., *In what way is a roof like a drum?*). Notice also the onomatopoeia.

READING (Dictionary Skills)

▶ 1. Turn to a page in the dictionary and have your child read the guide words. (You may choose to cover the rest of the page for this activity.) Ask your child which word is most likely to be on this page: *goat, money* or *time* (fill in your own words here). One of the three you mention should fall between the guide words. Repeat with a new page and three new option words. As your child gains experience, include words that begin with the same letter as the guide words, but do not fall on that page.

▶ 2. On lined paper, write a list of page numbers from the dictionary. Have your child find each page listed and write the guide words from that page on the lined paper. Then, have your child look up each word and write the guide words from that page.

▶ 3. On the chalkboard, write two guide words in one color chalk. Off to the side, write three entry words that would fall between the guide words, using a different color chalk. Have your child arrange them in alphabetical order under the guide words.

▶ 4. On the chalkboard, write two guide words in one color chalk. Write four entry words, three that would fall between the guide words and one that would not. Have your child cross out one that does not belong and alphabetize the others.

▶ 5. A character web should include as much as you know about that character—appearance, character traits, roles in life, family, etc.

Learn at Home, Grade 2

MATH (Time)

BACKGROUND

The best method for helping your child gain a sense of time is by maintaining a schedule and by thinking aloud about the time and how long things did or will take. Time includes time of day, as measured on a clock, as well as days, months and years, as measured on a calendar. Each day, look at a calendar with your child and review the day and date. Look ahead on the calendar for family events, birthdays or holidays. Discuss how much time will pass before these events occur.

▶ 1. Have your child show three o'clock on the clock. Have your child set other times on the hour. Show your child how to write the time. Then, you set the time and have your child identify it.

▶ 2. Show your child how the minute hand revolves around the clock 60 times before the hour hand moves from one hour to the next. The hour hand revolves around the clock only two times in a day. Have your child count hours with you as you discuss what you might be doing at each hour. When you reach twelve, tell your child that is only half a day. The clock has to go around again until it gets back to twelve for a day to have gone by. Have your child continue around the clock again; this time count that there are 24 hours in a day.

▶ 3. Show your child a traditional clock face and a digital clock face. Compare them. Write a digital time and have your child set the clock. Set the clock and tell your child to write the digital time.

263

Inching Along

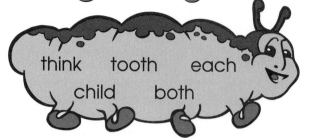
think   tooth   each
child   both

inch   thing   change
teach   thank

Write the spelling words that begin like **cheese**.

_____   _____

Write the spelling words that begin like **thumb**.

_____   _____   _____

Write the spelling words that end like **branch**.

_____   _____   _____

Write the spelling words that end like **teeth**.

_____   _____

Circle the misspelled word. Then, **write** the spelling word correctly on the line.

1. Which team do you thick will win the game?   _____

2. The dentist filled the cavity in her toth.   _____

3. We will boff ride on the train.   _____

4. A baby kangaroo is about 1 itch long when it is born.   _____

5. There is an apple for eack person.   _____

6. Theo had to chanj his clothes after he fell in the mud.   _____

7. What is that furry ting under the table?   _____

8. A star soccer player will teech us how to kick the ball.   _____

9. She wrote a letter to tank her grandmother for the gift.   _____

10. Mom helped the lost cilde find his mother.   _____

Learn at Home, Grade 2

Turtle Time

Write the time each clock shows.

Language Skills	Spelling	Reading
Monday **Review Week** **Researching and Writing a Report:** Help your child choose a topic. Keep the topic small. Rather than "All About Monkeys," narrow the scope down to a topic such as "Monkey Diet" or "Gorillas." *See* Language Skills, Week 27.	**Review Week** *See* Spelling, Week 27, numbers 1–4 for review ideas for the week.	**Review Week** Review vowel combinations. Write *ou/ow, oo, au/aw* and *oi/oy* on four index cards. Say a word that contains one of these vowel sounds. Have your child hold up the card that spells the sound he/she hears in the word. At this time, do not be concerned about whether the word is spelled with *au* or *aw*. This is a listening activity.
Tuesday Have your child think of five questions to have answered in his/her research. Have him/her write each question on the top of an index card. When your child finds an answer, have him/her write the facts on the appropriate card. Have him/her include the page number so he/she can look it up again later, if necessary.	Write homophones on index cards. Dictate a sentence to your child and have him/her point to the index card with the correct spelling of the homophone used in the sentence.	Review prefixes and suffixes. Write the following words on paper or the board. Have your child circle the prefix or suffix and underline the root word. sitter biker misbehave unwrap packer unearth misfire disobey remake misguide washer disrespect unfair rejoin unruly mistreat unplug replant
Wednesday Have your child continue his/her research. You may need to adjust the focus of the topic if the research reveals too much or too little information for your child. You may want to help him/her change the focus of the report as he/she collects more information but don't change the topic.	Write the spelling words from each week on a different color of paper. Cut apart the letters in each word. (Do not split blends and digraphs.) Mix up the letters. Have your child sort the letters and unscramble each spelling word.	Review reading for details. Reread one of the biography books read recently. Ask specific questions that can be answered in the text.
Thursday Have your child write a rough draft of his/her report. The introduction should be interesting and may include the questions posed at the beginning of research. Remind your child to include the facts researched in the body of the report. Model how to paraphrase. It must be written in your child's own words. Have him/her end the report with a summary, evaluation or thought-provoking question.	Write a short story incorporating several spelling words from the past 8 weeks. Misspell some of the spelling words. Have your child read the story and circle the misspelled words. Have your child write the correct spelling above each circled word.	Review dictionary skills and guide words. Have your child complete a guide words activity described in Reading, Week 27, number 1.
Friday Help your child read and revise the report. Then, your child may want to read it to someone else and ask for suggestions and specific praise or criticism. He/she should then revise his/her report again.	Give a review test of 25–50 words to assess whether your child has remembered the spelling of words from the beginning of the school year.	Have your child list books read in the past 8 weeks. Have your child complete **Guide Words** (p. 270).

Learn at Home, Grade 2

Math	Science	Social Studies
Review Week In sequence, write the variations of time: 60 seconds = 1 minute, 60 minutes = 1 hour, 24 hours = 1 day, 7 days = 1 week, 365 days = 1 year (except leap year) and 12 months = 1 year. Review 3-digit place value. Have your child roll three dice and record the smallest and largest number that can be made from the three numerals. Use **Numbers Small and Large** (p. 134).	**Review Week** Help your child continue working on the habitats and birds. Review what has been learned about birds so far.	**Review Week** Review geographical areas in relation to where you live. Each day, read a section of *Where Do I Live?* by Neil Chesanow. Keep a written account of geographic words and meanings highlighted in the book. With your child, read and discuss pages 4–13 and record *room, home, land, street* and *neighborhood* with their meanings.
Review 3-digit addition. Obtain several dollar bills, dimes and pennies. On large paper, have your child draw three large (money) trees. Write *hundreds* above the first tree, *tens* above the second and *ones* above the last tree. Write a 3-digit addition problem to be solved using the money, placing the coins and bills on the correct trees. Repeat several times, giving your child practice with and without regrouping.	Help your child continue working on the habitats and birds.	With your child, read and discuss pages 14 –21 and record *town, city, suburbs, country* (rural), *state* and *country* (USA) with their meanings.
Review greater than and less than. Have your child use the **<** and **>** cards to place between pairs of three place numbers. *See* Math, Week 21 numbers 1 and 2.	Help your child continue working on the habitats and birds.	With your child, read and discuss pages 22–31 and record *continent, world, planet* and *solar system* with their meanings.
Review 3-digit subtraction. Write several 3-digit addition problems for your child to solve. Have place-value materials available for your child to use. Your child may choose to solve the problems without the manipulatives. If so, have him/her check the work with the manipulatives.	Have your child neatly write each prepared paragraph and attach it to the appropriate background. He/she should also make a cover and title page for the book. Staple all the pages together.	With your child, read and discuss pages 32–37 and record *galaxy* and *universe* with their meanings.
Review telling time with your child. Have your child complete **It's About Time!** (p. 271).	Have your child complete **Birds of a Feather** (p. 272).	With your child, read and discuss pages 38–48. Review where you live. Then, have your child complete **Where Do I Live?** (p. 273).

TEACHING SUGGESTIONS AND ACTIVITIES

LANGUAGE SKILLS (Researching and Writing a Report)

The first step in the process is choosing a topic. You should narrow the field to an area, such as plants, animals or famous people. Teach your child to browse the library shelves for the topic that most interests him/her. Interest can be increased if there are several resources, including a video and/or a person to talk to. Research can include looking at pictures; reading books, encyclopedias and magazines; watching an informational video; or speaking to an expert. Teach your child to use the table of contents to narrow the search. Having the questions he/she wrote down on Tuesday will help your child know what to focus on while researching the topic. The scope of information provided can be overwhelming—be sure to give your child plenty of guidance and encouragement.

SPELLING

▶ 1. Write ten sentences containing spelling words that end with *ck, mp* or *nd*. Replace those endings in the sentences with a blank line. Then, have your child write *ck, mp* or *nd* in the blanks to complete the spelling words.
   Examples:
   Dad will take the garbage to the du____.
   Sam will sta____ between Pete and Sara.
   We watched the du___ swim around the pond.
   How much money may we spe____ for the gift?

▶ 2. Write some riddles for words that contain blends for your child.
   Examples:
   I rhyme with *tell*. You learn to do this when you read and write. What word am I? _____ (spell)
   I rhyme with *tag*. I hang on a pole outside. What word am I? _____ (flag)
   I rhyme with *tub*. I am another word for *bat*. What word am I? _____ (club)
   I rhyme with *rain*. I am driven by a conductor. What word am I? _____ (train)

▶ 3. Write some riddles for words that contain digraphs.
   Examples:
   It is another word for *boat*. It rhymes with *tip*. _____ (ship)
   It is covered with soft wool. It rhymes with *keep*. _____ (sheep)
   It is another word for *money*. It rhymes with *dash*. _____ (cash)

▶ 4. Help your child make a crossword puzzle using words from the spelling lists.

Learn at Home, Grade 2

READING

▶ 1. Write the following three sets of guide words at the top of lined paper: *deep* and *elephant, moth* and *nice,* and *water* and *white.* The list provided below contains words that fall on the three dictionary pages. Have your child write each word under the correct set of guide words. For an added challenge, have your child write each list in alphabetical order.

Word list:

droop	where	neighbor	mouse	dirt	east
wheat	nasty	what	earth	mother	went
drink	neat	west	donut	much	whisper
wave	edit	dream	echo	destroy	while

MATH

▶ 1. Concentrate on reviewing the following skills with your child:
- time words and concepts
- 3-digit addition and subtraction
- greater than and less than concepts

▶ 2. Give your child plenty of practice in the skills in which he/she is weak. Do not spend excess time on concepts in which he/she demonstrates proficiency.

Guide Words

Circle the words that would be found on these dictionary pages. Remember to use the guide words to help you. One has already been done for you.

save		**seal**
(seafood)	sass	sea
seafarer	scene	season
scuba	seam	salt
savage	scurry	say

thirsty		**today**
thirst	toddle	tiff
toad	time	togs
tissue	third	thumb
thirty	thread	toboggan

what		**whet**
where	whey	wheezy
whiff	wham	wheel
wheat	wart	wharf
west	whatever	when

Learn at Home, Grade 2

It's About Time!

Trace each mouse with red if it has a time word.

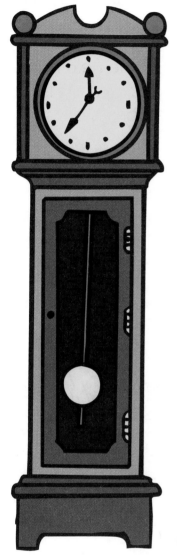

minute

week

flower

month

hour

day

catch

second

patch

year

Circle the correct answer.

1. There are 60 seconds in a   *1* minute.   year.

2. There are 60 minutes in an   second. *2* hour.

3. There are 24 hours in a   minute. *3* day.

4. There are 365 days in a   *4* year.   week.

5. There are 7 days in a   *5* week.   hour.

6. There are 12 months in a   year.   week.

© 1999 Tribune Education. All Rights Reserved.

Birds of a Feather

Birds are the only animals that have feathers. All birds have wings but not all can fly. They all hatch from eggs, have backbones and are warm-blooded.

The eggs in the nest contain the names of different birds. When filling in the puzzle, the last letter of one name becomes the first letter of the next name. Write the names of the birds in the puzzle in the correct order. Start at the outside edge and spiral in toward the center. The first three names are written for you.

Complete this story. **Write** the letters from the sections with numbers in the blanks.

    A sly and hungry fox quietly crept into the hen house one night. Carefully, he took a basket and began filling it with eggs. As he turned to leave, he tripped on a rake and went tumbling down, eggs and all. The hens awoke, laughed loudly and said,

" $\overline{\rule{1em}{0.4pt}}$ $\overline{\rule{1em}{0.4pt}}$ $\overline{\rule{1em}{0.4pt}}$ $\quad$ $\overline{\rule{1em}{0.4pt}}$ $\overline{\rule{1em}{0.4pt}}$ $\overline{\rule{1em}{0.4pt}}$ $\overline{\rule{1em}{0.4pt}}$ $\overline{\rule{1em}{0.4pt}}$ $\quad$ $\overline{\rule{1em}{0.4pt}}$ $\overline{\rule{1em}{0.4pt}}$ $\quad$ $\overline{\rule{1em}{0.4pt}}$ $\overline{\rule{1em}{0.4pt}}$ $\overline{\rule{1em}{0.4pt}}$! "

  1 2 3   4 5 6 7 8   9 10   4 12 13

Learn at Home, Grade 2

Where Do I Live?

1. My name is _____

2. My house number is _____

3. My street's name is _____

4. I live in the city or town of _____

5. I live in the state of _____

6. My country's name is _____

7. I live on the continent of _____

8. I live on the planet _____

9. The name of my galaxy is _____

10. The name of all the galaxies together is the _____

	Language Skills	**Spelling**	**Reading**
Monday	Read through your child's report and suggest punctuation, spelling or grammar errors he/she should watch out for. Choose one or two areas where you see many mistakes. It is important not to overwhelm your child with "red marks." Help your child repair any errors in punctuation, spelling and grammar.	Pretest your child on these spelling words: book took cook push pull look wood put foot full Discuss the vowel sounds in this week's list. Draw attention to the fact that the *oo* sound is similar to the short *u* sound.	**Folktales From Other Countries** **Japan:** Read and discuss *Peach Boy* by William H. Hooks. *See* Reading, Week 28.
Tuesday	Before your child makes the final copy of the report, edit the story for accuracy. Write your corrections above your child's words. Talk about what you are doing as you work so your child can learn from your modeling. Have your child copy his/her report neatly and accurately onto lined paper. You may have him/her include illustrations and a cover, if desired.	Have your child write the spelling words in sentences.	**Japan:** Read and discuss *The Magic Fan* by Keith Baker. Have your child create and design a "magic" fan and write a paragraph telling about its magic.
Wednesday	Have your child write his/her report in his/her best handwriting.	Have your child spell each word aloud while writing large letters in the air. Have your child complete **Baking Cookies** (p. 278).	**Korea:** Read and discuss *Sim Chung and the River Dragon: A Folktale From Korea* by Ellen Schecter. Choose one of the folktales read this week and help your child practice oral reading skills by reading character parts like a play. Someone else in your family could read the part of the narrator.
Thursday	Have your child share the finished report with someone again. Display his/her report at home on the coffee table or bookshelf.	Have your child alphabetize the spelling words.	**China:** Read and discuss *Tikki Tikki Tembo* retold by Arlene Mosel. Both you and your child should create a long name for yourselves.
Friday	Watch a fictional movie about a topic similar to that of your child's report.	Give your child the final spelling test.	**China:** With your child, read and discuss *The Emperor and the Kite* by Jane Yolen. Help your child make a kite from paper and sticks.

Learn at Home, Grade 2

Math	Science	Social Studies
Graphing Choose a collection of objects that is meaningful to your child, such as marbles or buttons. Have your child sort the collection into groups and name them. Write the group names at the bottom of a grid (with individual boxes large enough to hold a piece of the collection). Above each name, have your child line up the group, one object per box. Discuss and compare the real graph. *See* Math, Week 28, numbers 1–2.	**Rocks** The Earth is constantly changing. Some changes are very fast, such as changes caused by an earthquake or volcano. Some changes are very slow, such as the formation of rocks in the Earth's crust. *See* Science, Week 28, numbers 1 and 2.	**Global Awareness: People in Other Societies** Read and discuss *A Ticket to Japan* by Tom Streissguth. Have your child begin writing a list of Japanese words and their English meanings. Have your child start **New Words I Learned About Japan** (p. 282).
Using a copy of **Individual Graph Boards** (p. 279), teach your child to make a picture graph. Have your child count pencils, pens and markers (not more than ten each). *See* Math, Week 28, number 3. To make this a picture graph activity, have your child draw circles in the boxes rather than coloring them in. Have your child complete **Turtle Spots** (p. 280).	Collect and observe rocks. Teach your child to recognize differences in rocks. *See* Science, Week 28, number 3. Have your child write in his/her log about where you both found the rocks. Have him/her describe some of the rocks.	With your child, read and discuss *Colors of Japan* by Holly Littlefield. Have your child add the color words to **New Words. . . .**
Use **Honey Bear's Bakery** (p. 281) to create a bar graph. Have your child color in the number of boxes above each bakery treat, to match the number of treats on the bakery shelves. **Alternative:** Use **Honey Bear's Bakery** to create a picture graph. Fill in the boxes with pictures of the treats. *See* Math, Week 28, numbers 4 and 5.	Have your child continue yesterday's lesson.	With your child, read and discuss *Count Your Way Through Japan* by Jim Haskins. Have your child add the new words to **New Words . . .** from Monday and Tuesday.
Provide your child with a small bag of stickers (4–9 different designs) for making a pictograph. For this graph, there should be no more than nine of any one design. Ask your child to sort the stickers by design, name the designs and write the names at the bottom of **Individual Graph Boards**. Above each name, place the matching stickers. Discuss the statistics of the graph. **Example:** There are six more dog stickers than food stickers.	Explain the meaning of "unique." Have your child describe a rock, highlighting its uniqueness. *See* Science, Week 28, number 4.	With your child, read and discuss *C Is for China* by Sungqan So. Have your child begin **New Words I Learned about China** (p. 283).
Make a bar graph using the sticker graph (*See* Thursday) as a model. Copy **Individual Graph Boards** (p. 279). Have your child write the sticker names along the bottom of the graph. Have your child color in a box for every sticker on the sticker graph. Discuss the statistics of the graph as before. Compare the pictograph to the bar graph.	**Writing:** With your child, brainstorm adjectives that describe the size, shape, texture, color, luster and weight of rocks. Write the adjectives on a chart as a reference. Ask your child to write a short descriptive paragraph about his/her favorite rock, using adjectives from the chart.	With your child, read and discuss *Count Your Way Through China* by Jim Haskins. Have your child add the new words to **New Words. . . .**

275

TEACHING SUGGESTIONS AND ACTIVITIES

READING   (Folktales From Other Countries)

BACKGROUND
During Weeks 28, 29 and 30, your child will read a variety of folktales from other countries. A folktale is a traditional story handed down by word of mouth among a group of people. As each book is read, review with your child its story elements (characters, settings, problems, events and solution) and magic in the tale.

MATH (Graphing)

BACKGROUND
Graphing is used to present information in an organized manner. Some graphs are used to compare amounts. If graphing is a new concept for your child, provide the first experiences with real graphs. With more experience, your child will understand the purpose of a picture graph. Then, you may present information in bar graph form.

A real graph is made up of actual objects organized in equally spaced columns. You will need to ask a question about a set of objects that can be best answered if the actual objects are sorted and organized on a large graph. Pictorial graphs, drawn on paper, may contain the same information, but actual objects are represented by pictures. Symbolic graphs, the most abstract, contain marked spaces that represent the actual objects. To make the connection, have your child graph the same information using the three forms.

▶   1.   Start a real graph project by posing one of the following questions: *Are there more raisins, nuts or pieces of cereal in this (small) bag of trail mix? How many more blue blocks than red blocks are in your set of blocks? If we collect all the shoes in your closet, how many will there be of each kind?*

▶   2.   To make a picture graph of the above information, your child should leave the real graph intact and fill in a copy of the **Individual Graph Boards** (p. 279) to match. For the trail-mix graph, write the column names at the bottom of the page (raisins, nuts and pieces of cereal). For each food object counted, your child should draw a circle in a box. Discuss the relative lengths of the rows. For the blocks, have your child draw squares. For the shoes, have your child draw the shape of the shoe outline.

▶   3.   Have your child make a picture graph of the pens, markers and pencils found in a desk drawer. Your child should draw a pencil on a copy of the **Individual Graph Boards** (p. 279) to represent each pencil, pen and marker he/she counted. Discuss and compare the statistics of the graph. **Examples:** There are ____ more pencils than pens. There are _____ markers and pens together. Other picture graphs to draw include neighborhood pets, furniture in the house and flowers in the yard.

▶   4.   **Writing:** Have your child write story problems about a graph. **Example:** There are 8 pencils and 4 markers. How many pencils and markers are there in all? How many more pencils are there than markers?

▶   5.   To make a symbolic bar graph, use one of the picture graphs created above as a model. Make an identical graph, except everywhere there is a picture, have your child color in a square of the graph. The resulting graph will look like bars of color rather than columns of pictures.

SCIENCE (Rocks)

BACKGROUND

Rock is the solid part of Earth's crust. Rocks are formed in the Earth through heat and pressure and are made up of many different minerals. The three types of rock formations are igneous, sedimentary and metamorphic. Igneous rocks are formed when melted rock inside Earth cools and hardens. Sedimentary rocks are formed over time with layers of sand, mud, gravel and decayed plants and animals. Metamorphic rocks are rocks that have been changed through pressure and heat to a different form.

▶ 1. Read *The Big Rock* by Bruce Hiscock. Discuss the rock's age, as well as changes in the past and changes that may occur in the future. The Earth is covered by a thin skin of rock called the crust. The crust may be as thin as 5 miles or as thick as 25 miles. The crust contains tall mountains and runs under the oceans.

▶ 2. Go for a walk with your child. Find a big rock. Speculate with your child about how that rock got to where it is. Help your child become aware of all rocks, large and small and think about the rocks' origins.

▶ 3. Collect rocks wherever you go. Try to gather a large variety. Look around lakes, rivers, in woods and along country roads. Wash the rocks and sort them by size and color.

▶ 4. Select a rock from your collection. Describe the rock to your child. Describe a feature on it that none of the other rocks has. Ask your child to point to the rock you described. Have your child describe a rock for you to guess. Take turns describing two or three more each.

SOCIAL STUDIES (Global Awareness: People in Other Societies)

BACKGROUND

The world is getting smaller everyday due to a mobile population, modern technology and readily accessible transportation. Learning about other countries and cultures can help societies become more aware of their differences and similarities and also helps us to better understand ourselves as humans. Your child will learn about different Asian cultures in China and Japan this week.

Baking Cookies

wood   book   push

put   took   pull   foot

cook   look   full

Write the spelling words with **double o** that make the sound you hear in the middle of **hook**.

_____   _____   _____

_____   _____   _____

Write the spelling words with **u** that make the sound you hear in the middle of **foot**.

_____   _____

_____   _____

Write the correct spelling word on each line.

1. You do this with your eyes.   _____

2. Opposite of empty   _____

3. You burn this in a fireplace.   _____

4. A part of your body   _____

5. Something to read   _____

6. Opposite of push   _____

7. Did take   _____

8. To set something down   _____

9. To fix food for a meal   _____

10. Opposite of pull   _____

Learn at Home, Grade 2

Turtle Spots

Color the boxes to show how many spots are on each turtle's shell.

1	2	3	4	5	6	7	8

1	2	3	4	5	6	7	8

1	2	3	4	5	6	7	8

1	2	3	4	5	6	7	8

1	2	3	4	5	6	7	8

Learn at Home, Grade 2

Honey Bear's Bakery

Fill in the graph to show how many of each treat are in the bakery.

Number of Bakery Treats

12						
11						
10						
9						
8						
7						
6						
5						
4						
3						
2						
1						

New Words I Learned About . . .
Japan

Word

English Meaning

_____   _____

_____   _____

_____   _____

_____   _____

_____   _____

_____   _____

_____   _____

_____   _____

_____   _____

_____   _____

_____   _____

Learn at Home, Grade 2

New Words I Learned About . . .
China

Word   English Meaning

_____   _____

_____   _____

_____   _____

_____   _____

_____   _____

_____   _____

_____   _____

_____   _____

_____   _____

_____   _____

Learn at Home, Grade 2

	Language Skills	Spelling	Reading
Monday	Good writing includes details that show rather than tell. Teach your child to use adjectives and words related to the five senses in his/her writing. Read *The Relatives Came* by Cynthia Rylant. Discuss how the author includes details about sounds, tastes and smells to portray the mood and feelings of the characters.	Pretest your child on these spelling words: food　huge　room soon　zoo　school use　cute　rude moon Discuss the vowel sounds in this week's list. Note that the *oo* sound is similar to the long *u* sound.	**Abbreviations** Write the days of the week on the board. Underline the first letters of each to show your child how abbrevi-ations are formed. **Mexico:** With your child, read and discuss *The Tale of Rabbit and Coyote* by Tony Johnston. Review the story elements in this folktale (*see* Week 7). Have your child add the Spanish expressions to **New Words I Learned About Mexico** (p. 291).
Tuesday	With your child, read the sentences below. Discuss which sentences tell and which ones show. 1. My aunt smiled. I hugged her. 2. When I caught my aunt's eye from across the room, the corners of her mouth turned up while a glimmer lit up her eyes. I ran to her open arms and hugged her tightly. Have your child write about a recent experience with relatives. Have him/her include the smells, sounds and tastes of the visit.	Have your child write the spelling words in sentences.	Teach your child common abbreviations such as months, titles, A.M. and P. M., and address words. Teach proper spelling and punctuation. *See* Reading, Week 29, number 1. **Mexico:** Read and discuss *Cuckoo: Cucu* by Lois Ehlert. Review the story elements. Have your child create an animal using cut paper. Have your child add the Spanish expressions to **New Words . . .** (p. 291).
Wednesday	**Adverbs:** Have your child read his/her story to another person. Have your child ask him/her: *How would you communicate the mood of the event using words? What words could you use to show rather than tell? What sentences could you add or take away?* Teach your child about adverbs. *See* Language Skills, Week 29. Have your child complete **Adverbs** (p. 288).	Have your child spell each word aloud in a "shivery" voice. Have your child complete **Super Cool!** (p. 290).	**Mexico:** Read and discuss *The Moon Was at a Fiesta* by Matthew Gollub. Review the story elements in this folktale and the Spanish words in the glossary. Have your child add the Spanish expressions to **New Words . . .** (p. 291).
Thursday	Using adjectives and adverbs helps create a clearer image in writing. Read the sentences below with your child. Discuss which sentence communicates a clearer image. 1. The car door shut. 2. The heavy car door slammed shut with a bang.	Draw four columns on a sheet of paper. Write *noun, verb, adjective* and *adverb* at the top of the columns. Have your child write the spelling words in the correct columns and be ready to explain his/her reasons for placing each word in its specific column.	Teach your child to write the date correctly. (You may use abbreviations.) Teach your child that there are several appropriate ways to write the date. **Italy**: Read and discuss *Days of the Blackbird: A Tale of Northern Italy* by Tomie dePaola. With your child, review the story elements in this book. Have your child begin **New Words I Learned About Italy** (p. 292).
Friday	Review adjectives and adverbs. *Adjectives* describe nouns (color, number, size and character). An *adverb* describes a verb (when, where and how). The more specific the adjective or adverb, the clearer the image will be. Have your child complete **Using Exact Adjectives** (p. 289).	Give your child the final spelling test.	**Italy**: Read and discuss *Strega Nona* by Tomie dePaola. Then, read *Strega Nona: Her Story as told to Tomie dePaola*. Have your child complete a copy of **Venn Diagram** (p. 293) comparing the two stories. Have your child add the Italian expressions to **New Words . . .** (p. 292).

Learn at Home, Grade 2

Math	**Science**	**Social Studies**
Create a line graph to display information that is meaningful to your child. A line graph works well to show changes, growth or improvement over time. **Ideas for Graphing:** your child's growth, measured weekly over a 3–6 month period; spelling test scores or math speed test scores; depth of water in a jar placed by the window for several days. *See* Math, Week 29, number 1.	Classify rocks using a copy of the **Venn Diagram** (p. 293). *See* Science, Week 29, number 1.	Your child will learn about Mexico. With your child, read and discuss *A Ticket to Mexico* by Tom Streissguth. Begin writing a list of Spanish words and their English meanings. Help your child make a *papel picado*, a brightly colored paper with cutout designs (see the book for directions). Have your child begin **New Words I Learned About Mexico** (p. 291).
Give your child one die and a copy of **Individual Graphing Boards** (p. 279). Have your child write the numbers from the die in boxes A–F. Each time your child rolls the die, color one box above that number on the graph. Discuss the results on the graph.	**Art:** Have your child make a rock character. *See* Science, Week 29, number 2.	**Mexico:** Read and discuss *Count Your Way Through Mexico* by Jim Haskins. Have your child add the number words to the list of Spanish words on **New Words. . . .**
Give your child a small bag of colored jellybeans, chocolate candies or other kind of colored candy and a copy of **Individual Graphing Boards** (p. 279). Then, write the colors in boxes A–F and color one box for each piece above that color on the graph. Discuss the results on the graph.	**Creative Writing:** Have your child write a short story about his/her rock character.	**Mexico:** Read and discuss *Colors of Mexico* by Lynn Ainsworth Olawsky. Have your child add the color words to the list of Spanish words from Monday and Tuesday.
Play "Heads and Tails" with a penny, a nickel and a dime and a copy of **Individual Graphing Boards** (p. 279). Have your child write 1¢-heads, 1¢-tails, 5¢-heads, 5¢-tails, 10¢-heads, 10¢-tails in boxes A–F. Toss each coin twelve times and color in a box for heads or tails each time. Discuss the results shown on the graph. Have your child write and describe how the graph looks.	Learn about igneous, sedimentary and metamorphic rocks. With your child, read *Let's Go Rock Collecting* by Roma Gans. Then, help your child define and show examples of these three kinds of rocks. *See* Science, Week 29, number 3.	**Italy:** Read and discuss *Count Your Way Through Italy* by Jim Haskins. Begin a list of Italian words and their English meanings. Have your child begin **New Words I Learned About Italy** (p. 292).
Help your child form a question that can be answered differently by different people. Write six answer choices in boxes A–F of **Individual Graphing Boards** (p. 279). Have your child survey several people and fill in the graph with their responses. Discuss the results of the survey graph. Have your child write a response to the survey. Ask what he/she learned about the topic or the people he/she questioned.	**Art:** Your child will make a stratification bottle with colored sand. Make different colors of sand by adding food coloring to white sand in separate containers. Give your child a small glass bottle with a lid. Have him/her fill it with layers of colored sand. Compare the layers of stratification in the bottle with the layers in the Grand Canyon. Reread *Grand Canyon: A Trail Through Time* by Linda Vieira. *See* Social Studies, Week 11.	**Italy:** Have your child add new Italian words to the list from the books, *Strega Nona* and *Strega Nona: Her Story* read today. *See* today's Reading plans.

TEACHING SUGGESTIONS AND ACTIVITIES

LANGUAGE SKILLS (Adverbs)

BACKGROUND
Adverbs are describing words for verbs, just like adjectives are describing words for nouns. Adverbs also modify adjectives with words such as *very*, but your child does not need to know this yet. Adverbs tell how, where or when something happened. **Examples:** *now, very, quickly, gently, soon, thoughtfully*

READING (Abbreviations)

BACKGROUND
An abbreviation is a shortened form of a word. It usually ends with a period. Provide experience with several common abbreviations so your child will recognize them when they come up in future reading.

▶ 1. Write the days of the week in a column. In a second column, write the abbreviation for each (out of sequence). Have your child match the word with its abbreviation. Repeat the activity with the months of the year, familiar states and common titles (Mr., Ms. and Dr.).

MATH (Graphing)

▶ 1. A line graph works well for showing change over time. Choose an activity for your child to perform every day for 2 weeks, such as jumping rope, shooting baskets, kicking a soccer ball or running. Each day have your child perform the activity, record the number performed or distance traveled. Set up the line graph with dates along the bottom and numbers or measurements up the left side. Place a dot where the appropriate date and number meet. At the end of the 2 weeks, connect the dots with a line and observe the change over time. Discuss the results of the graph. Discuss other ways a graph like this could be helpful.

▶ 2. Have your child look in magazines and newspapers for graphs of different kinds. Cut them out and glue them on a large sheet of paper. Discuss the different types of graphs with your child.

Learn at Home, Grade 2

SCIENCE (Rocks)

▶ 1. Draw a large Venn diagram on an 18" x 24" sheet of paper. Provide a dozen or more rocks of different colors, shapes, textures and sizes. Choose two adjectives from the descriptions made last week (activity 4). Write one adjective describing the rocks above each circle of the diagram. Have your child sort the rocks into the two circles. If the categories were *shiny* and *pink*, your child would place a rock that is pink *and* shiny in the intersection of the circles. A rock that is dull and brown would be placed outside both circles. Choose two different adjectives and sort the rocks again.

▶ 2. **Art:** Your child will design a character by gluing 3–6 rocks together. The different rocks form the head, body and arms of the rock character. Features can be drawn on with permanent marker or paint. Use an epoxy glue (under adult supervision). Let the glue between two rocks dry before adding the next rock. When the glue and paints are dry, help your child shellac the entire figure.

▶ 3. Give your child a piece of pumice to observe. Pumice is an igneous rock. It forms when lava is frothy and bubbly with gases. Give your child a bowl of water and have him/her discover a property of pumice.

An **adverb** describes a verb. It tells *how, when* or *where* an action takes place.

Example:

The space shuttle blasted off **yesterday**. (when)
It rose **quickly** into the sky. (how)
We watched **outdoors**. (where)

Write how, when or **where** to explain what each adverb tells.

1. I run **today**. _____

2. I run **outside**. _____

3. I run **tomorrow**. _____

4. I run **around**. _____

5. I run **nearby**. _____

6. I run **sometimes**. _____

7. I run **there**. _____

8. I run **far**. _____

9. I run **happily**. _____

10. I run **weekly**. _____

11. I run **swiftly**. _____

12. I run **first**. _____

13. I run **next**. _____

14. I run **gracefully**. _____

Circle the adverb in each pair of words. Remember, an adverb describes an action.

1. soon, supper

2. neatly, nine

3. proudly, prove

4. help, easily

5. warmly, wonder

6. quilt, quickly

7. finally, feather

8. quietly, quacks

9. sail, safely

Learn at Home, Grade 2

Using Exact Adjectives

Use an **adjective** that best describes the noun or pronoun. Be specific.

Example: David had a nice birthday.
David had a **fun** birthday.

Rewrite each sentence, replacing nice or good with a better adjective from the box or one of your own.

| sturdy | new | great | chocolate | delicious | special |

1. David bought a nice pair of in-line skates.

_____

2. He received a nice helmet.

_____

3. He got nice knee pads.

_____

4. Father baked a good cake.

_____

5. David made a good wish.

_____

6. Mom served good ice cream.

_____

Learn at Home, Grade 2

Super Cool!

food huge room soon zoo
school use cute rude moon

Write the **double o** words that make the **oo** sound.

_____ _____ _____

_____ _____ _____

Write the spelling words ending with **e** that make the **oo** sound.

_____ _____

_____

Complete the puzzle.

Across

2. Rhymes with choose
4. A place where you learn
6. Opposite of polite
7. A place to see many different animals
9. It shines in the sky at night

Down

1. Pretty
3. In a short time
5. Very, very big
6. Part of a house
8. You eat this

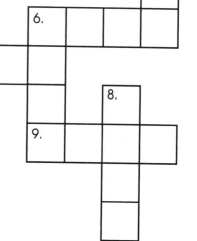

Learn at Home, Grade 2

Mexico

Word   English Meaning

New Words I Learned About . . .
Italy

Word

English Meaning

_____   _____

_____   _____

_____   _____

_____   _____

_____   _____

_____   _____

_____   _____

_____   _____

_____   _____

_____   _____

_____   _____

Learn at Home, Grade 2

Venn Diagram

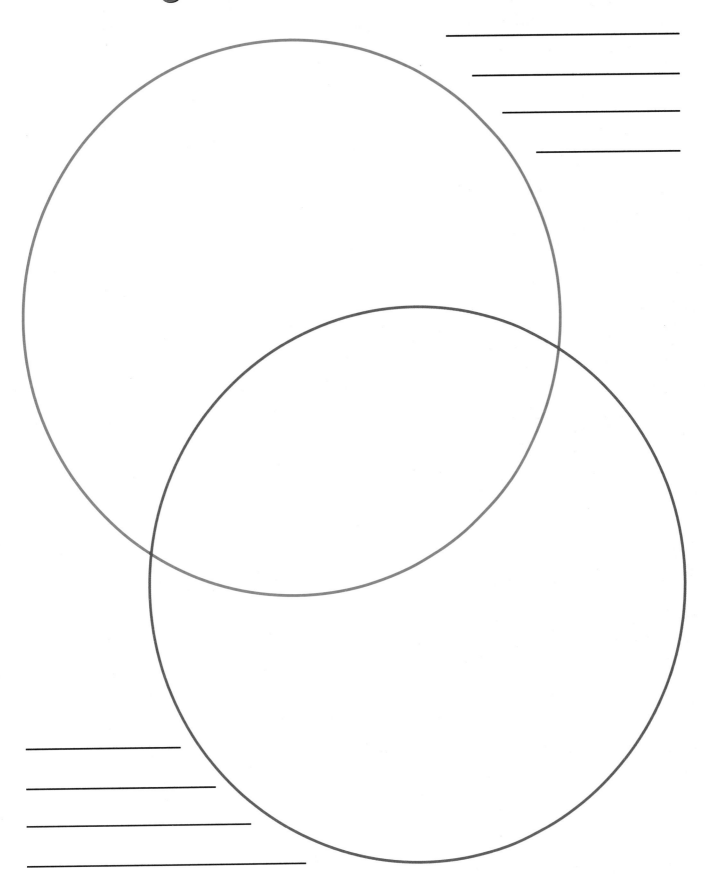

Language Skills	Spelling	Reading
Monday This week your child will write an original folktale as he/she follows the steps in the writing process. **Prewriting:** Have your child brainstorm ideas for characters, setting, problem, details and resolution. The story should be divided into three parts: beginning, middle and end. Have your child plan the story on a copy of **My Story Map** (p. 298).	Pretest your child on these spelling words: clown our down count how town house about now out Teach the *ou* (or *ow*) sound.	**Library Skills** **Germany:** With your child, read and discuss *Rumpelstiltskin* by Marie-Louise Gay. Review the story elements of the book. Have your child identify the parts and specifics of the book: cover, end covers, spine, title page, copyright date, number of pages, price, etc.
Tuesday **Drafting:** Have your child write a rough draft of his/her tale using **My Story Map** from Monday.	Have your child write the spelling words in sentences.	**Russia:** With your child, read and discuss *Babushka: Baba Yaga* by Patricia Polacco. Review the story elements of the book. Visit the public library and familiarize your child with its system of locating books by author, title or subject. *See Reading, Week 30.*
Wednesday **Revising:** Have your child read the rough draft of his/her story to someone to be sure it makes sense and to get new ideas or suggestions. Then, have your child revise the rough draft.	Have your child spell each word aloud as you write it on the chalkboard. Have your child complete **Clowning Around** (p. 299).	**Africa:** With your child, read and discuss *How Giraffe Got Such a Long Neck and Why Rhino Is So Grumpy*, retold by Michael Rosen. Review the story elements and the magic in this tale.
Thursday **Editing:** Have your child proofread the story to correct capitalization, punctuation and spelling. Then, he/she should meet with someone and proofread the story again.	**Poetry:** Have your child write a four-line rhyme, using words that contain the *ou* sound at the end of each line.	**Africa:** With your child, read and discuss *Zomo the Rabbit: A Trickster Tale From West Africa* by Gerald McDermott. Review the story elements in this tale. With your child, research more trickster tales about rabbits, spiders and tortoises at the library.
Friday **Publishing:** Have your child write the final draft which will be published into a book next week.	Give your child the final spelling test.	Choose one of the folktales read this week and help your child practice oral reading skills like a play. Someone else in your family could play the part of the narrator.

Learn at Home, Grade 2

Math	Science	Social Studies
Checking Answers Using Opposite Operations Teach your child to check addition with the opposite subtraction problem and subtraction with the opposite addition problem. *See* Math, Week 30, numbers 1 and 2. Have your child find the mistakes on the worksheets you prepared.	**Weathering** Observe the effect of rubbing two rocks together. *See* Science, Week 30, number 1.	**Germany:** With your child, read and discuss *Count Your Way Through Germany* by Jim Haskins. Have your child begin a list of German number words and other words and their meanings. Have your child start **New Words I Learned About Germany** (p. 303).
Teach the checking method with 2-digit problems. *See* Math, Week 30, number 3. Have your child complete **Airport Action** (p. 300).	Have your child continue yesterday's lesson.	**Russia:** With your child, read and discuss *Count Your Way Through Russia* by Jim Haskins. Have your child write a list of Russian number words and other words and their meanings on **New Words I Learned About Russia** (p. 304).
Ordinal Numbers: Teach your child to use ordinal numbers and relate them to cardinal numbers. *See* Math, Week 30, numbers 4 and 5.	Observe a rock breaking apart. *See* Science, Week 30, number 2.	**Africa (Swahili):** With your child, read and discuss *Jambo Means Hello: Swahili Alphabet Book* by Muriel Feelings. Have your child write a list of Swahili words and their meanings on **New Words I Learned About Africa** (p. 305).
Have your child complete **My First Treat Will Be . . .** (p. 301).	**Field Trip:** Walk in an area known to have a lot of rock cover. Have your child take his/her Science Log. Your child should look for evidence of rock erosion and draw different rocks and write a short explanation of each.	**Africa:** With your child, read and discuss *A Is for Africa* by Ifeoma Onyefulu. Have your child compare the similarities and differences of living in Africa to his/her way of life. Have your child continue adding words to **New Words. . . .**
Help your child make **Bookette Pattern** (p. 302). Use something that comes in a certain order, such as days of the week, the ingredients in a recipe or events in a story. On each page, have your child use an ordinal number and one part of the series. **Examples:** The first day of the week is Monday. Third, I mixed the eggs and milk. *See* Math, Week 30, number 6. Make sure your child colors and writes before gluing.	Make an artificial sandstone rock and watch it break down in the weather over several months. *See* Science, Week 30, number 3.	Review new words and cultures with your child. *See* Social Studies, Week 30.

TEACHING SUGGESTIONS AND ACTIVITIES

READING (Library Skills)

BACKGROUND
Library skills are critically important for the twenty-first century. As the volume of information available to us increases, so must our ability to access information in a variety of ways. Your child must learn to find information in books, newspapers, magazines, encyclopedias, technology networks and other resources. All these resources can be accessed at the public library.

MATH (Checking Answers Using Opposite Operations)

▶ 1. Write 3 + 5 = 8. Tell your child that although he/she already knows this math sentence is correct, you are going to prove that it is correct. Reverse the number order and change the operation sign; write 8 − 5 = 3. If this sentence is correct, then the first sentence is also correct. Repeat with several equations, addition and subtraction. Throw in some incorrect equations for your child to catch. Write some equations vertically as well.

▶ 2. Write down ten addition and ten subtraction problems and complete each problem. Complete some of the problems with incorrect answers. Give the page to your child to check each problem with the opposite operation. Have your child circle your mistakes.

▶ 3. Write 16 + 32 = 48. Prove that the equation is accurate by solving 48 − 32 = 16.

Ordinal Numbers

BACKGROUND
Ordinal numbers are used to indicate order in a series, such as *fifth* in line, *second* place and *first* born. Cardinal numbers are used in counting and showing how many. Teach your child the meaning of the words as well as the spelling.

▶ 4. Write the numerals 1–12 on twelve index cards. Mix them up and have your child put them in order. Have your child name each numeral. Tell your child that each of these cards has a place in order. Point to 1 and say "first;" point to 2 and say "second;" continuing through 12. Write the ordinal number below the numeral on each card (first, second, third, fourth, etc.). Look at each word with your child and discuss the similarity between the cardinal number words and the ordinal number words. **Example:** nine and ninth

▶ 5. Cut up comic strip pictures. Have your child put the comic strip in order and verbalize which box is first, second and third.

▶ 6. Directions for making the **Bookette** (minibook):
   • Copy page 302.
   • Cut out the minipages on the dotted lines.
   • Fold each piece in half on the heavy solid line. Glue the ends.
   • Put the pages in the following order:
      Place page 1/10 on the table faceup.
      Place page 3/8 over that.
      Place page 5/6 on top.
      Fold on the solid line so page 5/6 is in the center.
      Staple on the fold.
      Fold on the staple.

Learn at Home, Grade 2

SCIENCE (Weathering)

▶ 1. a. Have your child predict what will happen when you rub two sandstone rocks together. Have your child write a hypothesis in his/her log. Have him/her rub the two together over a sheet of white paper and observe the particles of sand that are rubbed off. Have your child draw and describe in his/her log what happened. Ask your child to think of something in nature that would cause the same effect.

   b. Have your child predict what will happen when you rub two hard rocks together. Have your child write a hypothesis in his/her log. Have him/her rub the two together over a sheet of white paper and observe. Tell your child that if two hard rocks such as these did rub against each other over a really long period of time, there would be a wearing away, but it can't be seen in this sampling.

   c. Observe a smooth rock taken from the shore of a large lake or ocean. Ask your child to make a hypothesis about what might cause a rock to be so smooth by the shore. When your child understands that water is able to wear away rock, show a picture of the Grand Canyon.

   d. Define *erosion*. Erosion is the weathering of rock and the movement of the weathered material. Erosion is caused mainly by water, ice and wind.

▶ 2. Show your child a piece of limestone. Let him/her hold it and observe it carefully. Have your child draw the rock and make a hypothesis about what will happen when you tap it with a hammer. Wrap the rock in a rag and hit it with a hammer. Open the towel and observe the debris left from the tapping. Have your child draw and describe what happened. Ask your child to think of something in nature that would cause the same effect. Some connections include earthquakes, freezing and thawing and roots from plants and trees that break through rocks.

▶ 3. Mix 1 cup of sand, $\frac{1}{2}$ cup water and $\frac{1}{2}$ cup of plaster of Paris in a large paper cup. If the mixture is too thick to stir, add a little more water. Allow the mixture to harden overnight. Remove the paper cup. Have your child put the artificial sandstone rock outside where it will be exposed to the weather. Ask your child to write a hypothesis about what will happen to the rock and why. Your child should describe and draw the rock in his/her log at least once a week over the next few months.

SOCIAL STUDIES (Global Awareness: People in Other Societies)

Postcards From . . . , a series of simple, descriptive and informational travel books about different countries is published by Raintree-Steck Vaughn Publishers, Austin, Texas. Countries included in this series are Australia, Brazil, Canada, China, France, Germany, Great Britain, Japan, Mexico, Russia, South Africa and Spain.

Learn at Home, Grade 2

My Story Map

1. Title _____

Beginning

2. The main characters _____

_____

3. The settings _____

4. When does the story take place? _____

Middle

5. The problem _____

_____

6. What do the characters do to try to solve it? _____

_____

_____

_____

_____

End

7. How is the problem solved? _____

_____

Learn at Home, Grade 2

Clowning Around

clown
our   down
count   how   town
house   about   now   out

Write the **ou** words that make the vowel sound you hear in **mouse**.

_____   _____   _____

_____   _____

Write the **ow** words that make the vowel sound you hear in **cow**.

_____   _____   _____

_____   _____

Write the missing spelling words in the boxes.

1. Sally lives in the _____ on the corner.

2. Do you know _____ to make a robot?

3. Please take the towels _____ of the dryer.

4. We must leave for the airport _____ !

5. It is _____ time for the race to start.

6. They rode the elevator _____ to the bottom floor.

7. This is _____ new four-wheel drive truck.

8. The big funny _____ rode a tiny bike.

9. Can you _____ to 100?

10. The farmer took his fresh fruit to _____ .

Learn at Home, Grade 2

Airport Action

To find out if the answer to a subtraction problem is correct, add the answer to the number taken away. If the sum is the same as the first number in the subtraction problem, then the answer is correct.

Example 1

$$
\begin{array}{r} {\scriptstyle 3\ 13} \\ \cancel{43} \\ -\ 27 \\ \hline 16 \end{array}
\qquad
\begin{array}{r} {\scriptstyle 1} \\ 16 \\ +\ 27 \\ \hline 43 \end{array}
$$

Since the sum is the same as the first number in the subtraction problem, the answer must be correct.

Example 2

$$
\begin{array}{r} {\scriptstyle 6\ 11} \\ \cancel{71} \\ -\ 28 \\ \hline 43 \end{array}
\qquad
\begin{array}{r} {\scriptstyle 1} \\ 43 \\ +\ 28 \\ \hline 71 \end{array}
$$

Check the subtraction by adding.

$$
\begin{array}{r} 52 \\ -\ 37 \\ \hline 25 \end{array}
\qquad +\ \underline{\hspace{1cm}}
$$

Is the subtraction problem correct? _____
How do you know?

Subtract. Then, add to check.

$$
\begin{array}{r} 52 \\ -\ 37 \\ \hline \end{array}
\quad +\ \underline{\hspace{1cm}}
\qquad
\begin{array}{r} 80 \\ -\ 26 \\ \hline \end{array}
\quad +\ \underline{\hspace{1cm}}
\qquad
\begin{array}{r} 64 \\ -\ 48 \\ \hline \end{array}
\quad +\ \underline{\hspace{1cm}}
$$

Learn at Home, Grade 2

My First Treat Will Be . . .

Circle the ordinal number word for each treat.

1

16

15

14

13

2

third, sixteenth, (fifth)

fifteenth, fourth, first

twelfth, second, seventh

third, eleventh, fifteenth

eighth, first, tenth

sixteenth, thirteenth, third

ninth, second, thirteenth

sixth, seventh, ninth

3

4

5

6

7

12   11   10   9   8

301

Bookette Pattern

10

8

6

1

3

5

2

4

Title: _____

_____

By: _____

11

9

7

New Words I Learned About . . .

Germany

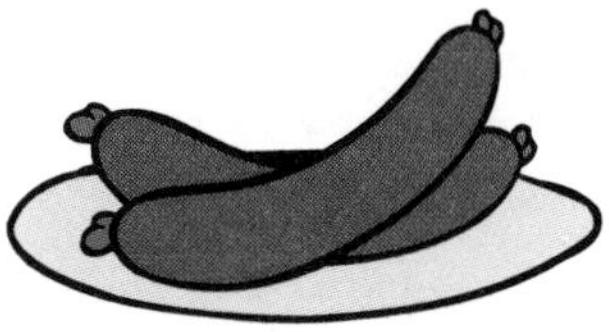

Word

English Meaning

_____   _____

_____   _____

_____   _____

_____   _____

_____   _____

_____   _____

_____   _____

_____   _____

_____   _____

_____   _____

_____   _____

_____   _____

_____   _____

New Words I Learned About . . .
Russia

Word   English Meaning

_____   _____

_____   _____

_____   _____

_____   _____

_____   _____

_____   _____

_____   _____

_____   _____

_____   _____

_____   _____

Learn at Home, Grade 2

New Words I Learned About . . .
Africa

Word   English Meaning

_____   _____

_____   _____

_____   _____

_____   _____

_____   _____

_____   _____

_____   _____

_____   _____

_____   _____

_____   _____

_____   _____

305

	Language Skills	Spelling	Reading
Monday	Have your child illustrate and publish the folktale written during Week 30 into book form. Reread the folktale together and break down the text into pages. Help your child decide how many pages are needed, including cover, title page, dedication page, etc. Fold 11" x 17" sheets of construction paper to form the book and staple.	Pretest your child on these spelling words: Sunday Monday Tuesday Wednesday Thursday Friday Saturday weekday weekend Analyze each word, breaking it into syllables to help your child remember the spelling. Notice the capital letter at the beginning of each weekday.	**Nonfiction Books** Discuss nonfiction books. What is nonfiction? When might you read a nonfiction book? What are some of your child's interests? *See* Reading, Week 31. Begin reading the biography *Tiger Woods: Golf's Young Master* by S. A. Kramer. Have your child complete **Nonfiction Books** (p. 310).
Tuesday	Have your child write the text on the pages and begin the illustrations.	Have your child write the spelling words in sentences.	Teach your child that nonfiction books are organized by subject. They are sometimes grouped by numbers in the library (100s–900s). Have your child continue reading about Tiger Woods. Visit the library and look at the numbers on the books in the nonfiction section, from the 100s to the 900s if your library uses that system.
Wednesday	Have your child continue illustrating the folktale.	Have your child write each word neatly on lined paper. Have your child spell each word aloud while tracing the letters in a pan of sand.	Poetry is found in the 800s of the nonfiction section. With your child, read from several books of poetry. You may both enjoy *A Light in the Attic* by Shel Silverstein.
Thursday	Have your child design the cover, title page (include a publication date), dedication page and an "About the Author" section inside the backcover.	Have your child write each day of the week on a sheet of paper. After each day, write about a small goal that he/she would like to accomplish. Help your child work to accomplish each goal over the next week.	Help your child make a mobile illustrating the important events from the life of Tiger Woods.
Friday	Have your child complete the book. With your child, read and share it with family and friends.	Give your child the final spelling test.	Have your child finish the mobile.

Learn at Home, Grade 2

Math	**Science**	**Social Studies**
Geometry Review the names of common shapes such as triangle, square, circle, oval, diamond and rectangle. *See* Math, Week 31, numbers 1 and 2. Have your child complete **How Many?** (p. 311).	**Identifying Rocks** **Math:** Have your child compare weights of rocks using a balance scale and ounce weights. *See* Science, Week 31, number 1.	**Global Education** This week your child will create a nonfiction ABC book *My ABC World,* which will consist of global information gathered the past 3 weeks. Have your child review the **New Words I Learned About . . .** lists and choose a foreign word for as many letters of the alphabet as possible.
Discuss the attributes of shapes with your child. *See* Math, Week 31, numbers 3 and 4. Also expose your child to shapes in space (solids) such as a cone, cylinder, cube, sphere and rectangular prism.	Have your child continue yesterday's lesson.	Decide how many pages are needed, including title page and dedication page. Use large 5" x 7" index cards for the pages. Design a special ABC letter for each card. Have your child write the foreign word, then the language's name. Then, write its English meaning. **Example:** R is for rojo in Spanish. In English it means red. Then, have your child illustrate the word.
With your child, read and discuss *Three Pigs, One Wolf and Seven Magic Shapes* by Grace Maccarone. Cut the tangram into seven pieces. *See* Math, Week 31, number 5. Then, reread the story. As you come to a tangram animal or shape, have your child form it with the tangram pieces. Copy **Tangram** (p. 189).	Have your child order the rocks from lightest to heaviest. Have him/her use the balance scale to confirm.	Have your child continue working on *My ABC World.*
Provide a geoboard and rubber bands for your child to make geometric shapes. Your child can create designs from several basic shapes. *See* Math, Week 31, number 6. Reproduce your geometric designs on dot paper.	Rocks are made up of minerals. With your child, read about minerals. Have your child copy a list of familiar minerals in his/her log. *See* Science, Week 31, number 2.	Have your child continue working on *My ABC World.*
Teach your child symmetry. Cut out a large variety of shapes. Teach your child to attempt to fold each shape in half. If the two halves are equal, the shape is symmetrical. Lines of symmetry can run up and down, across or diagonally. *See* Math, Week 31, number 7.	Teach your child to evaluate the hardness of rocks. *See* Science, Week 31, number 3.	Have your child complete *My ABC World* and share it with family and friends. Visit another country on the Internet. If you do not have access at home, your community library should have computers set aside for your use.

READING (Nonfiction Books)

BACKGROUND

A *nonfiction book* is any book that has not been made-up. These include history, how-to, encyclopedias, cookbooks and sheet music books. Some libraries still use the Dewey Decimal System to organize their nonfiction section. You may teach your child the different numbers if your library uses it.

MATH (Geometry)

▶ 1. On index cards, write the names of the common shapes and draw a matching shape card for each. Have your child match the shapes with the names.

▶ 2. Introduce other shapes. Show your child a picture of the U.S. Pentagon building. Discuss its shape. Show a picture of a stop sign. Discuss its shape (hexagon). Show your child a parallelogram and trapezoid. Discuss their characteristics.

▶ 3. **Center:** Cut several of each shape of different sizes from red, yellow and blue paper. Make attribute cards that say *red, yellow, blue, large, medium, small, not red, not yellow, not blue, one side, two sides, three sides, four sides* and *more than four sides*. Put attribute cards and shapes in an envelope. **Directions:** Select an attribute card. Find all shapes that have that attribute. **Variations:** First, let your child choose two attribute cards and sort the shapes under the two headings. Repeat with two new cards. Then, have your child choose two attribute cards and find all the shapes that have both attributes. Repeat with two new cards.

▶ 4. *See* the model below for problem solving with shapes.
   All of these have something in common.   None of these has it.

   Which of these has it? (parallel sides)

▶ 5. Have your child cut out a copy of **Tangram** (p. 189). Discuss the shapes in the tangrams. Direct your child to use two pieces to make a triangle, to make a square, a tree, etc. Let your child experiment with tangrams to make his/her own recognizable figures.

▶ 6. Use a rubber band to make a geometric figure on the geoboard. Teach your child to measure the area of the figure in units. One unit equals one small square (the space between four nails).

▶ 7. Stretch a rubber band down the center nails. Make a pattern on one side of the band. Your child should make the symmetrical shape on the other side of the band.

Learn at Home, Grade 2

SCIENCE (Identifying Rocks)

▶ 1. **Math:** Let your child feel how heavy a 1-ounce weight is. Then, have your child to pick up each rock from his/her collection and estimate if it weighs less or more than an ounce or if it is about the same. Have your child sort the rocks into three piles: those that (he/she thinks) weigh less than an ounce, about the same as an ounce and more an ounce. Using a balance scale, your child should weigh each rock to confirm his/her prediction. Teach your child to read the measurements carefully.

▶ 2. To identify minerals, a geologist will rub a rock on a square of unglazed tile. The color of the streak may help determine the minerals present. Have your child rub rocks from his/her collection across the back of a piece of ceramic tile to see if they leave a streak.

▶ 3. A mineralogist by the name of Friedrich Mohs developed a hardness scale of minerals. The scale lists ten minerals from the softest to the hardest. His scale is used to help identify minerals. Draw three columns on a sheet of paper and write *Soft, Medium* and *Hard* at the top. Your child will use three "tools" to check the hardness: a fingernail, a penny or a steel penknife and a glass plate. Your child will first try scratching every rock with his/her fingernail. If the fingernail leaves a scratch on the rock, it is soft. Your child should put the rock in the *Soft* column. Next, your child will scratch the remaining rocks with a copper penny or penknife. If any of the rocks were marked by the penny or penknife, your child should put them in the *Medium* column. Finally, your child will test the remaining rocks with a glass plate. If the rock scratches the glass, put it in the *Hard* column.

Nonfiction Books

The characters below need a book that will show them how to bake cakes. "How to" books are also called **Nonfiction**. These books are not make-believe, they are true.

Circle the book titles that are nonfiction.

The Cat in the Hat

Treasure Island

Building a Doghouse

The Ugly Duckling

History of Baseball

Where the Wild Things Are

How to Make Doll Clothes

Alice in Wonderland

Peter Rabbit

The Incredible Journey

Animals in the Jungle

Baking Made Easy

Now, decorate the cake!

Learn at Home, Grade 2

How Many?

Find the shapes and **color** them using the code.

▲ **red** ⬤ **blue** ◆ **yellow**

⬭ **green** ▬ **orange** ▬ **black**

	Language Skills	**Spelling**	**Reading**
Monday	**Writing Process** During the remaining weeks, allow your child to work with relative freedom with the writing process. Try to follow the five steps of writing. *See* Language Skills, Week 32. As you monitor your child's writing, encourage the practicing of writing skills learned. **Writing prompt**: *Pretend you are going to immigrate to another country.* Have your child brainstorm a prewriting activity and write a journal, letter or story.	Pretest your child on these spelling words: nice then would with once close every many saw goes With your child, read over these commonly misspelled words several times.	**Antonyms and Synonyms** Teach your child antonyms. Have your child brainstorm and write a list of antonyms. Have your child complete **Who's Afraid?** (p. 317). **Caldecott Medal Award Books 1998:** With your child, read and discuss *Rapunzel* by Paul Zelinsky. Review the story elements. Examine and talk about the illustrations. Have your child complete a copy of **Caldecott Critique** (p. 318).
Tuesday	Have your child write a rough draft (or first draft) of the story idea from yesterday.	Have your child write the spelling words in sentences.	Play "The Antonym Card Game." *See* Reading, Week 32, number 2. **1997:** With your child, read and discuss *Golem* by David Wisniewski. Review the five story elements. Examine and talk about the cut-paper illustrations. Have your child complete a copy of **Caldecott Critique** (p. 318).
Wednesday	Have your child revise his/her own story.	Have your child spell each word aloud in a silly voice. Have your child complete **Keep Control of These** (p. 316).	Teach your child synonyms. With your child, brainstorm words with similar meanings. Have your child complete **Flower Fun** (p. 319). **1996:** With your child, read and discuss *Officer Buckle and Gloria* by Peggy Rathmann. Review the five story elements. Examine and talk about the bright full-color illustrations. Have your child complete a copy of **Caldecott Critique** (p. 318).
Thursday	Edit your child's story with him/her.	Have your child write a story that begins with "Once upon a time. . . ." Have him/her include and underline each of this week's spelling words.	Teach your child to use a thesaurus. Create a list of ten words and have your child find the words in the thesaurus, then write a synonym for each word. **1995:** With your child, read and discuss *Smoky Night* by Eve Bunting and David Diaz. Review the five story elements. Examine and talk about the acrylic and collage illustrations. Have your child complete a copy of **Caldecott Critique** (p. 318).
Friday	Have your child publish his/her story in the correct form. For example, if he/she chose to write a letter, it should be in letter form on stationery.	Give your child the final spelling test.	**1994:** With your child, read and discuss *Grandfather's Journey* by Allen Say. Review the five story elements. Examine and talk about the watercolor illustrations. Have your child complete a copy of **Caldecott Critique** (p. 318).

Learn at Home, Grade 2

Math	Science	Social Studies
Money Review coin values. Give your child practice adding coins up to 99¢. *See* Math, Week 32, number 1.	Have your child organize his/her rock collection. He/she could sort the rocks into egg cartons. Have your child write a number inside each cup of the carton to label the rock. On a sheet of paper, have him/her write the corresponding number with a description of the rock in that cup. Have him/her refer to a book with colored pictures to help identify the rocks.	Where did your family come from? Discuss immigration. With your child, read and discuss pages 1–12 in the book *Where Did Your Family Come From?: A Book About Immigrants* by Melvin and Gilda Berger. Learn about immigrants and the process for becoming a citizen of the United States.
Prepare a play store with real objects or magazine pictures. Put a price tag on each object. Provide your child with real money to "buy" single objects. **Extension:** Have your child choose two or three products, add the cost and purchase the objects. *See* Math, Week 32, number 2.	Have your child measure, weigh and describe each rock in his/her collection accurately.	Visit or contact a government office to inquire about obtaining a passport or visa.
Teach your child to write money values correctly. *See* Math, Week 32, numbers 3 and 4.	Have your child measure the size of the rocks in the collection by placing each rock next to a centimeter ruler. To measure circumference, wrap a string around the rock; then measure the string against a centimeter ruler.	Have your child finish reading *Where Did Your Family Come From?* and learn about Boris, Maria, Rosa and Chang and how they all immigrated to our country.
See Math, Week 32, numbers 5 and 6. Have your child complete **Here's Your Order** (p. 320).	Visit a rock shop. It may be fun to browse and observe a variety of rocks and minerals. Your child may also purchase rocks to add to his/her collection. Ask the salesperson about a good place to go rock hunting in the area.	With your child, research your family's history and where they came from.
See Math, Week 32, numbers 7 and 8. Have your child complete **So Many Choices!** (p. 321)	Have your child make a "reading rock." *See* Science, Week 32, number 1.	With your child, create a family tree showing the names of your relatives.

TEACHING SUGGESTIONS AND ACTIVITIES

LANGUAGE SKILLS (Writing Process)

BACKGROUND
The five steps of the writing process are prewriting, drafting, revising, editing and publishing.

Prewriting: (Brain Drain) Brainstorming about the topic. This may include a topic web, flowchart for a story, etc.

Drafting: (Sloppy Copy) Writing the paper or story.

Revising: (Goof Proof) Going over the completed paper and making changes.

Editing: (Fix 'n' Nix) Proofreading and changing the paper. This might be done with the help of someone else.

Publishing: (Neat Sheet) Writing the final copy of the paper.

READING (Caldecott Medal Award Books)

BACKGROUND
In the next 3 weeks, your child will read, compare and evaluate Caldecott Medal Award Books. The Caldecott Medal is awarded annually to the artist of the most distinguished American picture book for children.

▶ 1. The project will begin with the most recent award book and continue backward through the years. After reading each winner, have your child complete a **Caldecott Critique** (p. 318). Make fifteen copies and staple them together to form a book.

Antonyms and Synonyms

BACKGROUND
Antonyms are words of opposite meanings. **Examples:** *hot* and *cold, up* and *down*
Synonyms are words that mean the same thing or nearly the same thing. **Examples:** *small* and *little, under* and *below*

▶ 2. **The Antonym Card Game:** Take the antonym list from Monday and write each word on a different index card. Shuffle the cards and give each person five cards. Place the remaining cards facedown. Turn over the top card. The player with the matching antonym card takes the card and places the pair in front of him/herself. The next card is turned up and the game continues. If no player has a match, the next card is turned over. The player that matches all his/her antonym pairs first, wins the game.

MATH (Money)

▶ 1. In an envelope, put an index card and some change (pennies, nickels and dimes). Tell your child to count the change and use the index card to design a stamp worth that amount of money. You may want to have some stamps available as examples. To coordinate this activity with Social Studies, have your child select a famous person or well-known event to draw on the stamp.

Learn at Home, Grade 2

2. On the chalkboard, write a 2-digit addition problem using money. **Example:**

    $$\begin{array}{r} \$ \quad .25 \\ \underline{.53} \\ \$ \quad . \end{array}$$

    Point out the placement of the dollar sign and the decimal point. Give your child several dimes and pennies. Have your child count out twenty-five cents and fifty-three cents and add. Create a worksheet adding values that total under a dollar.

3. Write $ .07 on the chalkboard and have your child read the amount. Discuss the purpose of the zero in the tens place. (Why can't you write $ .7?) Display a group of coins totalling under $ .10. Have your child write the value correctly.

4. Introduce the cents (¢) symbol. Explain that a decimal point is not needed.

5. Have your child count change orally (including quarters). Demonstrate how to count the larger coins first. **Example:** Begin with one quarter. Say, "twenty-five cents." As you add two dimes say, "thirty-five cents, forty-five cents." Add a nickel. Say, "fifty cents." Add three pennies. Say, "fifty-one cents, fifty-two cents, fifty-three cents" as you add each coin to the count.

6. Challenge your child to think of all the coin combinations that total 25¢.

7. Introduce your child to the dollar bill as an equivalent to one-hundred cents. Have your child count out 100 pennies. Have your child make 100 cents using different combinations of coins. Teach your child how to write $1.00. Have your child explain how a dollar is written differently from writing only cents.

8. On the chalkboard, write a 3-digit addition problem using money. **Example:**

    $$\begin{array}{r} \$ \, 4.07 \\ \underline{+ \, 3.42} \\ \$ \quad . \end{array}$$

    Point out the placement of the dollar sign and the decimal point. Give your child several dollars, dimes and pennies. Have your child count out $4.07 and $3.42. and add, starting with the pennies. Create a worksheet adding values that total under $10.00.

SCIENCE (Identifying Rocks)

1. **Art:** Choose a large smooth rock. Wash and dry the rock. Set it on newspaper and decorate it. Acrylic paints, brushes, markers, glue, scissors, yarn and buttons will transform the rock into a "reading rock." A reading rock is useful when there is no one else available to listen to your child read.

315

Keep Control of These

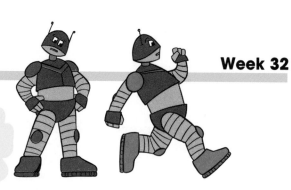

nice	every	with	many	then
once	saw	would	close	goes

Write the spelling words on the lines. Then, use the numbered letters to solve the code.

1. All

$\underset{1}{\rule{1cm}{0.4pt}}\ \rule{1cm}{0.4pt}\ \rule{1cm}{0.4pt}\ \underset{2}{\rule{1cm}{0.4pt}}\ \rule{1cm}{0.4pt}$

2. Only one time

$\underset{3}{\rule{1cm}{0.4pt}}\ \rule{1cm}{0.4pt}\ \underset{4}{\rule{1cm}{0.4pt}}\ \rule{1cm}{0.4pt}$

3. Opposite of comes

$\underset{5}{\rule{1cm}{0.4pt}}\ \rule{1cm}{0.4pt}\ \rule{1cm}{0.4pt}\ \rule{1cm}{0.4pt}$

4. A tool for cutting

$\rule{1cm}{0.4pt}\ \underset{6}{\rule{1cm}{0.4pt}}\ \rule{1cm}{0.4pt}$

5. Opposite of open

$\rule{1cm}{0.4pt}\ \rule{1cm}{0.4pt}\ \rule{1cm}{0.4pt}\ \rule{1cm}{0.4pt}\ \rule{1cm}{0.4pt}$

6. Next, or at that time

$\underset{7}{\rule{1cm}{0.4pt}}\ \rule{1cm}{0.4pt}\ \rule{1cm}{0.4pt}\ \underset{8}{\rule{1cm}{0.4pt}}$

7. Pleasing and agreeable

$\rule{1cm}{0.4pt}\ \underset{9}{\rule{1cm}{0.4pt}}\ \rule{1cm}{0.4pt}\ \rule{1cm}{0.4pt}$

8. Was willing to

$\rule{1cm}{0.4pt}\ \rule{1cm}{0.4pt}\ \underset{10}{\rule{1cm}{0.4pt}}\ \underset{11}{\rule{1cm}{0.4pt}}\ \underset{12}{\rule{1cm}{0.4pt}}$

9. She will go ____ her mother.

$\underset{13}{\rule{1cm}{0.4pt}}\ \rule{1cm}{0.4pt}\ \rule{1cm}{0.4pt}\ \underset{14}{\rule{1cm}{0.4pt}}$

10. Several

$\rule{1cm}{0.4pt}\ \underset{15}{\rule{1cm}{0.4pt}}\ \rule{1cm}{0.4pt}\ \underset{16}{\rule{1cm}{0.4pt}}$

$\underset{4}{\rule{0.7cm}{0.4pt}}\ \underset{3}{\rule{0.7cm}{0.4pt}}\ \underset{8}{\rule{0.7cm}{0.4pt}}\ \underset{5}{\rule{0.7cm}{0.4pt}}\ \underset{2}{\rule{0.7cm}{0.4pt}}\ \underset{15}{\rule{0.7cm}{0.4pt}}\ \underset{7}{\rule{0.7cm}{0.4pt}}\ \underset{10}{\rule{0.7cm}{0.4pt}}\ \underset{11}{\rule{0.7cm}{0.4pt}}\ \underset{15}{\rule{0.7cm}{0.4pt}}\ \underset{7}{\rule{0.7cm}{0.4pt}}\ \underset{9}{\rule{0.7cm}{0.4pt}}\ \underset{3}{\rule{0.7cm}{0.4pt}}\ \underset{8}{\rule{0.7cm}{0.4pt}}\ \underset{6}{\rule{0.7cm}{0.4pt}}$ **!**

$\underset{16}{\rule{0.7cm}{0.4pt}}\ \underset{3}{\rule{0.7cm}{0.4pt}}\ \underset{10}{\rule{0.7cm}{0.4pt}}\ \ \underset{13}{\rule{0.7cm}{0.4pt}}\ \underset{2}{\rule{0.7cm}{0.4pt}}\ \underset{3}{\rule{0.7cm}{0.4pt}}\ \underset{7}{\rule{0.7cm}{0.4pt}}\ \underset{1}{\rule{0.7cm}{0.4pt}}\ \ \underset{15}{\rule{0.7cm}{0.4pt}}\ \underset{11}{\rule{0.7cm}{0.4pt}}\ \underset{11}{\rule{0.7cm}{0.4pt}}\ \ \underset{7}{\rule{0.7cm}{0.4pt}}\ \underset{14}{\rule{0.7cm}{0.4pt}}\ \underset{1}{\rule{0.7cm}{0.4pt}}$

$\underset{13}{\rule{0.7cm}{0.4pt}}\ \underset{3}{\rule{0.7cm}{0.4pt}}\ \underset{2}{\rule{0.7cm}{0.4pt}}\ \underset{12}{\rule{0.7cm}{0.4pt}}\ \underset{6}{\rule{0.7cm}{0.4pt}}\ \ \underset{4}{\rule{0.7cm}{0.4pt}}\ \underset{3}{\rule{0.7cm}{0.4pt}}\ \underset{2}{\rule{0.7cm}{0.4pt}}\ \underset{2}{\rule{0.7cm}{0.4pt}}\ \underset{1}{\rule{0.7cm}{0.4pt}}\ \underset{4}{\rule{0.7cm}{0.4pt}}\ \underset{7}{\rule{0.7cm}{0.4pt}}\ \underset{11}{\rule{0.7cm}{0.4pt}}\ \underset{16}{\rule{0.7cm}{0.4pt}}$ **!**

Learn at Home, Grade 2

Who's Afraid?

Help Frog and Toad escape from the snake. Read the two words in each space. If the words are antonyms, color the space green. Do not color the other spaces.

go
stop

large
small

wide
narrow

dinner
supper

scared
afraid

brave
afraid

shut
close

happy
sad

dark
light

fall
rise

outside
inside

higher
lower

leap
jump

none
all

tremble
shake

fast
quick

happy
glad

stones
rocks

look
see

top
bottom

covers
blankets

friend
pal

down
up

shout
whisper

loud
soft

under
over

Toad's House

Caldecott Critique

1. Title _____

2. Author _____

3. Illustrator _____

4. Caldecott Award in _____

5. Art Technique Used in Illustrations _____

6. I liked/disliked the illustrations because _____

_____

_____

7. I liked/disliked the storyline because _____

_____

_____

8. My favorite part was _____

_____

_____

Flower Fun

Write the words from the box that are **synonyms** for the words in the flower pots.

yell
_____

pick   start   easy   sky
kind   rain   afraid fall
close   hard   scream awake
put   whisper dirt   tired

begin
_____

scared
_____

drop
_____

nice
_____

sleepy
_____

soil
_____

near
_____

place
_____

difficult
_____

Here's Your Order

Count the money on each tray. **Write** the name of the food that costs that amount.

hamburger.. **$2.45** hot dog......... **$1.77** sandwich.... **$1.55**

milk .... **$.64** soda pop...... **$1.26** milkshake.... **$1.89**

cake........... **$2.85** pie............... **$2.25** sundae......... **$.95**

_____

_____

_____

Learn at Home, Grade 2

You want to buy 3 different items in the hobby store. You have $16.00. **Write** all the different combinations of items you can buy using the entire $16.00.

1._____ 1._____ 1._____ 1._____

2._____ 2._____ 2._____ 2._____

3._____ 3._____ 3._____ 3._____

1._____ 1._____ 1._____ 1._____

2._____ 2._____ 2._____ 2._____

3._____ 3._____ 3._____ 3._____

	Language Skills	**Spelling**	**Reading**
Monday	Read over your child's drafts from the beginning of the year, middle of the year and current writing. Look for improvements and discuss them with your child. Look for areas that have not improved and teach a mini-lesson.	Pretest your child on these spelling words: off than people new going went again some another want Discuss the meaning of each word, its vowel sounds and any hints for remembering how to spell it.	Help your child choose a topic for a project. Visit the library and research necessary information for the project. Have your child work on the project throughout the week. **1993:** With your child, read and discuss *Mirette on the High Wire* by Emily Arnold McCully. Review the story elements. Examine and talk about the watercolor illustrations. Have your child complete a copy of **Caldecott Critique** (p. 318).
Tuesday	Have your child write a sequel to the book, *Tuesday. See* Reading plans for today. **Writing prompt:** *Imagine what might happen "next Tuesday, at 7:58 p.m." when the pigs leave the barn.*	Have your child write the spelling words in sentences.	Have your child continue working on his/her research project. Remind your child to write the information in his/her own words. **1992:** With your child, read and discuss *Tuesday* by David Weisner. Review the five story elements. Examine and talk about the watercolor illustrations. Have your child complete a copy of **Caldecott Critique** (p. 318).
Wednesday	Teach your child to use a word-processing program to publish an edited story if you have one available to you. Otherwise have your child type it on a typewriter. With your child, choose a form of publishing from **Bookmaking** (p. 326).	Have your child spell each word aloud as he/she writes the letters on a soft bed sheet using his/her index finger as a pencil. Have your child complete **Don't Stand in the Fog!** (p. 327).	Have your child continue working on the research project. **1991:** With your child, read and discuss *Black and White* by David Macaulay. Review the five story elements happening in each of the four stories in the book. Examine and talk about the collage and watercolor illustrations. Have your child complete a copy of **Caldecott Critique** (p. 318).
Thursday	Have your child finish typing his/her story.	Have your child create a code giving every letter of the alphabet a different symbol. Then, have him/her write the spelling words using this code.	Have your child complete the research project and write a report about it. **1990:** With your child, read and discuss *Lon Po Po: A Red Riding Hood Story From China* by Ed Young. With your child, compare it to the traditional Little Red Riding Hood tale. Examine and talk about the watercolor and pastel illustrations. Have your child complete a copy of **Caldecott Critique** (p. 318).
Friday	An important part of writing is having a real audience. Have your child think about who he/she would like to write a story for. Have your child write letters, posters and books for special people.	Give your child the final spelling test.	Have your child present the project and report to family or friends. **1989:** With your child, read and discuss *Song and Dance Man* by Karen Ackerman and Steven Gammell. Discuss the five story elements and the term *vaudeville.* Compare how is it different and similar to today's entertainment. Have your child complete a copy of **Caldecott Critique** (p. 318).

Learn at Home, Grade 2

Math	Science	Social Studies
Measurement Allow your child to study and compare a ruler, yardstick, meterstick and tape measure. Ask him/her questions about the numbers and spaces on the "tools." What is the meaning of these marks and what types of things could you measure with one of these tools? *See* Math, Week 33, numbers 1–3. Have your child complete **Jumping Jelly Beans** (p. 328).	**Electricity** Find out what your child already knows about electricity. Have him/her write in his/her Science Log a description of how a light works.	**Transportation** Help your child name ways of transportation that move people and goods. Sort the list into different modes of transportation: land, water and air. *See* Social Studies, Week 33.
Using a ruler or meter/yardstick, teach your child to measure the length of several objects in and around his/her desk. *See* Math, Week 33, numbers 4 and 5. Have your child record the name of the object measured and its length in inches or centimeters on lined paper.	Have your child write a creative story, making up an explanation for what causes a light or television to work.	With your child, read and discuss *Things That Go: A Traveling Alphabet* by Seymour Reit. Add to the list any other means of transportation. Research other modes at the library or on the Internet.
Assess your child's ability with a ruler. Using a tape measure in inches or centimeters, work together to measure parts of your child's body. Measure around his/her head, the length of an arm or leg and the distance from head to toe. *See* Math, Week 33, number 6. Have your child record the measured lengths on a sketch of him/herself.	Static electricity is similar to current electricity which will be discussed next week. *See* Science, Week 33, number 1 for an explanation. Create static electricity with a comb. Have your child complete **Unpeppering the Salt** (p. 330).	With your child, classify the different modes of transportation on the list by the purpose it serves. **Examples:** pleasure, transporting goods, transporting people, etc.
Have your child compare the volume of different liquid measures. Ahead of time you will need to save cup, pint, quart and gallon containers. Label each container clearly. *See* Math, Week 33, number 7. Have your child complete **Liquid Limits** (p. 329).	Static electricity is produced when you rub an object in one direction. *See* Science, Week 33, number 2. Have your child complete **Dancing Parsley** (p. 331).	Have your child create a transportation collage using pictures from magazines, newspapers, catalogs, etc.
Show your child what happens to the mercury in a thermometer when it is heated and cooled. Discuss the units of measure on the thermometer and why standard units are necessary. Teach your child to read the temperature in Celsius and Fahrenheit. *See* Math, Week 33, numbers 8–11.	Have your child cut out bug, fish or snake shapes from tissue paper. Lay two or three shapes on a flat surface. Then, have your child rub a plastic ruler over a piece of silk or wool in one direction. He/she should then pass the ruler over the shapes and observe the effects.	Have your child imagine what would be different in your lives without the development of transportation. Have your child draw a picture of him/herself in a world without cars, planes, trains and buses.

323

TEACHING SUGGESTIONS AND ACTIVITIES

MATH (Measurement)

BACKGROUND

Measurement is a broad category which may include linear measurement, volume, weight, time and temperature. When your child is introduced to a measurement concept, it is usually with non-standard units. Soon he/she changes to the American standard units of measurement, such as inches, pounds and degrees Fahrenheit. You may also want to teach him/her metric units, such as meters, grams and degrees Celsius. Unless you live where metric is used more often, concentrate on American standard units. Look for opportunities in your shopping and daily activities to explore and discuss measurement concepts.

▶   1.   Have your child compare inches on a ruler, yardstick and tape measure. Lead him/her to discover that an inch is always the same. Have your child show with his/her index finger and thumb the approximate length of an inch. Have an "Inch Scavenger Hunt" by having your child find some objects that measure approximately 1 inch.

▶   2.   Repeat the above activity with centimeters.

▶   3.   Discuss when a tape measure would be more appropriate than a ruler.

▶   4.   Draw an 8-inch line on the chalkboard. Show your child how to align the beginning of the ruler with the beginning of the line. Teach your child to read the ruler. Draw several lines on the board for your child to measure with a ruler. Observe your child carefully to make sure he/she is holding and reading the ruler correctly.

▶   5.   Make a worksheet listing objects in the classroom. Have your child measure objects and record the length in inches and centimeters.

▶   6.   Discuss ways that a person is measured (height, weight, circumference). Discuss units of measurement for each. Weigh your child and measure his/her height. Keep a record (line graph) of his/her height and weight over time.

▶   7.   Provide volume containers and a "liquid" substance for your child to explore. Rice, sand, water and flour can each be poured easily from one container to another. Be sure to prepare the work area for spills. Label a teaspoon, tablespoon, cup, pint, quart and gallon. Read each label with your child. Allow your child to pour the substance back and forth among the containers repeatedly. After quite a bit of exploration, ask your child to find out how many of each smaller container fill each larger container.

▶   8.   Show your child a variety of thermometers (inside, outside, meat, candy and body thermometers). Discuss their uses and how to read them.

▶   9.   Have your child draw five large outdoor thermometers on a sheet of paper. Tell your child to read the outside thermometer every day at the same time. Your child should write the date under each thermometer and then color in the mercury line to the number indicated that day.

▶   10.   Have your child compare indoor/outdoor temperatures daily.

▶   11.   Take your child's body temperature. Discuss "normal." Have your child record temperature daily to see if he/she runs a close to "normal" temperature (98.6° F). Discuss when a person is ill what happens to body temperature.

Learn at Home, Grade 2

SCIENCE (Electricity)

BACKGROUND

Electricity is an important form of energy. It produces light and heat. It provides power for household and industrial machines. The power produced by electricity enables us to have computers, televisions and radios. Electricity consists of a flow of tiny particles called electrons, the smallest units of electricity. Most energy is produced by generators situated in power plants. Thick wires carry the electricity from the plants to the users, such as homes, factories and schools. Teach your child to be very careful around electricity since it is very powerful.

▶ 1. Static electricity is related to current electricity. They are both made up of the same particles, but static electricity does not move like current electricity. Static electricity is not used as a source of power. Static electricity can be created when you walk across a carpet or comb your hair on a dry day. These actions create positively and negatively charged particles that crackle harmlessly.

▶ 2. In the Dancing Parsley experiment (p. 331), your child placed a charge on the cup. Have your child rub the cup back and forth on his/her hair and clothing and notice the results. The back and forth action removes the charge placed on the cup.

SOCIAL STUDIES (Transportation)

BACKGROUND

Transportation involves moving people and goods from one place to another. Its development has made the world a smaller, more united place. With the development of vehicles, people and goods can now travel far and quickly. Now, we can exchange, buy and sell goods and foodstuffs with people all over the world and become aware of the diversity of people that make up this world. How does advanced transportation make the world a better and a more interesting place?

Bookmaking

Index Card Books

Index card books are simple to make and easy to use. Use several 5" X 7" pieces of colored posterboard for the covers. Two holes can be punched in the left side of all the cards, and covers and notebook rings can be inserted. The first page is lined for writing the title and author. Page two will be blank which will be perfect for an illustration of the text on page three. Continue in the same pattern throughout the book. More cards can easily be added for longer stories. The title and author's name should be written on the front cover and may be decorated using colored markers. You might want to make some index card books for the writing center. Extra cards, notebook rings and a hole punch could also be kept there.

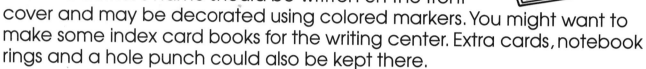

Word Processors

Word processors make publishing easy. After writing your rough drafts and making revisions, dictate your stories to someone. Print out a copy. Make a cover with graphics imported from software.

Scrolls

Scrolls are wonderful for publishing poems and proclamations. First, write your poems or proclamations on writing paper and glue them to construction paper. (Be careful not to use too much glue because it may make the paper too stiff to roll nicely.) After the glue has dried, roll the paper from the bottom and tie the scroll with fancy ribbon. Heavy holiday gift wrapping paper is nice for fancier scrolls with appropriate holiday writings. Glue the poems on the back.

326

Learn at Home, Grade 2

Don't Stand in the Fog!

people   off   want   new
again   going
than   some   another   went

Unscramble the letters to **write** a spelling word.

1. g a i a n   _again_
2. e t n w   _went_
3. s e m o   _some_
4. e p o e l p   _people_
5. n o i g g   _going_
6. e w n   _new_
7. n o a h r t e   _another_

8. f f o   _off_
9. a w n t   _want_
10. h t n a   _than_

Complete the puzzle.

Across
2. A few
5. One more
7. Do a second time
9. Opposite of old

Down
1. Persons
3. Opposite of on
4. Wish to have
6. She would rather swim _____ ride a bike.
8. Opposite of coming
10. Did go

Jumping Jelly Beans

Use an inch ruler to measure the line segments. **Write** the total length on each candy jar.

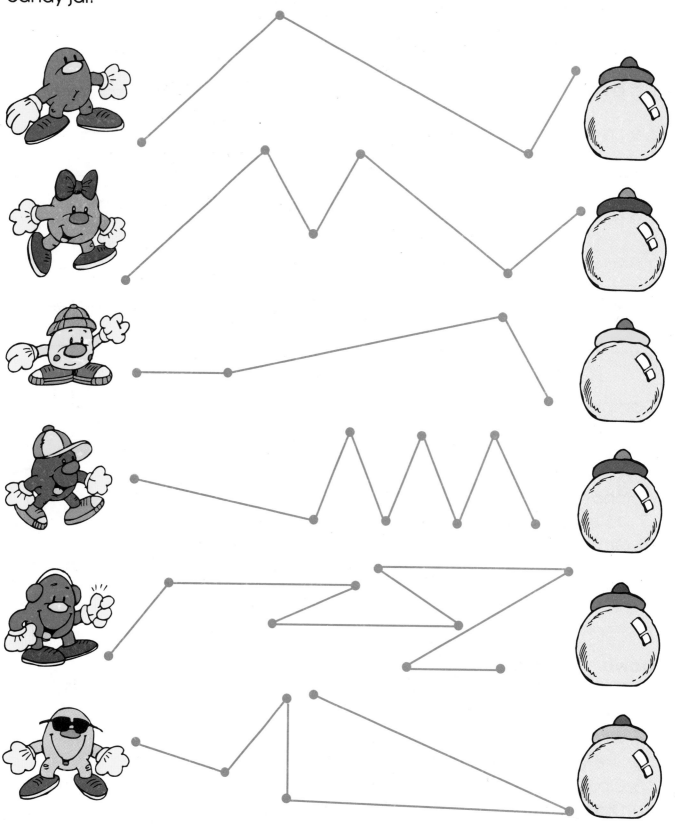

Learn at Home, Grade 2

Liquid Limits

Draw a line from the containers on the left to the containers on the right that will hold the same amount of liquid. **Hint:** 2 pints = 1 quart

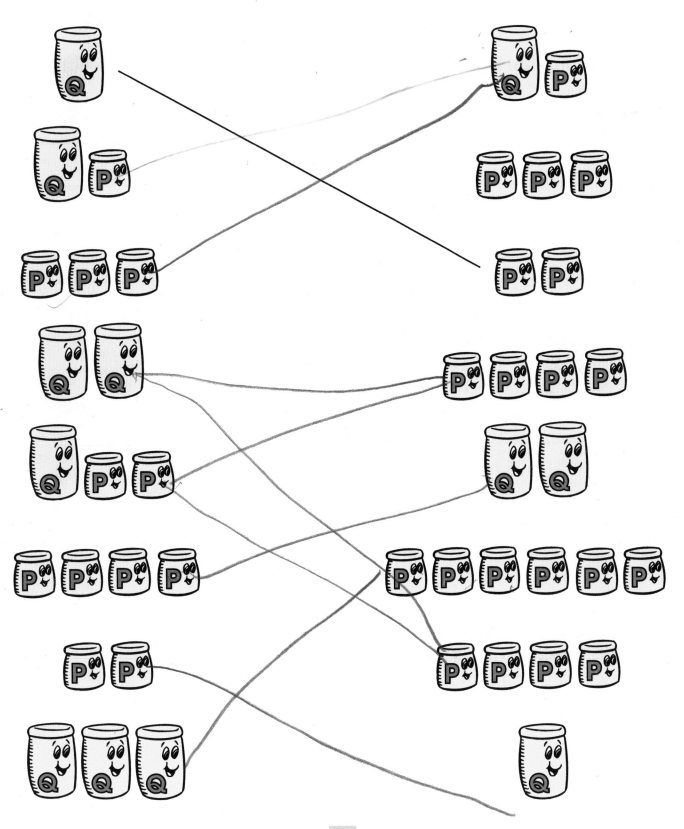

Unpeppering the Salt

You need a teaspoon of salt on a sheet of paper. Place a pinch of pepper on top of the salt. Stir them together.

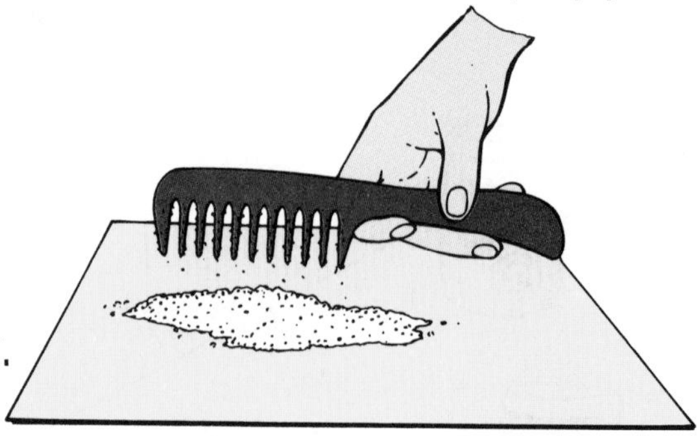

Unpeppering the Salt
Comb your hair 20 to 30 times.
Hold the comb over the salt-and-pepper mix.
What happened?

_____

_____

_____

Brush your hair 20 to 30 times.
Hold the brush over the salt-and pepper mix.
Did more pepper jump onto the comb or the brush?

_____

Brush your hair again.
Hold the brush over the salt and pepper.
How high can you make the pepper jump? _____

Rub your comb on a sweater or a shiny blouse or shirt.
Rub only one way about 20 to 30 times.
Now, does the comb make the pepper jump? _____

Rub the comb on your arm only one way.
Now, does the comb make the pepper jump? _____

Dancing Parsley

There is a lot of electricity in nature. This is called static electricity. Static electricity cannot be used to run machines.

This is one way you can make static electricity:
1. Put one pinch of parsley flakes in a foam cup.
2. Rub the cup against your hair, your arm, a piece of silk or a piece of wool.
   Rub only one way.
   Rub about 30 times.
3. Look inside the cup.
   What happened to the flakes?

_____

_____

_____

_____

Try This
Rub the cup against something else.
What happened?

_____

_____

Think About It
Where else do you see static electricity?

_____

_____

	Language Skills	**Spelling**	**Reading**
Monday	If you have access to the Internet, you can find kid's pages that provide an audience for writing. Have your child write an e-mail to someone. If you don't know anyone on e-mail, there are many sites that will hook your child up with a pen pal.	Pretest your child on these spelling words: said are because little very have were friend coming they Discuss the meaning of each word, its vowel sounds and any hints for remembering how to spell it.	**Homophones** Teach your child about homophones. *See* Reading, Week 34, number 1. Write the words *two, to* and *too* on the chalkboard. Write three sentences to demonstrate the usage of each of the words. **1988:** With your child, read and discuss *Owl Moon* by Jane Yolen and John Schoenherr. Review the five story elements and examine the illustrations. Have your child complete a copy of **Caldecott Critique** (p. 318).
Tuesday	Have your child design his/her own Web site.	Have your child write the spelling words in sentences.	Write ten single words on index cards (one word from ten homophone pairs). Show one word at a time to your child. Make up a sentence using that word. Have your child make up a sentence using its homophone. **1987:** With your child, read and discuss *Hey, Al* by Arthur Yorinks and Richard Eglielski. Review the five story elements Discuss the illustrations. Have your child complete a copy of **Caldecott Critique** (p. 318).
Wednesday	Have your child check his/her e-mail and write a response.	Have your child spell each word aloud while tapping two keys on the piano—one key for consonants and another key for vowels. Have your child complete **Wrap It Up With These** (p. 336).	Write four pairs of homophones on the chalkboard and discuss the meaning of each word. Fold a 12" x 18" sheet of paper into eight sections. Have your child copy one word in each section and draw pictures illustrating the meanings of the homophones. **1982:** With your child, read and discuss *Jumanji* by Chris Van Allsburg. You could rent the movie as well. Have your child complete a copy of **Caldecott Critique** (p. 318).
Thursday	Find a children's chat room on the Internet. Visit it with your child.	Have your child write silly sentences using a pair of homophones with each spelling word. **Example:** The big hare had very little hair.	Play a homophone game. *See* Reading, Week 34, numbers 2 and 3. **1970:** With your child, read and discuss *Sylvester and the Magic Pebble* by William Steig. Review the five story elements and examine and talk about the illustrations. Have your child complete a copy of **Caldecott Critique** (p. 318).
Friday	Look in magazines and newspapers for writing contests and opportunities to have your child's writing published. The magazines *Highlights* and *Cricket* often publish children's writing.	Give your child the final spelling test.	Find different older Caldecott Medal books at the library, such as **1949:** *The Big Snow* by Berta and Elmer Hader; **1963:** *The Snowy Day* by Ezra Jack Keats; **1967:** *Sam, Bangs and Moonshine* by Evaline Ness or **1972:** *One Fine Day* by Nonny Hogrogian. With your child, read and discuss the storylines and compare the illustrations with the more recent winners.

Learn at Home, Grade 2

Math	**Science**	**Social Studies**
Problem Solving Review different forms of measurement. Compare and list standard and non-standard units of measurements. **Examples:** inches, cups, pounds, minutes and standard paper clips, pencils, Unifix cubes and non-standard With your child, read *Measuring Penny* by Loreen Leedy. Discuss and compare the standard and non-standard units Lisa used to measure her dog, Penny.	**Complete Circuits** Describe the parts of a circuit to your child. *See* Science, Week 34, number 1.	**Field Trip** Visit the library and research the history of transportation. Help your child begin to create a pictorial time line about transportation in the United States from 1700 to 2000.
Present an addition and subtraction story problem. Have your child name the clues and the operation needed to solve the problem. Repeat with other one and two operation story problems.	Help your child make a complete circuit. *See* Science, Week 34, number 2. Have your child draw a complete circuit in his/her Science Log. Have your child complete **Complete Circuits** (p. 338).	Have your child continue the study of the history of transportation and the pictorial time line.
Problem Solving: Help your child read and solve problems. *See* Math, Week 34, number 1. Have your child complete **Problems! Problems! Problems!** (p. 337).	Explore different arrangements of the three parts of the circuit. Have your child draw a picture in his/her Science Log of any arrangements that light the bulb.	Discuss the problems that engine powered transportation has created. With your child, read *Just a Dream* by Chris Van Allsburg. Suggest solutions to our transportation problems, such as traffic jams, pollution, traffic safety, exhaustion of energy sources, etc.
With your child, read and discuss *Betcha!* by Stuart J. Murphy. Discuss the methods the boys used to estimate. Have your child complete some of the estimating activities at the end of the book.	A conductor is anything an electric current can flow through. Explore a variety of objects to determine whether they are conductors. *See* Science, Week 34, number 3. Have your child complete **Conductors and Non-Conductors** (p. 339).	Have your child complete the history of transportation time line. Compare past and present modes of transportation and their affects on society.
Teach your child to estimate answers to 2-digit addition problems before solving them. *See* Math, Week 34, number 2.	Discuss how life might have been different 300 years ago when people did not use electricity. With your child, read about the work of Michael Faraday, Count Volta, Benjamin Franklin, Thomas Edison and Samuel Morse.	With your child, imagine what would be different in your lives without transportation. Have your child draw a picture of him/herself in a world without cars, planes, trains and buses.

TEACHING SUGGESTIONS AND ACTIVITIES

READING (Homophones)

BACKGROUND

Homophones are words which sound alike but are spelled differently and have different meanings. *See* number 1 for examples.

▶ 1. For your convenience, some homophones are listed below.

pair, pear	whole, hole	dear, deer	no, know	tail, tale	passed, past
week, weak	tow, toe	I, eye	hour, our	peace, piece	knead, need
ate, eight	nose, knows	some, sum	hare, hair	write, right	weight, wait
not, knot	do, due	heard, herd	haul, hall	mail, male	pause, paws

▶ 2. **Game:** Write the individual word of each of twenty-four homophone pairs on an index card. Deal twelve cards to each player. Place the remaining cards upside-down on the table. Turn over the top card. If the first player is holding the homophone of the faceup card, he/she may discard it, turn over the next card and continue playing. If he/she does not have the homophone, he/she picks up the top card of the pile and play goes to the other player. The player to discard his/her hand first is the winner of the game.

▶ 3. Play "Concentration" with the homophone pair cards.

MATH (Problem Solving)

BACKGROUND

Problem solving is an integral part of mathematics. Problem solving teaches reasoning, critical thinking skills and other strategies essential in mathematics. Problem solving also provides your child with a reason to use current math skills, such as finding patterns, using manipulatives and graphs, choosing an operation and estimating.

▶ 1. Based on the information on the table, answer the questions below.
   Push-ups

Brad	Jen	Lynn	Dave	Todd	Jo
28	30	33	26	34	31

   Which pair of children did the most push-ups, Brad and Todd, Dave and Lynn or Jen and Jo? Which child did the most? Least? What was the difference between those two? Who did three more push-ups than Jen? Who did six less than Todd?

Estimation

BACKGROUND

Your child may be uncomfortable with estimation because he/she wants to give the right answer. Help your child understand that estimating is not making a wild guess but involves a reasonable, "educated" guess. Never make your child feel his/her estimate is wrong. You can teach estimation throughout math lessons when you have your child predict answers first before counting or solving. Teach your child to use terms such as *about, between, a little more* and *a little less*. You can give hints to help your child make reasonable estimates. **Example:** Show one book and say, "There are 200 pages in this book." Show another book and say, "This book is half as big." Ask, "About how many pages *do you think* there are in this book?"

Learn at Home, Grade 2

2. Write a 2-digit addition problem on the chalkboard. Tell your child to estimate the answer first. Have your child explain his/her estimate. After your child gives an estimate, have him/her actually solve the problem. Estimating an answer first will help your child see if an answer is way off.

SCIENCE (Complete Circuits)

BACKGROUND

A battery provides a source of electricity and a wire conducts electricity. The three parts of an electric circuit are the source, the conductor and the use. In this case, the use will be a lightbulb. Electric current conveys energy from one point to another.

1. The electricity that powers things in our homes is called *current electricity*. An electric current is the movement of particles, called *electrons*. In order to have electrical energy, the electrons must flow in an uninterrupted loop, called an electrical circuit. To make a complete circuit, you will need a size C or D battery (electric source), a 6" piece of insulated wire and a flashlight bulb.

2. Strip an inch of the plastic coating off each end of a 6" wire using sandpaper. To do this, bend a piece of sandpaper over the last inch of the wire and twist and pull as you hold the sandpaper between thumb and forefinger.

3. Gather several objects for this experiment. Suggestions include a key, pencil, eraser, plastic glass, fork, nail, cloth, scissors, button, glass, mirror and penny. Have your child predict which will be the best conductors of electricity. Have your child add each object to the complete circuit to test if it does.

Wrap It Up With These

because   very

little   coming   friend

they   said   have   were   are

Write the spelling words in alphabetical order.

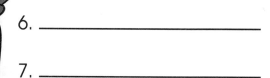

1. _____

2. _____

3. _____

4. _____

5. _____

6. _____

7. _____

8. _____

9. _____

10. _____

Circle the misspelled words. Then, **write** the words correctly on the lines.

Pat and Robin ar vere excited. Thae hav worked all week to plan the perfect birthday party for their frend Karen. Robin baked a chocolate cake, becuze it is Karen's favorite. The presents are wrapped—big ones, littl ones and even odd-shaped ones. All who where invited sed they are kuming. It will be the best party ever!

1. _____

2. _____

3. _____

4. _____

5. _____

6. _____

7. _____

8. _____

9. _____

10. _____

Learn at Home, Grade 2

Problems! Problems! Problems!

Read and solve these problems on another sheet of paper.

1. Craig went to the pond. He kept a tally of the animals he saw there. Which kind of animal did he see most often?_____ Which kind of animal did he see least often?_____
   Frog ⊞ Duck III Bug ⊞ ⊞ II Bird ⊞ II Lizard II Fish ⊞ III

2. Ellen went to the library. She checked out five books on zoo animals, three books on fish, eight books on airplanes and two books on dogs. How many animal books did Ellen check out?_____ How many books did she check out altogether?_____ If she returns the books on dogs and airplanes, how many books will she have then? _____

3. Complete this sequence of numbers: 14, 24, 34,_____ ,_____ , 64

4. Debbie and Missy have twelve pieces of candy. If they share equally, how many pieces of candy should each girl get?_____ Suppose they decide to share equally the twelve pieces of candy with Kimberly, too. Now, how many pieces of candy will each girl get? _____

5. Mike has forty cents. Lynette has twenty-three cents. How much more money does Lynette need to have as much money as Mike?_____ If she had the same amount as Mike, how much money would they have altogether?_____ Does Mike have enough money to purchase a ball for 50¢?_____

6. Use a number line. Start at zero. Count up twelve, back three, up two, back eight, up four. What number are you on now?_____

337

Complete Circuits

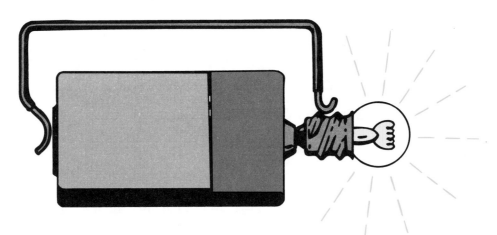

Lighting the Bulb
(Have an adult help.)

1. Use a pocket knife to strip the insulation off 1 inch of the wire at each end.
2. Place one bare end of the wire on the bottom of the battery.
3. Place the base of the bulb on the top center of the battery.
4. Touch the other bare end of the wire to the brass of the flashlight bulb.
5. Draw two pictures which show other ways to make the bulb light.

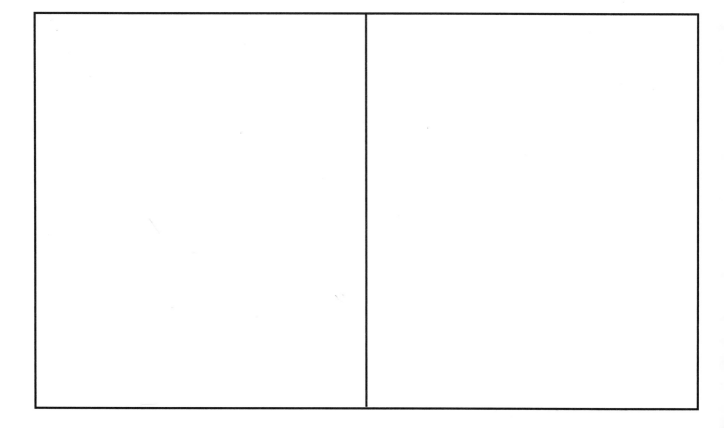

Learn at Home, Grade 2

Conductors and Non-Conductors

With an adult, make a complete circuit and light the bulb. Then, put each of these materials, one at a time, between the bulb and the battery. If the bulb still lights, put a check mark in front of that material.

_____ scissors

_____ eraser

_____ nail

_____ pencil

_____ pen

_____ toothpick

_____ tagboard

_____ large paper clip

_____ thumbtack

_____ chalk

_____ crayon

_____ marker

_____ ruler

_____ book

_____ button

_____ cloth

_____ finger

_____ penny

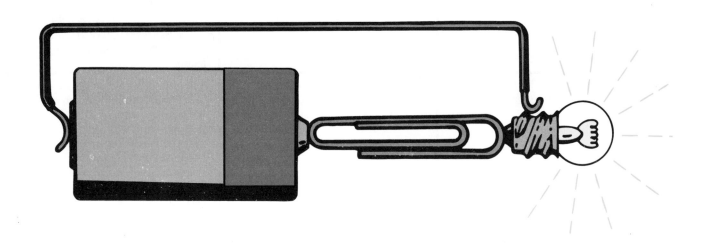

339

	Language Skills	**Spelling**	**Reading**
Monday	Brainstorm ideas for a mystery story that your child will write this week. Decide what the mystery will be, the clues to its solution and how the mystery will be solved. Refer to **My Story Map** (*see* p. 298).	Pretest your child on these spelling words: from any thought been upon could has them away inside Discuss the meaning of each word, its vowel sounds and any hints for remembering how to spell it.	Provide examples of similes and discuss the implied meaning. *See* Reading, Week 35, number 1. Your child will begin a mystery book, *Cam Jensen and the Chocolate Fudge Mystery* by David A. Adler. Read and discuss chapter 1. Discuss photographic memory and how Cam used it. Have your child complete a **Chapter Book Report** (p. 345) by writing the title and main idea for each chapter.
Tuesday	Have your child write a rough draft of a mystery story.	Have your child write the spelling words in sentences.	Write several similes on the chalkboard and discuss their meanings. *See* Reading, Week 35, number 1. Then, have your child draw a picture of four similes. He/she may draw either the intended meaning or the literal meaning of the simile. With your child, read and discuss chapter 2 in *Cam Jensen and the Chocolate Fudge Mystery*. Discuss why Cam and Eric were suspicious of the woman they followed.
Wednesday	Have your child read the rough draft to someone to be sure it makes sense and to get new ideas and suggestions. Have your child revise his/her draft.	Have your child spell each word aloud while using American sign language to form the letters. Have your child complete **Build Yourself Up With Words** (p. 344).	Introduce idioms. Write "It is raining cats and dogs" on the chalkboard. Ask your child if he/she has ever seen dogs and cats falling out of the sky. Ask what such words mean. *See* Reading, Week 35, number 2. With your child, read and discuss chapter 3 in *Cam Jensen and the Chocolate Fudge Mystery*. Discuss why Cam and Eric were skeptical about the yellow horse.
Thursday	Have your child proofread the mystery story to correct capitalization, punctuation and spelling. Then, he/she should meet with someone and together they can proofread the mystery again.	Have your child write the spelling words in alphabetical order.	Review and discuss the art media used in the Caldecott Medal Award books read last week: acrylic, pencil, watercolor, collage and colored pencil. Have your child pick one medium and create a picture. With your child, read and discuss chapter 4 in *Cam Jensen and the Chocolate Fudge Mystery*. Discuss why Cam thought someone was hiding in the house.
Friday	Have your child write the final draft and share it with a small audience.	Give your child the final spelling test.	Have your child create a picture using two of the art media mentioned on Thursday. With your child, read and discuss chapter 5 in *Cam Jensen and the Chocolate Fudge Mystery*. Review the clues Cam recognized as she tried to convince everyone that someone was hiding in the house.

Learn at Home, Grade 2

Math	Science	Social Studies
Multiplication Teach the concept of multiplication using an egg carton and marbles. Have your child show you two sets of 3 by placing three marbles in each of two egg sections and counting the total. Repeat with three sets of 2, four sets of 3 and so on. Each time, have your child count the total number of marbles used.	On the complete circuit created last week, show your child how a switch works. *See* Science, Week 35.	**Communication** Ask your child to define communication. With your child, brainstorm a list of ways people and animals communicate. *See* Social Studies, Week 35, number 1. Classify them as either reading/writing or speaking/listening.
Have your child continue the concept of multiplication. *See* Math, Week 35, number 1.	Help your child make an electronic quiz board. Gather the following materials: two 9" x 12" pieces of cardboard, three 6" pieces of insulated wire, a size C or D battery, a flashlight bulb, aluminum foil cut into 1" wide strips, masking tape and insulated tape, a paper punch. *See* Science, Week 35, numbers 1 and 2.	Discuss the different silent and spoken ways that your child communicates with a friend. Have your child try to play with a friend for an hour without speaking. Discover new ways to communicate. *See* Social Studies, Week 35, numbers 2 and 3.
Make multiplication flash cards vertically and horizontally on index cards, through 5 x 5 = 25. Have your child draw the sets for each problem on the card. Use the cards for multiplication practice.	Have your child continue working on the quiz board for the rest of the week.	Offer a variety of messages. Have your child recommend the best way to communicate the message. *See* Social Studies, Week 35, number 4.
With your child, read and discuss *Too Many Kangaroo Things To Do* by Stuart J. Murphy. Review how multiplication is applied to the story. Choose some of the activities at the end of the book to have your child complete.	Have your child continue working on the quiz board for the rest of the week.	Discuss when a letter is the best form of communication. Have your child write a letter to someone. Depending on the technology you have access to, show your child how to fax or e-mail. Send instant written messages to people far away.
Have your child write and illustrate story problems using multiplication facts from 1 to 5. **Example:** I had 4 cats. Each cat has 4 legs. How many legs in all?	Have your child finish the quiz board today.	Communication takes two parties: a sender of the message and a receiver of the message. Discuss: Is there communication if the receiver ignores or doesn't understand the message?

Learn at Home, Grade 2

TEACHING SUGGESTIONS AND ACTIVITIES

READING (Similes and Idioms)

BACKGROUND

Teach this colorful use of language as a method for making writing more interesting. Teach your child to recognize the meaning of the phrase beyond the literal meaning. A simile is a phrase in which two unlike things are compared and the words *like* or *as* are used to link them. Idioms are colorful expressions that, when interpreted literally, can seem pretty ridiculous.

▶ 1. Write a sentence containing a simile such as M*other was busy as a bee an hour before the guests arrived.* Ask your child to tell what Mother is being compared to and why. Write another simile such as *After the guests came, Mother was cool as a cucumber.* Ask your child what the simile is and why Mother is being compared to a cucumber. Look for other examples of similes in poetry. Similes should not be read literally but interpreted and discussed. Some similes are listed below for your convenience.

sharp as a tack	sweet as honey	cold as ice
slow as a turtle	sly like a fox	strong as an ox
snug as a bug in a rug	hungry as a bear	flat as a pancake
fast like a jack rabbit	red as a beet	busy like a bee
hard as a rock	loud like thunder	black as night

▶ 2. Discuss the literal meaning and what is really meant by the following groups of words (idioms).

caught a cold	look sharp	two-faced
time flies	driving me crazy	saw red
face the music	stick with you	feels blue
see eye to eye	on the ball	held up (a bank)

MATH (Multiplication)

BACKGROUND

Multiplication is repeated addition. At this level, your child will learn what multiplication means and how it is useful.

▶ 1. Put two blocks on the table. Ask your child how many are in the set of blocks. Write and say, "One set of two." Put three more sets of two markers below the first set so it looks like four rows of two. Ask your child how many sets of two are on the table now. Write and say, "Four sets of two." Have your child count the total. Count by twos (2, 4, 6, 8). Write 4 x 2 = 8 on the chalkboard. Tell your child this is another way of counting to eight. Read the problems as *four sets of two* and as *four times two*. Repeat with other sets, keeping the number of sets below five.

▶ 2. Write multiplication problems on the chalkboard. Have your child read and illustrate them with pictures or manipulatives. **Example:** (3 x 2) "three sets of two."

SCIENCE (Complete Circuits)

BACKGROUND

When a complete circuit is closed, the bulb lights. When a wire is separated at one point, the circuit is no longer closed and the bulb does not light. Relate this to a light switch. The switch can interrupt the flow of electrons by separating conductors somewhere in a closed circuit.

Learn at Home, Grade 2

1. To set up the battery for the quiz board, strip both ends off three insulated wires. Attach the first wire to the positive end (or tip) of a flashlight bulb and the positive end of the battery. Attach the second wire to the negative end of the battery. Attach the third wire to the common (or metal) side of the lightbulb.

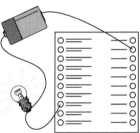

2. Make the electronic quiz board.

   a. Using the paper punch, make ten holes along the left (12") side of the cardboard. Make ten holes along the right side. Have your child write ten questions alongside the holes on the left side of the cardboard. The questions may be from any area of the curriculum (math, vocabulary or science). Have your child write the answers along the left side in a different order.

   b. Turn the cardboard over. Fold each strip of foil in half so the strips are $\frac{1}{2}$" wide. Place one strip of foil across the back connecting the first hole on the left side with the hole on the right which holds the answer. Turn the card back to confirm that the correct holes are matched. (This is a two-person job.) Cut the foil to the length required to reach from hole to hole. Cover the foil completely with a piece of masking tape. Be careful not to cover any of the other holes with the tape. Repeat with the other pieces of foil, connecting each matching question and answer across the back of the card. Always tape completely before moving on to the next connection.

   c. When all the pairs of holes are connected, secure the second piece of cardboard over the back of the first to hide the tape.

   d. Rest the battery (set up in number 1 above) on the desk near the card. To answer a question on the front of the card, your child should touch the free end of one wire to the question on the left and the free end of the other wire to the answer on the right. If your child has matched them correctly, the light will go on.

SOCIAL STUDIES (Communication)

BACKGROUND
Communication is an exchange of messages and ideas that involves telling, listening, reading and responding. Long ago people lived in small groups and communicated by using speech, gestures and sounds. As language and writing developed, runners carried messages between small communities, but news traveled slowly. With modern day technology, communication between people around the world is quick and allows for instant interactive experiences among diverse societies.

1. Some ways in which we communicate are signs, gestures, music, writing letters, newspapers, books, magazines, fax and e-mail, telephone, typewriter, tape and CD players, radio, television, Internet, etc.

2. **Creative Dramatics:** Role-play a telephone conversation.

3. **Creative Dramatics:** Write out simple behaviors or acts on cards for your child to pantomime. Have your child choose a card and then act it out.

4. State each of the following type of messages and ask your child how each could be sent.
   •Information about a new product.
   •Greet a friend across the street.
   •Information about what to bring on the picnic tomorrow.
   •To let someone know you are thinking of them.
   •You want to have a garage sale.

Build Yourself Up With Words

Week 35

Unscramble the letters to spell a word.

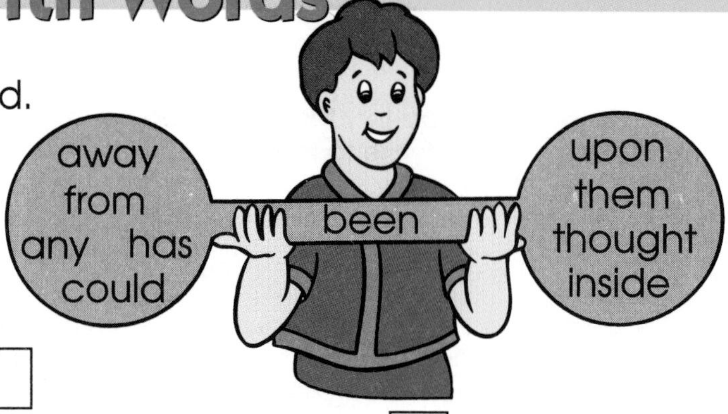
away
from
any has
could
been
upon
them
thought
inside

1. r o f m
2. y a a w
3. s h a
4. i d n s i e
5. h m e t
6. y n a
7. c u l d o
8. e n b e
9. n o p u
10. h g t h o u t

Write the words on the lines.

1. On top ___ ___ ___ ___
2. Opposite of outside ___ ___ ___ ___ ___ ___
3. Where have you ___? ___ ___ ___ ___
4. Please stay ___ from the fire. ___ ___ ___ ___
5. Opposite of to ___ ___ ___ ___
6. Do you have ___ pets? ___ ___ ___
7. Was able to ___ ___ ___ ___ ___
8. An idea ___ ___ ___ ___ ___ ___ ___
9. She ___ a new bike. ___ ___ ___
10. Those people over there ___ ___ ___ ___

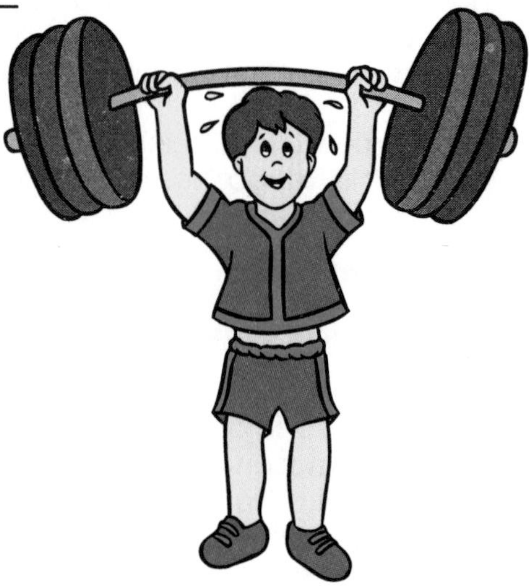

Chapter Book Report Form

Book Title _____

Chapter 1	Chapter 5
Chapter 2	Chapter 6
Chapter 3	Chapter 7
Chapter 4	Chapter 8

Learn at Home, Grade 2

Language Skills	**Spelling**	**Reading**
Monday **Review Week** In this last week of school, help your child organize his/her writing folder. *See* Language Skills, Week 36. He/she may decide to organize his/her folder into a book or to create a writing journal for the summer. *See* **Bookmaking** (p. 350).	**Review Week** Have your child sort and write the spelling words from the past 8 weeks in ABC order.	**Review Week** Review adverbs. Choose an action that your child can perform such as run or jump. Have your child act out different adverbs with that action. **Examples:** run quickly, run outside or run noisily. Continue to read *Cam Jensen and the Chocolate Fudge Mystery* by David A. Adler this week. Continue to have your child complete a **Chapter Book Report** for each chapter (p. 345).
Tuesday Have your child continue organizing his/her writing folder.	Have your child sort and write the spelling words the past 8 weeks into nouns, verbs, adjectives, adverbs, pronouns and prepositions. Refer to the dictionary for correct classifications if needed.	Review abbreviations. Write a list of abbreviations for days of the week, months of the year, titles and familiar states. Have your child identify each abbreviation and use it in context. Have your child write a silly story using many abbreviations. With your child, read and discuss chapter 7 in *Cam Jensen and the Chocolate Fudge Mystery*. Discuss how "the mystery woman" escaped them in the supermarket.
Wednesday Have your child continue organizing his/her writing folder.	Have your child write sentences using two to four spelling words in one sentence.	**Field Trip:** Review library skills. Visit the library and locate various fiction and nonfiction books. With your child, read and discuss chapter 8 in *Cam Jensen and the Chocolate Fudge Mystery*. Discuss how Cam's photographic memory helped the police capture the mysterious woman.
Thursday Adverbs describe verbs. With your child, brainstorm verbs and then add adverbs. **Examples:** walk - quickly eat - slowly Have your child add adverbs to tongue twisters. **Example:** Sally saw seven silly slippery silver seals swimming slowly.	Write a story using several spelling words from the previous 8 weeks. Include misspelled spelling words in your story. Have your child circle and correct the misspelled words.	Review homophones, synonyms, antonyms, similes and idioms. Write silly sentences using these terms. **Example:** My aunt's ant was as busy as a bee. Reread the complete **Chapter Book Report**. Help your child check to see if he/she has photographic memory. Show him/her a picture or photo for ten seconds. Remove the picture and ask him/her to describe it. Re-examine it to see if he/she would be a good detective.
Friday **Post-Writing Activity:** On construction paper, have your child draw the characters from one of the stories. Have him/her cut out each character and glue it on a craft stick. Have your child tell the story using the puppets.	Give a review spelling test.	Have your child review the running record of the books he/she read in the past 8 weeks. Have him choose five favorites and tell why he/she enjoyed them.

Learn at Home, Grade 2

Math	Science	Social Studies
Review Week Review graphing. Have your child collect data and graph the data on a bar or line graph. Discuss the information organized on the graph. Have your child write sentences describing the information. *See* Math, Week 36, number 1.	**Review Week** Review weathering. Have your child check the artificial sandstone for weathering (*see* Science, Week 30, number 3). Discuss the impact of weather on the rock.	**Review Week** Communication includes entertainment such as books, radio, videos, movies, CDs, television, Internet, etc. Ask your child to imagine in what ways his/her life would be different without television. If possible, invite an older adult to talk about life before television.
Review geometry. Show pictures of different shapes' outlines that exist in our environment. Have your child create and color a picture that includes several shapes. *See* Math, Week 36, number 2.	Review identifying rocks. Have your child sort rocks by different characteristics. *See* Science, Week 36, number 1. Have your child complete **Comparing and Classifying Rocks** (p. 353).	Read and discuss *Better Than TV* by Sara Swan Miller. Ask: *Why did Chris, Erin and Fred have more fun with no electricity than with full electricity and being able to watch their favorite TV show?* Talk about a time when the electricity went out at your home.
Review money. Set up a real or imaginary budget with your child. Include money earned by your child and money spent. Have your child keep track of how much money he/she has at all times. *See* Math, Week 36, number 3. Have your child complete **Earnings Add Up!** (p. 351).	**Art:** Have your child make a pebble mosaic with his/her rock collection. Begin the lesson by showing your child mosaics or pictures of mosaics. *See* Science, Week 36, number 2.	Have your child role play a news story for radio or television. Have him/her write a news story about what happened to him/her, your family or in the neighborhood. Tape record or video tape his/her presentation or have him/her present it in front of a live audience.
Field Trip: Go to the grocery store. Have your child practice money skills. Look also for measurement vocabulary on products. Read labels for information on length, width, volume, weight and time. *See* Math, Week 36, number 4. Take a journal along and have your child write some story problems using products and people that you see.	Draw several diagrams of circuits. Some of the diagrams should illustrate complete circuits and some incomplete circuits. Have your child identify which ones are complete. *See* Science, Week 34 for information on complete circuits.	If you have access to a computer, allow your child to "surf" (browse) the Internet under your supervision. There are many excellent kids pages with interesting information and connections. *See* Social Studies, Week 36.
Review ordinal numbers. Have your child write an account of what he/she learned this year using the ordinal numbers to organize the information. Review multiplication. *See* Math, Week 36, number 5. Have your child complete **Amy's Things** (p. 352) to review problem solving.	Gather several small objects that your child did not explore with the complete circuit in Week 34. Ask him/her to predict which objects are conductors of electricity. Have your child add each object to a complete circuit to test it. *See* Science, Week 34, number 3.	Read *What a Wonderful World* by George David Weiss and Bob Thiele, containing the lyrics of the famous song sung by Louis Armstrong. Then, play the original song sung by Louis Armstrong as your child rereads the book silently. Each page corresponds with the lyrics. Talk about why we live in a wonderful world, and what your child likes about it.

TEACHING SUGGESTIONS AND ACTIVITIES

LANGUAGE ARTS

In this last week of school, help your child organize his/her writing folder. Read through and talk about the stories. Put them in order by date. This folder is a portfolio demonstrating a year's growth and thinking. What a treasure! Your child may wish to continue writing over the summer. You may keep the folder active or purchase a notebook for summer writing.

MATH

▶ 1. Make a reading graph. Have your child list and sort the books he/she has read this year. Your child should graph the books by category (biography, animal, fantasy, etc.). Discuss and compare the number of books read in each category. Discuss how the graph makes the information easy to read and understand.

▶ 2. Ask your child to name some things that are round (clock, ball and face) and things that are square (box, block and computer keys). **Art:** Prepare a page with six circles and a page with six squares. Have your child turn each shape into a picture using crayons.

▶ 3. Make dollar bills and coins available for your child's use. Have your child count out given amounts of money. For a challenge, have your child make one amount in several different ways.

▶ 4. **Field Trip:** Design a grocery store scavenger hunt. Have your child look for objects at specific costs. **Hint:** Scan the store's ads the day ahead to prepare the scavenger hunt so you know the prices of some specific objects to include. **Sample problems:** *Find a vegetable selling for 89¢. What is the cost of three peaches? Find two objects that total $3.89.*

▶ 5. Draw a group of objects on the chalkboard. Have your child circle sets. **Example:** *Draw twenty apples.* Have your child circle sets of five apples each.

Learn at Home, Grade 2

SCIENCE

▶ 1. Give your child a small bag filled with assorted pebbles and rocks. Have your child make patterns on his/her tabletop. A pattern may read as follows: large rock, small rock, large rock, small rock, etc. You may also have your child sort and classify rocks using a Venn diagram (*see* Science, Week 29, number 1).

▶ 2. **Art:** Have your child put all the pebbles on the tabletop and look at them. Have your child think about their shapes and colors and what sort of a design or picture could be made with them. Give your child a piece of 5" square cardboard. First, your child should design the mosaic on top of the table. When the mosaic plan is ready, mix some thick plaster of Paris. Spread a little of the plaster at a time on the cardboard. Your child should transfer the design from the table to the cardboard.

SOCIAL STUDIES (Global Education)

BACKGROUND
As communication and travel increase in this country, the need for globally literate citizens increases. We encounter people of diverse beliefs every day. It is important to prepare your child to respect others and seek knowledge about the other cultures that share this world.

Learn at Home, Grade 2

Bookmaking

Wallpaper Book Covers

Assorted-sized wallpaper book covers are great. Ask an adult to help. First, get outdated wallpaper books from a local store. Textured papers are desirable. Follow the steps below to make a 4" X 6" book. Or you can adapt them to make any size book.

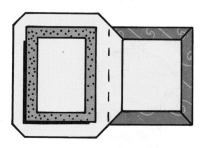

1. Cut out a wallpaper piece 5" X 7". Fold it in half, reopen and cut off the corner at each fold. Then, cut off each outside corner. Lay it flat.

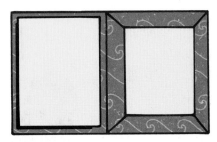

2. Cut out two pieces of tagboard $3\frac{7}{8}$" X 7". Lay the pieces $\frac{1}{2}$" from the edges of the wallpaper, leaving a small space in the center.

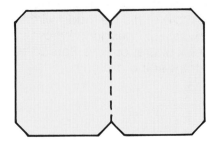

3. Apply a thin strip of rubber cement on the outer edges of the tagboard. Fold the edges of the wallpaper over the pieces of tagboard, making sharp corners. Press it until it sticks.

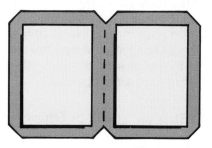

4. Cut out two pieces of manila drawing paper $3\frac{3}{4}$" X $5\frac{3}{4}$". Glue the two pieces on the tagboard to finish the inside cover leaving a small space in the center.

5. Use a long-reach stapler to staple lined pages in some books and blank pages in others. Leave a cover empty until your book is ready to publish. If the texture of the wallpaper is too rough to write a book's title and author on it, type or write the information on a colorful label and stick it on.

Learn at Home, Grade 2

Earnings Add Up!

Wash dishes **$1.50**

Feed cat **$.95**

Mow lawn **$3.50**

Mop floors **$1.25**

Pick tomatoes **$2.75**

Wash windows **$2.85**

Use the pictures above to help you find out how much you can earn by doing each set of jobs. **Write** the total amount for each set.

1. pick tomatoes _____

2. wash windows _____

3. mow the lawn _____

1. wash windows _____

2. mop floors _____

3. mow the lawn _____

1. feed the cat _____

2. pick tomatoes _____

3. wash dishes _____

1. pick tomatoes _____

2. wash windows _____

3. feed the cat _____

Fill in the table. Then, answer the questions.

Toy	How Many?

1. How many books and balls are there altogether? _____

2. How many more teddy bears are there than cars? _____

3. Are there more dolls or animals? _____

4. Amy has 4 more _____ than _____ .

5. Are there enough cars for each doll? _____

Learn at Home, Grade 2

Comparing and Classifying Rocks

Size
Arrange your rocks in three piles by size. **Count** the rocks in each pile.

Number of large rocks _____

Number of medium rocks _____

Number of small rocks _____

Color
Arrange your rocks in three piles by color. **Count** the rocks in each pile.

Number of dark-colored rocks _____

Number of medium-colored rocks _____

Number of light-colored rocks _____

List every color you see on these rocks. _____

_____

Feel
Arrange your rocks in three piles by feel. **Count** the rocks in each pile.

Number of smooth rocks _____

Number of rough rocks _____

Number of rough and smooth rocks _____

Learn at Home
Grade 2
Answer Key

page 16

Catch an Act!

gas mad bag
sat rag had bat
pat bad wag

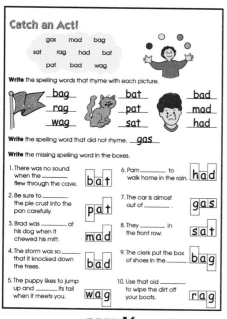

Write the spelling words that rhyme with each picture.

bag
rag
wag

bat
pat
sat

bad
mad
had

Write the spelling word that did not rhyme. _gas_

Write the missing spelling word in the boxes.

1. There was no sound when the _____ flew through the cave. **b a t**

2. Be sure to _____ the pie crust into the pan carefully. **p a t**

3. Brad was _____ at his dog when it chewed his mitt. **m a d**

4. The storm was so _____ that it knocked down the trees. **b a d**

5. The puppy likes to jump up and _____ its tail when it meets you. **w a g**

6. Pam _____ to walk home in the rain. **h a d**

7. The car is almost out of _____ . **g a s**

8. They _____ in the front row. **s a t**

9. The clerk put the box of shoes in the _____ . **b a g**

10. Use that old _____ to wipe the dirt off your boots. **r a g**

page 17

Common Nouns

A **common noun** names a person, place or thing.

Example: The **boy** had several **chores** to do.

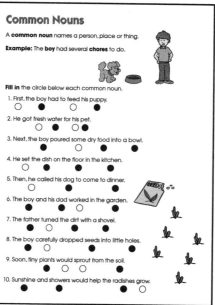

Fill in the circle below each common noun.

1. First, the boy had to feed his puppy.

2. He got fresh water for his pet.

3. Next, the boy poured some dry food into a bowl.

4. He set the dish on the floor in the kitchen.

5. Then, he called his dog to come to dinner.

6. The boy and his dad worked in the garden.

7. The father turned the dirt with a shovel.

8. The boy carefully dropped seeds into little holes.

9. Soon, tiny plants would sprout from the soil.

10. Sunshine and showers would help the radishes grow.

page 18

Proper Nouns

A **proper noun** names a specific or certain person, place or thing. A proper noun always begins with a capital letter.

Example: Becky flew to **St. Louis** in a **Boeing 747**.

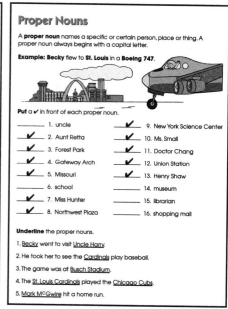

Put a ✔ **in front of each proper noun.**

✔ 1. uncle
✔ 2. Aunt Retta
✔ 3. Forest Park
✔ 4. Gateway Arch
✔ 5. Missouri
___ 6. school
✔ 7. Miss Hunter
✔ 8. Northwest Plaza
✔ 9. New York Science Center
✔ 10. Ms. Small
✔ 11. Doctor Chang
✔ 12. Union Station
✔ 13. Henry Shaw
___ 14. museum
___ 15. librarian
___ 16. shopping mall

Underline the proper nouns.

1. <u>Becky</u> went to visit <u>Uncle Harry</u>.
2. He took her to see the <u>Cardinals</u> play baseball.
3. The game was at <u>Busch Stadium</u>.
4. The <u>St. Louis Cardinals</u> played the <u>Chicago Cubs</u>.
5. <u>Mark McGwire</u> hit a home run.

Learn at Home, Grade 2

Singular Nouns

A **singular noun** names one person, place or thing.

Example: My **mother** unlocked the old **trunk** in the **attic**.

If the noun is singular, **draw** a line from it to the trunk. If the noun is not singular, **draw** an **X** on the word.

teddy bear   hammer   picture   sweater
bonnet   ~~letters~~   ~~seashells~~   fiddle
kite   ring   feather   ~~books~~
postcard   crayon   doll   ~~dishes~~
~~blocks~~   ~~hats~~   bicycle   blanket

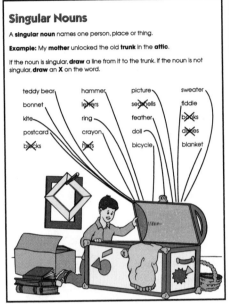

page 19

Plural Nouns

A **plural noun** names more than one person, place or thing.

Example: Some **dinosaurs** ate **plants** in **swamps**.

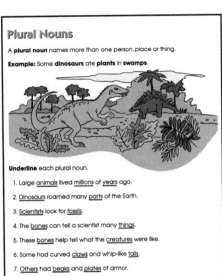

Underline each plural noun.

1. Large <u>animals</u> lived <u>millions</u> of <u>years</u> ago.
2. <u>Dinosaurs</u> roamed many <u>parts</u> of the Earth.
3. <u>Scientists</u> look for <u>fossils</u>.
4. The <u>bones</u> can tell a scientist many <u>things</u>.
5. These <u>bones</u> help tell what the <u>creatures</u> were like.
6. Some had curved <u>claws</u> and whip-like <u>tails</u>.
7. <u>Others</u> had <u>beaks</u> and <u>plates</u> of armor.
8. Some <u>dinosaurs</u> lived on the <u>plains</u>, and <u>others</u> lived in <u>forests</u>.
9. You can see the <u>skeletons</u> of <u>dinosaurs</u> at some <u>museums</u>.
10. We often read about these <u>animals</u> in <u>books</u>.

page 20

Addition
Facts to 10

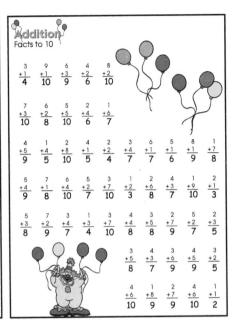

3 +1 = 4	9 +1 = 10	6 +3 = 9	4 +2 = 6	8 +2 = 10
7 +3 = 10	6 +2 = 8	5 +5 = 10	2 +4 = 6	1 +6 = 7

4 +5 = 9	1 +4 = 5	2 +8 = 10	4 +1 = 5	2 +2 = 4	3 +4 = 7	6 +1 = 7	5 +1 = 6	8 +1 = 9	1 +7 = 8

| 5 +4 = 9 | 7 +1 = 8 | 6 +4 = 10 | 5 +2 = 7 | 3 +7 = 10 | 1 +2 = 3 | 2 +6 = 8 | 4 +3 = 7 | 1 +9 = 10 | 2 +1 = 3 |

| 5 +3 = 8 | 7 +2 = 9 | 3 +4 = 7 | 1 +3 = 4 | 3 +7 = 10 | 4 +4 = 8 | 3 +5 = 8 | 2 +7 = 9 | 5 +2 = 7 | 2 +3 = 5 |

3 +5 = 8	4 +3 = 7	3 +6 = 9	4 +5 = 9	3 +2 = 5

| 4 +6 = 10 | 1 +8 = 9 | 2 +7 = 9 | 4 +6 = 10 | 1 +1 = 2 |

page 21

Subtraction
Facts to 10

10 -5 = 5	7 -2 = 5	6 -3 = 3	4 -3 = 1	9 -1 = 8

| 3 -2 = 1 | 8 -6 = 2 | 10 -7 = 3 | 7 -1 = 6 | 8 -5 = 3 |

| 10 -1 = 9 | 7 -4 = 3 | 2 -1 = 1 | 6 -4 = 2 | 8 -4 = 4 | 9 -5 = 4 | 8 -1 = 7 | 9 -2 = 7 | 7 -6 = 1 | 5 -3 = 2 |

| 10 -3 = 7 | 8 -7 = 1 | 9 -6 = 3 | 5 -4 = 1 | 10 -6 = 4 | 7 -3 = 4 | 4 -2 = 2 | 6 -2 = 4 | 9 -7 = 2 | 4 -1 = 3 |

| 10 -8 = 2 | 5 -1 = 4 | 7 -5 = 2 | 9 -3 = 6 | 8 -5 = 3 | 7 -3 = 4 | 6 -4 = 2 | 5 -2 = 3 | 8 -2 = 6 | 7 -4 = 3 |

page 22

Topic Web

Write the topic of the web in the center oval. **Write** four subheadings in the small ovals. **Write** details of each subheading on the spokes.

Example:

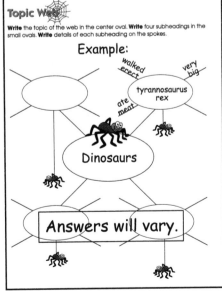

walked   very
erect   big

ate meat   tyrannosaurus rex

Dinosaurs

Answers will vary.

page 23

Nestlings

wet   fell   tell
men   rest   well   set
met   best   pen

Write the spelling words that rhyme with the pictures.

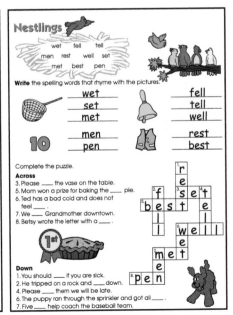

wet	fell
set	tell
met	well
men	rest
pen	best

Complete the puzzle.

Across
3. Please ____ the vase on the table.
5. Mom won a prize for baking the ____ pie.
6. Ted has a bad cold and does not feel ____.
7. We ____ Grandmother downtown.
8. Betsy wrote the letter with a ____ .

Down
1. You should ____ if you are sick.
2. He tripped on a rock and ____ down.
4. Please ____ them we will be late.
6. The puppy ran through the sprinkler and got all ____ .
7. Five ____ help coach the baseball team.

Crossword: rest, set, fell, best, well, wet, met, pen

page 28

Action Verbs

A **verb** is a word that can show action.

Example: I **jump.**   He **kicks.**   He **walked.**

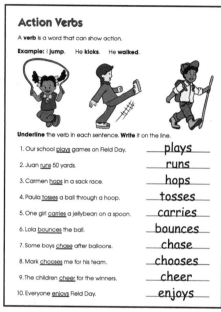

Underline the verb in each sentence. **Write** it on the line.

1. Our school <u>plays</u> games on Field Day.   **plays**
2. Juan <u>runs</u> 50 yards.   **runs**
3. Carmen <u>hops</u> in a sack race.   **hops**
4. Paula <u>tosses</u> a ball through a hoop.   **tosses**
5. One girl <u>carries</u> a jellybean on a spoon.   **carries**
6. Lola <u>bounces</u> the ball.   **bounces**
7. Some boys <u>chase</u> after balloons.   **chase**
8. Mark <u>chooses</u> me for his team.   **chooses**
9. The children <u>cheer</u> for the winners.   **cheer**
10. Everyone <u>enjoys</u> Field Day.   **enjoys**

page 29

Irregular Verbs

Verbs that do not add **ed** to show what happened in the past are called **irregular verbs**.

Example: **Present**   **Past**
run, runs   ran
fall, falls   fell

Jim **ran** past our house yesterday.
He **fell** over a wagon on the sidewalk.

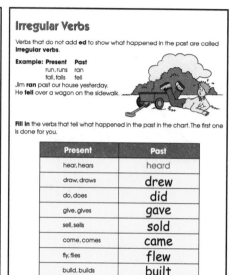

Fill in the verbs that tell what happened in the past in the chart. The first one is done for you.

Present	Past
hear, hears	heard
draw, draws	drew
do, does	did
give, gives	gave
sell, sells	sold
come, comes	came
fly, flies	flew
build, builds	built
know, knows	knew
bring, brings	brought

page 30

Linking Verbs

A **linking verb** does not show action. Instead, it links the subject with a word in the predicate. **Am, is, are, was** and **were** are linking verbs.

Example: Many people **are** collectors.
(**Are** connects **people** and **collectors.**)
The collection **was** large.
(**Was** connects **collection** and **large.**)

Underline the linking verb in each sentence.

1. I <u>am</u> happy.
2. Toy collecting <u>is</u> a nice hobby.
3. Mom and Dad <u>are</u> helpful.
4. The rabbit <u>is</u> beautiful.
5. Itsy and Bitsy <u>are</u> stuffed mice.
6. Monday <u>was</u> special.
7. I <u>was</u> excited.
8. The class <u>was</u> impressed.
9. The elephants <u>were</u> gray.
10. My friends <u>were</u> a good audience.

page 31

Playing in the Summer Sun

Circle the missing word. Then, **write** it on the line.

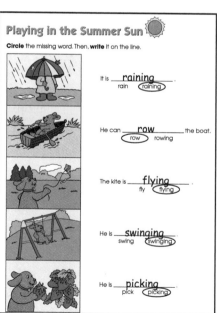

It is **raining** .
rain (raining)

He can **row** the boat.
(row) rowing

The kite is **flying** .
fly (flying)

He is **swinging** .
swing (swinging)

He is **picking** .
pick (picking)

page 32

Addition and Subtraction
Facts to 10

10 −6 **4**	7 +3 **10**	4 −2 **2**	6 −2 **4**	9 −7 **2**
4 +1 **5**	10 −8 **2**	5 −1 **4**	6 +4 **10**	2 −1 **1**
5 +4 **9**	7 −1 **6**	6 −3 **3**	5 +2 **7**	3 +7 **10**

9 −2 **7**	2 +6 **8**	4 +3 **7**	1 +9 **10**	2 −1 **1**	8 −6 **2**	2 +1 **3**	10 −3 **7**	4 +2 **6**	7 +2 **9**
9 −4 **5**	3 +5 **8**	2 +8 **10**	6 −3 **3**	5 +5 **10**	5 −3 **2**	8 +2 **10**	5 −4 **1**	3 +7 **10**	8 −1 **7**

page 33

Addition and Subtraction
Facts to 10

7 +2 **9**	9 −3 **6**	2 +5 **7**	10 −7 **3**	5 −1 **4**
7 −3 **4**	4 +3 **7**	6 +3 **9**	8 −3 **5**	1 +6 **7**
7 −6 **1**	9 −8 **1**	10 −2 **8**	3 +5 **8**	4 +6 **10**

10 −2 **8**	2 +5 **7**	5 +3 **8**	3 +3 **6**	9 −6 **3**	6 −3 **3**	4 +5 **9**	8 −5 **3**	7 −5 **2**	8 +1 **9**
6 −2 **4**	10 −9 **1**	8 −2 **6**	7 +1 **8**	6 +2 **8**	3 −1 **2**	8 −2 **6**	9 −7 **2**	2 +2 **4**	5 +2 **7**

page 34

Learn at Home, Grade 2

Getting To Know You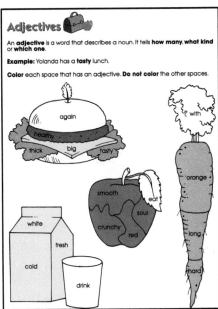

Name: _____ Date: _____

Address: _____

Why did you choose to live in this neighborhood?
_____

Who else lives with you here?
_____

Describe your work.
_____

Tell about your ~~interests and hobbies.~~

Answers will vary.

Describe any changes you have seen in the neighborhood.
_____

What do you think would make this neighborhood a better place to live?
_____

page 35

It's a Dilly!

fix still sit
win tin fit hit
will hill bill

Write the spelling words that rhyme with the pictures. **Circle** the letters that rhyme.

st**ill** w**ill** h**ill** b**ill**
s**it** f**it** h**it**
w**in** t**in**

Write the spelling word that did not rhyme. **fix**

Write the missing spelling word in the boxes.

1. The cat stood _____ as the dog walked by him. **still**
2. Do the new shoes _____ you? **fit**
3. My sister helped me _____ the broken toy. **fix**
4. When _____ we go on our trip? **will**
5. Willy wants his friend to _____ the contest. **win**
6. We walked to to the top of the _____ . **hill**
7. Minna swung the bat and _____ the ball into the field. **hit**
8. Some cans are made of _____ . **tin**
9. Mom paid the phone _____ . **bill**
10. We want to _____ next to each other. **sit**

page 40

Adjectives

An **adjective** is a word that describes a noun. It tells **how many**, **what kind** or **which one**.

Example: Yolanda has a **tasty** lunch.

Color each space that has an adjective. **Do not color** the other spaces.

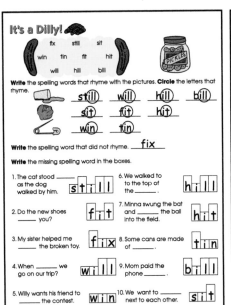

page 41

Add the Adjectives

Write a describing word on each line. **Draw** a picture to match each sentence.

Example: high mountain

The **American** flag waved over the **tall** building.

A _____ lion searched for food in the _____ jungle.

We saw _____ fish _____ the _____ car was parked _____ the _____ van.

Answers will vary.

The _____ dog barked and chased the _____ truck.

The _____ building was filled with _____ packages.

page 42

Something's Missing

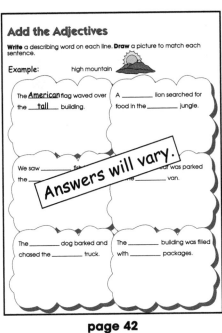

In the forest, 10 animals have a picnic. Skunk brings 8 sandwiches. How many sandwiches should Raccoon bring so that each animal can have one?

$$8 + ? = 10$$

What number added to 8 equals 10?
To find the missing addend, find the difference of 10 and 8.
That is, subtract the given addend (8) from the sum (10).

$$10 - 8 = 2$$

Since $10 - 8 = 2$, then $8 + 2 = 10$.
Raccoon should bring 2 sandwiches.

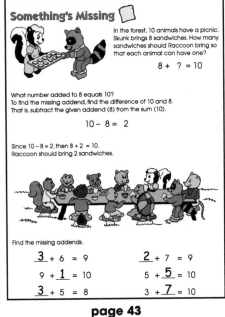

Find the missing addends.

$$\underline{3} + 6 = 9 \qquad \underline{2} + 7 = 9$$
$$9 + \underline{1} = 10 \qquad 5 + \underline{5} = 10$$
$$\underline{3} + 5 = 8 \qquad 3 + \underline{7} = 10$$

page 43

Buoyancy

Things I think will sink: (Place them here.)

Things I think will float: (Place them here.)

Answers will vary.

Things I ~~know sink:~~ (Draw a ~~picture of~~ each here.)

Things I know float: (Draw a picture of each here.)

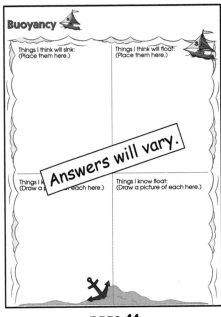

page 44

City Streets

Every town has some interesting street names. Streets can get their names in many different ways. They are often named after presidents, states, trees and flowers. What are some of the interesting street names in your town?

People's Names	Places	Funny Names
Natural Features		Animals
Plants and Trees	Directions	Other

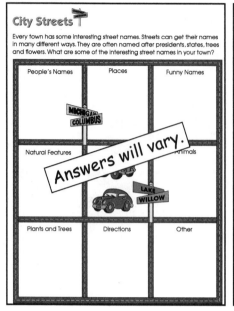

Answers will vary.

page 45

Subjects of Sentences

The **subject** of a sentence tells **who** or **what** does something.

Example: Some people eat foods that may seem strange to you.

Underline the subject of each sentence.

1. Some people like crocodile steak.
2. The meat tastes like fish.
3. Australians eat kangaroo meat.
4. Kangaroo meat tastes like beef.
5. People in the Southwest eat rattlesnake meat.
6. Snails make a delicious treat for some people.
7. Some Africans think roasted termites are tasty.
8. Bird's-nest soup is a famous Chinese dish.
9. People in Florida serve alligator meat.
10. Almost everyone treats themselves with ice cream.

page 50

Rocketing Off!

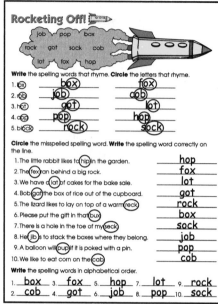

job   pop   box
rock   got   sock   cob
lot   fox   hop

Write the spelling words that rhyme. **Circle** the letters that rhyme.

1. box   box   fox
2. rob   job   cob
3. hot   got   lot
4. cop   pop   hop
5. block   rock   sock

Circle the misspelled spelling word. **Write** the spelling word correctly on the line.

1. The little rabbit likes to hip in the garden. — hop
2. The fex ran behind a big rock. — fox
3. We have a lat of cakes for the bake sale. — lot
4. Bob gat the box of rice out of the cupboard. — got
5. The lizard likes to lay on top of a warm reck. — rock
6. Please put the gift in that bux. — box
7. There is a hole in the toe of my seck. — sock
8. He jib is to stack the boxes where they belong. — job
9. A balloon will pup if it is poked with a pin. — pop
10. We like to eat corn on the cab. — cob

Write the spelling words in alphabetical order.

1. box   3. fox   5. hop   7. lot   9. rock
2. cob   4. got   6. job   8. pop   10. sock

page 51

Short and Long
ă e ĭ o u

˘ means short vowel sound   ¯ means long vowel sound

Color the correct pictures in each box.

ă blue	
ā orange	
ĕ red	
ē yellow	
ĭ green	
ī purple	
ŏ yellow	
ō blue	
ŭ green	
ū orange	

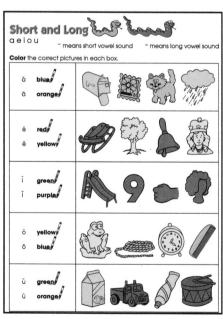

page 52

Missing Subtrahends and Minuends

Fill in the missing part of the subtraction.

10 − ⑦ = 3   ⑩ − 7 = 3   ⑦ − 4 = 3   10 − ⑧ = 2

Fill in the missing numbers in the problems below.

10 − **7** = 3   **11** − 7 = 4   3 − **2** = 1

9 − **3** = 6   7 − **2** = 5   **8** − 6 = 2

4 − 2 = 2   **9** − 5 = 4   8 − **5** = 3

6 − **4** = 2   7 − **1** = 6   **10** − 8 = 2

10 − **6** = 4   **9** − 6 = 3   **9** − 2 = 7

Fill in the missing numbers in the problems below.

5	8	9	**9**	**9**	**9**	6
−**3**	−**4**	−**3**	− 3	− 8	− 4	−**3**
2	4	6	6	1	5	3

8	7	**10**	9	**3**	**10**	4
− 3	−**6**	− 4	−**5**	− 2	− 7	−**2**
5	1	6	4	1	3	2

page 53

Food Fun

The table below tells what each animal brought to the picnic. **Fill in** the missing numbers.

Animal	Vegetables	Fruits	Total
Skunk	8	6	14
Raccoon	9	8	17
Squirrel	7	8	15
Rabbit	6	7	13
Owl	7	9	16
Deer	9	9	18

Write the name of the animal that answers each question.

1. Who brought the same number of vegetables as fruits? — Deer
2. Who brought two more fruits than vegetables? — Owl
3. Who brought two more vegetables than fruits? — Skunk
4. Which two animals brought one more fruit than vegetables?
   Squirrel and Rabbit
5. Which two animals brought the most vegetables?
   Raccoon and Deer
6. Which two animals brought the most fruit?
   Owl and Deer
7. Which animal brought the least vegetables? — Rabbit
8. Which animal brought the least fruit? — Skunk

page 54

Learn at Home, Grade 2

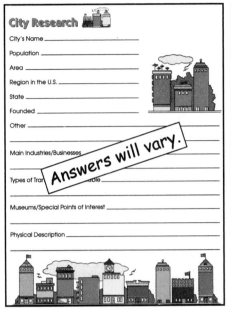

City Research

City's Name _____

Population _____

Area _____

Region in the U.S. _____

State _____

Founded _____

Other _____

Main Industries/Businesses _____

Types of Tran_____ _____

Museums/Special Points of Interest _____

Physical Description _____

Answers will vary.

page 55

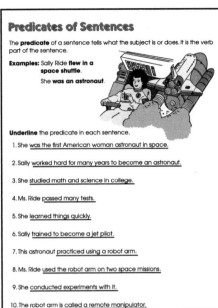

Predicates of Sentences

The **predicate** of a sentence tells what the subject is or does. It is the verb part of the sentence.

Examples: Sally Ride **flew in a space shuttle.**

She **was an astronaut.**

Underline the predicate in each sentence.

1. She was the first American woman astronaut in space.
2. Sally worked hard for many years to become an astronaut.
3. She studied math and science in college.
4. Ms. Ride passed many tests.
5. She learned things quickly.
6. Sally trained to become a jet pilot.
7. This astronaut practiced using a robot arm.
8. Ms. Ride used the robot arm on two space missions.
9. She conducted experiments with it.
10. The robot arm is called a remote manipulator.

page 60

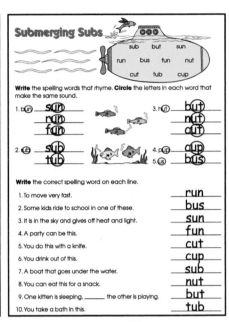

Submerging Subs

sub but sun
run bus fun nut
cut tub cup

Write the spelling words that rhyme. **Circle** the letters in each word that make the same sound.

1. b(un) s(un) r(un) f(un)
2. t(ub) s(ub) t(ub)
3. h(ut) b(ut) n(ut) c(ut)
4. p(up) c(up)
5. b(us) b(us)

Write the correct spelling word on each line.

1. To move very fast. — run
2. Some kids ride to school in one of these. — bus
3. It is in the sky and gives off heat and light. — sun
4. A party can be this. — fun
5. You do this with a knife. — cut
6. You drink out of this. — cup
7. A boat that goes under the water. — sub
8. You can eat this for a snack. — nut
9. One kitten is sleeping, ___ the other is playing. — but
10. You take a bath in this. — tub

page 62

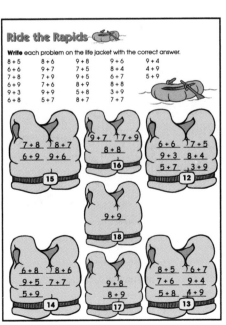

Ride the Rapids

Write each problem on the life jacket with the correct answer.

8+5 8+6 9+8 9+6 9+4
6+6 9+7 7+5 8+4 4+9
7+8 7+9 9+5 6+7 5+9
6+9 7+6 8+9 8+8
9+3 9+9 5+8 3+9
6+8 5+7 8+7 7+7

15: 7+8 8+7 6+9 9+6
16: 9+7 7+9 8+8
12: 6+6 7+5 9+3 8+4 5+7 3+9
18: 9+9
14: 6+8 8+6 9+5 7+7 5+9
17: 9+8 8+8
13: 8+5 6+7 7+6 9+4 5+8 4+9

page 63

The Numbers Game

Roll the dice or cubes to find 2 addends. **Write** them on the first two lines. Then, add to find the sum.

1. ___ + ___ = ___
2. ___ + ___ = ___
3. ___ + ___ = ___
4. ___ + ___ = ___
5. ___ + ___ = ___
6. ___ + ___ = ___
7. ___ + ___ = ___
8. ___ + ___ = ___
9. ___ + ___ = ___
10. ___ + ___ = ___

Answers will vary.

page 64

Addition
Facts to 18

2+9=11 6+6=12 4+9=13 5+4=9 8+7=15
5+9=14 7+7=14 3+5=8 9+9=18 7+9=16
9+8=17 6+5=11 8+5=13 9+6=15 9+4=13 4+4=8 8+6=14 9+7=16 4+8=12 4+7=11
4+6=10 5+3=8 4+5=9 9+9=18 7+3=10 6+8=14 7+8=15 3+8=11 6+3=9 2+6=8
8+3=11 4+4=8 6+7=13 3+2=5 7+5=12 3+4=7 8+8=16 5+2=7 3+9=12 6+8=14

page 66

Complete Sentences

A **sentence** is a group of words that tells a whole idea. It has a subject and a predicate.

Examples: Some animals have stripes.
(sentence)
Help to protect.
(not a sentence)

Write S in front of each sentence. **Write No** if it is **not** a sentence.

_S_ 1. There are different kinds of chipmunks.

_No_ 2. They all have.

_S_ 3. They all have stripes to help protect them.

_S_ 4. The stripes make them hard to see in the forest.

_S_ 5. Zebras have stripes, too.

_No_ 6. Some caterpillars also.

_S_ 7. Other animals have spots.

_S_ 8. Some dogs have spots.

_No_ 9. Beautiful, little fawns.

_S_ 10. Their spots help to hide them in the woods.

page 72

Sail Away

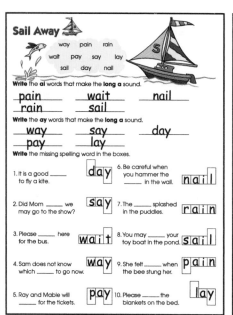

way   pain   rain
wait   pay   say   lay
sail   day   nail

Write the **ai** words that make the **long a** sound.

pain   wait   nail
rain   sail

Write the **ay** words that make the **long a** sound.

way   say   day
pay   lay

Write the missing spelling word in the boxes.

1. It is a good _____ to fly a kite. **day**

2. Did Mom _____ we may go to the show? **say**

3. Please _____ here for the bus. **wait**

4. Sam does not know which _____ to go now. **way**

5. Ray and Mable will _____ for the tickets. **pay**

6. Be careful when you hammer the _____ in the wall. **nail**

7. The _____ splashed in the puddles. **rain**

8. You may _____ your toy boat in the pond. **sail**

9. She felt _____ when the bee stung her. **pain**

10. Please _____ the blankets on the bed. **lay**

page 73

Double or Nothing

Circle the endings in the words below. **Draw** a line under each root word.

tripp(ed)   help(ed)   class(es)   lett(ing)   plann(ed)   drumm(ed)
matt(ed)   dress(ed)   bagg(ing)   flagg(ed)   jamm(ed)   guess(es)
cuff(s)   pinn(ed)   cutt(ing)   zipp(ed)   tugg(ing)   tell(s)
popp(ed)   sitt(ing)   plugg(ed)   hunt(ed)   tann(ed)   start(ing)

Write each word in the correct column.

Only ending added to the root word	Final consonant doubled before adding ending
cuffs	tripped letting
helped	matted flagged
dressed	popped zipped
classes	pinned planned
hunted	sitting jammed
guesses	bagging tugging
tells	cutting tanned
starting	plugged drummed

page 74

Connect the Facts

Subtract. **Write** the answer.

page 75

Subtraction
Facts to 18

11 −9 2	12 −6 6	13 −9 4	9 −4 5	15 −7 8
14 −9 5	14 −7 7	8 −5 3	11 −2 9	14 −9 5
17 −1 16	11 −5 6	13 −5 8	15 −6 9	8 −4 4	14 −6 8	16 −7 9	12 −8 4	11 −7 4
10 −6 4	8 −3 5	9 −5 4	18 −9 9	10 −3 7	14 −8 6	15 −8 7	11 −8 3	9 −3 6	8 −6 2
11 −3 8	14 −4 10	13 −7 6	5 −2 3	12 −5 7	7 −4 3	16 −8 8	7 −2 5	12 −9 3	11 −6 6

page 76

Compound Subjects

A **compound subject** has two or more subjects joined by the word **and**.

Example: Owls are predators. Wolves are predators.
Owls and wolves are predators. (compound subject)

If the sentence has a compound subject, **write CS**. If it **does not**, **write No**.

_No_ 1. A predator is an animal that eats other animals.

_No_ 2. Prey is eaten by predators.

_CS_ 3. Robins and bluejays are predators.

_No_ 4. Some predators eat only meat.

_CS_ 5. Crocodiles and hawks eat meat only.

_CS_ 6. Raccoons and foxes eat both meat and plants.

Combine the subjects of the two sentences to make a compound subject. **Write** the new sentence on the line.

1. Snakes are predators. Spiders are predators.

Snakes and spiders are predators.

2. Frogs prey on insects. Chameleons prey on insects.

Frogs and chameleons prey on insects.

page 84

Learn at Home, Grade 2

Compound Predicates

A **compound predicate** has two or more predicates joined by the word **and**.

Example: Abe Lincoln was born in Kentucky. Abe Lincoln lived in a log cabin there.
Abe Lincoln **was born in Kentucky and lived in a log cabin there.**

Kentucky

If the sentence has a compound predicate, **write CP**. If it **does not, write No.**

CP 1. Abe Lincoln cut trees and chopped wood.

No 2. Abe and his sister walked to a spring for water.

CP 3. Abe's family packed up and left Kentucky.

No 4. They crossed the Ohio River to Indiana.

No 5. Abe's father built a new home.

CP 6. Abe's mother became sick and died.

No 7. Mr. Lincoln married again.

CP 8. Abe's new mother loved Abe and his sister and cared for them.

page 85

Seeing the Sea Life

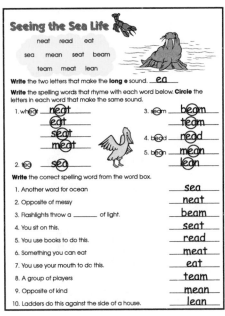

neat   read   eat
sea   mean   seat   beam
team   meat   lean

Write the two letters that make the **long e** sound. **ea**

Write the spelling words that rhyme with each word below. **Circle** the letters in each word that make the same sound.

1. wheat — n**ea**t, **ea**t, s**ea**t, m**ea**t
2. flea — s**ea**
3. seam — b**ea**m, t**ea**m
4. bead — r**ea**d
5. bean — m**ea**n, l**ea**n

Write the correct spelling word from the word box.

1. Another word for ocean — **sea**
2. Opposite of messy — **neat**
3. Flashlights throw a _____ of light. — **beam**
4. You sit on this. — **seat**
5. You use books to do this. — **read**
6. Something you can eat — **meat**
7. You use your mouth to do this. — **eat**
8. A group of players — **team**
9. Opposite of kind — **mean**
10. Ladders do this against the side of a house. — **lean**

page 86

A Fork in the Road

Write the words below on the correct "road."

sky   jelly   try   kitty   fly   my
fry   cry   funny   dry   penny
candy   by   sleepy   happy   lazy   baby
sly   fuzzy   shy   many   why

jelly	sky
kitty	try
funny	fly
penny	my
candy	fry
sleepy	cry
happy	dry
lazy	by
baby	sly
fuzzy	shy
many	why

Y sounds like **long e.**   **Y** sounds like **long i.**

page 87

Missing Numbers

Fill in the missing addend.

$9 + \textcircled{8} = 17$ $\textcircled{7} + 5 = 12$ $8 + \textcircled{6} = 14$ $5 + \textcircled{6} = 11$

$7 + \textcircled{6} = 13$ $8 + \textcircled{8} = 16$ $\textcircled{6} + 6 = 12$ $\textcircled{9} + 9 = 18$

Fill in the missing subtrahends.

$12 - \mathbf{9} = 3$ $11 - \mathbf{7} = 4$

$14 - \mathbf{8} = 6$ $17 - \mathbf{12} = 5$

$17 - \mathbf{9} = 8$ $15 - \mathbf{5} = 10$

$16 - \mathbf{7} = 9$ $15 - \mathbf{9} = 6$

$18 - \mathbf{9} = 9$ $15 - \mathbf{6} = 9$

Fill in the missing subtrahends and minuends.

15	18	12	**13**	**11**
−**6**	−**9**	−**6**	− 7	− 8
9	9	6	6	3

13	15	**10**	13	**15**
− 8	−**7**	− 4	−**9**	− 9
5	8	6	4	6

page 88

My Special Home

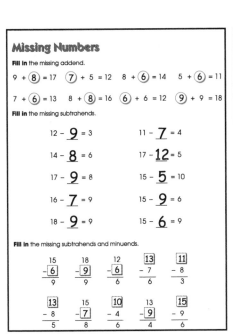

Draw a picture of your home in the box. Then, answer the questions.

Pictures and answers will vary.

1. How old is your home?

2. What building materials were used to build your home?

3. Does your home have special features to make it attractive? (Example: flower boxes, walkway, decorated door.) List them.

4. What do you like best about your home?

5. Do you think there are homes similar to yours in other parts of the country? Why or why not?

page 89

Numbers and Number Words

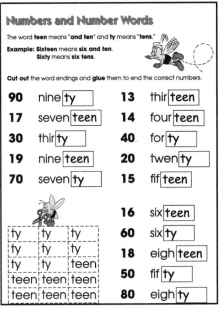

The word **teen** means "**and ten**" and **ty** means "**tens.**"

Example: Sixteen means **six and ten. Sixty** means **six tens.**

Cut out the word endings and **glue** them to end the correct numbers.

90	nine|**ty**	**13**	thir|**teen**
17	seven|**teen**	**14**	four|**teen**
30	thir|**ty**	**40**	for|**ty**
19	nine|**teen**	**20**	twen|**ty**
70	seven|**ty**	**15**	fif|**teen**
		16	six|**teen**
		60	six|**ty**
		18	eigh|**teen**
		50	fif|**ty**
		80	eigh|**ty**

ty	ty	ty
ty	ty	ty
ty	ty	teen
teen	teen	teen
teen	teen	teen

page 94

Training With Facts

Use the numbers on each train to **write** the fact families.

8 6 14

$6 + 8 = 14$
$8 + 6 = 14$
$14 - 6 = 8$
$14 - 8 = 6$

6 15 9

$6 + 9 = 15$
$9 + 6 = 15$
$15 - 6 = 9$
$15 - 9 = 6$

17 8 9

$8 + 9 = 17$
$9 + 8 = 17$
$17 - 9 = 8$
$17 - 8 = 9$

9 5 14

$5 + 9 = 14$
$9 + 5 = 14$
$14 - 5 = 9$
$14 - 9 = 5$

page 95

Predicates of Sentences

The **predicate** of a sentence tells what the subject is or does.

Example: Cars **pollute the air.**
Cars **are helpful machines.**

Color each piece **red** that holds a predicate. **Color** the other pieces **blue.**

our next car
the engine
four new tires
a steering wheel
air pollution
electric cars
a battery
some vans
uses gasoline
is used everyday
looks neat
adds to smog
carries people
burns fossil fuels
costs a lot of money
makes pollution

page 100

Down to Basics

In each sentence, **circle** the nouns, **draw** an **X** above the verbs and **draw two lines** under all adjectives.

1. The children saw a black cloud in the sky.
2. Rain fell from the enormous black cloud.
3. Lightning flashed and thunder crashed.
4. The rain made puddles on the ground.
5. Moving cars splashed water.
6. The children raced into the house.

7. Ten boys and six girls belong to the Wildcat team.
8. The Wildcats played the Greyhounds from Central City.
9. The Wildcats won the big game.
10. The coach said, "The Wildcats made two more goals than our team."

11. The circus came to town on Thursday.
12. On Friday the circus had a parade.
13. The silly monkeys rode in a cage and did tricks.
14. The huge elephants pulled heavy wagons.
15. People laughed at the funny clowns.

page 101

Y as a Vowel

Y as the long sound of **e.**
Y as the long sound of **i.**

Color the spaces:
purple – **y** sounds like **i.**
yellow – **y** sounds like **e.**

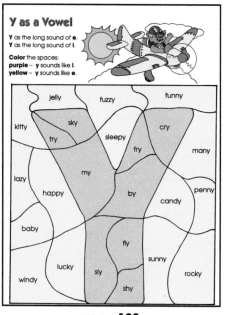

jelly fuzzy funny
kitty sky cry
try sleepy
fry many
lazy my
happy by penny
candy
baby
fly
lucky sly sunny rocky
windy shy

page 102

A Hidden Message

Add or subtract. Use the code to find out your new motto!

Code:

9	18	6	15	13	12	16	11	8	7	14	17
H	Y	D	E	V	T	S	O	A	M	N	I

9 +8		16 -7	16 -8	8 +5	6 +9		14 -7	9 +9
17		9	8	13	15		7	18
I		H	A	V	E		M	Y

17 -8	15 -7	9 +5	13 -7	8 +8
9	8	14	6	16
H	A	N	D	S

4 +7	6 +8		12 -5	17 -9	6 +6	15 -6
11	14		7	8	12	9
O	N		M	A	T	H

page 103

Addition

Facts to 18

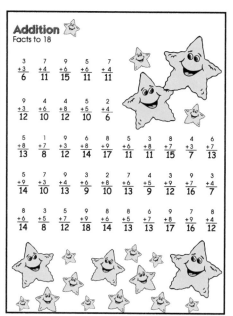

$3 + 3 = 6$ $7 + 4 = 11$ $9 + 6 = 15$ $5 + 6 = 11$ $7 + 4 = 11$

$9 + 3 = 12$ $4 + 6 = 10$ $4 + 8 = 12$ $5 + 5 = 10$ $2 + 4 = 6$

$5 + 8 = 13$ $1 + 7 = 8$ $9 + 3 = 12$ $6 + 8 = 14$ $8 + 9 = 17$ $5 + 6 = 11$ $3 + 8 = 11$ $8 + 7 = 15$ $4 + 3 = 7$ $6 + 7 = 13$

$5 + 9 = 14$ $7 + 3 = 10$ $9 + 4 = 13$ $3 + 6 = 9$ $2 + 8 = 10$ $7 + 6 = 13$ $4 + 5 = 9$ $3 + 9 = 12$ $9 + 7 = 16$ $3 + 4 = 7$

$8 + 6 = 14$ $3 + 5 = 8$ $5 + 7 = 12$ $9 + 9 = 18$ $8 + 6 = 14$ $6 + 5 = 13$ $9 + 7 = 13$ $8 + 9 = 17$ $7 + 9 = 16$ $8 + 4 = 12$

page 105

Learn at Home, Grade 2

Subtraction
Facts to 18

6−3=3	11−4=7	15−6=9	11−6=5	11−4=7
12−3=9	10−6=4	12−4=8	10−5=5	6−4=2
13−5=8	8−7=1	12−3=9	14−8=6	17−9=8	11−6=5	11−8=3	15−7=8	7−3=4	13−7=6
14−9=5	10−3=7	13−4=9	9−6=3	10−8=2	13−6=7	9−6=3	12−9=3	16−7=9	7−4=3
14−6=8	8−5=3	12−7=5	18−9=9	14−6=8	13−8=5	13−6=7	17−8=9	16−9=7	12−4=8

page 106

All Aboard
Add or subtract. Match the related facts.

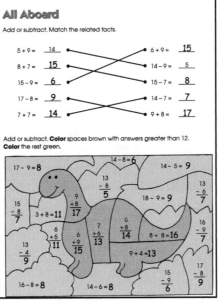

5 + 9 = __14__   6 + 9 = __15__
8 + 7 = __15__   14 − 9 = __5__
15 − 9 = __6__   15 − 7 = __8__
17 − 8 = __9__   14 − 7 = __7__
7 + 7 = __14__   9 + 8 = __17__

Add or subtract. **Color** spaces brown with answers greater than 12. **Color** the rest green.

17 − 9 = 8   14 − 8 = 6   14 − 5 = 9
9+8=17   13−8=5   18−9=9   13−6=7
15−8=7   3+8=11   7+6=13   6+8=14   8+8=16   16−7=9
6+5=11   6+9=15   9+4=13
13−4=9
16−8=8   14−6=8   15−9=6   17−8=9

page 107

Summer Camp
A **statement** is a telling sentence. It begins with a capital letter and ends with a period. **Write** each statement correctly on the lines.

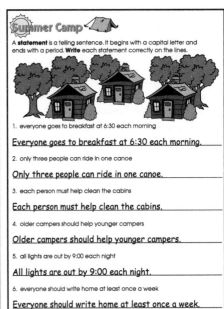

1. everyone goes to breakfast at 6:30 each morning

Everyone goes to breakfast at 6:30 each morning.

2. only three people can ride in one canoe

Only three people can ride in one canoe.

3. each person must help clean the cabins

Each person must help clean the cabins.

4. older campers should help younger campers

Older campers should help younger campers.

5. all lights are out by 9:00 each night

All lights are out by 9:00 each night.

6. everyone should write home at least once a week

Everyone should write home at least once a week.

page 112

Wind It Up
Write the missing spelling word in the boxes.

side wind mind
mile line kind bike
fine find time

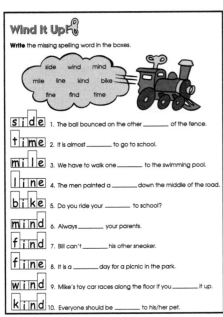

s i d e	1. The ball bounced on the other _____ of the fence.
t i m e	2. It is almost _____ to go to school.
m i l e	3. We have to walk one _____ to the swimming pool.
l i n e	4. The men painted a _____ down the middle of the road.
b i k e	5. Do you ride your _____ to school?
m i n d	6. Always _____ your parents.
f i n d	7. Bill can't _____ his other sneaker.
f i n e	8. It is a _____ day for a picnic in the park.
w i n d	9. Mike's toy car races along the floor if you _____ it up.
k i n d	10. Everyone should be _____ to his/her pet.

page 113

Unpack the Teddy Bears
Cut out the bears at the bottom of the page. **Glue** them where they belong in number order.

39	40	41	29	30	31
10	11	12	78	79	80
84	85	86	64	65	66

65 41 11 80
30 86 84 39 78

page 114

Count the Continents
Color:
Europe – green   North America – orange
Asia – purple   South America – brown
Australia – red   Antarctica – blue
Africa – yellow

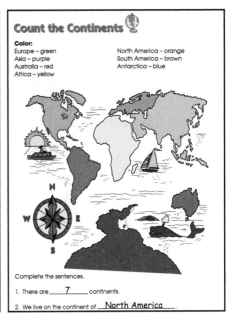

Complete the sentences.

1. There are __7__ continents.

2. We live on the continent of __North America__.

page 115

Learn at Home, Grade 2

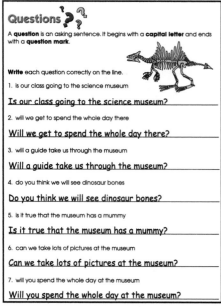

Questions

A **question** is an asking sentence. It begins with a **capital letter** and ends with a **question mark**.

Write each question correctly on the line.

1. is our class going to the science museum

Is our class going to the science museum?

2. will we get to spend the whole day there

Will we get to spend the whole day there?

3. will a guide take us through the museum

Will a guide take us through the museum?

4. do you think we will see dinosaur bones

Do you think we will see dinosaur bones?

5. is it true that the museum has a mummy

Is it true that the museum has a mummy?

6. can we take lots of pictures at the museum

Can we take lots of pictures at the museum?

7. will you spend the whole day at the museum

Will you spend the whole day at the museum?

page 120

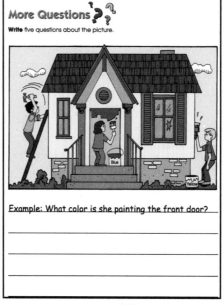

More Questions

Write five questions about the picture.

Example: What color is she painting the front door?

_____

_____

_____

page 121

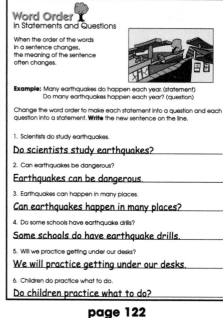

Word Order
in Statements and Questions

When the order of the words in a sentence changes, the meaning of the sentence often changes.

Example: Many earthquakes do happen each year. (statement)
Do many earthquakes happen each year? (question)

Change the word order to make each statement into a question and each question into a statement. **Write** the new sentence on the line.

1. Scientists do study earthquakes.

Do scientists study earthquakes?

2. Can earthquakes be dangerous?

Earthquakes can be dangerous.

3. Earthquakes can happen in many places.

Can earthquakes happen in many places?

4. Do some schools have earthquake drills?

Some schools do have earthquake drills.

5. Will we practice getting under our desks?

We will practice getting under our desks.

6. Children do practice what to do.

Do children practice what to do?

page 122

Completing Sentences

Read each sentence. **Write** a word or words to tell **who** or **when** on each line.

Example:

1. Mary's little ___sister___ is starting her first day at school ___today___

2. Aunt _____ is moving to Florida _____.

3. It was almost _____ arrived at the party

Answers will vary.

4. _____ wants to meet with the soccer team next _____

5. We have an appointment at _____ to have our teeth checked by Dr. _____

6. _____ and _____ are going to the movies _____ instead of _____.

page 123

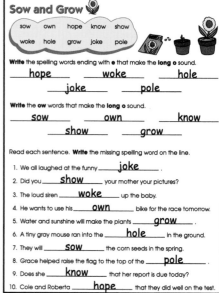

Lighting the Sky

sky   might   dry   by   night
sight   cry   light   right   fly

Write the **igh** words that make the **long i** sound.

___might___   ___night___
___sight___   ___light___   ___right___

Write the spelling words ending in **y** that make the **long i** sound.

___sky___   ___dry___
___by___   ___cry___   ___fly___

Circle the misspelled word in each sentence. Then, **write** the word correctly on the line.

1. We will (lite) the campfire when it gets dark.   light
2. Hang the wet towel on the rack so it will (dri.)   dry
3. Diane likes to walk (bi) the candy store.   by
4. The Moon and stars can be seen on a clear (nite)   night
5. Bright flashes of lightning lit up the dark (ski)   sky
6. A baby will (kri) when it is frightened.   cry
7. You can see a deer behind the tree on the (rite)   right
8. Wild geese (fli) to the river every morning.   fly
9. Mike (mite) catch the bus if he runs.   might
10. Quickly, the groundhog jumped into the hole and was out of (syte)   sight

page 124

Sow and Grow

sow   own   hope   know   show
woke   hole   grow   joke   pole

Write the spelling words ending with **e** that make the **long o** sound.

___hope___   ___woke___   ___hole___
___joke___   ___pole___

Write the **ow** words that make the **long o** sound.

___sow___   ___own___   ___know___
___show___   ___grow___

Read each sentence. **Write** the missing spelling word on the line.

1. We all laughed at the funny ___joke___.
2. Did you ___show___ your mother your pictures?
3. The loud siren ___woke___ up the baby.
4. He wants to use his ___own___ bike for the race tomorrow.
5. Water and sunshine will make the plants ___grow___.
6. A tiny gray mouse ran into the ___hole___ in the ground.
7. They will ___sow___ the corn seeds in the spring.
8. Grace helped raise the flag to the top of the ___pole___.
9. Does she ___know___ that her report is due today?
10. Cole and Roberta ___hope___ that they did well on the test.

page 130

Learn at Home, Grade 2

Hard and Soft c and g

Circle as many words in each word search as you can find. List them in the correct column. Hint: the words going up and down have the hard sound, and the words going across and backwards are soft.

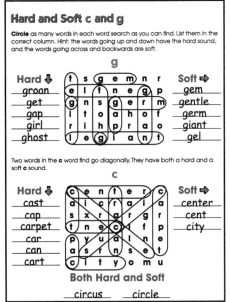

g

Hard ⬇
- groan
- get
- gap
- girl
- ghost

Soft ➡
- gem
- gentle
- germ
- giant
- gel

Two words in the **c** word find go diagonally. They have both a hard and a soft **c** sound.

c

Hard ⬇
- cast
- cap
- carpet
- car
- can
- cart

Soft ➡
- center
- cent
- city

Both Hard and Soft
- circus
- circle

page 131

Tens and Ones

Write the number indicated by tally marks.

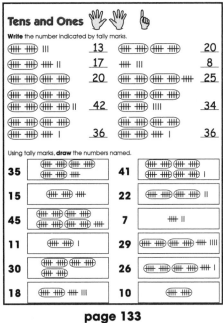

13	20
17	8
20	25
42	34
36	36

Using tally marks, **draw** the numbers named.

35		41	
15		22	
45		7	
11		29	
30		26	
18		10	

page 133

A Fish Story

Fish live almost anywhere there is water. Although fish come in many different shapes, colors and sizes, they are alike in many ways.

- All fish have backbones.
- Fish breathe with gills.
- Most fish are cold-blooded.
- Most fish have fins.
- Many fish have scales and fairly tough skin.

Use the clues to unscramble the fish names. **Write** each name correctly at the top of the bubble. Then, use your imagination to draw each fish.

Drawings will vary.

- **parrot** — rparto fish (a talking bird)
- **lion** — oinl fish (king of the beasts)
- **king** — gkni fish (opposite of queen)
- **butterfly** — tbturelfy fish (an insect with colorful wings)
- **goat** — ogat fish (a nanny– or a billy–)
- **porcupine** — opprucnei fish (animal with quills)

page 135

Kinds of Sentences

A **statement** ends with a period. **.** A **question** ends with a question mark. **?**
Write the correct mark in each box.

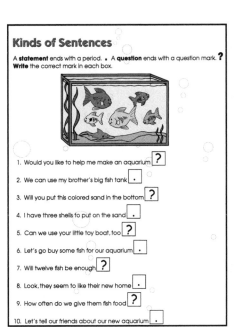

1. Would you like to help me make an aquarium **?**
2. We can use my brother's big fish tank **.**
3. Will you put this colored sand in the bottom **?**
4. I have three shells to put on the sand **.**
5. Can we use your little toy boat, too **?**
6. Let's go buy some fish for our aquarium **.**
7. Will twelve fish be enough **?**
8. Look, they seem to like their new home **.**
9. How often do we give them fish food **?**
10. Let's tell our friends about our new aquarium **.**

page 140

Writing Sentences

Every sentence begins with a capital letter.

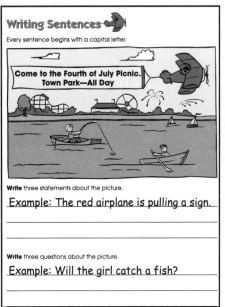

Come to the Fourth of July Picnic.
Town Park—All Day

Write three statements about the picture.

Example: The red airplane is pulling a sign.

Write three questions about the picture.

Example: Will the girl catch a fish?

page 141

Four Kinds of Sentences

A **statement** tells something. A **question** asks something. An **exclamation** shows surprise or strong feeling. A **command** tells someone to do something.

Example: The shuttle is ready for takeoff. (statement)
Are all systems go? (question)
What a sight! (exclamation)
Take a picture of this. (command)

Use the code to color the spaces.

Code
statement—**yellow**
question—**red**
exclamation—**blue**
command—**gray**

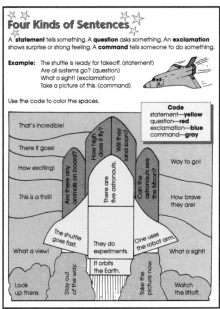

page 142

Loading Cargo

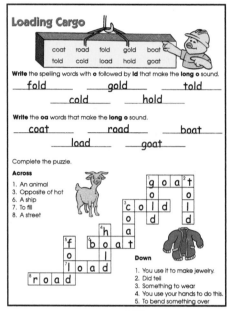

| coat | road | fold | gold | boat |
| told | cold | load | hold | goat |

Write the spelling words with **o** followed by **ld** that make the **long o** sound.

fold   gold   told

cold   hold

Write the **oa** words that make the **long o** sound.

coat   road   boat

load   goat

Complete the puzzle.

Across

1. An animal
3. Opposite of hot
6. A ship
7. To fill
8. A street

Down

1. You use it to make jewelry.
2. Did tell
3. Something to wear
4. You use your hands to do this.
5. To bend something over

page 143

Book Evaluation

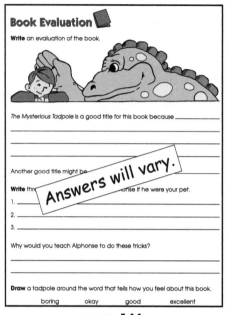

Write an evaluation of the book.

The Mysterious Tadpole is a good title for this book because _____

Another good title might be _____

Write three _____ _____ if he were your pet.

1. _____
2. _____
3. _____

Why would you teach Alphonse to do these tricks?

_____

Draw a tadpole around the word that tells how you feel about this book.

boring   okay   good   excellent

Answers will vary.

page 144

Compound Your Effort

Find the word in the word box that goes with the words numbered below to make a compound word. Cross it out. Then, **write** the compound word on the line.

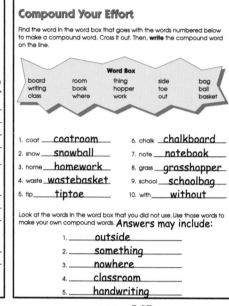

Word Box

board	room	thing	side	bag
writing	book	where	toe	ball
class	where	work	out	basket

1. coat   coatroom
2. snow   snowball
3. home   homework
4. waste   wastebasket
5. tip   tiptoe

6. chalk   chalkboard
7. note   notebook
8. grass   grasshopper
9. school schoolbag
10. with   without

Look at the words in the word box that you did not use. Use those words to make your own compound words. **Answers may include:**

1. outside
2. something
3. nowhere
4. classroom
5. handwriting

page 145

Contractions

A **contraction** is a word made up of two words joined together with one or more letters left out. An **apostrophe** is used in place of the missing letters.

Examples: I am—**I'm**
do not—**don't**
that is—**that's**

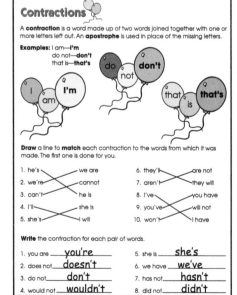

Draw a line to **match** each contraction to the words from which it was made. The first one is done for you.

1. he's — we are
2. we're — cannot
3. can't — he is
4. I'll — she is
5. she's — I will

6. they'll — are not
7. aren't — they will
8. I've — you have
9. you've — will not
10. won't — I have

Write the contraction for each pair of words.

1. you are   you're
2. does not   doesn't
3. do not   don't
4. would not   wouldn't

5. she is   she's
6. we have   we've
7. has not   hasn't
8. did not   didn't

page 146

Alphonse's First Year

Number the sentences in the correct order. Then, **draw** a picture to go with each set.

4   There was a tadpole in the jar.
2   Louis opened the door.
1   There was a knock at the door.
3   The postman handed Louis a jar.

Picture will vary.

2   Alphonse grew and had to be moved to the sink.
1   Louis named his pet Alphonse.
3   Alphonse kept growing and had to be moved to the bathtub.
4   Eventually, he was even too big for the bathtub.

Picture will vary.

4   They used the money to build a swimming pool for Alphonse.
1   Miss Seevers, the librarian, had an idea to help Louis and Alphonse.
2   She located information about a sunken treasure.
3   Alphonse brought up the treasure.

Picture will vary.

page 147

Circus Fun

Add. Remember to add the ones first.

tens	ones
2	5
+ 1	4
3	9

tens	ones
5	3
+ 3	2
8	5

tens	ones
7	1
+ 2	8
9	9

tens	ones
4	4
+ 3	2
7	6

tens	ones
5	1
+ 3	7
8	8

tens	ones
2	6
+ 5	2
7	8

tens	ones
2	6
+ 4	2
6	8

tens	ones
3	7
+ 5	1
8	8

tens	ones
1	9
+ 3	0
4	9

page 148

Learn at Home, Grade 2

Recording Sheet

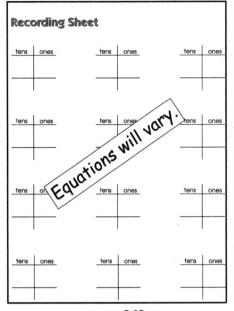

Equations will vary.

page 149

A Sensational Scent

Circle the letters that should be capital letters. Then, **write** them in the matching numbered blanks below to answer the question.

1. Eddie, Homer's friend, lives on Elm Street.
2. Homer's aunt lives in Kansas City, Kansas.
3. Are you sure Aunt Aggie is coming?
4. Old Rip Van Winkle came to town.
5. The doughnuts were made by Homer Price.
6. Miss Terwillinger and Uncle Telly saved yarn.
7. *Homer Price* was written by Robert McCloskey.
8. Uncle Ulysses owned a lunch room.
9. The Super-Duper was a comic book hero.
10. Doc Pelly lived in Homer's town.
11. Money was stolen by the robbers.
12. Now you have the answer to the question.

Who is hiding in the suitcase?

A R O M A   T H E   P E T   S K U N K
3 7 4 11 3   6 5 1   10 1 6   9 2 8 12 2

page 154

Punctuation Magic

Write the sentences correctly. Be sure to use capital letters, periods and question marks.

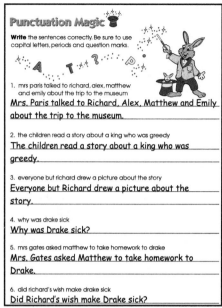

1. mrs paris talked to richard, alex, matthew and emily about the trip to the museum

Mrs. Paris talked to Richard, Alex, Matthew and Emily about the trip to the museum.

2. the children read a story about a king who was greedy

The children read a story about a king who was greedy.

3. everyone but richard drew a picture about the story

Everyone but Richard drew a picture about the story.

4. why was drake sick

Why was Drake sick?

5. mrs gates asked matthew to take homework to drake

Mrs. Gates asked Matthew to take homework to Drake.

6. did richard's wish make drake sick

Did Richard's wish make Drake sick?

page 155

Horsing Around

| story | park | corn | part | north |
| horse | far | farm | hard | start |

Write the spelling words with the same vowel sound as in **horn**. Then, **circle** the letters that make that sound.

story   corn   north   horse

Write the spelling words with the same vowel sound as in **jar**. Then, **circle** the letters that make that sound.

park   far   hard
part   farm   start

Complete the puzzle.

Across
1. Opposite of near
2. A place to play
3. Opposite of stop
4. A yellow vegetable
7. An animal you can ride

Down
1. A place to raise animals and crops
2. A piece of something
3. Something you can read or write
5. Opposite of south
6. Opposite of soft

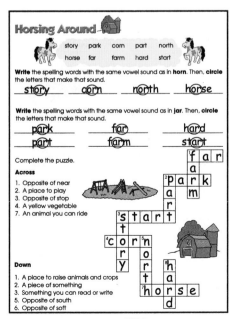

page 156

Christmas Around the World

1. Title _____
2. Author _____
3. Illustrator _____
4. Country _____
5. Continent _____
6. New words I learned _____

Answers will vary.

7. I learned that _____

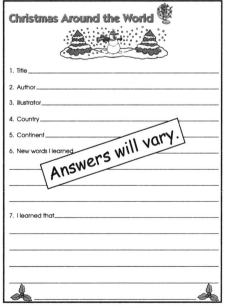

page 157

Picking Pronouns

The words **he**, **she**, **it** and **they** can be used in place of a noun.

Write the correct pronoun in each blank.

He   **She**   **It**   **They**

1. John won first place.
   He got a blue ribbon.

2. Janet and Gail rode on a bus.
   They went to visit their grandmother.

3. Sarah had a birthday party.
   She invited six friends to the party.

4. The kitten likes to play.
   It likes to tug on shoelaces.

5. Ed is seven years old.
   He is in the second grade.

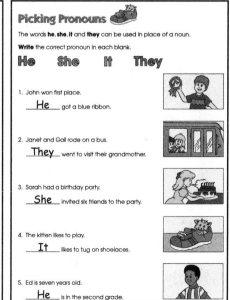

page 158

Add an Apostrophe

Add 's to a noun to show who or what **owns** something.

Circle the correct word under each picture.

The ___ nose is big.
clown clowns (clown's)

This is ___ coat.
Bettys (Betty's) Betty

I know ___ brother.
(Burt's) Burt Burts

The ___ hat is pretty.
girl girl (girl's)

That is the ___ ball.
(kitten's) kitten kittens

My ___ shoe is missing.
sisters sister (sister's)

The ___ coach is Mr. Hall.
team (team's) team

The ___ cover is torn.
(book's) books book

page 159

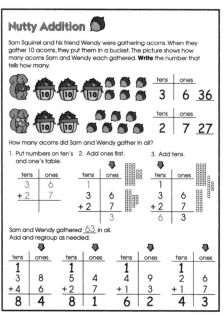

Nutty Addition

Sam Squirrel and his friend Wendy were gathering acorns. When they gather 10 acorns, they put them in a bucket. The picture shows how many acorns Sam and Wendy each gathered. **Write** the number that tells how many.

tens	ones	
3	6	36

tens	ones	
2	7	27

How many acorns did Sam and Wendy gather in all?

1. Put numbers on ten's and one's table.

tens	ones
3	6
+2	7

2. Add ones first.

tens	ones
	1
3	6
+2	7
	3

3. Add tens.

tens	ones
1	
3	6
+2	7
6	3

Sam and Wendy gathered _63_ in all.
Add and regroup as needed.

tens	ones	tens	ones	tens	ones	tens	ones
1		1		1		1	
3	8	5	4	4	9	2	6
+4	6	+2	7	+1	3	+1	7
8	4	8	1	6	2	4	3

page 160

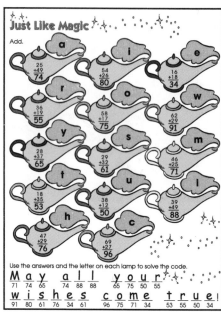

Just Like Magic

Add.

a: 25 +49 = 74
i: 54 +26 = 80
e: 16 +18 = 34
r: 36 +19 = 55
o: 58 +17 = 75
w: 62 +29 = 91
y: 28 +37 = 65
s: 29 +32 = 61
m: 46 +25 = 71
t: 18 +35 = 53
u: 38 +12 = 50
l: 39 +49 = 88
h: 47 +29 = 76
c: 69 +27 = 96

Use the answers and the letter on each lamp to solve the code.

M a y   a l l   y o u r
71 74 65   74 88 88   65 75 50 55

w i s h e s   c o m e   t r u e!
91 80 61 76 34 61   96 75 71 34   53 55 50 34

page 161

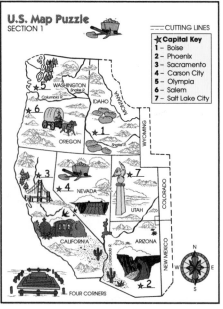

U.S. Map Puzzle
SECTION 1

CUTTING LINES

★ **Capital Key**
1 – Boise
2 – Phoenix
3 – Sacramento
4 – Carson City
5 – Olympia
6 – Salem
7 – Salt Lake City

page 162

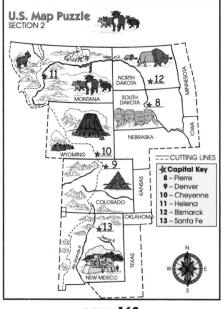

U.S. Map Puzzle
SECTION 2

CUTTING LINES

★ **Capital Key**
8 – Pierre
9 – Denver
10 – Cheyenne
11 – Helena
12 – Bismarck
13 – Santa Fe

page 163

Subject Pronouns

I, you, he, she, it, we and **they** are **subject pronouns**. They take the place of nouns or noun phrases in the subject part of the sentence.

Example: Cinderella is my favorite fairy tale character.
She is my favorite fairy tale character.

Write the pronoun that takes the place of the underlined words.

1. A prince was looking for a wife.
   _He_ was looking for a wife.

2. A big ball was held at the palace.
   _It_ was held at the palace.

3. Cinderella's stepmother wouldn't let her go.
   She wouldn't let her go.

4. Cinderella was left at home to work.
   She was left at home to work.

5. A fairy godmother came to help her go to the ball.
   She came to help her go to the ball.

6. The prince fell in love with Cinderella.
   _He_ fell in love with Cinderella.

7. The prince and Cinderella were married.
   They were married.

page 168

Learn at Home, Grade 2

Object Pronouns
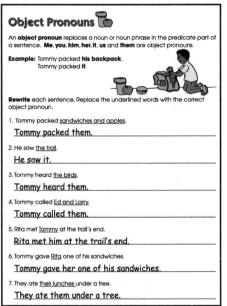

An **object pronoun** replaces a noun or noun phrase in the predicate part of a sentence. **Me, you, him, her, it, us** and **them** are object pronouns.

Example: Tommy packed **his** backpack.
Tommy packed **it**.

Rewrite each sentence. Replace the underlined words with the correct object pronoun.

1. Tommy packed <u>sandwiches and apples</u>.
   Tommy packed them.

2. He saw <u>the trail</u>.
   He saw it.

3. Tommy heard <u>the birds</u>.
   Tommy heard them.

4. Tommy called <u>Ed and Larry</u>.
   Tommy called them.

5. Rita met <u>Tommy</u> at the trail's end.
   Rita met him at the trail's end.

6. Tommy gave <u>Rita</u> one of his sandwiches.
   Tommy gave her one of his sandwiches.

7. They ate <u>their lunches</u> under a tree.
   They ate them under a tree.

page 169

Stir Up a Dessert

stir   girl   verb
skirt   herd   her   clerk
first   bird   jerk

Write the spelling words with **er** that make the sound you hear in the middle of **fern**.
verb   herd   her
clerk   jerk

Write the spelling words with **ir** that make the sound you hear in the middle of **shirt**.
stir   girl   skirt
first   bird

Write the missing spelling word in the boxes.

1. Our class will sing the _____ song in the program. first

2. The cowboys will drive the cattle _____ to the range. herd

3. Sara wore her new _____ to the party. skirt

4. A tiny _____ chirped when it hatched from its egg. bird

5. A part of speech that describes an action is called a _____. verb

6. Trudy met _____ grandmother at the train station. her

7. You must _____ the cake batter before you put it in the pan. stir

8. The car started to _____ as it ran out of gas. jerk

9. Mother paid the _____ for my new shirt. clerk

10. That _____ lives next door to me. girl

page 170

Just Like Magic . . . Again

Subtract.

i 90 −24 = 66
a 52 −15 = 37
r 52 −19 = 33
o 98 −59 = 39
w 43 −29 = 14
y 95 −37 = 58
s 80 −8 = 72
m 73 −26 = 47
n 82 −28 = 54
u 93 −48 = 45
d 52 −26 = 26
h 57 −29 = 28
c 81 −38 = 43

Use the answers and the letter on each lamp to solve the code.
Your   wish
58 39 45 33   14 66 72 28
is   my   command!
66 72   47 58   43 39 47 47 37 54 26

page 171

Articles
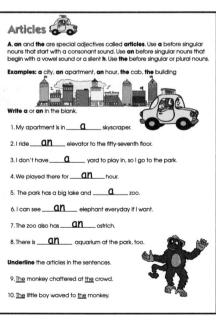

A, an and **the** are special adjectives called **articles**. Use **a** before singular nouns that start with a consonant sound. Use **an** before singular nouns that begin with a vowel sound or a silent **h**. Use **the** before singular or plural nouns.

Examples: a city, an apartment, an hour, the cab, the building

Write a or **an** in the blank.

1. My apartment is in a skyscraper.
2. I ride an elevator to the fifty-seventh floor.
3. I don't have a yard to play in, so I go to the park.
4. We played there for an hour.
5. The park has a big lake and a zoo.
6. I can see an elephant everyday if I want.
7. The zoo also has an ostrich.
8. There is an aquarium at the park, too.

Underline the articles in the sentences.

9. <u>The</u> monkey chattered at the crowd.
10. <u>The</u> little boy waved to <u>the</u> monkey.

page 176

Mixing a Compound

sometimes   downtown   girlfriend
everybody   maybe   myself   lunchbox
baseball   outside   today

Write the correct compound word on the line. Then, use the numbered letters to solve the code.

1. Opposite of inside   o u t s i d e
                          1
2. Another word for me   m y s e l f
                                    2
3. A girl who is a friend   g i r l f r i e n d
                             4   5   3
4. Not yesterday or tomorrow, but . . .   t o d a y
                                           6
5. All of the people   e v e r y b o d y
                                7   8
6. A sport   b a s e b a l l
7. The main part of a town   d o w n t o w n
                                  10   9
8. Not always, just . . .   s o m e t i m e s
                             12   13   11
9. A box for carrying your lunch   l u n c h b o x
                                           14
10. Perhaps or might   m a y b e
                             15

W o n d e r f u l ! Y o u
10 8 11 6 15 7 3 1 9   2 8 1
f o u n d   t h e
6   13 14 15
r i g h t   s o l u t i o n !
7 5 4 14 13   12 3 9 1 13 5 8 11

page 177

Subtraction
With Regrouping

Use manipulatives to find the difference.

1. | Tens | Ones |
   |---|---|
   | 4̶ | 1̶4̶ |
   | − 1 | 7 |
   | 3 | 7 |

2. | Tens | Ones |
   |---|---|
   | 2̶ | 1̶3̶ |
   | − 1 | 5 |
   | 1 | 8 |

3. | Tens | Ones |
   |---|---|
   | 5̶ | 1̶1̶ |
   | − 3 | 3 |
   | 2 | 8 |

4. | Tens | Ones |
   |---|---|
   | 2̶ | 7̶ |
   | − 1 | 6 |
   | 1 | 1 |

5. | Tens | Ones |
   |---|---|
   | 3̶ | 1̶2̶ |
   | − 2 | 4 |
   | 1 | 8 |

6. | Tens | Ones |
   |---|---|
   | 4̶ | 1̶2̶ |
   | − 2 | 6 |
   | 2 | 6 |

7. | Tens | Ones |
   |---|---|
   | 8̶ | 1̶4̶ |
   | − 3 | 8 |
   | 4 | 6 |

8. | Tens | Ones |
   |---|---|
   | 7̶ | 7̶ |
   | − 3 | 4 |
   | 4 | 3 |

9. | Tens | Ones |
   |---|---|
   | 5̶ | 1̶5̶ |
   | − 2 | 6 |
   | 3 | 9 |

page 178

Turtle Venn Diagram

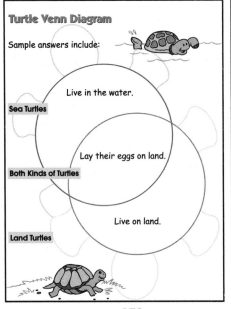

Sample answers include:

Sea Turtles

Live in the water.

Both Kinds of Turtles

Lay their eggs on land.

Land Turtles

Live on land.

page 179

U.S. Map Puzzle
SECTION 3

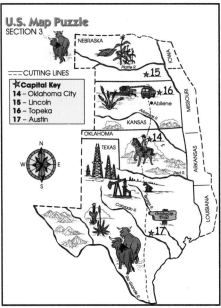

CUTTING LINES

★ **Capital Key**
14 – Oklahoma City
15 – Lincoln
16 – Topeka
17 – Austin

page 180

U.S. Map Puzzle
SECTION 4

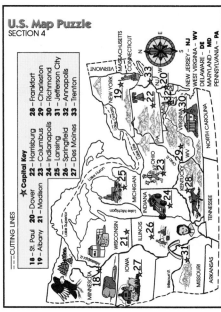

★ **Capital Key**
18 – St. Paul
19 – Albany
20 – Dover
21 – Madison
22 – Harrisburg
23 – Columbus
24 – Indianapolis
25 – Lansing
26 – Springfield
27 – Des Moines
28 – Frankfort
29 – Charleston
30 – Richmond
31 – Jefferson City
32 – Annapolis
33 – Trenton

NEW JERSEY – NJ
WEST VIRGINIA – WV
DELAWARE – DE
MARYLAND – MD
PENNSYLVANIA – PA

page 181

Something Is Missing!

doesn't it's she's
don't aren't who's he's
didn't that's isn't

Write the correct contraction for each set of words. Then, **circle** the letter that was left out when the contraction was made.

1. he i**s** — he's
2. are n**o**t — aren't
3. do n**o**t — don't
4. who i**s** — who's
5. is n**o**t — isn't
6. did n**o**t — didn't
7. it i**s** — it's
8. she i**s** — she's
9. does n**o**t — doesn't
10. that i**s** — that's

Write the missing spelling word on the line.

1. **She's** on her way to school.
2. There **isn't** enough time to finish the story.
3. Do you think **it's** too long?
4. We **aren't** going to the party.
5. Donna **doesn't** like the movie.
6. **Who's** going to try for a part in the play?
7. Bob said **he's** going to run in the big race.
8. They **don't** know how to bake a cake.
9. Tom **didn't** want to go skating on Saturday.
10. Look, **that's** where they found the lost watch.

page 186

Is It a World Record?

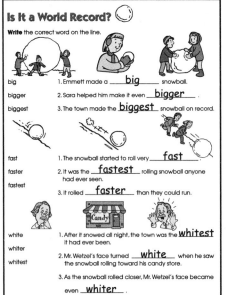

Write the correct word on the line.

big
bigger
biggest

1. Emmett made a **big** snowball.
2. Sara helped him make it even **bigger**.
3. The town made the **biggest** snowball on record.

fast
faster
fastest

1. The snowball started to roll very **fast**.
2. It was the **fastest** rolling snowball anyone had ever seen.
3. It rolled **faster** than they could run.

white
whiter
whitest

1. After it snowed all night, the town was the **whitest** it had ever been.
2. Mr. Wetzel's face turned **white** when he saw the snowball rolling toward his candy store.
3. As the snowball rolled closer, Mr. Wetzel's face became even **whiter**.

page 187

Book Report Form

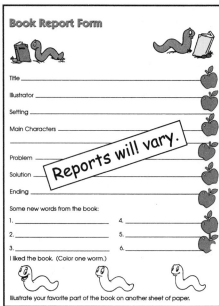

Title _____

Illustrator _____

Setting _____

Main Characters _____

Problem _____

Solution _____

Ending _____

Reports will vary.

Some new words from the book:
1. _____   4. _____
2. _____   5. _____
3. _____   6. _____

I liked the book. (Color one worm.)

Illustrate your favorite part of the book on another sheet of paper.

page 188

Learn at Home, Grade 2

Pronouns

Rewrite each sentence. Replace the underlined words with the correct pronoun.

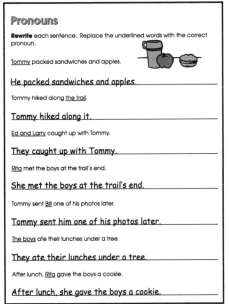

Tommy packed sandwiches and apples.

He packed sandwiches and apples.

Tommy hiked along the trail.

Tommy hiked along it.

Ed and Larry caught up with Tommy.

They caught up with Tommy.

Rita met the boys at the trail's end.

She met the boys at the trail's end.

Tommy sent Bill one of his photos later.

Tommy sent him one of his photos later.

The boys ate their lunches under a tree.

They ate their lunches under a tree.

After lunch, Rita gave the boys a cookie.

After lunch, she gave the boys a cookie.

page 194

Word Magic

Maggie Magician announced, "One plus one equals one!" The audience giggled. So Maggie put two words into a hat and waved her magic wand. When she reached into the hat, Maggie pulled out one word and a picture. "See," said Maggie, "I was right!"
Use the box to help **write** a compound word for each picture below.

| ball | door | rain | star | shirt | bell | fish | shoe | book | foot | basket |
| bow | lace | box | stool | light | sun | cup | mail | tail | cake | worm |

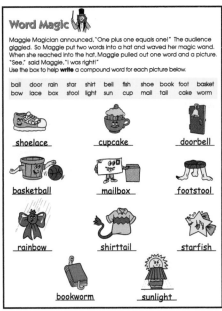

shoelace   cupcake   doorbell

basketball   mailbox   footstool

rainbow   shirttail   starfish

bookworm   sunlight

page 195

Addition Chart

+	0	1	2	3	4	5	6	7	8	9
0	0	1	2	3	4	5	6	7	8	9
1	1	2	3	4	5	6	7	8	9	10
2	2	3	4	5	6	7	8	9	10	11
3	3	4	5	6	7	8	9	10	11	12
4	4	5	6	7	8	9	10	11	12	13
5	5	6	7	8	9	10	11	12	13	14
6	6	7	8	9	10	11	12	13	14	15
7	7	8	9	10	11	12	13	14	15	16
8	8	9	10	11	12	13	14	15	16	17
9	9	10	11	12	13	14	15	16	17	18

page 196

Keep On Truckin'

Write each sum. **Connect** the sums of 83 to make a road for the truck.

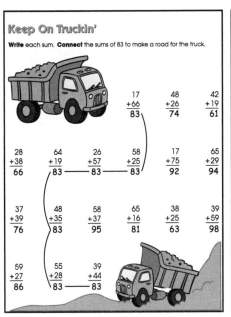

17 +66 83	48 +26 74	42 +19 61

28 +38 66	64 +19 83	26 +57 83	58 +25 83	17 +75 92	65 +29 94

37 +39 76	48 +35 83	58 +37 95	65 +16 81	38 +25 63	39 +59 98

59 +27 86	55 +28 83	39 +44 83

page 197

Subtraction on the Beach

Subtract. Regroup as needed. **Color** the spaces with differences of:

10–19 **red**   20–29 **blue**   30–39 **green**
40–49 **yellow**   50–59 **brown**   60–69 **orange**

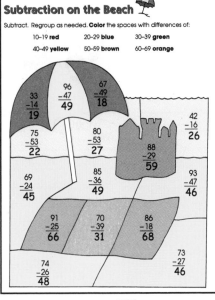

96
−47
49

67
−49
18

33
−14
19

42
−16
26

75
−53
22

80
−53
27

88
−29
59

69
−24
45

85
−36
49

93
−47
46

91
−25
66

70
−39
31

86
−18
68

74
−26
48

73
−27
46

page 198

Anti-Freeze

Water turns into a solid at a temperature of 32°F. This is called the freezing point. Does all water freeze at 32°F?

You will need:
2 small paper cups
4 teaspoons of salt
water
marking pen
freezer

1. Fill both cups with water.

2. Mix 4 teaspoons of salt in one of the cups. Write "salt" on that cup.

3. Put both cups in the freezer. Check on them every hour for four hours.

I found out . . . Results will vary.

the cup of plain water froze quickly.

the cup of salt water took longer to freeze.

page 199

Review of Sentences

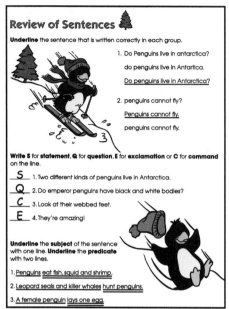

Underline the sentence that is written correctly in each group.

1. Do Penguins live in antarctica?
   do penguins live in Antarctica.
   <u>Do penguins live in Antarctica?</u>

2. penguins cannot fly?
   <u>Penguins cannot fly.</u>
   penguins cannot fly.

Write S for **statement, Q** for **question, E** for **exclamation** or **C** for **command** on the line.

<u>S</u> 1. Two different kinds of penguins live in Antarctica.

<u>Q</u> 2. Do emperor penguins have black and white bodies?

<u>C</u> 3. Look at their webbed feet.

<u>E</u> 4. They're amazing!

Underline the **subject** of the sentence with one line. **Underline** the **predicate** with two lines.

1. <u>Penguins</u> <u>eat fish, squid and shrimp.</u>

2. <u>Leopard seals and killer whales</u> <u>hunt penguins.</u>

3. <u>A female penguin</u> <u>lays one egg.</u>

page 204

Sentence Combining

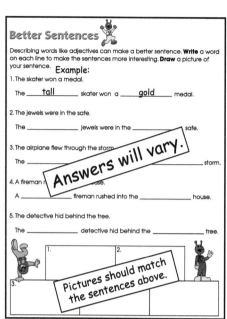

Two sentences can become one sentence. **Write** two sentences as one sentence.

The bird lives in a nest.
The bird lives in the tree.

<u>The bird lives in a nest in the tree.</u>

The music teacher is wearing a blue dress.
The music teacher is wearing white pearls.

<u>The music teacher is wearing a blue dress and white pearls.</u>

I will meet you at the park.
I will meet you by the balloon stand.

<u>I will meet you at the park by the balloon stand.</u>

My name is ...

My first name is Brian.
My last name is Williams.

<u>My name is Brian Williams.</u>

page 205

Better Sentences

Describing words like adjectives can make a better sentence. **Write** a word on each line to make the sentences more interesting. **Draw** a picture of your sentence. **Example:**

1. The skater won a medal.
   The <u>tall</u> skater won a <u>gold</u> medal.

2. The jewels were in the safe.
   The _____ jewels were in the _____ safe.

3. The airplane flew through the storm.
   The _____ storm.

4. A fireman rushed into the house.
   A _____ fireman rushed into the _____ house.

5. The detective hid behind the tree.
   The _____ detective hid behind the _____ tree.

Answers will vary.

1.   2.

3.

Pictures should match the sentences above.

page 206

Hear It Here!

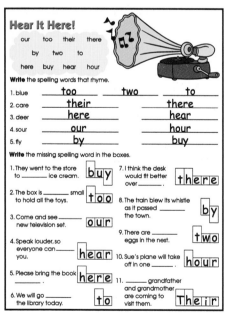

our	too	their	there
by	two	to	
here	buy	hear	hour

Write the spelling words that rhyme.

1. blue __too__ __two__ __to__
2. care __their__ __there__
3. deer __here__ __hear__
4. sour __our__ __hour__
5. fly __by__ __buy__

Write the missing spelling word in the boxes.

1. They went to the store to _____ ice cream. **buy**

2. The box is _____ small to hold all the toys. **too**

3. Come and see _____ new television set. **our**

4. Speak louder, so everyone can _____ you. **hear**

5. Please bring the book _____ here **here**

6. We will go _____ the library today. **to**

7. I think the desk would fit better over _____. **there**

8. The train blew its whistle as it passed _____ the town. **by**

9. There are _____ eggs in the nest. **two**

10. Sue's plane will take off in one _____. **hour**

11. _____ grandfather and grandmother are coming to visit them. **Their**

page 207

Fairy Tale Trivia

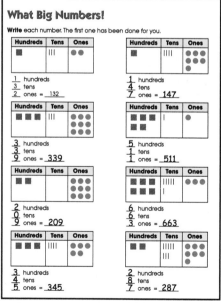

Title _____

Author _____

Illustrator _____

Setting _____

Beginning _____

Royal Charac _____

Evil Characters _____

Special Number _____

Magic _____

Answers will vary.

page 208

What Big Numbers!

Write each number. The first one has been done for you.

Hundreds	Tens	Ones
■	|||	●●

<u>1</u> hundreds
<u>3</u> tens
<u>2</u> ones = 132

Hundreds	Tens	Ones
■	||||	●●● ●

<u>1</u> hundreds
<u>4</u> tens
<u>7</u> ones = 147

Hundreds	Tens	Ones
■■■	|||	●●● ●●● ●●●

<u>3</u> hundreds
<u>3</u> tens
<u>9</u> ones = 339

Hundreds	Tens	Ones
■■■ ■■			●

<u>5</u> hundreds
<u>1</u> tens
<u>1</u> ones = 511

Hundreds	Tens	Ones
■■		●●● ●●● ●●●

<u>2</u> hundreds
<u>0</u> tens
<u>9</u> ones = 209

Hundreds	Tens	Ones
■■■ ■■■			●●●

<u>6</u> hundreds
<u>6</u> tens
<u>3</u> ones = 663

Hundreds	Tens	Ones
■■■	||||	●●● ●●

<u>3</u> hundreds
<u>4</u> tens
<u>5</u> ones = 345

Hundreds	Tens	Ones
■■	||||| |||	●●● ●●●

<u>2</u> hundreds
<u>8</u> tens
<u>7</u> ones = 287

page 209

372

My Bird List

Bird watchers keep a list of all the different kinds of birds they have seen. They also keep track of the date and location. Keep a list of your own using the chart below.

BIRD	DATE	LOCATION

List will vary.

page 210

Backpacking

kite   sick   key   pick   king
back   call   cake   duck   candy

Write the spelling words beginning with **c** that make the **k** sound.

call   cake   candy

Write the spelling words beginning with **k** that make the **k** sound.

kite   key   king

Write the spelling words ending with **ck** that make the **k** sound.

sick   pick   back   duck

Write the missing spelling word in the boxes.

1. Which _____ will open the lock? — key
2. The front and _____ of the folder look the same. — back
3. A mother _____ waddled to the pond. — duck
4. Many people are needed to _____ the ripe apples. — pick
5. The wind blew the _____ high into the sky. — kite

6. Kate had to stay home because she was — sick
7. The _____ and queen live in a castle. — king
8. Buck gave his mom a box of chocolate — candy
9. Let's _____ our friends and invite them to a party. — call
10. There are eight candles on her birthday _____ . — cake

page 216

U.S. Map Puzzle
SECTION 5

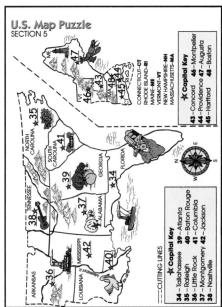

★ **Capital Key**
43 — Concord   46 — Montpelier
44 — Providence   47 — Augusta
45 — Hartford   48 — Boston

CONNECTICUT-**CT**
RHODE ISLAND-**RI**
MAINE-**ME**
VERMONT-**VT**
NEW HAMPSHIRE-**NH**
MASSACHUSETTS-**MA**

★ **Capital Key**
34 — Tallahassee   39 — Atlanta
35 — Raleigh   40 — Baton Rouge
36 — Little Rock   41 — Columbia
37 — Montgomery   42 — Jackson
38 — Nashville

page 217

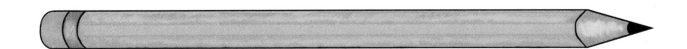

Sentence Sequence

Sentences can tell a story. **Color, cut out** and **glue** the pictures in order to tell a story. **Write** a sentence on each line that tells what is happening in the pictures.

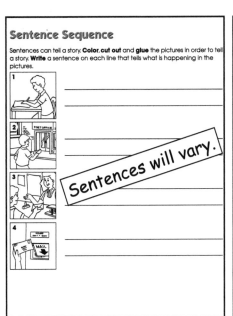

Sentences will vary.

page 222

Bumper Cars

jump   pond   kind   hand   land   stamp   bump   send   camp   ramp

Write the spelling words that end with the same consonants as sand.

hand   land   pond   send   kind

Write the spelling words that end with the same consonants as stump.

jump   stamp   bump   camp   ramp

Write the spelling words on the lines. Then, use the numbered letters to solve the code.

1. To run into — b u m p (1)
2. Not mean — k i n d (2 3)
3. To live in a tent in the woods — c a m p (4)
4. A small lake — p o n d (5)
5. A walkway that slopes — r a m p (6)
6. To leap — j u m p (7)
7. The ground — l a n d (8)
8. A part of your body — h a n d (9 10)
9. To make or order someone to leave — s e n d (11 12)
10. You need this to mail a letter — s t a m p (13)

Y o u   h a n d l e d
5   4   12   10   8   11   10

i t   l i k e   a   p r o!
3   13   8   3   2   11   4   7   6   5

page 223

Forgetful Fred

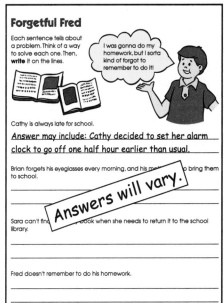

Each sentence tells about a problem. Think of a way to solve each one. Then, **write** it on the lines.

I was gonna do my homework, but I sorta kind of forgot to remember to do it!

Cathy is always late for school.

Answer may include: Cathy decided to set her alarm clock to go off one half hour earlier than usual.

Brian forgets his eyeglasses every morning, and his mother has to bring them to school.

Sara can't find her book when she needs to return it to the school library.

Answers will vary.

Fred doesn't remember to do his homework.

page 224

Our House

Choose two words from the box that describe each character. Then, complete each sentence to tell why you chose those words.

understanding spoiled responsible lazy helpful upset happy
busy caring kind mean confused unhappy patient nice

Answer may include:
The girl is __happy__ and __kind__
because she __likes to help people and__
__makes a lot of friends that way.__
_____

Mother is _____
because _____

Answers will vary.

Father is _____ and _____
because he _____
_____
_____

page 225

Number Lines

Write the circled numbers in the correct order on the lines.

A.
0 1 2 3 4 ⑤ 6 7 8 9 10 11 ⑫ 13 14 15 16 17 18 19 20

__12__ > __5__

B.
10 11 12 13 14 15 16 17 ⑱ 19 20 21 22 23 24 25 26 27 28 29 ㉚

__18__ < __30__

C.
20 ㉑ 22 ㉓ 24 25 26 27 28 29 30 31 32 33 34 35 36 37 38 39 40

__23__ > __21__

D.
30 31 32 33 34 35 36 37 38 ㊴ 40 41 42 ㊸ 44 45 46 47 48 49 50

__39__ < __43__

E.
40 41 ㊷ 43 44 45 46 47 ㊽ 49 50 51 52 53 54 55 56 57 58 59 60

__48__ > __42__

F.
50 51 52 53 54 55 ㊶ 57 58 59 60 �61 62 63 64 65 66 67 68 69 70

__56__ < __61__

page 226

"Mouth" Math

Write < or > in each circle. Make sure the "mouth" is open toward the greater number!

36 < 49   35 < 53

20 > 18   74 > 21

53 < 76   68 < 80

29 > 26   45 > 19

90 > 89   70 > 67

page 227

A Friendly Letter

          Date _____

Greeting _____

_____   Body _____

_____

_____

_____

_____

_____

_____

_____

          Closing _____

          Signature _____

page 232

Right on Track

free   drop   truck   drive   train
from   grass   brag   grade   bring

Write the spelling words on the lines. Then, use the numbered letters to solve the code.

1. Operate a car   d r i v e
                                             1
2. Transportation that moves on a track   t r a i n
                                           2   3
3. To take something to someone   b r i n g
                                                   4
4. A kind of plant   g r a s s
                                              5   6
5. To let fall   d r o p
                                              7 8
6. At no cost to you   f r e e
                                             9 10
7. To boast   b r a g
                                               11
8. Transportation that travels on a road t r u c k
                                             12
9. You are in the second ...   g r a d e
                                               13
10. Opposite of to   f r o m
                                              14

G r e a t! y o u a r e
11 9 10 5 2   7 12 5 9 10

m o v i n g a t t o p s p e e d!
14 7 1 3 4 11 5 2 2 7 8 6 8 10 10 13

page 233

Chapter Book Report Form

Book Title _____   by _____

Main idea of each chapter should be stated or drawn.

page 234

Learn at Home, Grade 2

Recording Sheet
Addition of 2-Digit and 3-Digit Numbers

H = hundreds   T = tens   O = ones

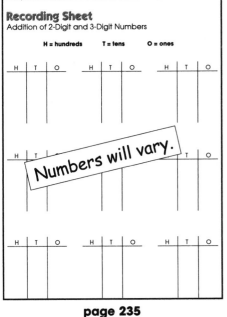

Numbers will vary.

page 235

Loosey Goosey

Find the names of the birds at the bottom of the page that will rhyme with the words given.

Example: Loose goose

narrow	sparrow	bobbin	robin
hairy	canary	dark	lark
men	wren	pinch	finch
pork	stork	muffin	puffin
love	dove	beagle	eagle
pleasant	pheasant	frail	quail
perky	turkey	hull	gull
soon	loon	lay	jay
luck	duck	howl	owl
darling	starling		

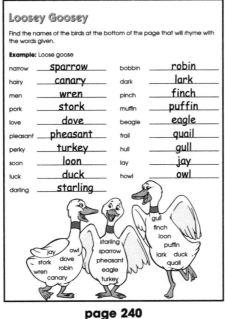

page 240

Smile, Please! 😊

sleep small speak snap slow
smart spin smile spell snow

Write the spelling words that begin with the sound you hear at the beginning of the pictures.

sleep   speak
slow   spin
small   spell
smart
smile   snap
             snow

Write the missing spelling word on the line.

1. Can you **spell** all the words correctly?
2. The clown has a big **smile** painted on his face.
3. A baby needs lots of **sleep**.
4. Steve likes sledding on the fresh white **snow**.
5. A **small** white bunny hid behind the bush.
6. Studying and learning will help make you **smart**.
7. Bike wheels **spin** when you pedal.
8. Do you know how to **snap** your fingers?
9. Cars must **slow** down near a school.
10. Please **speak** louder, so that everyone can hear you.

page 241

Adding Strategies

When adding three numbers, add two numbers first, then add the third to that sum. To decide which two numbers to add first, try one of these strategies.

Look for doubles.

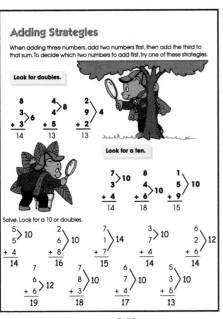

$$\begin{array}{r} 8 \\ 3 \\ +3 \\ \hline 14 \end{array}\Big\rangle 6 \qquad \begin{array}{r} 4 \\ 4 \\ +5 \\ \hline 13 \end{array}\Big\rangle 8 \qquad \begin{array}{r} 2 \\ 9 \\ +2 \\ \hline 13 \end{array}\Big\rangle 4$$

Look for a ten.

$$\begin{array}{r} 7 \\ 3 \\ +4 \\ \hline 14 \end{array}\Big\rangle 10 \quad \begin{array}{r} 8 \\ 4 \\ +6 \\ \hline 18 \end{array}\Big\rangle 10 \quad \begin{array}{r} 1 \\ 5 \\ +9 \\ \hline 15 \end{array}\Big\rangle 10$$

Solve. Look for a 10 or doubles.

$$\begin{array}{r} 5 \\ 5 \\ +4 \\ \hline 14 \end{array}\Big\rangle 10 \quad \begin{array}{r} 2 \\ 6 \\ +8 \\ \hline 16 \end{array}\Big\rangle 10 \quad \begin{array}{r} 7 \\ 1 \\ +7 \\ \hline 15 \end{array}\Big\rangle 14 \quad \begin{array}{r} 3 \\ 7 \\ +4 \\ \hline 14 \end{array}\Big\rangle 10 \quad \begin{array}{r} 6 \\ 2 \\ +6 \\ \hline 14 \end{array}\Big\rangle 12$$

$$\begin{array}{r} 7 \\ 6 \\ +6 \\ \hline 19 \end{array}\Big\rangle 12 \quad \begin{array}{r} 7 \\ 8 \\ +3 \\ \hline 18 \end{array}\Big\rangle 10 \quad \begin{array}{r} 6 \\ 7 \\ +4 \\ \hline 17 \end{array}\Big\rangle 10 \quad \begin{array}{r} 5 \\ 3 \\ +5 \\ \hline 13 \end{array}\Big\rangle 10$$

page 242

U.S. Map Puzzle
SECTION 8

ALASKA

Haida plank house

Peninsula   Kodiak Island   Gulf of Alaska   50

page 243

Fluttering Flags

floor glue blink play glad
flag club plant blow clean

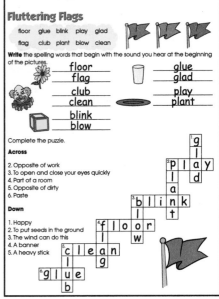

Write the spelling words that begin with the sound you hear at the beginning of the pictures.

floor   glue
flag   glad
club   play
clean   plant
blink
blow

Complete the puzzle.

Across
2. Opposite of work
3. To open and close your eyes quickly
4. Part of a room
5. Opposite of dirty
6. Paste

Down
1. Happy
2. To put seeds in the ground
3. The wind can do this
4. A banner
5. A heavy stick

Crossword:
- ²p l a y / g l a d
- ³b l i n k
- ⁴f l o o r
- c l e a n
- ⁶g l u e

page 248

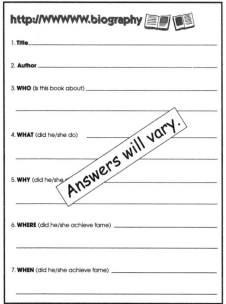

http://WWWW.biography 📖

1. **Title** _____

2. **Author** _____

3. **WHO** (is this book about) _____

_____

4. **WHAT** (did he/she do) _____

5. **WHY** (did he/she) _____

6. **WHERE** (did he/she achieve fame) _____

_____

7. **WHEN** (did he/she achieve fame) _____

_____

Answers will vary.

page 249

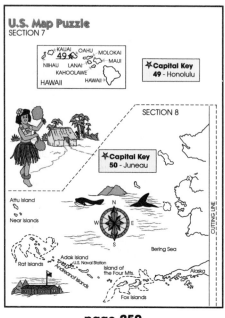

U.S. Map Puzzle
SECTION 7

★**Capital Key**
49 - Honolulu

SECTION 8

★**Capital Key**
50 - Juneau

page 250

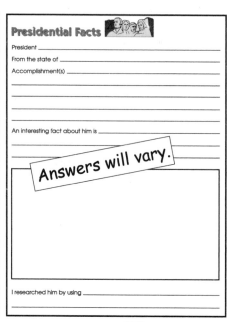

Presidential Facts

President _____

From the state of _____

Accomplishment(s) _____

_____

An interesting fact about him is _____

Answers will vary.

I researched him by using _____

page 251

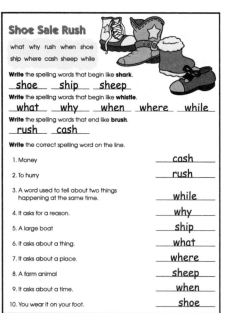

Shoe Sale Rush

what   why   rush   when   shoe
ship   where   cash   sheep   while

Write the spelling words that begin like **shark**.
shoe   _ship_   _sheep_

Write the spelling words that begin like **whistle**.
what   _why_   _when_   _where_   _while_

Write the spelling words that end like **brush**.
rush   _cash_

Write the correct spelling word on the line.

1. Money _____ _cash_

2. To hurry _____ _rush_

3. A word used to tell about two things happening at the same time. _____ _while_

4. It asks for a reason. _____ _why_

5. A large boat _____ _ship_

6. It asks about a thing. _____ _what_

7. It asks about a place. _____ _where_

8. A farm animal _____ _sheep_

9. It asks about a time. _____ _when_

10. You wear it on your foot. _____ _shoe_

page 256

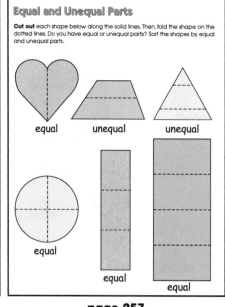

Equal and Unequal Parts

Cut out each shape below along the solid lines. Then, fold the shape on the dotted lines. Do you have equal or unequal parts? Sort the shapes by equal and unequal parts.

equal   unequal   unequal

equal   equal   equal

page 257

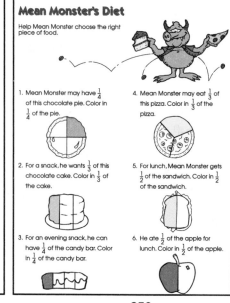

Mean Monster's Diet

Help Mean Monster choose the right piece of food.

1. Mean Monster may have $\frac{1}{4}$ of this chocolate pie. Color in $\frac{1}{4}$ of the pie.

2. For a snack, he wants $\frac{1}{3}$ of this chocolate cake. Color in $\frac{1}{3}$ of the cake.

3. For an evening snack, he can have $\frac{1}{4}$ of the candy bar. Color in $\frac{1}{4}$ of the candy bar.

4. Mean Monster may eat $\frac{1}{3}$ of this pizza. Color in $\frac{1}{3}$ of the pizza.

5. For lunch, Mean Monster gets $\frac{1}{2}$ of the sandwich. Color in $\frac{1}{2}$ of the sandwich.

6. He ate $\frac{1}{2}$ of the apple for lunch. Color in $\frac{1}{2}$ of the apple.

page 258

Learn at Home, Grade 2

Fortunate Fractions

Color the correct number of fortune cookies to show each fraction.

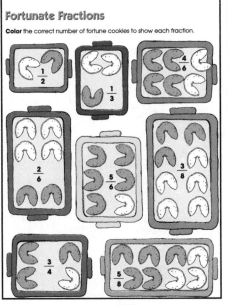

page 259

Inching Along

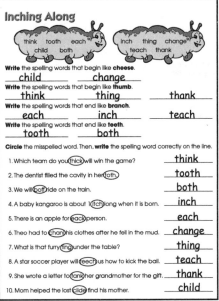

think tooth each
child both

inch thing change
teach thank

Write the spelling words that begin like **cheese**.
child   change

Write the spelling words that begin like **thumb**.
think   thing   thank

Write the spelling words that end like **branch**.
each   inch   teach

Write the spelling words that end like **teeth**.
tooth   both

Circle the misspelled word. Then, **write** the spelling word correctly on the line.

1. Which team do you (thick) will win the game?   think
2. The dentist filled the cavity in her (tooth).   tooth
3. We will (boff) ride on the train.   both
4. A baby kangaroo is about 1 (itch) long when it is born.   inch
5. There is an apple for (each) person.   each
6. Theo had to (chanj) his clothes after he fell in the mud.   change
7. What is that furry (ting) under the table?   thing
8. A star soccer player will (teech) us how to kick the ball.   teach
9. She wrote a letter to (tank) her grandmother for the gift.   thank
10. Mom helped the lost (cilde) find his mother.   child

page 264

Turtle Time

Write the time each clock shows.

9:10   8:25

10:05   8:20   1:45   7:55

8:15   3:50   2:35   7:30

page 265

Guide Words

Circle the words that would be found on these dictionary pages. Remember to use the guide words to help you. One has already been done for you.

save		seal
(seafood)	sass	(sea)
(seafarer)	(scene)	season
(scuba)	seam	salt
savage	(scurry)	(say)

thirsty		today
thirst	toddle	(tiff)
(toad)	(time)	togs
(tissue)	third	(thumb)
(thirty)	(thread)	(toboggan)

what		whet
(where)	whey	(wheezy)
whiff	wham	(wheel)
(wheat)	wart	wharf
west	(whatever)	(when)

page 270

It's About Time!

Trace each mouse with red if it has a time word.

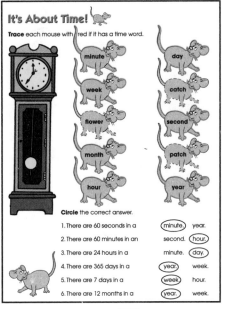

minute   day
week   catch
flower   second
month   patch
hour   year

Circle the correct answer.

1. There are 60 seconds in a   (minute.) year.
2. There are 60 minutes in an   second. (hour.)
3. There are 24 hours in a   minute. (day.)
4. There are 365 days in a   (year.) week.
5. There are 7 days in a   (week.) hour.
6. There are 12 months in a   (year.) week.

page 271

Birds of a Feather

Birds are the only animals that have feathers. All birds have wings but not all can fly. They all hatch from eggs, have backbones and are warm-blooded.

The eggs in the nest contain the names of different birds. When filling in the puzzle, the last letter of one name becomes the first letter of the next name. Write the names of the birds in the puzzle in the correct order. Start at the outside edge and spiral in toward the center. The first three names are written for you.

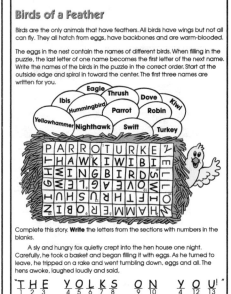

Eagle Thrush Dove Kiwi
Ibis Hummingbird Parrot Robin
Yellowhammer Nighthawk Swift Turkey

Complete this story. **Write** the letters from the sections with numbers in the blanks.

A sly and hungry fox quietly crept into the hen house one night. Carefully, he took a basket and began filling it with eggs. As he turned to leave, he tripped on a rake and went tumbling down, eggs and all. The hens awoke, laughed loudly and said,
"THE YOLKS ON YOU!"
1 2 3 4 5 6 7 8 9 10 4 12 13

page 272

Where Do I Live?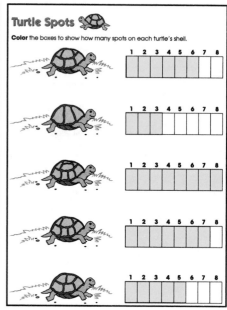

1. My name is _____Answers will vary._____

2. My house number is _____Answers will vary._____

3. My street's name is _____Answers will vary._____

4. I live in the city or town of _____Answers will vary._____

5. I live in the state of _____Answers will vary._____

6. My country's name is _____U.S.A._____

7. I live on the continent of _____North America_____

8. I live on the planet _____Earth_____

9. The name of my galaxy is _____Milky Way_____

10. The name of all the galaxies together is the _____Universe_____

page 273

Baking Cookies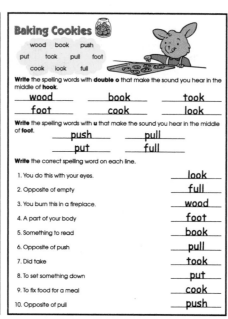

wood   book   push
put   took   pull   foot
cook   look   full

Write the spelling words with **double o** that make the sound you hear in the middle of **hook**.

wood   _book_   _took_
foot   _cook_   _look_

Write the spelling words with **u** that make the sound you hear in the middle of **foot**.

push   _pull_
put   _full_

Write the correct spelling word on each line.

1. You do this with your eyes. _____look_
2. Opposite of empty _____full_
3. You burn this in a fireplace. _____wood_
4. A part of your body _____foot_
5. Something to read _____book_
6. Opposite of push _____pull_
7. Did take _____took_
8. To set something down _____put_
9. To fix food for a meal _____cook_
10. Opposite of pull _____push_

page 278

Turtle Spots

Color the boxes to show how many spots on each turtle's shell.

1 2 3 4 5 6 7 8

page 280

Honey Bear's Bakery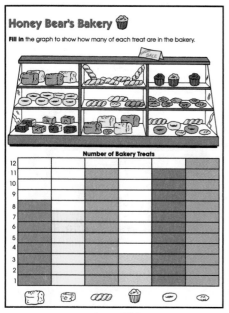

Fill in the graph to show how many of each treat are in the bakery.

Number of Bakery Treats

page 281

New Words I Learned About . . . Japan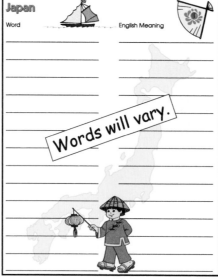

Word   English Meaning

Words will vary.

page 282

New Words I Learned About . . . China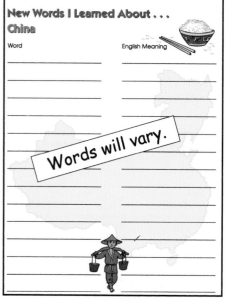

Word   English Meaning

Words will vary.

page 283

Learn at Home, Grade 2

Adverbs

An **adverb** describes a verb. It tells *how, when* or *where* an action takes place.

Example:

The space shuttle blasted off **yesterday**. (when)
It rose **quickly** into the sky. (how)
We watched **outdoors**. (where)

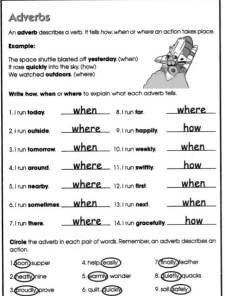

Write how, when or **where** to explain what each adverb tells.

1. I run **today**. _____when_____
2. I run **outside**. _____where_____
3. I run **tomorrow**. _____when_____
4. I run **around**. _____where_____
5. I run **nearby**. _____where_____
6. I run **sometimes**. _____when_____
7. I run **there**. _____where_____
8. I run **far**. _____where_____
9. I run **happily**. _____how_____
10. I run **weekly**. _____when_____
11. I run **swiftly**. _____how_____
12. I run **first**. _____when_____
13. I run **next**. _____when_____
14. I run **gracefully**. _____how_____

Circle the adverb in each pair of words. Remember, an adverb describes an action.

1. (Soon) supper
2. (neatly) nine
3. (proudly) prove
4. help (easily)
5. (warmly) wonder
6. quilt, (quickly)
7. (finally) feather
8. (quietly) quacks
9. sail (safely)

page 288

Using Exact Adjectives

Use an **adjective** that best describes the noun or pronoun. Be specific.

Example: David had a nice birthday.
David had a **fun** birthday.

Rewrite each sentence, replacing nice or good with a better adjective from the box or one of your own.

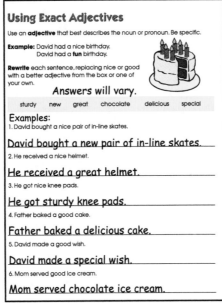

Answers will vary.

| sturdy | new | great | chocolate | delicious | special |

Examples:

1. David bought a nice pair of in-line skates.

David bought a new pair of in-line skates.

2. He received a nice helmet.

He received a great helmet.

3. He got nice knee pads.

He got sturdy knee pads.

4. Father baked a good cake.

Father baked a delicious cake.

5. David made a good wish.

David made a special wish.

6. Mom served good ice cream.

Mom served chocolate ice cream.

page 289

Super Cool!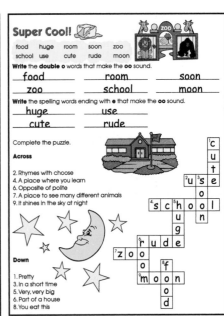

| food | huge | room | soon | zoo |
| school | use | cute | rude | moon |

Write the **double o** words that make the **oo** sound.

| food | room | soon |
| zoo | school | moon |

Write the spelling words ending with **e** that make the **oo** sound.

| huge | use |
| cute | rude |

Complete the puzzle.

Across

2. Rhymes with choose
4. A place where you learn
6. Opposite of polite
7. A place to see many different animals
9. It shines in the sky at night

Down

1. Pretty
3. In a short time
5. Very, very big
6. Part of a house
8. You eat this

Crossword answers:
- ¹cute
- ²use
- ⁴school
- huge
- ⁶rude
- ⁷zoo
- ⁸food
- ⁹moon

page 290

New Words I Learned About . . .
Mexico

Word   English Meaning

Words will vary.

page 291

New Words I Learned About . . .
Italy

Word   English Meaning

Words will vary.

page 292

Venn Diagram

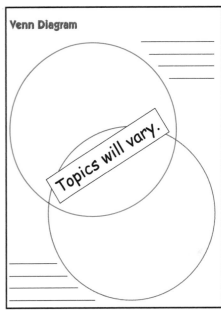

Topics will vary.

page 293

Learn at Home, Grade 2

My Story Map

1. Title _____

Beginning

2. The main characters _____

_____

3. The settings _____

4. When does the story take place? _____

Middle

5. The problem _____

_____

6. What do th~~~~ ~~~~d to try to solve it? _____

Answers will vary.

_____

_____

_____

_____

End

7. How is the problem solved? _____

page 298

Clowning Around

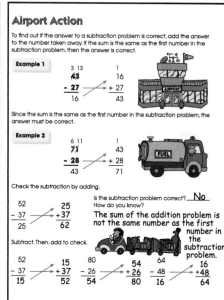

clown
our down
count how town
house about now out

Write the **ou** words that make the vowel sound you hear in **mouse**.

<u>our</u> <u>count</u> <u>house</u>

<u>about</u> <u>out</u>

Write the **ow** words that make the vowel sound you hear in **cow**.

<u>clown</u> <u>down</u> <u>how</u>

<u>town</u> <u>now</u>

Write the missing spelling words in the boxes.

1. Sally lives in the ____ on the corner. house

6. They rode the elevator ____ to the bottom floor. down

2. Do you know ____ to make a robot? how

7. This is ____ new four-wheel drive truck. our

3. Please take the towels ____ of the dryer. out

8. The big funny ____ rode a tiny bike. clown

4. We must leave for the airport ____ I now

9. Can you ____ to 100? count

5. It is ____ time for the race to start. about

10. The farmer took his fresh fruit to ____ . town

page 299

Airport Action

To find out if the answer to a subtraction problem is correct, add the answer to the number taken away. If the sum is the same as the first number in the subtraction problem, then the answer is correct.

Example 1

```
  3 13        1
  43          16
- 27    →   + 27
  16          43
```

Since the sum is the same as the first number in the subtraction problem, the answer must be correct.

Example 2

```
  6 11        1
  71          43
- 28    →   + 28
  43          71
```

Check the subtraction by adding.

```
  52          25
- 37    →   + 37
  25          62
```

Is the subtraction problem correct? How do you know? **No**

The sum of the addition problem is not the same number as the first number in the subtraction problem.

Subtract. Then, add to check.

```
  52          15       80          54       64          16
- 37    →   + 37     - 26    →   + 26     - 48    →   + 48
  15          52       54          80       16          64
```

page 300

My First Treat Will Be . . .

Circle the ordinal number word for each treat.

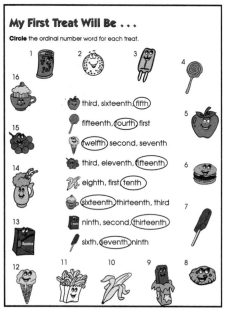

third, sixteenth, (fifth)

fifteenth, (fourth) first

(twelfth) second, seventh

third, eleventh, (fifteenth)

eighth, first, (tenth)

(sixteenth) thirteenth, third

ninth, second, (thirteenth)

sixth, (seventh) ninth

page 301

New Words I Learned About . . .
Germany

Word _____ English Meaning _____

Words will vary.

page 303

New Words I Learned About . . .
Russia

Word _____ English Meaning _____

Words will vary.

page 304

Learn at Home, Grade 2

New Words I Learned About . . .
Africa

Word   English Meaning

Words will vary.

page 305

Nonfiction Books

The characters below need a book that will show them how to bake cakes. "How to" books are also called **Nonfiction**. These books are not make-believe, they are true.

Circle the book titles that are nonfiction.

The Cat in the Hat   (*How to Make Doll Clothes*)
Treasure Island   *Alice in Wonderland*
(*Building a Doghouse*)   *Peter Rabbit*
The Ugly Duckling   *The Incredible Journey*
(*History of Baseball*)   (*Animals in the Jungle*)
Where the Wild Things Are   (*Baking Made Easy*)

Now, decorate the cake!

page 310

How Many?

Find the shapes and **color** them using the code.

△ red   ⬭ blue   ◇ yellow
⬭ green   ▢ orange   ▮ black

page 311

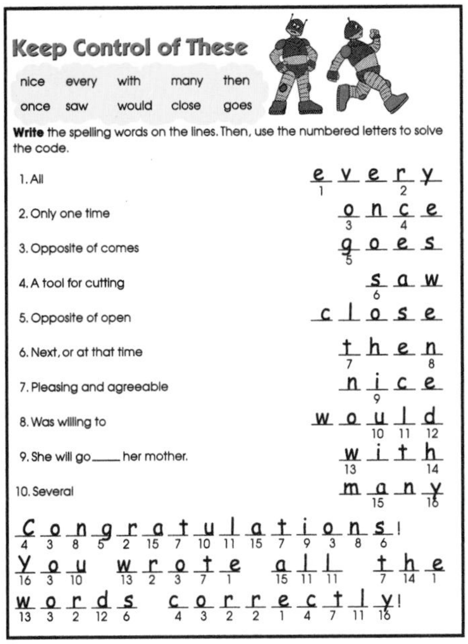

Keep Control of These

| nice | every | with | many | then |
| once | saw | would | close | goes |

Write the spelling words on the lines. Then, use the numbered letters to solve the code.

1. All — e v e r y
2. Only one time — o n c e
3. Opposite of comes — g o e s
4. A tool for cutting — s a w
5. Opposite of open — c l o s e
6. Next, or at that time — t h e n
7. Pleasing and agreeable — n i c e
8. Was willing to — w o u l d
9. She will go ____ her mother. — w i t h
10. Several — m a n y

C o n g r a t u l a t i o n s !
Y o u   w r o t e   a l l   t h e
w o r d s   c o r r e c t l y !

page 316

Who's Afraid?

Help Frog and Toad escape from the snake. Read the two words in each space. If the words are antonyms, color the space green. Do not color the other spaces.

page 317

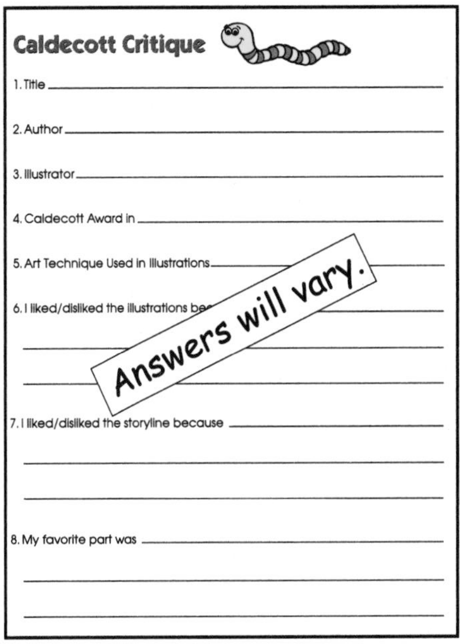

Caldecott Critique

1. Title _____
2. Author _____
3. Illustrator _____
4. Caldecott Award in _____
5. Art Technique Used in illustrations _____
6. I liked/disliked the illustrations be____

7. I liked/disliked the storyline because _____

8. My favorite part was _____

Answers will vary.

page 318

page 319

page 320

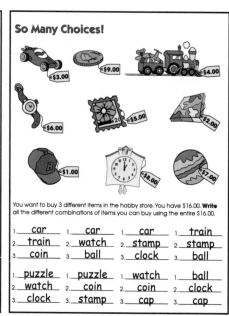

page 321

page 327

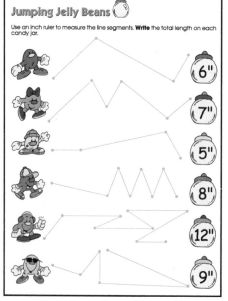

page 328

page 329

Learn at Home, Grade 2

Unpeppering the Salt

You need a teaspoon of salt on a sheet of paper. Place a pinch of pepper on top of the salt. Stir them together.

Unpeppering the Salt
Comb your hair 20 to 30 times.
Hold the comb over the salt-and-pepper mix.
What happened?

<u>Results may vary.</u>
<u>The pepper and some salt were picked up</u>
<u>by the comb.</u>

Brush your hair 20 to 30 times.
Hold the brush over the salt-and-pepper mix.
Did more pepper jump onto the comb or the brush?

<u>The brush.</u>

Brush your hair again.
Hold the brush over the salt and pepper.
How high can you make the pepper jump? <u>About 2 inches.</u>

Rub your comb on a sweater or a shiny blouse or shirt.
Rub only one way about 20 to 30 times.
Now, does the comb make the pepper jump? <u>No.</u>

Rub the comb on your arm only one way.
Now, does the comb make the pepper jump? <u>No.</u>

page 330

Dancing Parsley

There is a lot of electricity in nature. This is called static electricity. Static electricity cannot be used to run machines.

This is one way you can make static electricity:
1. Put one pinch of parsley flakes in a foam cup.
2. Rub the cup against your hair, your arm, a piece of silk or a piece of wool.
   Rub only one way.
   Rub about 30 times.
3. Look inside the cup.
   What happened to the flakes?

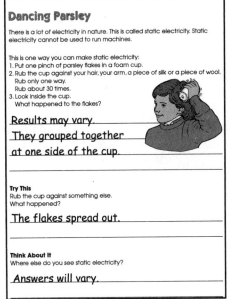

<u>Results may vary.</u>
<u>They grouped together</u>
<u>at one side of the cup.</u>

Try This
Rub the cup against something else.
What happened?

<u>The flakes spread out.</u>

Think About It
Where else do you see static electricity?

<u>Answers will vary.</u>

page 331

Wrap It Up With These

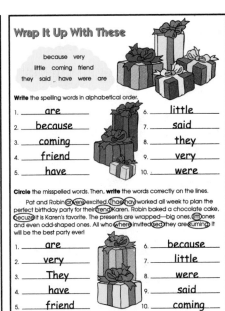

because   very
little   coming   friend
they   said   have   were   are

Write the spelling words in alphabetical order.

1. are
2. because
3. coming
4. friend
5. have
6. little
7. said
8. they
9. very
10. were

Circle the misspelled words. Then, **write** the words correctly on the lines.

Pat and Robin are excited. They worked all week to plan the perfect birthday party for their friend Karen. Robin baked a chocolate cake, because it is Karen's favorite. The presents are wrapped—big ones. Little ones and even odd-shaped ones. All who where invited said they are coming. It will be the best party ever!

1. are
2. very
3. They
4. have
5. friend
6. because
7. little
8. were
9. said
10. coming

page 336

Problems! Problems! Problems!

Read and solve these problems on another sheet of paper.

1. Craig went to the pond. He kept a tally of the animals he saw there.
   Which kind of animal did he see most often? <u>bug</u> Which kind of animal did he see least often? <u>lizard</u>

Frog ꟾꟾꟾꟾ ꟾ	Duck ꟾꟾꟾ	Bug ꟾꟾꟾꟾ ꟾꟾꟾꟾ ꟾꟾ	Bird ꟾꟾꟾꟾ ꟾꟾ	Lizard ꟾꟾ	Fish ꟾꟾꟾꟾ ꟾꟾꟾ
5	3	12	7	2	8

2. Ellen went to the library. She checked out five books on zoo animals, three books on fish, eight books on airplanes and two books on dogs.
   How many animal books did Ellen check out? <u>10</u> How many books did she check out altogether? <u>18</u> If she returns the books on dogs and airplanes, how many books will she have then? <u>8</u>

3. Complete this sequence of numbers: 14, 24, 34, <u>44</u>, <u>54</u>, 64

4. Debbie and Missy have twelve pieces of candy. If they share equally, how many pieces of candy should each girl get? <u>6</u> Suppose they decide to share equally the twelve pieces of candy with Kimberly, too. Now, how many pieces of candy will each girl get? <u>4</u>

5. Mike has forty cents. Lynette has twenty-three cents. How much more money does Lynette need to have as much money as Mike? <u>17¢</u>
   If she had the same amount as Mike, how much money would they have altogether? <u>80¢</u> Does Mike have enough money to purchase a ball for 50¢? <u>no</u>

6. Use a number line. Start at zero. Count up twelve, back three, up two, back eight, up four. What number are you on now? <u>7</u>

page 337

Complete Circuits

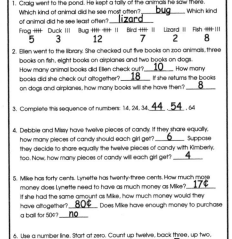

Lighting the Bulb
(Have an adult help.)
1. Use a pocket knife to strip the insulation off 1 inch of the wire at each end.
2. Place one bare end of the wire on the bottom of the battery.
3. Place the base of the bulb on the top center of the battery.
4. Touch the other bare end of the wire to the brass of the bulb.
5. Draw two pictures which show other ways to make the bulb light.

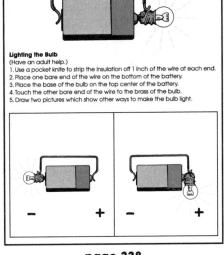

page 338

Conductors and Non-Conductors

With an adult, make a complete circuit and light the bulb. Then, put each of these materials, one at a time, between the bulb and the battery. If the bulb still lights, put a check mark in front of that material.

✔ scissors	___ chalk
___ eraser	___ crayon
✔ nail	___ marker
___ pencil	only a metal ruler ___ ruler
___ pen	___ book
___ toothpick	only a metal button ___ button
___ tagboard	___ cloth
✔ large paper clip	___ finger
✔ thumbtack	✔ penny

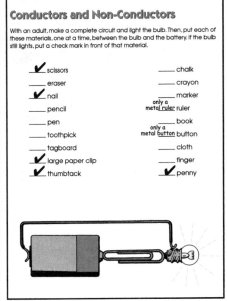

page 339

Build Yourself Up With Words

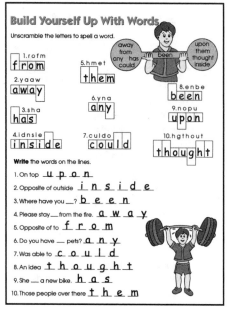

Unscramble the letters to spell a word.

1. r o f m **from**
2. y a a w **away**
3. s h a **has**
4. i d n s l e **inside**
5. h m e t **them**
6. y n a **any**
7. c u l d o **could**
8. e n b e **been**
9. n o p u **upon**
10. h g t h o u t **thought**

Write the words on the lines.

1. On top **upon**
2. Opposite of outside **inside**
3. Where have you ___? **been**
4. Please stay ___ from the fire. **away**
5. Opposite of to **from**
6. Do you have ___ pets? **any**
7. Was able to **could**
8. An idea **thought**
9. She ___ a new bike. **has**
10. Those people over there **them**

page 344

Chapter Book Report Form

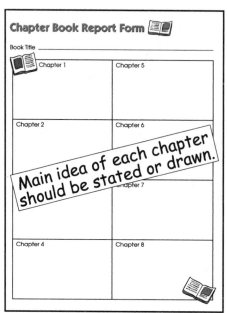

Book Title _____

Chapter 1	Chapter 5
Chapter 2	Chapter 6
	Chapter 7
Chapter 4	Chapter 8

Main idea of each chapter should be stated or drawn.

page 345

Earnings Add Up!

Wash dishes **$1.50**   Feed cat **$.95**   Mow lawn **$3.50**

Mop floors **$1.25**   Pick tomatoes **$2.75**   Wash windows **$2.85**

Use the pictures above to help you find out how much you can earn by doing each set of jobs. **Write** the total amount for each set.

1. pick tomatoes **$2.75**
2. wash windows **$2.85**
3. mow the lawn **$3.50**
$9.10

1. wash windows **$2.85**
2. mop floors **$1.25**
3. mow the lawn **$3.50**
$7.60

1. feed the cat **$.95**
2. pick tomatoes **$2.75**
3. wash dishes **$1.50**
$5.20

1. pick tomatoes **$2.75**
2. wash windows **$2.85**
3. feed the cat **$.95**
$6.55

page 351

Amy's Things

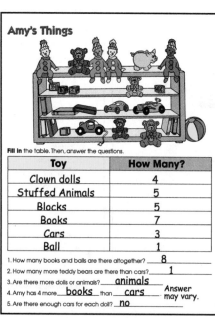

Fill in the table. Then, answer the questions.

Toy	How Many?
Clown dolls	4
Stuffed Animals	5
Blocks	5
Books	7
Cars	3
Ball	1

1. How many books and balls are there altogether? **8**
2. How many more teddy bears are there than cars? **1**
3. Are there more dolls or animals? **animals**
4. Amy has 4 more **books** than **cars**   Answer may vary.
5. Are there enough cars for each doll? **no**

page 352

Comparing and Classifying Rocks

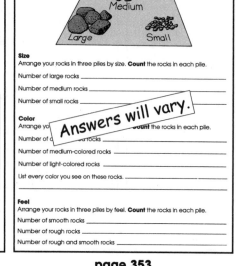

Medium   Large   Small

Size
Arrange your rocks in three piles by size. **Count** the rocks in each pile.

Number of large rocks _____
Number of medium rocks _____
Number of small rocks _____

Color
Arrange yo... ...ount the rocks in each pile.
Number of d... ...rocks _____
Number of medium-colored rocks _____
Number of light-colored rocks _____
List every color you see on these rocks. _____

Answers will vary.

Feel
Arrange your rocks in three piles by feel. **Count** the rocks in each pile.
Number of smooth rocks _____
Number of rough rocks _____
Number of rough and smooth rocks _____

page 353

Learn at Home, Grade 2